CONTEMPORARY RATIONALIST
ISLAM IN TURKEY

CONTEMPORARY RATIONALIST ISLAM IN TURKEY

The Religious Opposition to Sunni Revival

Gokhan Bacik

I.B.TAURIS
LONDON • NEW YORK • OXFORD • NEW DELHI • SYDNEY

I.B. TAURIS
Bloomsbury Publishing Plc
50 Bedford Square, London, WC1B 3DP, UK
1385 Broadway, New York, NY 10018, USA
29 Earlsfort Terrace, Dublin 2, Ireland

BLOOMSBURY, I.B. TAURIS and the I.B. Tauris logo are trademarks of Bloomsbury Publishing Plc

First published in Great Britain 2021
This paperback edition published 2023

Copyright © Gokhan Bacik, 2021

Gokhan Bacik has asserted his right under the Copyright, Designs and Patents Act, 1988, to be identified as Author of this work.

For legal purposes the Acknowledgments on p. viii constitute an extension of this copyright page.

Series design by Adriana Brioso
Cover image © MISHA SOTNIKOV / 500px

All rights reserved. No part of this publication may be reproduced or transmitted in any form or by any means, electronic or mechanical, including photocopying, recording, or any information storage or retrieval system, without prior permission in writing from the publishers.

Bloomsbury Publishing Plc does not have any control over, or responsibility for, any third-party websites referred to or in this book. All internet addresses given in this book were correct at the time of going to press. The author and publisher regret any inconvenience caused if addresses have changed or sites have ceased to exist, but can accept no responsibility for any such changes.

A catalogue record for this book is available from the British Library.

A catalog record for this book is available from the Library of Congress.

ISBN: HB: 978-0-7556-3674-7
PB: 978-0-7556-3678-5
ePDF: 978-0-7556-3675-4
eBook: 978-0-7556-3676-1

Typeset by Deanta Global Publishing Services, Chennai, India

To find out more about our authors and books visit www.bloomsbury.com and sign up for our newsletters.

CONTENTS

List of Illustrations	vii
Acknowledgments	viii
INTRODUCTION	1
The Political Context: The Islamic Movement in Turkey	5
What Is Contemporary Islamic Rationalism?	6
Between Historicism and Universalism: Explaining and Categorizing the Rationalists	11
From Sunnism to Rationalism	14
The Structure of the Book	21
Chapter 1	
THE FUNDAMENTALS: QURAN AND HADITH	25
The Rationalists on Quran	25
The Rationalists on Hadith	51
Conclusion	58
Chapter 2	
LAW: DEMYSTIFYING SHARI'A	61
The Nature and the Status of Shari'a	62
A Rationalist Interpretation of Shari'a	64
Who Is a Good Muslim? A Moralistic Theory of Piety	88
The Comprehensive Sunnah	94
A Religious Theory of Political Opposition	97
Conclusion	101
Chapter 3	
HISTORY: DE-ISLAMIZING ISLAMIC HISTORY	103
The Rationalists on Causation in History	105
Revisionism on the History of Quran	108
Revisionism on Muhammad	116
Revisionism on Early Islamic History	124
Conclusion	133

Chapter 4
POLITICS AND SOCIETY: WHAT WENT WRONG?   135
- The Mainstream Theory of Decay   136
- Ash'arism: The Paradigmatic Obstacle   139
- al-Shafi'i: "The Villain"   139
- The Umayyads: The Distortion of Islam   140
- Sufism: The Popularization of Anti-Rationalism   144
- Islamic Social Movements: A False Theory of Revival   145
- Conclusion   146

CONCLUSION   149
- The Rationalists as Moderns   149
- The Impact: The Crisis of Sunnism and the Rationalists   151
- The Rationalists and the Quandary of Change in Islamic Thought   153

Notes   155
Bibliography   212
Index   237

ILLUSTRATIONS

1	The rationalists between universalism and historicism	13
2	The birthplaces of the rationalists	16
3	The list of universities where the rationalists had their theology education	19
4	The hierarchy of Islamic norms according to Kırbaşoğlu	62
5	The literal and the historicist readings of the *zihar* verses	78
6	Comparing the "prime antagonism" for Sunnis and the rationalists	101
7	The spectrum of Islamic history in the context of the "what went wrong" debate	147

ACKNOWLEDGMENTS

The research for this book began in 2016, the year I left Turkey for political reasons. A restart in life is never easy in such a situation. Survival is difficult if one's state is not cooperating with you. We are living in a modern international system where citizenship is *the* organizing institution. Once your citizenship is no longer functional, you are in the hands of other nations' mercy. Thus, my academic survival has been possible thanks to so many people whom I have met in the past four years of transition. If I try to thank them in name, I will probably need an independent section. But in general, I would like to emphasize my personal gratitude to, what I call, the European hospitality. Indeed, Europe has its own problems. However, comparatively speaking, Europe is still one of the best places, where people like me are welcomed with an open arm.

Likewise, I am grateful to the Institute of International Education's Scholar Rescue Fund (IIE-SRF), which supported me during the difficult times of my transition. Global institutions like the SRF have played vital roles in the survival of many persecuted Turkish academics in recent years. I am also equally indebted to the Palacky University in Czech Republic, an institution of higher education that should be globally appreciated for its historical role in supporting scholars at risk from different countries. It is in this vein, I owe much to my Czech colleagues Jaroslav Miller, Jiri Lach, and Tomas Lebeda, who offered their unwavering support to have me settled in Olomouc. They played key roles in my professional survival, which I will never forget.

INTRODUCTION

Back in the nineteenth century, a vivid school of religious thought emerged, its ambitious goal the revival of Islamic thought with the renowned voices of the likes of Muhammad Abduh (d. 1905), Sayyid Ahmad Khan (d. 1898), Jamal al-Din al-Afghani (d. 1897), and Hasan al-Attar (d. 1835). This tradition in the making was later continued by scholars like Fazlur Rahman (d. 1988), Taha Hussain (d. 1973), and Muhammad Taha (d. 1985), who might be called the second-generation intellects. Today, prominent names such as Ebrahim Moosa, Khaled Abou El Fadl, Abdulaziz Sachedina, Abdullahi Ahmed An-Na'im, and Amina Wadud continue the same intellectual mission. Meanwhile, a parallel scholarship is observed also in the individual voices in/from Iran, like those of Mohsen Kadivar, Abdolkarim Soroush, and Hasan Yousefi Eshkevari.[1]

The nineteenth-century Ottoman scholarly climate was no different: Istanbul was an intellectual hub of rich discussions of Islam, in which leading reformists played significant roles. For example, al-Afghani was received by the Sultan.[2] He influenced the Young Turks, who were also enthusiastic about Islamic revivalism. Ali Pasha (d. 1871), a dominant figure of nineteenth-century Ottoman reformism, wanted al-Afghani to shape Ottoman education, as well as to stir up the ulema.[3] Hasan al-Attar, the grand imam of al-Azhar known for reformist views, lived in Ottoman Egypt and continued his studies in other Ottomans cities, like Istanbul and Damascus.[4] There were many other people, namely Ahmed Hilmi (d. 1914), Said Halim Pasha (d. 1921), Ferit Kam (d. 1944), Musa Kazım (d. 1920), and İsmail Fenni (d. 1946), whose works influenced the late Ottoman- and the early Republican-period discussions of Islam. In fact, the general reformist spirit of the Ottoman intellectuals in the nineteenth century always included a search for a better interpretation of Islam. Reading Ottoman thinkers such as Ziya Pasha (d. 1880), Ali Suavi (d. 1878), and many others, one always notices a critical engagement with Islam. This had its roots in the belief among Ottoman intellectuals that how Islam is being interpreted in their times generates serious problems.[5]

In contrast, Turkey today appears to be an intellectual vacuum to anyone in search of ongoing discussions on Islam in the tradition of the people I named earlier as the second- and the present-generation scholars. There is almost no systematic reference to Turkish scholarship in the global literature on reformist Islam. References to scholarly thought are rare, or the odd citations of their works are bent to assist readings of Turkey through political and social movements, not through religious theoretical constructs. Consequently, unlike in the late nineteenth and early twentieth centuries, we do not detect invocations of the leading Turkish names of Islamic thought in the global debate on Islam, particularly after the 1950s. The global literature on reformist Islam is now silent on the Turkish stage. This is a serious deficit, given this country's historical and current impact in the Muslim world.

The main purpose of this book is to demonstrate that despite appearances, a critical intellectual scholarship on Islam does exist in Turkey. I study it under the rubric "contemporary Islamic rationalists," or "the rationalists" for short. This scholarship challenges the Islamic tradition, and provides an alternative methodology for interpreting Islam in regard of the law, theology, and history. The rationalists accept that the interpretation and the practice of Islam in line with the Islamic tradition generates problems that can be healed only in a fresh religious paradigm.[6] To this end, the rationalists propose a new interpretation of Islam based on the primacy and supremacy of reason in any approach to Islamic texts, including Quran and the works of foregone scholars. This results in a radical critique of Sunnism, the mainstream religious paradigm in Turkey. In this book, I study the output of nine prominent rationalist names to illustrate the scope and the depth of critical Islamic thought in there:

Hüseyin Atay
Yaşar Nuri Öztürk (d. 2016)*
Ömer Özsoy
M. Hayri Kırbaşoğlu
İlhami Güler
İhsan R. Eliaçık
Mustafa Öztürk
İsrafil Balcı
Mehmet Azimli

The rationalists engage with the global discussions of Islam by incorporating their arguments as well as developing them in their context. On this account, they are the Turkish representatives of the critical thought on Islam represented by the second- and third-generation scholars like Fazlur Rahman, Taha Hussain, and Abdullahi Ahmed An-Naʿim.

The absence of interested attention to the rationalists is due first to the fact that most of their writing is in Turkish. Their works amount to some 200 volumes and many articles, but almost all are published in Turkish only. Another reason is that studies of Islam in the Turkish context usually focus on major cases, like the Justice and Development Party (JDP) and the Gülen movement, the political and social impacts of which are more decisive. However, it is impossible to detect critical Islamic thought by studying such cases, for they follow the typical Sunni

---

* Since two rationalists have the same surname, Yaşar Nuri Öztürk will be quoted as Yaşar Nuri throughout the book.

paradigm. Worse, those groups' pragmatic and political engagement with Islam, which never offers an intellectual critique of the Sunni tradition, is brought to the global public with hackneyed nominals like "revivalism" and "reformism."[7] Finally, the global scholarship on Turkey is comparatively less interested in intellectual approaches than it was in the late Ottoman period. Unlike the discourse of the late Ottoman period, intellectual discussions today either occupy less space in Turkish studies or are analyzed as the secondary elements of the political dynamic.

A distinguishing feature of contemporary Islamic rationalism is its break with Sunnism. Basically, the rationalists see Sunnism as either an outdated or a mistaken paradigm that cannot provide a correct interpretation of Islam. Therefore, methodologically, the critique of Sunnism is an inseparable element of their works, since they develop their alternative paradigm principally by engaging critically with Sunnism: they challenge it on all possible grounds, from theology to Islamic history. These challenges can be summarized under seven headings:

1. Historically, the relationship between Sunnism and the state has put religion into the service of politics. Sunnism is not successful at defining its distance and relationship with the political power. The state-oriented characteristic of Sunnism transformed Islam into a kind of right-wing paradigm where individualism and opposition are sacrificed to communalism and stability.
2. Sunnism has marginalized rationalist scholars and survived as an anti-rationalist paradigm. It has stayed primarily a text-based reasoning.
3. Sunnism has failed to develop a moral paradigm because it has reduced Islam into a religion of law, and of the rituals of worship.
4. The Sunni methods of interpreting the major Islamic texts (Quran and the traditions) are not updated, thus they no longer provide efficient solutions for today's issues. Besides, they generate anachronic and damaging religious opinions and judgments.
5. Several fundamental Sunni arguments and opinions, including those on the basic theological topics such as the nature of Quran, are wrong.
6. The Sunni narrative of early Islamic history has deficits and methodological limits that make it anachronic, and therefore useless for contemporary Muslims. More, Sunni history is itself a major source of problems, and deepens political and social divisions among Muslims.
7. Sunnism has failed to differentiate the universal elements and the contextual/temporary elements of Islam, which results in a puzzling concept of shari'a as a set of fixed and universal laws. Such an understanding of shari'a is wrong, and a major cause of stagnancy in the Islamic world.

As I noted earlier, the alternative Islamic paradigm that we encounter in the works of the rationalists is drawn mainly from their critique of Sunnism, which can also be summarized under seven headings:

1. Criticizing the historical power relations between Sunnism and the state, the rationalists propose the turning upside down of the relationship between

them. Accordingly, Islam requires Muslims to be interested in politics through moral norms. Thus, it is a religious obligation upon Muslims to be critical of corrupt and authoritarian rulers. Unlike the amicable relationship between Islam and state on the Sunni model, the rationalists propose that Islam become a theory of opposition.

2. Challenging and even disapproving the legacy of traditionalist scholars, the rationalists propose a new interpretation that reconnects Islam with prior and contemporary rationalists, such as the Muʿtazila, as well as present-day Muslim and Western philosophers. As rationalists, they promote Islamic reasoning as the superior of the Islamic texts.

3. Denouncing Sunnism for transforming Islam into a religion of *fiqh*/law, Islam is redefined first as a religion of morality in contemporary Islamic rationalism. The rationalists define "moral act" as the highest religious deed. They propose a moralistic piety where formal worships are given only secondary status.

4. Unsatisfied by traditional Sunni methods of interpreting Quran and the traditions, the rationalists introduce alternative methods, such as historicism, hermeneutics, and the social sciences.

5. The rationalists' opinions on the various substantial theological and legal issues are different. Thus, a radical departure from Sunni theology and law is observed, such as the defense of the Muʿtazili thesis of the "created Quran."

6. The rationalists are revisionists of early Islamic history. Accordingly, they explain early Islamic history, including the life of Muhammad, in terms of natural and historical causation. The method requires rejecting miracles, exceptionalism, and other Sunni methods, such as approaching the Islamic past as a Golden Age. They challenge pragmatically the narration of early Islamic history according to Sunni theological and political arguments.

7. Defining Shariʿa as a historical and contextual/temporary example derived from Arab practices, the rationalists argue that its content, including the penal rules as well as the rules of worships, can be changed in other contexts. In contemporary Islamic rationalism, Islam is not equal to shariʿa, and therefore the latter is subject to change in a different context.

A significant point about the rationalists is that though they develop their alternative religious interpretation through a critical engagement with Sunnism, their objective is not to correct it. For them, *Sunnism is no longer a viable framework in Islamic reasoning.* In fact, by undertaking an ambitious agenda of critical scholarship on Sunnism, the rationalists challenge the equation between Islam and Sunnism in Turkey. For the rationalists, a new paradigm is only possible by going beyond Sunnism. They entertain opinions on theology and law that are seen by Sunnism as tantamount to heresy. However, breaking with Sunnism is never a rejection of the Islamic tradition. The rationalists often remind that reviving Islamic civilization requires going back to the origins. But they take an approach other than Sunnism when engaging with the Muslim scholars of yore. For the rationalists, Sunnism does not take many of those scholars into consideration, so it cannot represent the whole Islamic tradition.⁸ Thus, the rationalists do not abide by Sunni judgments or priorities while engaging with the tradition. They incorporate many scholars' opinions into their works, for example, those of Zaydi and Mu'tazili, who are normally excluded by Sunnis. On this account, contemporary Islamic rationalism is also a quest for an alternative engagement with Islamic tradition.

The Political Context: The Islamic Movement in Turkey

The rationalists have developed their opinions in response to the interpretation and practice of Islam in Turkey, which is determined predominantly by Sunnism. And particularly, the rise of Sunni Islamic actors and Turkey's going through complex problems (such as authoritarianism and corruption of the political executive of the last two decades) is a significant element in this context.⁹ On this account, contemporary Islamic rationalism is a theory of religious opposition to the Sunni revival in Turkey, a country where Islam is traditionally a theory of political legitimacy. However, paradoxically, the failure of Islamic actors has helped contemporary Islamic rationalism. Their failure, and particularly the concomitant growing reaction to Islamic politics, has naturally increased the social reception of the rationalists by a larger number of people. Particularly young people, frustrated by Islamist authoritarian policies, are drawn away from the traditional Sunni understanding toward alternative religious interpretations.¹⁰

However, more attention grabbing is how the rationalists correlate the failure of Islamic actors and the interpretation of Islam. Accordingly, Islamic actors like the JDP and the Gülen movement repeated the same mistakes that the Sunni paradigm has repeated over the ages.¹¹ Therefore, ironically, the failure of Islamic actors is due to their successful practice of Islam according to Sunnism.¹² What happened in the last two decades, a period which one may dub as the "Islamic movement in Turkey," is yet another episode in the history of Sunnism. So, on many accounts, from the relationship between state and religion¹³ to the economic mentality of Islamic actors,¹⁴ Islamic politics in Turkey is a repetition of historical Sunni patterns. Actors like R. Tayyip Erdoğan, Necmettin Erbakan, Fethullah Gülen, and Ahmet Davutoğlu are therefore public faces of Sunnism.¹⁵ In a prelude to one of his books, Güler informed his readers that the book was written as a protest against the JDP and the Gülen movement, for they created their Sunni tutelage, which had ironically promised to destroy the previous Kemalist-military tutelage.¹⁶ For Güler, even the fight between the Gülen movement and the JDP, which started in 2013 and concluded in the brutal purge of the Gülenists after the failed 2016 coup by declaring them terrorists, is a typical case where we observe the historical Sunni patterns.¹⁷ Yaşar Nuri lays equal blame at the feet of the JDP and the Gülen movement for transforming Turkey into a field of oppression where freedom and justice are under systematic assault.¹⁸ Kırbaşoğlu criticizes the JDP and the Gülen movement—which he presents as group loyal to traditional Sunnism—for their pathological secularization that manifests itself as corruption, billionaire Islamists, and their intricate relationships through banks and big financial conglomerates.¹⁹

As such examples show, the substantial critique of Islamic actors is to carry on with Sunnism, which for the rationalists is outdated as well as mistaken on many counts. In view of this, Öztürk summarizes the Turkish case as "Sunni fundamentalism" recognizable for three typical characteristics: agreeing only to a limited and pragmatic reformism in politics; rejecting any substantial change in Islamic thought; and never being genuinely interested in the social purposes of Islam, such as social equality and justice.[20]

The rationalists' critique, through Sunnism, of the Islamic movement in Turkey provides a completely new perspective. Usually, Islam in the Turkish case is studied as an antagonism of Islam *versus* secularism. Or more recently, Islamic authoritarianism *versus* democracy has emerged as a second popular antagonism. Logically, those studies could only provide insights into Islam from external perspectives of the secularization or democratization theories. Besides, approaching Islam as a monolithic phenomenon, they deal primarily with how Islamic actors respond to external or contextual situations. However, studying Islam from an external perspective does not yield knowledge of the inner determinants that realize Islam as we observe it in Turkey, independently of the political fight between Islamists and seculars. Islam in the Turkish context, as elsewhere, derives its characteristics and practices from how Muslims interpret theology, law, and history. That is, the religious critique of Sunnism provides us with insight that we would not get from secular or liberal approaches into how the Turkish Islamic actors' policies in the various fields are linked to their interpretations of Islam.

What Is Contemporary Islamic Rationalism?

I do not prefer "reformism" as a suitable characterization of what happens in this book's study of nine scholars. "Reformism" is used open-endedly to identify any kind of Islamic interpretation that sounds liberal, progressive, or critical. In practice, it is not clear what exactly is meant by "reformism." Besides, the generosity of Western Islamic scholarship in using synonyms for it, such as "enlightenment" and "liberalism," worsens the case.[21] Many scholars, including several rationalists I study in this book, also reject "reformism" as a suitable representation of their works.[22] Finally, given this word's negative connotations among Muslims, and its controversial social baggage, it is best to do without it.

"Rationalism" is the better fitting label for the scope and methodology of the works of the nine scholars. Besides, a coherent and technically accurate definition of rationalism is doable, given that there already is an established perspective explaining the trajectory of Islamic intellectual history in terms of the polarization of traditionalism and rationalism. The scholars I analyze in this book also often refer to this taxonomy when explaining their case in the Turkish context.[23]

Islamic thought is historically classified as two grand categories into which the relationship of reason and texts, that is, Quran and tradition, is distilled.[24] The taxonomy, which traces back to the time of the companions, imagined them into two groups: *ahl ra'y*, who favor independent reasoning, and *ahl hadith*, who prefer adherence to the text. While the companions like Umar, Aisha, and Ibn Abbas are categorized as *ahl ra'y*, companions like Salamah ibn al-Akwaʻ, and Abdullah ibn Umar are categorized as *ahl hadith*.[25] Later, the difference evolved into the traditionists-jurisprudents, who proposed that the law be inferred from traditions, and from what the earlier companions reported, and rationalistic jurisprudents, who used reasoning-based methods along with traditions.[26] As a matter of fact, in the eighth century, the isolation of the differences between the Kufa School and the Hijaz School, a major early differentiation in Islamic legal tradition, was a typical ramification of the same debate: The Kufa School was the symbol of *ahl ra'y*, and the latter was composed of traditionists.[27]

Though they both employ reasoning, the main difference between *ahl ra'y* and *ahl hadith* is the status of reason. The text is subject to reason for the former, whereas, for the latter, the basis of religion is the text to be followed.[28] This taxonomy is significant to the extent that the whole history of Islamic thought tends to be imagined as a competition of rationalists and traditionalists.[29] While scholars like al-Ghazali (d. 1111), al-Shafiʻi (d. 820), al-Ashʻari (d. 936), and Ahmad ibn Hanbal (d. 855) belong to the latter trajectory, scholars like Abu Hanifa (d. 767), al-Maturidi (d. 944), and al-Shatibi (d. 1388) belong to the former. However, the definition of traditionalism and rationalism is always contextual and comparative. Not all traditionalists are traditionalist in the same way. Similarly, what is meant by "rationalist" changes from age to age. For example, al-Ghazali, who deserves to be hailed as the champion of the use of reason, is nonetheless a traditionalist, given his legacy—the role he played, particularly vis-à-vis Aristotelian Muslim scholars. Therefore, the historical polarization of traditionalists and rationalists would usually present al-Ghazali as a traditionalist, and Ibn Rushd (d. 1198) as a rationalist. But al-Ghazali was quite closed to rationalism if compared with the traditional Ashʻarism before him.[30] Again, while the Ashʻari school is famous for reasoning, it is regarded as traditionalists in comparison to with the Muʻtazila and the Maturidi.[31]

The nine Turkish scholars, given that they recognize the primacy and supremacy of reason over text, are definitely on the rationalist track. However, living in modern times, the definition of their rationalism is naturally different from the classical rationalists like the Muʻtazila, who lived before modernity. Contemporary Islamic rationalists were trained in modern institutions, so they are in intellectual interaction with classical and modern Western thought, such as that of Immanuel Kant, John Searle, Ludwig Wittgenstein, and William Dilthey. This is a typical feature of contemporary Islamic rationalism, since the first-generation reformists like Muhammad Iqbal (d. 1938), who were inspired by Western scholars like Bernard Russell and Henry Bergson.[32] Like Iqbal, others such as Sayyid Ahmad Khan were also given to engaging with Western rationalism.[33] Unlike the pre-moderns such as al-Ghazali or the Muʻtazila, contemporary Islamic rationalists thus study Islam on the intellectual stretcher of a modern methodology. Logically, the usual warning that the use of rationalism in the Islamic context requires caution, given that rationalism emerged in the Western context during the seventeenth and eighteenth centuries, is not a matter of direct concern for contemporary Islamic rationalists.[34] Rationalism in contemporary Islamic thought should be distinguished from classical Islamic rationalism.[35]

In this regard, the difference between *reasoning* and *rationalism* is a critical subject in the distinguishing of contemporary Islamic rationalism from the classical Islamic rationalism. Reasoning is the using of the human capacity to think in various ways: Typically, those ways are to compare, to deduce, to induce, to accept, or to reject, and to conclude. Logically, reasoning is a natural human cognitive activity, necessarily practiced also by traditionalists, no matter how anti-rationalist they are. Reasoning is not rationalism. An eloquent statement on this equation came down to us from al-Maturidi in *Kitab al-Tawhid*, where he wrote that denying reason is also an act of reasoning.[36] For example, we encounter typical examples of successful reasoning in al-Ghazali. However, he was not promoting rationalism knowingly. In *Al-Qistas Al-Mustaqim*, al-Ghazali proposed that an analogy should be constructed as it is explained in Quran. And he rejected the appeal to reason (*qiyas*) and opinion (*ra'y*) as the "rules of the devil," and insisted that these faculties be exercised according to "the rule of God (*qistas al-mustaqim*)."[37] Although in saying this, al-Ghazali degrades human reasoning to a subordinate role, the sequence in which he speaks is nonetheless a sequence of reasoning.[38] In fact, al-Ghazali was generally distrustful not only of the human faculty of reasoning, but also of the human feelings that erupt as sensations. As he wrote in his autobiography, he had searched for an infallible body of knowledge, but ultimately found that he "could no longer trust sense-perception."[39] Having culled reason and sensation from the field of meritorious quest for knowledge, al-Ghazali then advanced the concept "inner knowledge," which did not come about by systematic demonstration or marshaled argument, but by a light that God cast into his breast.[40] For him, those who reach for inner knowledge—that is, the mystics—can quickly achieve the intellectual progress that al-Ghazali himself only accomplished over a long time.[41] For al-Ghazali, the mystics' ability to acquire knowledge is beyond doubt, since it depends on and is bestowed by God's grace.[42] Indeed, given such crucial conclusions, al-Ghazali's legacy consolidated traditionalism against rationalism in Islam.[43] Mohammed Abed al-Jabri, for example, likened his legacy to a deep wound inside reason, which is still bleeding.[44]

A more radical brand of reasoning against rationalism is observed in al-Shafi'i, who confined reasoning into the boundaries of the texts, that is, Quran and the traditions.[45] His method was to replace theology with legal theory, since there is no need for the former when "Islamic" is equated with text-oriented effort.[46] Thus, for al-Shafi'i, reasoning is by nature a deficiency, for it repeatedly displays that it has failed to acquire the quality answers that are already available in the text.[47] Even if reason notices what appears to be a contradiction, for example in a tradition, then that contradiction should be assigned to various facts, such as that an incomplete transmission distorted a truth.[48] For al-Shafi'i, the texts are perfect; thus, it is required to follow them. Containing all solutions, the texts do not leave any need to go beyond them. In traditionalism as we read in al-Shafi'i, to reason is therefore to follow *al-salaf al-salih*, the righteous predecessors, whose territory abhors deviation.

In stark contrast, rationalism recognizes human reason as being capable of articulating solutions beyond the texts' capacity. Accordingly, human reason understands what is meant in the text. But that understanding could well contradict how foregone readings had understood the same text. That phenomenon confers the license to deviate from tradition. In the Islamic tradition, the Muʿtazila is usually recognized as the typical rationalist school.[49] For the Muʿtazila, it is possible to develop a successful rational method to understand nature, and even to know good and evil solely through human reason.[50] Though they are vehement to a lesser degree, the rationalist track in Islamic thought has other prominent proponents, such as Abu Hanifa and al-Maturidi.

As already noted, contemporary Islamic rationalists propose an Islamic methodology where reasoning towers above the texts. In view of this, the rationalists' case against Sunnism is a vibrant chapter in this perennial grand debate. While the rationalists are critical of traditionalists, they make many positive references to names whom they see as rationalists, starting with the early companions like Umar, who is known as *ahl ra'y*. To elaborate on this: The rationalists set themselves apart from scholars whom they define as traditionalists. In regard to traditionalists' impact, as we read in Güler, they criticize the Islamic tradition for sacrificing human reason to the text.[51] Thus, the rationalists particularly see the Shafiʿ-Sufi-Ashʿari axis, that is, the al-Shafiʿi method, the Ashʿari theology, and the al-Ghazali's incorporation of Sufism into mainstream Islam, as the major paradigmatic reason for explaining the problems in the Muslim world.[52] However, unlike the typical critical works of contemporary Islamic literature, which usually challenge al-Ghazali first, it is al-Shafiʿi who is treated as the "villain" in the works of the rationalists, for one simple reason: His methodology is regarded as the foundation of what is known as Sunnism today.[53] Al-Shafiʿi symbolizes the apex of traditionalism for the rationalists, for it is his method that reduced the role of reasoning in the understanding the text, thereby sidelining rationalists like Abu Hanifa.[54] On the contrary, the rationalists are sympathetic to scholars whom they define as rationalists. The Muʿtazila is given big credit. Frequent references to Muʿtazila in the works of the rationalists vividly demonstrate that the school survives, despite efforts to present it as forgotten.[55] Öztürk's *The Muʿtazili Interpretation of Quran* presents a detailed analysis of the school, based on the views of Abu Muslim al-Isfahani (d. 934), a leading Muʿtazili scholar. Similarly, Eliaçık presents al-Isfahani as his master.[56] Güler has a book where he clearly underlines that the Muʿtazili perspective could provide solutions to contemporary Muslim problems.[57] Addressing the Muʿtazila as the exposers of the highest level of understanding Quran, Atay argues that, had Muʿtazila not existed, the Islamic civilization of the past might have not been so brilliant.[58] The rationalists are in intensive dialogue also with contemporary rationalist scholars such as Abdullahi al-Naʿim, Taha Hussain, Muhammad Iqbal, Sayyid Ahmad Khan, ʿAbed al-Jabiri, Hassan Hanafi, Muhammad Taha, Muhammad Arkoun, Nasser Abu-Zayd, and Izzat Darwaza. Unsurprisingly, Fazlur Rahman is on the list as a key person who influenced the rationalists.

However, looking closer, we detect in the works of the rationalists an ongoing negotiation of the various types of rationalism about the terms in which the supremacy of reason over the text is to be defined. For example, we observe in the rationalists Yaşar Nuri and Atay an approach similar to *classical rationalism*, where human reason is the prime agent of knowing and explaining.[59] Reflecting that, reason in Yaşar Nuri and Atay is the highest authority capable even of discerning truth by itself.[60] Atay calls reason "the natural revelation."[61] For Yaşar Nuri, reason is the first and the greatest prophet.[62] On this account, no other resource, not even the revelation, can be as solid as reason.[63] Moreover, reason's autonomy is not only a diminution of the revelation but also of the senses: Atay writes that reason comes before the senses.[64] Indeed, cooperation between reason and the revelation, or other resources, is welcomed. However, reason always retains its ability to decide unilaterally.[65] As Yaşar Nuri writes, reason can find what is good autonomously.[66] Having the ability to operate autonomously with no need of external resources, reason can arbitrate religious arguments.[67] Atay based this on the explanation that, unlike the revelation, which is contextual, reason is the universal authority that does not need a context.[68] Quoting the Muʿtazili scholar Qadi Abd al-Jabbar (d. 1025), Yaşar Nuri concludes that everything in religion should be tested by reason.[69]

However, there is another type of rationalism we detect in scholars like Öztürk, Güler, Özsoy, and Kırbaşoğlu, who are equally firm about identifying the senses, the sensitive part of the soul, as of primary importance. That positions them closer to *empiricism*.[70] To them, though they accept that human reason is the ultimate power in Islamic reasoning, they urge that external facts collected by senses be given due consideration. Accordingly, for them, knowledge of the external is an essential part of Islamic reasoning.[71] Thus reason, as Kırbaşoğlu underlines, should operate by considering concrete realities. He thus warns that the Western classical rationalism has no counterpart in the Islamic tradition. Accordingly, reason does not have an autonomous ability to discover truth. Instead, it operates only through concrete facts.[72] In this line of thinking, Islamic reasoning should not be conducted by reasoning alone; it should consider also the historical and the present context. Accordingly, knowledge acquired through senses affect sometimes limits, human reasoning. For example, Özsoy, Öztürk, Güler, and Kırbaşoğlu suggest interpreting the verses of Quran by considering their historical context as well as their relevance in the present context. Echoing empiricism, they believe that reasoning without reference to the social and historical contexts of the verses is a frameless and arbitrary reasoning.[73] In view of that, human reason does not have absolute authority to interpret the verses unilaterally, without taking account of external factors, like the meaning of the verses in their historical context.[74]

The rationalists' entertaining modern rationalism is indeed an important case, given that it is usually argued that modern rationalism is not compatible with Islam. For example, Georges Makdisi once argued that Islam does not tolerate a Western type of enlightened rationalism.[75] Similarly, it is argued that the Muʿtazila would have agreed with some of the principles of Enlightenment Rationalism.[76] I argue that the case of the rationalists can be explained in terms of two factors. Firstly, there is no standard rationalism in the Western example.[77] A Voltairean brand of rationalism is indeed not compatible with Islam, for it rejects the notion of deity. Principally, a rationalism that rejects the idea of God is not compatible with Islam. However, in the West, there are other rationalist approaches, like the British one, in which atheism is not axiomatic. That position takes issue with the Voltairean model.[78]

Secondly, the rationalists, no matter whether they are on the pure rationalist or empiricist track, pronounce a coherent rationalist paradigm, thanks to their understanding of causality. They explain the relationship of God and nature, as well of God and history, as the product of the natural laws. This enables them to entertain a full-blown rationalism.[79] They categorically reject the supernatural, which allows them to embrace the autonomy of human reason, as well as the concept of free will.[80] As I shall elaborate on this point in the following chapters, the rationalists are closed to Ibn Rushd on causality, which is the opposite of the Ash'ari/Ghazalian view of natural events. Accordingly, God does not influence nature as an agent, but as a transcendental power. Thus, recognizing the concept of natural causes does not necessarily contradict the concept of God's sovereignty. There are rules and standards in nature, and they can be discovered through rational observation. We have here a belief system in which atheism is not a prerequisite of enlightenment or rationalism. There is a God, but he does not suspend or destroy the natural order. Instead, as Ibn Rushd wrote, there is a continuum of causality underlying the structure of physical reality.[81] Logically, the rationalists' approach to nature as well history (which is radically different from the Ash'ari occasionalism that practically repudiates causation and explains all events in nature as caused by divine agency)[82] allows them to embrace a rationalist paradigm.

Between Historicism and Universalism: Explaining and Categorizing the Rationalists

The main selection rationale that collected the nine names discussed in this book is that they are typical and prominent, so apt cases to study in a quest of which the objective is to discern the nature of contemporary Islamic rationalism. There are a number of reasons to justify this rationale. Firstly, they are "rationalists" in the sense that they promote Islamic reasoning that is not confined to the texts. Secondly, despite their sociologically Sunni background, they are scholars who formulate their opinions outside of the parameters of Sunnism. Their scholarship represents a clean break with Sunnism. Thirdly, all the names on the list are well-known public intellectuals who dominate public discussions on the various platforms of the conventional and social media. All use YouTube, Twitter, and the newer outlets of the social media. In this regard, the rationalists can be glossed as the "visual" faces of the public debate on Islam.[83] Fourthly, the nine rationalists are influential scholars whose ideas are shaping Islamic thought in Turkey today. A major purpose of this book is to observe how Islam is interpreted and practiced in the present-day society; the purpose is not historical analysis. This discussion of the expressed views of nine prominent Turkish rationalists provides us with insights into the Islamic rationalism that is articulated now. Last but not least, these rationalists are also prominent in academic studies of Islam. Their books and articles are trendsetters for many academics, particularly for the young scholars who are interested in critical scholarship on Islam.

Concerned mainly with contemporary Islamic rationalism in Turkey, this book is also an attempt to insinuate notions of theory-building into Islamic studies. Islamic rationalism in the Turkish case is an area in which theory is vague or lacking; thus, the present time is the optimal beginning point for contributing to theory-building in the academic rationalist domain. The literature on Islamic rationalism derives its arguments mainly from classical studies, with almost no reference to contemporary contributions. This book thus demonstrates that contemporary Islamic rationalism is the fertile ground on which to study critical Islamic thought in Turkey.

As we observe throughout this book, there are major common precepts among the rationalists. For example, they criticize Sunnism, decline to regard shari'a as a fixed universal framework, and promote a moralistic piety rather than the ritualistic one. In fact, all the nine rationalists arrive at almost the same conclusions on many of the subjects under scrutiny in this book. However, they employ different methods of argumentation to justify their conclusions. For example, both Atay and Özsoy no longer accept that the chopping-off of hands is a part of Islamic law, but they come to that conclusion along different argumentative routes. They employ either historicism or universalism to justify their conclusions. This has its roots in preexisting methodological debates on how to interpret Quran.

Historicism, employed by several contemporary Islamic rationalists, is the method that insists on the prime importance of the historical context in an interpretation of Quran. By "historical context," historicism refers to the period when Muhammad received the revelation in the seventh century. Referring back to the earlier discussion on the variants of rationalism, historicism is comparable to empiricism, because reasoning proceeds through knowledge acquired from the past, and from the present, about how the verses were/are relevant. In other words, the reasoning procedure is empiricist, since reasoning in historicism is subjected to the knowledge acquired from external spaces. Historicism rejects the interpretation of the verses by reason alone: taking the historical context into consideration is obligatory.

The second framework used by other contemporary Islamic rationalists is universalism, according to which human reason is assigned an absolute authority to interpret the verses according to the general principles of Quran, even when there is no need to consider any information acquired by the senses. So universalism is comparable to classical rationalism. Thus, in universalism, reasoning can incorporate knowledge acquired by the senses. However, it is not obligatory to do that, since human reason is recognized as having absolute authority in the interpreting of Quran. In their method, universalists imagine reason as a mechanical process that can work independently of any context, for it always arrives at a correct and objective conclusion.

However, on the two trajectories of universalism and historicism that we detect in the works of the nine rationalists, we are not observing an exclusive

Empiricism			Classical Rationalism
Historicists	Closed to Historicism	Closed to Universalism	Universalists
Ömer Özsoy	İsrafil Balcı	İhsan Eliaçık	Hüseyin Atay
Mustafa Öztürk	Mehmed Azimli		Yaşar Nuri Öztürk
İlhami Güler	Hayri Kırbaşoğlu		

Figure 1 The rationalists between universalism and historicism.

epistemology. Though we have cases like that of Özsoy, who is strictly loyal to historicism, there are also cases like Eliaçık, who borrows from both universalism and historicism. And there are cases like Kırbaşoğlu's, who sometimes attempts to synthesize the two tracks.[84] So universalism and historicism should be treated as the two contending paradigms that the rationalists recognize, not as two necessarily divergent paradigms. Seen in this way, the rationalists can be categorized in regard to their stance vis-à-vis universalism and historicism as seen in Figure 1.

The preference for historicism and universalism is attributable to the rationalists' efforts to announce their opinions on Islam in a modern framework. Though they pay enormous attention to engaging with the previous Islamic scholars, they are committed to modern methods of argumentation. As expected, their methods are criticized by traditionalists as deviating from the Islamic tradition by incorporating Western methods. In response, the rationalists argue that modern methods have universal merit, no matter what their origin.[85] The rationalists are motivated by the opinion that traditional Sunni methods are no longer functional in Islamic reasoning. Simply, they see Sunnism as a Medieval paradigm that fails to satisfy modern Muslims. For instance, Kırbaşoğlu finds that the traditional Sunni methodology, in the various fields such as law and hadith, is still in its Medieval forms, and is therefore incapable of being effective today.[86] In this vein, Güler criticizes religious education in Turkey for being based on Medieval scholastic knowledge.[87]

Equally problematic for them is the blatant anachronism of the practice of employing Medieval methods to interpret living concepts, and no less blatantly anachronistic when that living concept is Islam. A brilliant case to illustrate this is Güler's writing on the methodology of several greats, like al-Shafi'i, al-Ash'ari, and Ahmad bin Hanbal, when they explain the relationship between God and man. Güler says that if their arguments are analyzed through the works of scholars like Fromm, Jung, and Freud, they would be condemned as authoritarian to the point of impeding human progress.[88] Güler's point is to emphasize how modern and traditional perspectives differ radically and to warn that traditional Islamic interpretations are often anachronic to the point that it is not easy to avoid identifying them as impediments to progress. In fact, Güler charges that Islamic discourse has failed to transform itself into a discourse of modern social science.[89] Basically, for the rationalists, the interpretation of Islam with Medieval methods generates only anachronic conclusions. For example, they explain various controversial issues, such as supernatural events, and the unequal status of women before the law (which they see as problems of Sunnism) as anachronic survivals of Medieval perceptions of Islamics.[90] Recalling such problems, Özsoy attributes these harmful Medievalizing (*ortaçağlaşma*) retentions in Islam to the failure to subject it to a methodological and paradigmatic update.[91] The same plea to update is formulized by Kırbaşoğlu as the synthesizing of the traditional and the modern.[92] It is in this vein that historicism and universalism come to the forefront as operational frameworks through which the rationalists fulfill their strategy of interpreting Islam by modern methods.

From Sunnism to Rationalism

İ. Hakkı İzmirli (d. 1946), an Ottoman scholar who later became a leading name of the New Theology Movement (*Yeni İlm-i Kelam*) in the early Republican period, is usually regarded in the literature as a typical example of the intellectual who searches for a new interpretation of Islam. Unlike law-oriented analysts, İzmirli underlined the importance of theology in the problems of Muslims.[93] Atay, however, thinks İzmirli a scholar who proposed solutions that did not go beyond the limits of the existing Islamic paradigm.[94] Like Atay, Eliaçık considers Said Nursi (d. 1960), who proclaimed himself the reviver of Islamic thought, and as an author satisfied with the existing Islamic paradigm. Accordingly, he did not challenge the Sunni paradigm, but he presented the existing Islamic paradigm on a different perspective, but substantively unchanged.[95] As we observe in these two cases, the rationalists believe that an intellectual revival in Islamic thought is only possible by going beyond the boundaries of the Sunni tradition.

Contemporary Islamic rationalism does not hesitate to leave the mainstream Islamic paradigm, that is, Sunnism, while basing its arguments on the various subjects of Islam. Basically, not content to see Sunnism as an outdated or even as a mistaken paradigm, the rationalists treat it as the problem per se. To them, the problems that emerge from how Muslims interpret Islam are in fact the consequences of the Sunni paradigm. As the solution, they propose a structural break with the Sunni paradigm, not only in the interpretation of Islamic law but also in theology. Therefore, as stated earlier, while criticizing Sunnism, the rationalists do not employ what I called "an external perspective" such as secular or liberal critiques. Instead, they criticize the Sunni status quo in Turkey by employing religious arguments. However, making the case more intricate, the rationalists come from a social and educational background which is associated with Sunnism. Naturally, the emergence of a religious critique of Sunnism from scholars who paradoxically come from a Sunni background requires in-depth analysis, which brings us to the formation of the elite in Turkey.

Modernization in the Ottoman Empire in the nineteenth century formed an elite polarization of reformists and conservatives.[96] The polarization later survived in the Republican period as the modernizing Kemalist elites and Islamic elites. Both groups had different worldviews and lifestyles.[97] The Kemalist elites represented the urban secular culture, the sociological foundation of Westernization. They were educated either in the West or in Turkey but in line with a Western curriculum.

Naturally, a typical Kemalist elite was a secular person with a minimal connection to Islam. The collective idea of Kemalist elites was to "enlighten people on the road to progress," which amounted to a plan to create a Western-style society in Turkey.[98] On the polar opposite were the counter-elites who were loyal to the traditional values, particularly the religious ones. Variously called the "Anatolian elites" or "Islamic elites," they espoused the opposite of the Kemalist worldview. After the monolithic Kemalist profile of Turkish elites in the early decades of the Republic, a deep polarization between Kemalist and Islamic elites came to the fore, particularly in the 1960s and 1970s, thanks mainly to rapid urbanization and social mobility.[99]

The antagonism between the two elite groups was not only about ideological commitment. A class difference also existed between them, which manifested as a resentment among Islamic elites of their inequality vis-à-vis the Kemalist elites. Particularly, young people from poor or lower-middle-class backgrounds felt themselves victimized for not being given an equal opportunity of upward social mobility. This was partially true. Historically, economic factors, mainly the derivatives of land ownership, were always a structural dynamic of elite formation. As Kemal Karpat wrote, both in the late Ottoman and in the early Republican periods, "many individuals among the intelligentsia and the civil and military bureaucracies were sons and grandsons of landowners, and their wealth derived from land provided them with the income that allowed them to attend school."[100] However, since the reign of Abdulhamid II (r. 1876–1908), there was also a state strategy to train elites on the basis of cultural capital, not on that of land ownership.[101] But, the amalgamation of economic factors with cultural capital through education was never satisfactory, particularly in Anatolian towns where it was usually the children of upper-middle-class families, that is, the rich, who found the opportunity to become part of the modernizing elites.[102] The Kemalist regime had, too, a sophisticated network with notables in Anatolia through whom those families' children could manage to participate in the network of the modernizing elites.[103] The alliance between the Kemalist regime and the notables fared well, particularly when Kemalism was strong. The notables, as Sinan Ciddi wrote, in return for acting as the local representatives of Kemalist regime, received various benefits.[104] Logically, one major benefit of this alliance was the incorporation of those families' children into the Kemalist elites.

However, when it came to the lower economic strata families, public education was the only opportunity for upward mobilization, which naturally led to a class resentment among their children. However, feeling somehow sidelined in the Kemalist elite formation, these children were the sociological base of the future counter-Islamic elites. As a matter of fact, the general recruitment strategy of the Turkish Islamic movement evolved through the supporting and the bringing of those children to upper positions in academies, bureaucracy, and society. To a great extent, the Islamic strategy was an infiltration tactic, where the goal was to create a new group and insert it into a higher stratum instead of into the existing [Kemalist] elites.[105] If there was not any exceptional reason to become Kemalist, the usual socialization of the lower-social-strata children turned them out as traditionalist, and even as Islamic/Islamist types, due to the networks they developed with various Islamic movements on their given tracks. Logically, unless subjected to an ideological change, the usual things that people bring with them to the center are religion and nationalism.

Studying nine rationalists on these parameters, we find that they are all of Anatolian background, without any social or economic networks that could link them to the Kemalist elites, or to their local extensions. In terms of the key parameters like economic background, birthplace, and education, the rationalists went through a socialization course which typically does not result in upward mobility, to "modernizing elites" status. To begin with the birthplaces, the rationalists were all born in Anatolian towns, villages, and cities (Figure 2). None of them was born in Istanbul, Ankara, or İzmir, the urban cultural centers where the typical modernizing elites are born and educated. Differently, born to Anatolian villages and towns, the rationalists grew up under the heavy influence of a religious and traditional lifestyle. What Carol Delaney wrote on daily life in an Anatolian village is informative in this vein, and could also be seen as a reference point even for towns: "There is no escape, it [Islam] is the very context in which daily life unfolds."[106] Poverty and underdevelopment should be highlighted as a second factor: the youngest of the nine, Azimli, was born in 1968, so we should imagine towns and villages in pre-1970 Turkey, where economic conditions and infrastructure were grimly below any respectable social standard. Basic infrastructural services in villages, such as water and electricity, were not even part of government agendas before 1967.[107] In 1964, only 250 villages, only 0.7 percent of all villages across Turkey, had electricity. In 1977, 7,462 villages had electricity, which was still only 20.6 percent of all villages. Even in 1980, only 50 percent of the villages had electricity.[108] As one would expect, villages and most towns had no access to the outer world via radio or television. Therefore, the social and economic setting in which the rationalists happened to be born can be summed up with several major characteristics: They were underdeveloped locations with very limited connection to the outer world, and they were closed societies where traditional values prevailed.

Öztürk, who was socialized in that Anatolian setting, provided us with a lifelike description of his case: Born into a poor family surviving in a village house with

	Western			Anatolian		
	City	Town	Village	City	Town	Village
Hüseyin Atay						•
Yaşar Nuri Öztürk				•		
Hayri Kırbaşoğlu				•		
İlhami Güler					•	
İhsan Eliaçık				•		
Ömer Özsoy					•	
Mustafa Öztürk						•
İsrafil Balcı					•	
Mehmet Azimli						•

Figure 2 The birthplaces of the rationalists.

two rooms, his mother was illiterate. Facing severe economic poverty, his father moved to Giresun—a northeastern coastal city—to work in a factory. The father bought land there and constructed a *gecekondu*, that is, slum house, to survive. In a shanty neighborhood, Öztürk experienced all sorts of social problems caused by economic poverty, such as muddy roads and drunk friends. Öztürk never even read a book during his high school years.[109] Güler's case was no difference: He was born in a poor villager family living in a house without electricity, toilet, and water. There was no elementary school in the village. Reading his memoires, one notices that Güler remembers his childhood as a nightmare. He was forced to clean the barns in winter and look after animals every day at an age where he was supposed to play like the child he was. Given the poor sanitary conditions, children were frequently infected with lice. The whole village had only one toilet for men. Women used the animal barns as toilets. Endemics were frequent among the children. Güler was able to leave his small village for the first time when he was thirteen years old.[110] Though they might not have had as rough a time as Güler and Öztürk, other rationalists also come from a similar Anatolian background, where similar economic and social conditions prevailed.

Despite some differences caused by socioeconomic parameters, all the provinces where the rationalists were born are typical conservative Anatolian places under the heavy impact of Islamic and nationalistic values. In general, Islamic lifestyle in all those provinces can be summarized as conservative Sunni Islamic, committed to a singular nationalism with a state-oriented political culture.[111] Given that political socialization is always determined by the local environment and its power relations, conservative and nationalist parties that dominate politics at local level are the natural products of local political culture. Additionally, conservative settings at the local level support an intensive network of Islamic groups in which many young people are socialized.[112] The sociological backgrounds of nine Turkish rationalists therefore allowed only for a certain type of socialization, one that turned out agents of Sunni religiosity and nationalistic ideas.

However, their Anatolian as well as economic background dictated another consequence for the rationalists: their upward mobility was possible only through public schools where middle-class and lower-middle-class families send their kids. In those years, and even now, middle-class and lower-middle-class families had three options for their children: normal high schools, that is, the *lycée*, the vocational schools, and İmam-Hatip schools. Normally, İmam-Hatip schools are also vocational schools, but their focus is on training students to be religious preachers and ministers alongside preparing them for higher education. The İmam-Hatip schools opened in 1951, and quickly assumed a special role, for they became a major venue for the entire Turkish Islamic movement. And they became popular among Anatolian conservative families who wanted their children to become educated while their traditional values were protected.[113]

All eight rationalists had their education in such public schools: Öztürk, Azimli, Balcı, and Yaşar Nuri are graduates of İmam-Hatip schools. Not graduates of İmam Hatip schools, Kırbaşoğlu, Güler, Eliaçık, and Özsoy were educated in other types of public schools in various Anatolian cities and towns. Though he later continued his higher education in Baghdad, Atay also began his education in an elementary school in an Anatolian village and continued in public schools in Istanbul. Either they were graduates of normal high schools or of the İmam-Hatip schools, none of the rationalists is therefore a graduate of private schools, nor of other prestigious English- or French-speaking colleges, nor of some other established Turkish public schools in the Western cities from where many Kemalist secular elites graduated. We thus see no Turkish rationalists among the graduates of schools like Galatasaray Lycée,[114] a prestigious institution from where the core modernizing elites, both of the Ottoman Empire and of the Republican period, graduated. Nor are the rationalists among the graduates of schools like Saint Benoit High School, Saint Joseph High School, or the German High School. Therefore, neither the sociological background nor the early schooling of the rationalists is the usual upwardly mobile track to membership of the modernizing elites' club.

The next delicate phase of the rationalists' socialization is their university education. This brings us to the faculty of theology, the *İlahiyat Fakültesi*. Faculties of theology are the only academic venues for religious education at university level. As expected, their graduates dominate religious life in Turkey at all levels: Diyanet (the Directorate of Religious Affairs), the gigantic body of official Islam with more than 110,000 employees, is ruled and staffed by the graduates of theology faculties. Nearly all academics with PhD degrees in Islamic sciences are graduates of theology faculties. It is they who are appointed as teachers to middle and high schools, where religious courses are constitutionally compulsory.

In fact, Turkish institutions such as the İmam Hatip schools, Diyanet, and the theology faculties are the contemporary embodiments of the historical alliance between Sunnism and the state.[115] In practice, the gigantic network created by the İmam Hatip schools, Diyanet, and the theology faculties are the Republican models of the "Sunni education and the ulema" that had been the Ottoman period's own. The alliance between the state and Islam, a key element of Sunni orthodoxy, thus still prevails in Turkey, and contributes to the persistence of particular interpretations of Islam over others. This alliance has even the constitutional power to define the Islamic orthodoxy of the Turkish state.[116] Enjoying the opportunities that the alliance delivers, the Sunni clergy are able to promote their particular interpretation, and to shape people's daily practices and beliefs. Through such institutions, we observe the continuum of Sunni theology supported by political authority. Typical of this system is that theology faculties tend to teach through a Sunni paradigm, as the state expects.[117] In a work published in 2018, Bayramali Nazıroğlu, a professor of Islamic studies at the newly established Recep Tayyip Erdoğan University Faculty of Theology in Rize, praised theology faculties for their work for the survival of the state, and for their graduates' cautious avoidance of behaviors that take issue with the state.[118]

With the notable exception of Eliaçık, who quit the theology faculty after the third year, all the rationalists are graduates of *İlahiyat Fakültesi* (Figure 3). Again, except Eliaçık, all of them hold doctorate degrees in Islamic sciences, and they were/are full professors at different theology faculties across Turkey.

	Undergraduate		Ph D	
	University	City	University	City
Hüseyin Atay	Baghdad University	Baghdad	Ankara University	Ankara
Yaşar Nuri Öztürk	Marmara University	Istanbul	Marmara University	Istanbul
Hayri Kırbaşoğlu	Ankara University	Ankara	Ankara University	Ankara
İlhami Güler	Ankara University	Ankara	Ankara University	Ankara
İhsan Eliaçık	Erciyes University	Kayseri	-	-
Ömer Özsoy	Ankara University	Ankara	Ankara University	Ankara
Mustafa Öztürk	Marmara University	Istanbul	Ondokuz Mayıs Üniversitesi	Samsun
İsrafil Balcı	Ondokuz Mayıs University	Samsun	Ondokuz Mayıs Üniversitesi	Samsun
Mehmet Azimli	Selçuk University	Konya	Selçuk University	Konya

Note 1. There were faculties of theology only in Istanbul, Ankara, Konya, Kayseri, İzmir, Erzurum, Bursa and Samsun until 1987.

Note 2. Yaşar Nuri also graduated from Istanbul University Law School.

Note 3. Eliaçık quit theology school after the junior year.

Figure 3 The list of universities where the rationalists had their theology education.

Once established in 1949, the Ankara University Faculty of Theology (AUFT) was quickly identified as a reformist school. Ali Fuat Başgil (d. 1967), a conservative Turkish politician, criticized the school for training not scholars of religion but critics of religion.[119] Islamic groups and religious circles have kept up an attitude of skepticism toward AUFT, and they criticize it for championing reformist and Muʿtazili views, which traditional Sunnism disdains.[120] For example, as a young high school graduate Kırbaşoğlu was influenced by the negative propaganda on AUFT, and at first tried to register at the Atatürk University Faculty of Theology in Erzurum, attracted by its traditional stance.[121] Those used to the traditional methods would have met academic studies of Islam at theology faculties with skepticism. Studies of intricate subjects such as the Muʿtazila were naturally introduced first at AUFT during the 1950s.[122] For example, Mehmed S. Hatiboğlu, whose works laid out a rationalist analysis of key Islamic subjects, was received with criticism by traditionalist Islamic scholars as well as by the Islamic movements.[123] Atay rejected the Sunni concept of destiny in his PhD thesis at AUFT. Theology faculties established later continued on the same scholarly track. But approaching Islam as a scholarly subject was indeed not a charming move in the eyes of the Turkish public, be they Islamic movements or old-school clergy. Undoubtedly, their expectation of theology faculties was not explication of religion but its preaching and its defense. Logically, it was the early studies conducted on modern scholarship lines that sparked a negative feeling about theology faculties. Yet it should be kept in mind, as Güler also notes, that at its establishment in 1949, AUFT had a philosophy-dominated curriculum that remained until the 1970s. This was a reflection of the secular characteristics of the Kemalist regime.[124]

However, though the Kemalist regime expected the schools to become the agents of a modern interpretation of Islam, it is not correct to see them as ever having adopted that mission wholeheartedly.[125] In his speech in parliament as a deputy on the establishment of a theology faculty in 1949, İ. Hakkı Baltacıoğlu (d. 1978), a pioneering name in education reform, underlined that the purpose was not to revive the *madrasa* but to create a theology school that teaches according to modern methods.[126] However, despite such plans, theology faculties have mostly repeated the existing religious literature rather than renewed it. Güler, for example, apparently does not even see them as schools of theology, but rather as schools of *tafsir* and *hadith*, that is, as exegeses and traditions.[127] Confirming Güler in general, it was traditional Sunni scholars who later dominated the theology faculties. But still, theology faculties have helped several scholars who promote critical thinking on Islam to survive in the academic system. No matter who dominates the school, theology faculties have operated as legitimate spaces that bring the required elements and opportunities to the support of critical scholarship, albeit viewed as a deviant case. Thus, by introducing modern scholarship into Islamic studies, theology faculties somehow provided a suitable academic milieu for a rationalist track of Islamic scholarship. The study of Islamic disciplines in a modern format has also helped several scholars develop critical engagements with Islamic classics, as well as with modern discussion on Islam. Many graduate students are socialized in a modern academic methodology where it is inevitable to engage with Western works while writing doctoral dissertations. In those studies, Islam was also a subject under inquiry along with being a divine instruction. Consequently, modern methods introduced new approaches, such as the sociology of religion, where there is excessive quotation of Western scholarship. This gave rise to serious intellectual debates. For example, the first PhD thesis set in the sociology of religion was defended before an academic jury at AUFT in 1969 by M. Rami Ayas, who studied Islamic orders through the lens of the sociology of religion.[128]

Theology faculties also became the venues where a new generation of Turkish scholars of religious studies developed an academic network with the global intelligentsia. To give only a few examples: Atay was sent to Israel in 1962 to learn Hebrew, where he studied the impact of Hebrew translations, for the Western readership, of classical Islamic philosophy. Atay later spent academic years in prestigious American institutions such as Harvard University and Chicago University. A particular case that demonstrates how theology faculties operate as venues where people encounter alternative opinions is the meeting of young Atay with Muhammad Tanci (d. 1974)—a Moroccan professor of Islamic philosophy—who encouraged him to embrace critical opinions of Sunni theology.[129] Güler conducted postdoctoral studies at Cairo University. He later went to UK to carry out an academic project there. Kırbaşoğlu worked in various universities in Qatar and Saudi Arabia. Similarly, foreign scholars were invited by theology faculties. For example, Fazlur Rahman was invited to Turkey in 1979, and he exchanged opinions with the AUFT faculty. As such examples confirm, theology faculties have simply provided various institutional opportunities upon which one can develop a modern view of Islamic studies, as well as develop intellectual contacts with alternative paradigms. Therefore, despite the Sunni dominance of theology faculties, they have inevitably provided intellectual opportunities for critical thought, simply by bringing people and ideas together.

Remarkably, Fazlur Rahman predicted that modern religious education in Turkey might generate a new religious thought. The first thing that thrilled Rahman was "the impressive upward mobility of intellectual life in the new educational adventure of Islam in Turkey." For Rahman, mobility, which he defined as an inherent quality of the Turkish education system, could work as a positive social dynamic. In fact, the case of the rationalists—as I discussed earlier—could be proposed as proving Rahman's predictions. Secondly, Rahman, again remarkably, noticed astutely that the incorporation of new subjects, such as Islamic philosophy, into the curriculum has the potential to trigger intellectual discussion. He was even sure that "in the new Turkish Islamic education system, the bases were healthy from the beginning."[130] On my interpretation, Rahman was not optimistic about Turkey because he detected a strategy for the revival of Islamic thought. Instead, he discovered that the faculties of theology are turning into academic venues that gather a diversity of ideas. That will inevitably see them generate new thinking on religious themes, because they are set up as modern institutions with contemporary courses delivered with creative curriculum methods. This cannot but work as a dynamic in favor of critical thought. Rahman was sure that no matter how weighed down they remain by Sunnism, theology faculties in Turkey are much more advanced and modern than in any other Islamic country, including Pakistan and Egypt. He repeated this hope in his Introduction in 1977 to the Turkish translation of *Islam*. Again, citing the reforms of 1949 in higher-level religious education, Rahman wrote that Turkey is capable of stimulating an Islamic renaissance.[131] There is no doubt that what appealed to Rahman about the 1949 reforms was the introduction of a modern format to Islamic studies.

The Structure of the Book

The works of the rationalists provide a detailed and systematic paradigm on Islam from theology to history. Their works include a debate on all aspects of Islam that require a method that would provide a holistic view of contemporary Islamic rationalism. Therefore, I shall study the rationalists under the headings of (i) The fundamentals: Quran and traditions, (ii) law, (iii) history, and (iv) politics and society—the four major clusters that help span the aspects of religion comprehensively.

Chapter 1, "The Fundamentals: Quran and Hadith," introduces the rationalists' understanding of Quran and the traditions, that is, the fundamental resources of Islam. The chapter first describes the arguments of the rationalists on Quran and hadith in regard of their nature, status, and content; second, it explains the methodology that the rationalists propose for interpreting them. The rationalists accept that the failure of Sunnism is mainly because of the wrong paradigm it employs to understand and interpret Quran and hadith. Thus, they are of the opinion that an alternative Islamic paradigm is possible only with a new theological framework for the interpretation of the fundamentals. So they suggest a completely new theology for explaining Quran and hadith, and a new methodology for interpretation that effectively gives way to their breaks with Sunnism. For instance, they submit radically different opinions on the nature of Quran, such as on the subject of its createdness. The rationalists' arguments, particularly on the fundamentals, are methodologically important because those are the arguments that justify their approaches to other themes, such as shari'a.

Chapter 2, "Law: Demystifying Shari'a," explicates how the rationalists define shari'a, and its implications, in four fields: Islamic law, piety, politics, and sunnah. This chapter is concerned mainly with the practical implications of contemporary Islamic rationalism. As the basic principle, for the rationalists shari'a and Islam are not equal, for the former is not universal, and it is only a temporal form of Quran's message derived from Arab practices. Having defined shari'a as a temporal example, not as the ultimate model, the rationalists interpret Quran on such selected cases in a radical way, with completely different conclusions. Thus, for them, it is possible to interpret, and even to practice, shari'a in different forms in other contexts. The chapter then demonstrates the rationalists' different approach to shari'a, and how that impacts, on a practical level, their interpretation of Islamic law in regard of a number of cases, such as the punishment rules, polygamy, divorce, veiling, and jihad.

Piety is also analyzed in this chapter, for it is regarded by the rationalists as the practice of Islam in daily life. Unlike in Sunnism, which defines piety mainly through formal worship, for the rationalists, it is a matter of moral deeds. The rationalists are critical of Sunnism for promoting a piety based on formal worship, such as the five-times prayer. It is in this vein that they suggest that opposition to corrupt or unjust rulers is moral act of piety. The moralistic piety of the rationalists requires political opposition on moral grounds, as a part of religiosity. Unlike traditional Sunnism, which advices stability and loyalty, the rationalists reframe the relationship between politics and Islam as a theory of moral opposition. When it comes to sunnah, that is, Prophet Muhammad's deeds, the rationalists reject the Sunni view of sunnah for being a "photographic method," that is, an imitation of exactly what Muhammad did, without any elaboration on the moral purpose behind his deeds. Instead, for the rationalists, sunnah should be understood as a paradigm, not as a practice. Thus, the purpose of sunnah is not to imitate but to understand why Muhammad acted as he did.

Chapter 3, "History: De-Islamizing Islamic History," describes how the rationalists challenge the Sunni history, which they define as the third pillar of Sunnism, along with law and theology. For rationalists, the substantial problem of Sunni history is that it repudiates natural and historical causation in the constructions of its historical narrative. Their major reservation about Sunni historiography is therefore its stance on Medieval perceptions of causality. As a result, it is flawed, with problems such as the deployment of the supernatural, and of exceptionalism, with the result that they read the Islamic past exclusively through religious dynamics, and therefore underrate, sometimes even ignore, political and economic causes. In sharp contrast, the rationalists explain the Islamic past as a series of events of historical and natural causation. Theirs is thus a revisionist historiography on Islam. To exemplify various implications of their revisionism, the chapter studies how three major topics are differently narrated by the rationalists: the history of Quran, Muhammad's life, and the early Islamic period.

Naturally, the works of the rationalists are not indifferent from the grand debate that investigates the reasons for complex problems, such as the poverty and the authoritarianism in Muslim societies. Chapter 4, "Politics and Society: What Went Wrong?" studies the answers that the rationalists give to explain the general state of Muslim societies. Logically, they are interested in how the interpretation of Islam is related to those contemporary problems. As the chapter illustrates, they discuss various reasons, such as the rise of Sunni orthodoxy, the triumph of anti-rationalism in Muslim societies, the negative impact of the continuing legacy of Ash'arism, the problems caused by Sufism, and how contemporary Islamic movements worsen the general situation in the Muslim world. The book concludes with a general discussion of how its findings are relevant contributions to the critical global scholarship of Islamic studies.

Chapter 1

THE FUNDAMENTALS

QURAN AND HADITH

The trajectory of Islamic thought can be imagined as a discourse that plots the nature of Quran and hadith (the fundamentals), and the effects of that discourse in the various societal fields, such as law and politics. The rationalists, too, acquire their intellectual distinctiveness in general, and their reputations vis-à-vis Sunnism in particular, for their opinions on Quran and hadith. Logically, the top prerequisite of an inquiry into the works of the rationalists is an examination of their views on the fundamentals, and of the methods they propose for interpreting them. That is the subject matter of this chapter. In regard of the rationalists, it is a methodologically important chapter, for it will help them synthesize their views on other aspects of Islam, including Islamic law, with their understanding of Quran and hadith/traditions. The rationalists' position on Quran and traditions constitutes their theoretical framework.

The Rationalists on Quran

Quran (8:60)[1] asks Muslims to prepare whatever forces they can muster, including warhorses. Though it spells out "horses," Muslims interpret the verse broadly, and invest in modern weapons. Speaking of this broad interpretation, Özsoy states that the substantial question in Islamic thought is how Muslims interpret Quran.[2] But, what makes it possible to understand "warhorses" in Quran as "modern weapons"? Öztürk interjects that Muslims do not propose a similarly progressive interpretation on the status of women.[3] Such contending approaches to the interpretation of Quran reveal much about the nature of Islam in practice. However, interpreting Quran is essentially linked to another subject: the nature of Quran. Naturally, contending arguments on the nature of Quran enable different conclusions on the meaning of its verses.

With this in mind, I shall conduct my study of the rationalists in the light of how they answer two interrelated questions: What is the nature of Quran? What is the correct method of interpreting its verses? When analyzing rationalists in this regard, in the interest of clarity, I will study them separately as historicists and universalists according to the distinction I made in the previous chapter.

Historicists on the Nature of Quran

Historicism is a method that insists on the prime importance of the historical context to the interpretation of texts of all kinds.[4] Applied to the study of Quran, it is de rigueur to interpret the verses with reference to their historical context, the time of Prophet Muhammad, and of the early Muslims. Historicism recognizes the authentic meaning of a verse (i.e., how it was understood in its historical context) as the objective framework for understanding it now.[5] Thus, as I noted in the Introduction, historicism is comparable to empiricism inasmuch as both schools of thought are committed to the view that reasoning and the knowledge acquired through the senses together affect how one interprets a verse and draws religious conclusions. That the historicist method is at all possible is owed to a set of peculiar views on the nature of Quran. I shall first summarize those views, then explain the method in detail.

Quran Has No Divine Nature   Historicism rejects Quran's divine nature. Instead, it is created, and therefore not eternal.[6] In *The Muʿtazili Interpretation of Quran*, reminding of various verses like 50:38, which read as "we created the heavens, the earth, and everything between," Öztürk deduces that God could have spoken so only after he had created the earth, which entails that Quran is not eternal: Any argument that proposes that certain verses existed before the creation of the earth is committed to the conclusion that God made a claim that something that happened did not in fact happen. That, of course, is not in harmony with the nature of the deity.[7]

The "createdness" thesis is the foundational principle of historicism that proposes the hermeneutical method of interpreting Quran. As importantly, historicists exit Sunnism by embracing the thesis attributed to the Muʿtazila. Güler correctly alerts that Sunnis would brand them with the label "heretics."[8] In Sunnism, Quran is not created; it is divine and eternal. Quran is the Word of God in meaning and style.[9] *İlmihal*—the two-volume catechist book by the Diyanet prepared for households, mosques, and schools that shapes the popular understanding of Sunni Islam—defines Quran as a divine speech.[10] The origin of the Sunni dogma is a theological opinion promoted by Ashʿarism and Maturidism, the two major schools of Sunni theology. Accordingly, God's attributes, including his *kalam* (speech), are divine.[11] The logical conclusion is Quran's divinity, since it is God's speech.[12] In contrast, the Muʿtazila School accepts the "created Quran" tenet, and rejects its divinity, and the "God's speech" canon.[13]

A soft version of the Sunni dogma emerged later, arguing that there is an eternal Quran in heaven (*kalam nafsi*), and another in this world (*kalam lafdzi*).[14] The soft theory was advanced by Ibn Kullab (d. 855) as a compromising formula during the *Mihna*.[15] (The *Mihna* was introduced by the Abbasid caliph al-Maʾmun (d. 833) to enforce the doctrine of the createdness of the Quran. It eventually failed, due to the resistance of traditional scholars. Caliph al-Mutawakkil (d. 861) abandoned it altogether.[16]) However, historicists see the soft theory as a tactical attempt to challenge the Muʿtazili view.[17] Thus, they reject the heavenly Quran, too.[18] Öztürk dismisses the soft theory as a theological metaphor that brought no real change. He observes that Muslims are still loyal to the traditional Sunni dogma of the divine Quran.[19]

Indeed, the "uncreated Quran" is a strong theological argument. W. Cantwell Smith, commenting on the Sunni dogma, wrote that according to the "uncreated Quran" tenet, Quran is to Muslims as Jesus is to Christians.[20] As expected, attributing a divine nature to Quran is rigorously criticized by historicists. Lambasting Sunnis for proclaiming Quran a Godlike divinity, Güler condemns it as an idolatry.[21] Inspired by Naser Abu-Zayd, Öztürk finds the uncreated Quran incompatible with Islam, where a major commandment is to reject the dual nature of Jesus.[22] Beyond the theological reservations, the intellectual legacy of the divine Quran is also bothersome for historicists, who consider it a major obstacle, one that permanently undermines rationalism in Islamic thought.[23] Öztürk describes the uncreated Quran as a boundary within Islamic thought that is an impasse that puts human reason out of reach.[24] Likening it to a Sunni "end of history" thesis, Güler holds that the Sunni dogma is responsible for the popular belief among Muslims in a divine resource with perfect solutions to everything.[25] Therefore, historicists see the rejection of the divine Quran as the essential prerequisite of a rationalist turn in the Islamic tradition.

Quran Is Historical In Sunnism, Quran is an ahistorical message sent to this world, by divine intervention.[26] So, no historical event affected the formation of Quran; it does not belong to this world.[27] The diametric opposite is true for the rationalists, who adhere to the historicist view: Quran is historical and was determined by historical dynamics. Quran belongs to this world.[28] Özsoy summarizes the historicist principle: There is no ahistorical thing at human level; everything is part of history; and everything is subject to natural causation, so also is Quran.[29]

For historicists, social and political developments in Mecca and Medina affected Quran at all levels, including the content of its verses. Öztürk illustrates this by analyzing the changing attitude toward Jews in Quran. Accordingly, though earlier verses revealed in Mecca, like 21:7, 10:94, and 16:43, cite Jews in amicable terms, later verses revealed in Medina view them bitterly, due to the changing political status quo. For example, when Muslims, who were yet a small group, needed their support in Mecca, verse 10:94 mentions Jews affirmatively as reference group: "So if you are in doubt about what we have revealed to you, ask those who have been reading the scriptures before you." However, once the Muslims got a grip on power in Medina, the tone of the revelations toward the Jews changed, and turned into a humiliating depiction in Surah al-Baqarah.[30] The verse 2:120 speaks against Christians and Jews, for they are never pleased unless Muslims follow their ways. Or, while the earlier verses identify Abraham as a Jew, the Medina verses portray him as a *hanif* (monotheist). Öztürk asserts that the impact of the tense political atmosphere between Muslims and Jews caused even contradictions in Quran's verses: He points out verse 9:29, which describes Jews as the People of the Book who do not believe in God, and reads it as an oxymoron, for Jews cannot not believe in God while they are the People of the Book.[31] In another example, Öztürk expounds upon how economic dynamics affected the revelation: When non-Muslims were prohibited to approach Kaʻba (9:28), it sparked complaints among Muslims, for it caused them economic losses. Responding to them, the following verse (9:29) then introduced *jizyah*, a per capita yearly taxation levied on non-Muslims, and even asked Muslims to fight them "until they pay the taxes."[32] Such cases, for Öztürk, prove how historical developments determined the revelations. Otherwise, the only explanation would be to accept that God changed his mind, a contradiction of His deity. In like manner, the revelations' response to historical conjuncture also falsifies the concept of an eternal fixed-content Quran.[33]

"Historical Quran" also requires key Islamic concepts cited in the verses as determined in history by surrounding milieu and culture. So, the meanings of the key terms regarded as the foundation of Islamic faith have no eternally set meanings. For example, Güler presents God in Quran as a heavily anthropomorphic conceptualization reflecting the Arab mindset.[34] Similarly, Özsoy explains how various divine attributes like *muntaqim* (revenge taker) reflect the seventh-century Arab understanding of deity.[35] Having such facts in mind, Güler concludes that the Quranic God is a reflection of the Arab mentality, where He is imaged as a just king who has a master-slave relationship with people. Quoting R. E. Emerson's "the god of warriors is a warrior, the god of tradesmen is a tradesman," Güler deduces that the God of Quran is a reflection of Arab culture.[36] Logically, but still surprisingly, Güler does not then hesitate to warn that the Quranic God, having emerged in a specific social and historical context, might be unsatisfactory for later times or other cultures.[37] In practice, this is to accept that the concept of God in Quran is not a universal one. Historicists reuse this argument for other critical purposes. Öztürk detects *shirk* (polytheism) a term used in Quran in the context of an early Muslim society. That word does not speak for a universal perspective. It cannot be imagined to be referencing other practices, like the Iranian worship of fire.[38] In general, Güler spots that the religious vocabulary of Quran has no reference to distant religions like Hinduism or Shamanism.[39] In consequence, even key concepts of Quran are historical in the sense that their meanings were determined by social and political dynamics of their time and location. To illustrate the complicated interaction of Quran and its historical context, Güler likens it to the relationship of British pragmatism and the eighteenth-century Industrial Revolution, and to how Immanuel Kant was linked to the politics of the Prussian Empire. As in those contexts, Quran cannot be abstracted from the seventh-century Arab life and culture.[40] Similarly, there is an Arab anthropological shadow on Quran.[41] This is normal for Öztürk, since Quran was also exposed to the social and other dynamics of its society, like any other historical phenomenon.[42] Supporting this view, Kırbaşoğlu reminds that slavery in Quran can be explained only with reference to the complex relationship of Quran and the Arab society of the seventh century. Kırbaşoğlu warned that otherwise the only logical conclusion is to accept that slavery is a divine regulation.[43]

Quran Is Not Universal Sunnism defines Quran as a universal book, relevant for all ages and people.[44] Differently, not seeing Quran as universal, historicists define it as having a local scope limited by the Arab life around Mecca and Medina in the seventh century.[45] Accordingly, Quran addresses only those Arabs who were in conversation with Muhammad.[46] Therefore, Quran gives its universal messages through local people and events in a seventh-century Arab context.[47] So, Quran is a local interpretation of the universal message for historicists.[48] Logically, for historicists, other people in different times and places are not addressed by Quran.[49] Quran is therefore not in dialogue with all ages. Güler clarifies this by defining Quran as a collection of speeches that happened only "in Arab society, and on the Arab street."[50] Thus, it belongs to a specific time and geography.[51]

In this regard, expressions in Quran like "O, you people" are not interpreted as addressing all humanity. Instead, such utterances are like the politician's opening words to his audience, even in a small village: "Dear citizens . . ." That politician is not understood to be addressing all people in the country. In similar fashion, the Quran speech is local; hence, it cannot be imagined, for example, as addressing today's Turkish people. Thus, direct discourses in Quran—like "O, you . . ."—address only those who lived with Muhammad, including the polytheists, Muslims, and Christians.[52] Paul Ricoeur's approach might be helpful for a better view of historicists. Ricoeur categorizes pronouns in a conversation as having no objective or universal meaning. So, a pronoun—like *they* or *you*—has "meaning each time it is used, and each time it refers to a singular subject." So, we need to know whom it addresses in each conversation. However, writing gives way to a "universalization of the audience."[53] If we are not informed about the background, we tend to read a text as a universal speech addressing anyone who reads it. But, not defining Quran as a universal text, historicists interpret each *you* in Quran in terms of its singular subject in its historical context, which is Mecca and Medina during the prophethood of Muhammad.

The locality of Quran is not only a case of pronouns; the verses in Quran are meaningful only in their local context for historicists.[54] In other words, they do not have universal meanings independently of their local contexts. Alluding to John R. Searle, Kırbaşoğlu describes the Arab peninsula and the surrounding geography as the background of Quran without which we cannot interpret a verse.[55] The logical result of this reasoning is more important. Treating Quran as if it were a universal book would inevitably lead to wrong conclusions, like recognizing local elements in Quran as universal norms. Özsoy gives an example to demonstrate this problem: The literature is full of the virtues of breastfeeding a baby for two years. Yet this abstraction is the result of a false interpretation of verse (2:233), which reads as "mothers suckle their children for two whole years." In reality, it informs about an Arab tradition that has nothing to do with a universal health principle.[56] In the same way, Kırbaşoğlu writes that verse 5:2, which allows Muslims to hunt once they have completed pilgrimage rites, is about local and historical conditions that have no meaning at all today.[57] Similarly, many verses (like 17:11, 18:54, and 80:17) that define "human" as a very negative property are read as if they are axiomatic statements about human nature. However, Öztürk warns that those verses address some people who lived during Muhammad's time. But missing the significance of that contextual element, those local verses are read as if Quran presents a very negative view of human nature.[58] As the misinterpretation of the aforementioned verse illustrates, Öztürk notes that reading all verses as if they have universal content leads to another big problem: recognizing every verse as being equally a source of Islamic law. In fact, Quran has verses that cannot be thought to enunciate universal truths. As Öztürk believes, it is not logical to imagine God, "the creator of billions of galaxies," giving a universal message through person-specific verses, like 33:53, where a group of companions is asked not to talk long at Muhammad's home during a wedding, or verse 33:51, which regulates the nightly frequencies of Muhammad's being with his wives.[59] Güler too sees those verses that are on Muhammad's private life as having only local content, not universal messages. Even for him, they could trigger faith problem among Muslims if not well framed in a historicist logic.[60]

Many concepts in Quran that are understood to have universal application are in fact collected from the local Arab environment for the historicists.[61] For instance, Muslims understand the Paradise of Quran to be a divinely designed portrait of the legitimate universal expectation of the deserving. However, Öztürk remarks that the Quranic Paradise where rivers flow is a portrait of desire for Arabs whose life allotment is the desert. It does not work as such a portrait for a person who lives in countries like Bangladesh, where there are frequent floods.[62] Or, how Quran presents *houri*, the maiden who awaits Muslims in Paradise, is a typical Arabic concept of beauty dating back to pre-Islamic poets like Imru' al-Qais (d. c. 510). As we read in Azimli, similarities were recognized among the various verses and the al-Qais' poems even in earlier periods.[63] Then there is *sidr*, the tree that Quran describes in Paradise, which is also a theme of Arab poets like Umayyah ibn Abi Salt (d. 630), who composed similar depictions of Paradise that contain the same tree.[64] As a matter of fact, such discussions are known in various classics: Ibn Ishaq (d. 768) wrote that *kawthar*, a Quranic term which stands for the miraculous water of Paradise, was used by the poet Labid (d. 661).[65] Rationalists frequently underline that, as the examples of classical authors' creations demonstrate, Quran uses concepts familiar to the local Arab mind. Öztürk and Kırbaşoğlu explain this as the normal pattern, since the vocabulary of Quran was determined by its local context. They remind that the list of the names of various things like fruits, foods, and many other things in Quran are only local examples.[66] In consequence, for historicists, the meanings of words in Quran are also not universal. Thus, they are critical of the practice of seeking to understand such words as if they are universal terminology. Balcı, however, says that the later Sunni scholars redefined many of the local-phenomena words in Quran to build into them universal, or even metaphysical, ideas.[67]

Quran's Content It is axiomatic in Sunni dogma that Quran—the uncreated words of God—is perfect in all respects.[68] Muslims credit it with knowledge of everything, even of that which the human mind cannot conceive. Accordingly, even the smallest detail of Quran, for example a dot, is replete with meaning.

1. The Fundamentals

Attributing limitation to the content of Quran is a contempt of God.[69] Al-Ghazali describes Quran as the source from which "the sciences of the ancients and contemporaries branch off."[70] *İlmihal* states: "the sublime knowledge that Quran contains is enough to solve all human problems till the last day." Besides, its verses are sources of inspiration to reach for scientific truths and the natural law.[71]

Historicists dismiss the Sunni view of the content of Quran as an intellectual construction. Several scholars, like al-Razi (d. 1210), al-Zarkashi (d. 1392), and al-Suyuti (d. 1505), are the architects of the idea that Quran has infinite knowledge. Güler tackles al-Razi for his particular impact on the transformation of the exegesis tradition of Islam into an effort to discover endless meanings in Quran.[72] In an attitude of puzzlement, Öztürk quotes al-Razi, who claims that he can derive an understanding of thousands of subjects from al-Fatiha alone, a surah with only seven verses.[73] Öztürk takes a similar attitude to al-Zarkashi, who claims that one's life is not enough to study all the sciences in Quran.[74] We understand from the works of historicists that they are critical of the Sunni scholars who approach Quran as an encyclopedia containing all the sciences, which is the staple claim usually attributed to al-Suyuti.[75] Highly critical of al-Suyuti, historicists find that his argumentation makes of Quran a tract incomprehensible to the human mind. That stumbles into a contradiction, given that it was sent to be understood.[76] Alluding to Aristotle, Güler writes that if a verse has as many meanings as Sunni scholars claim, then it is meaningless.[77]

For historicists, al-Shafi'i has an exclusive significance in this regard. They see him as the key scholar whose method shaped the Sunni view of Quran. Al-Shafi'i is the chief symbol of traditionalism and of anti-rationalism. His methodological legacy is regarded by the historicists as having reduced reasoning to an intellectual effort within the tight boundaries of Quran and hadith, which was possible only after Quran was declared a book of infinite sciences.[78] As Öztürk summarizes this state of things, al-Shafi'i's legacy naturally weakens the influence of rationalists like Abu Hanifa, who suggested going beyond the text when reasoning.[79] But, for al-Shafi'i, going beyond the text became meaningless, since Muslim are told that they have a book that contains infinite knowledge. To illustrate the negative impact of al-Shafi'i on Islamic thought, Güler likens his method to sending Quran back to the heavens by declaring it to have infinite knowledge that is beyond the capacity of human reason to grasp.[80] Analyzing al-Shafi'i's impact from a different perspective, Öztürk asserts that it transformed Islamic literature into a repetition of previous works, since reasoning has been confined by the texts.[81] He adds that several ideas of the Mu'tazili scholar Abu Muslim al-Isfahani were rejected because nobody had voiced them before him.[82] I should note here that Fazlur Rahman, too, explained the legacy of the al-Shafi'i's methodology as a negative factor in regard of the trajectory of rationalism in Islamic thought.[83]

When it comes to the historicist view of the concept of knowledge in Quran, the quality of the expatiations on this subject is determined by the intellectual capacity of the person whom the revelation was speaking.[84] Thus "knowledge" in Quran is not a reflection of God's infinite knowledge but that of the limitations of the people whom were the subject of the revelation.[85] Deriving its discourse from the *jahilliya* mentality and life style, Quran did not bring anything that Arabs did not already know—according to the historicists.[86] So the tenet that Quran has complex knowledge of everything, and answers to all sorts of problems, is simply untenable.[87] According to Güler, solutions to various problems, such as to underdevelopment, are irrelevant on the Quran perspective.[88] Kırbaşoğlu agrees that Quran is not an encyclopedia providing solutions to political and economic problems.[89]

Historicists highlight a principle of communication in this vein: It is illogical to argue that Quran has knowledge that people do not know or understand.[90] Quran's having such knowledge would prove that the dialogue between revelation and the people is not successful, according to Öztürk.[91] Güler concludes that Quran does not have complex knowledge that the early Muslims could not understand.[92] For historicists, Quran is therefore a simple text. Öztürk thus evaluates the knowledge in Quran as the knowledge of the average person.[93] Historicists frequently quote "shari'a is illiterate," a maxim of al-Shatibi.[94] To prove the historicist argument, Güler and Öztürk remind that no complex knowledge or science survived from the early Muslims.[95]

Naturally, the historicist view on Quran's content has important implications. For example, *qissas* (the historical passages in Quran) give religious messages rather than accounts for historical events.[96] As Öztürk reminds, however, that the *qissas* are accounts of past events in Sunnism, given that God does not tell something that did not happen.[97] Nor does God tell a fictional story in Sunnism. In Egypt, Muhammad Ahmad Khalafallah's doctoral thesis was refused by Cairo University in 1947, for he presented *qissas* as mythological reports rather than historical facts. He was criticized for dealing with Quran as a work of literary art, presented as if Muhammad were speaking.[98] In deep contradiction with Sunnism, historicists too liken *qissas* to mythological stories.[99] Inspired by Taha Hussein, Özsoy approaches the historical stories in Quran as samples of Arab mythology, the content of which might be not historically correct.[100] To justify the argument in terms of Islamic tradition, Öztürk quotes various scholars like al-Qaffal al-Shashi (d. 976), for they read the passages on Adam and Eve in Quran as a metaphorical story.[101]

A second radical implication is the historicist view on the relationship between Quran and science. For historicists, neither in explicit nor in implicit ways does Quran contain sophisticated scientific information.[102] There is no reason for Öztürk to believe that Quran informs directly or indirectly on scientific subjects like quantum physics or astronomy.[103] In Güler's view, Quran is not a book of astronomy, medicine, or chemistry, and he therefore criticizes scholars who read the verses as if deep meanings are zipped into them.[104] Eliaçık dismisses such readings as presentism.[105] Sharing those views, Öztürk sarcastically questions why Muslims detect scientific clues in Quran only after scientific discoveries are publicized in the West.[106] As we read in Eliaçık, for historicists, passages in Quran on natural phenomena, like the stars, give various messages, not scientific information.[107] Thus, Güler does not find those passages eligible for a rating as scientific verification.[108] In this vein, historicists also refuse the translation as "science" of *'ilm* in Quran. Öztürk interprets *'ilm* as knowledge provided by revelation, like the Platonic logos. Rather than "knowing" in the language of modern science, *'ilm* is more like "faith."[109] The strategy of historicists—reflecting their empiricist tenet—is to develop a religious theory that addresses nature as the only source of scientific knowledge. Eliaçık contends that Quran addresses nature as the source of knowledge.[110] Sharing the same perspective, Özsoy defines the outer world, that is, nature, as the source confirmed by Quran as the knowledge of things (in the world).[111]

Historicists' insistent demand that a line be drawn between Quran and science is a matter of necessity, for that is the logical consequence of seeing the verses as historical. Passages on history and science in Quran might be factually wrong, just like mundane historical texts often are. Öztürk explains this as an inevitable cost of the dialogue between the revelations and the Arabs, which happened within the knowledge limits of the latter. Quran addresses the Arabs as if they knew of things, the past, and nature.[112] However, what Arabs knew might have been wrong information, and that would have caused errors of fact in Quran. Kırbaşoğlu gives the example of the Quranic account of Jews and Christians, where they are depicted according to the seventh-century Meccans' knowledge, which is not valid for all Jews and Christians.[113] Kırbaşoğlu here hints at various issues, such as the assertion in various verses that the Jews consider Uzair to be the son of God. One typical method to solve such problems is to argue that the assertion is based on some Meccan Jews' beliefs.[114] However, as a broader method, Öztürk suggests reading such verses for their message, and not with the intention of submitting them to historical verification.[115] The case gets more complicated when it comes to the passages on natural phenomena. What if Quran speaks of natural phenomena as its coeval Arabs knew them? Historicists again appeal to the principles of a dialogue that always require that revelation speaks on the knowledge level of the average Arab. To explain the principle, Azimli suggests that had Quran informed that, for example, the earth is a globe, Arabs would not have believed it.[116] Accordingly, when revelation chose to deliver a message through natural phenomena, then revelation deemed the Arab perception of nature capable of making that message understandable. But, Öztürk asserts that this caused various unfortunate outcomes, such as the Quranic depiction of a flat sky above the earth. The earth is also depicted as flat—the fixed soil of the entire universe. The Quranic descriptions, for Öztürk, are nothing other than the Bedouin Arab's comprehension that accumulates on the evidence of naked-eye observation.[117] To exemplify this, Öztürk cites verse 2:210, which asks, "Are these people waiting for God to come to them in the shadows of the clouds, together with the angels?" To him, the verse illustrates a typical Ptolemaic imagination of the universe.[118] Similarly, Özsoy argues that verse 18:86, which informs of the travels of Dhul-Qarnayn, particularly the verse on the setting of the Sun, resonates as a flat-earth theory.[119] In this vein, Öztürk reminds that the various scholars of the Islamic sciences—like al-Suyuti, Ibn Atiyya (d. 1146), al-Razi, and al-Qurtubi (d. 1273)—imagined earth as flat. And Abd al-Qahir al-Baghdadi (d. 1038) even declared that it is a requirement of faith to believe in a flat and stagnant earth.[120]

Öztürk quotes these names, since their recognition of the flat-earth theory cannot be imagined independently of how they understood Quran.

The more complicated aspect of the debate is the historical construction of an Islamic theology based on the literal understandings of the verses on nature. This construction fails to notice that those understandings are seventh-century Arab knowledge. Accordingly, for historicists, Islamic theology, on many counts, such as free will and causation, stands on a seventh-century Arab perception of nature.[121] Özsoy observes that even al-Ghazali made the same mistake while developing his influential opinions on causality.[122] Similarly, he dismisses the Ash'ari paradigm of nature, which repudiates causality, and gives little room to free will, as a theory based on the seventh-century Arab view of nature that is replete with mistakes.[123] Özsoy complains also that contemporary scholars keep repeating the same mistake.[124] The problem is that an idea of nature is a reflection of people's knowledge of "the natural world they live in," or "the cosmos they imagined."[125] On this account, for historicists, the key arguments of the Islamic idea of nature were developed before the unfolding of the modern scientific revolution, and are based mostly on the verses that reflect the seventh-century naked-eye Arab observations.

The Nature of Revelation Revelation in Sunnism is the transmission of the divine message from the heavens to the world.[126] Having an independent body, it is received via Gabriel as an external message. It is never a message relayed by Muhammad; he received it.[127] Additionally, the revelation is not a response to any event in human history. It is a divine intervention.[128] The Sunni view logically requires that revelation be different from reason, both in nature and priority.

Historicists have a radically different explanation of revelation. Öztürk portrays Sunni theory as a set of chaotic arguments in which he cannot find answers to several questions: How was Quran revealed? Was it revealed at once, or gradually? If it is sent from the heavens, did it descend directly to the world, or through intermediate layers, given that the revelation took twenty-two years? For him, the Sunni theory, far from giving satisfactory answers to such questions, is more like tactical space-occupying assertions that gainsay alternatives.[129]

On the historicist view, revelation is first and foremost not an external message. Historicists then question traditions where they present Gabriel's bringing of the revelation to Muhammad. Öztürk finds inaccurate, as well as simplistic and unrealistic, the famous hadith that narrates Gabriel's conveying of the revelation, having taken on the appearance of the companion Dihya ibn Khalifa.[130] Kırbaşoğlu, too, finds the Dihya traditions weak.[131] (Fazlur Rahman also refused revelation via an angel.)[132] For Öztürk, such traditions popped up as a response to the theological discussions that exploded in the second Islamic century. He contends that revelation as an external message is incompatible with verses like 2:97, according to which revelation was borne down into Muhammad's heart. However, Öztürk notes that scholars like al-Razi knowingly interpreted such verses as metaphorical discourses to justify the Sunni view of external revelation.[133]

Revelation for historicists is a kind of inner thought. It occurred within Muhammad. Öztürk thus writes that the verses were not revealed to Muhammad, neither in meaning nor in *lafdz* (form).[134] Güler likens revelation to inspiration.[135] As Eliaçık explains it, revelation is about Muhammad's instincts and inner thinking. It grew within Muhammad naturally, like "God's creation of a flower."[136] Reflecting rationalism, historicists limit their theory of revelation to the confines of natural law. Thus, as Eliaçık writes, it is simultaneously God's creation and Muhammad's work that reflects his personality.[137] So, the connection of revelation to God is not framed in contradiction of natural law. This is again clearly an impact of Fazlur Rahman, who defined revelation as emanating from God, but also connected it with Muhammad's personality. Rahman was also against the popular traditional accounts of the utter externality of the agency of revelation. For him, Quran is the divine response to Muhammad's mind.[138]

On this account, the historicist view of revelation has four major pillars, each unacceptable to Sunnism: Firstly, Muhammad is not a passive agent in the revelation. Instead, he is the one who gave revelation its human speech form.[139] Again echoing Mu'tazili arguments, historicists insist that God cannot be imagined speaking in Arabic; hence, there must be another agent to frame the divine message in human terms; and it is the Prophet who actualizes this.[140] Secondly, the text of Quran is now the words of man.[141] Thirdly, historical and cultural factors affected the revelation through Muhammad, who actualized God's message in a given historical and social context.[142] While putting the message in the human context, Muhammad's observations of his time and society, as well as their impact on him, played roles.[143] Finally, understanding revelation through Muhammad's agency, historicists now see no difference between reason and revelation—neither in form nor in degree.[144] Reflecting this, Güler writes that "reason is equal to revelation."[145]

Quran Is Not a Book   As another important deviation from Sunnism, historicists are against imagining Quran as a book.[146] Not designed or written as a book, Quran in historicists' view is a collection of speeches articulated as responses to various events during Muhammad's prophethood.[147] They are also of the opinion that Muhammad had no intention to compile the revelations into a book format. His goal was to leave a sample community to inspire Muslims.[148] Historicists opine that what made Muslims imagine Quran as a book was the compilation of the revelations in book format *after* Muhammad.[149] Quoting Arthur Jeffery, Kırbaşoğlu notes that Arabs were not even aware of books before Quran's compilation.[150] To him, imagining Quran as a book is only a populist idea to please the average Muslims.[151] Imagining Quran as a book has naturally significant consequences that impacts hugely on the interpretation of Islam. Güler observes that historicists are unhappy about its major consequence, which is the invitation to approach Quran as if it originated as a systematic book on theology.[152] Özsoy says that historicists discern correctly that the "Quran is a book" belief nurtures the popular thinking that a revelation is an external message.[153] Both beliefs are alarming for rationalists, since they are theological views advantageous to traditionalists.

For historicists, Quran is a collection of speech acts that early Muslims heard and adapted into their practice without imagining them as a systematic text.[154] Accordingly, the verses were not abstract sentences but acted-out speeches. Here

William A. Graham's definition, according to which a revelation is "an activity coextensive with the life of the bearer of revelation, the Prophet," might be explanatory.[155] A revelation is interwoven with action. Kırbaşoğlu explains this as imagining Quran as a life lived rather than as a book.[156] Inspired by Muhammad Arkoun, Güler writes likewise that Quran is a practical text, not a book of theory: Quran is not like Aristotle's *Metaphysics* or Spinoza's *Etica*—books that construct their messages as abstractions and general principles, but like Marx's *Capital*, a book that gives its message as practical solutions of the problems of society.[157] Güler's comparison says that the message of Quran is always delivered through contextual cases. Eliaçık thus proposes that early Muslims did not even pay attention to whether the revelations are consistent, since they did not see them as a coherent text. They were interested only in what God said to them.[158] And, they understood the revelations without a need for methodological explanation.[159] As proof that early Muslims did not regard the revelations as a book, Öztürk reminds that they were never shocked when a new revelation introduced a command different from a previous one. He thus held that there was an ontological relationship between Muslims and the revelation where the focus was on understanding and practicing rather than in search of an epistemic relationship that delivers systematic comprehension.[160] Öztürk produces this example to remind that despite the verse 9:36 prohibition to wage war during the four special months, Muslims did not interrupt their fights with their enemies.[161] Balcı's explanation is similar: The first Muslims were not interested in the discursive or linguistic aspects of a revelation; their purpose was simply to understand what it asks.[162] Öztürk gives also an interesting example to demonstrate how the first Muslims were indifferent to the textual and stylistic aspects of the revelations. (Contemporary Muslims respond to this with disdain.) Accordingly, they were not even alarmed by some formal changes in the transmission of a revelation with changed words.[163] We understand from the historicist arguments that the early Muslims did not imagine the revelation as a text. Instead, what mattered to them is what they were told. Eliaçık explains this with an analogy that makes out a "what to do" case in the event of a revelation. The premise of his argument by analogy is the image of a pointing forefinger: Rather than speculate on the forefinger, the early Muslims focused on the direction it is pointing to.[164]

For historicists, Quran's verses are speech acts, the meanings of which associate with the circumstances in which they were uttered. Güler illustrates them as examples of informal communication in a given setting where people already know the relevant contextual aspects of the speech, like the emotions it displays.[165] As Öztürk emphasizes, therefore, that the meaning of the verses—given that they are speech acts—naturally have limited connection with the noncontext.[166] In other words, they were not axioms to be understood in a universal context as a modern text. To clarify: by "contextual or complementary elements of meaning," historicists refer to the standard extralinguistic elements in a speech act that are all relevant to convey the intentions of the communicator.[167] Özsoy states that those extralinguistic elements are vital for a correct understanding of a speech act.[168] Similarly, emphasizing that language is not a mechanical transmitter,

Öztürk defines the interaction of language and its milieu as an essential aspect of communication.[169]

The most important problem for historicists is putting the verses, which were originally speech acts, into book format (*Mushaf*) despite that they did not come into being as systematic texts. The unavoidable consequence is the various gaps between a speech act and its written form, since the latter has no ability to incorporate all the complementary aspects of the former. There is no perfect match between the meaning a speech act makes and its transcription. Paul Ricoeur explains this phenomenon as the disappearance of the human facts in "writing up" what someone said. Unlike a speech act, "marks"—words, letters, dots, and so on—convey the text the message, but at the cost of detaching meaning from event. "Discourse as event disappears," and we get only a text, which is no longer able to transmit the relationship between the speech and the human context. Thus, for Ricoeur, writing does not fix the event of speaking, but records only what was said of the speaking.[170] This is what Graham explains as the verbal-noun revelation that becomes a concrete noun, and refers primarily to a text rather than to a happening (the context).[171] In consequence, reading the transcription of a speech act is never satisfactory.[172] Almost repeating Ricoeur, Özsoy defines a text only as a note on the meaning of the speech act.[173] Öztürk, too, repeats the perception that the transcription of a speech act is a picture that has lost the meaning-making power of its contextual elements.[174] Özsoy even reminds that the transition from the speech act to the text may even distort the meaning of the former.[175]

A second, but this time structural, consequence of making a book of the verses (which disturbs the historicists too) is the Muslim habit of regarding Quran as if it were sent as a systematic book of epistemological and other subjects.[176] For Öztürk, the book format of Quran wrongly became a reference in scholarly studies for interpreting the verses.[177] The historicists' reservation here is about the recognition of the book format, which is a human artifact, as a substantial framework in explaining the verses.[178] For the historicists, a format that was dictated by people after the revelations should not be taken as if it were the canonical framework to determine how the verses are understood. Özsoy reminds that the historical accounting for event of the revelation does not even provide satisfactory information on the rationale of the placement of the verses in Quran.[179] Similarly, for Öztürk, the purpose of the compilation of the verses was only to preserve them; hence, the existing format of Quran cannot be a systematic reference in any way when one is interpreting the verses.[180] As a consequence, reading Quran as a text has no reasonable explanation, save that the verses were placed between book covers.[181] Taking things one step further, Öztürk argues that the between-book-covers mistake caused Muslims to imagine Quran as a "reference text," but was not "a purpose and an intention of God." He is clear that the recognition of Quran as a reference text by Muslims is a result of their historical practice, which is nonetheless in contradiction of God's purpose.[182] In other words, apart from the troublesome effects of the book format on understanding the verses, it is also problematic to find out what is Islamic by looking at a reference book, even if it is Quran. Özsoy holds the same view: "I don't believe that God's intention is to send a reference book. Instead, his intention was to create a sample community that would inspire people."[183]

To summarize: According to historicists, the compilation of the verses into book format created three major problems:

1. The obfuscating gap between the verses as speech acts, and the verses in written format;
2. The recognition of the book format as the authoritative framework in explaining the verses; and
3. The recognizing of a book, that is, Quran, as the main framework of Islamic reasoning.

Alternatively, historicists suggest:

1. Interpreting the verses as speech acts;
2. Not being bound by how the verses are located in Quran while interpreting them; and
3. Not to accept that Islam commends Quran as the reference book in proposing solutions, but, instead, know that Quran commends to Muslims the community model that Prophet Muhammad and his friends developed by their practices.

If we return to the problems caused by *Mushaf*, we see that verses are now read as if their places in Quran were originally designed to generate a certain methodological importance. However, Öztürk reminds that each verse was revealed in a different context, so their locations in Quran cannot be taken as the parameters of their understanding.[184] Eliaçık asserts that it is possible even to get different meanings in Quran by changing the order of the verses. After studying the first thirty-seven of the revealed verses, he concludes that Islam's prime message is to criticize financial inequality in Mecca, rather than deal with rituals or worship.[185] Accordingly, the idols in Quran are symbols of economic exploitation.[186] Moreover, in Eliaçık's view, the current order of the verses in Quran, which does not correspond to the chronology of the revelation, gave way to the unfortunate conclusion that the prime focus of Quran is ritualistic piety, not social issues such as justice and equality.[187] If the verses are originally speech acts, their chronological order would indeed be important. However, historicists also find that information on the chronology of the verses is limited and contested.[188] For example, Öztürk reminds that traditions in *Sahih*, where Aisha—the prophet's wife—gives contradictory information on which verses were revealed first.[189] Kırbaşoğlu alerts to the discussions on Surah al-Maʻun, a short chapter with seven verses. For some, the surah was revealed in Mecca, but for others, in Medina. For a third group, some verses were revealed in Mecca, and others in Medina.[190] For historicists, the chronology problem proves that Quran in book format no longer transmits extralinguistic conditions such as the time aspects of the revelation.[191] Moreover, detached from their historical context, verses appear as equally important passages in Quran, with some sort of capacity to affect Islamic law.¹⁹² On the other hand, for the historicists, these are not only their theoretical discussions. Their negative impact is also observed among Muslims, since they are intra-Muslim conflict makers.¹⁹³ Reading the verses without reference to their historical context, which for historicists is a frameless interpretation, Muslims may find themselves justifying absurd or radical conclusions. Özsoy observes that, though it was easily understood by the early Muslims, Quran became the source of disagreements among Muslims after its compilation in book format during the reign of Caliph Uthman.¹⁹⁴ Simply, for historicists, embracing the revelations in book format triggered the chaos dynamic among Muslims. The compilation of Quran into book format has historically increased conflicts among Muslims rather than decrease them, Öztürk reflects.¹⁹⁵

For historicists, it is virtually impossible to generate a consistent text by compiling speech acts.¹⁹⁶ Logically, they find a number of problems in Quranic text. Doing that is impermissible only in Sunnism in which Quran is believed to have the perfect eloquence and the marvelous style challenging the most brilliant men of letters of humankind.¹⁹⁷ Not perturbed by this, Özsoy lists several structural and stylistic problems in Quran:

> There are contradictions and redundancies in Quran. It is not possible to discern the logic in the composition of the text; it does not have a chronological or a topical order. The whole text lacks inner consistency, nor is there consistency among the verses: often, even the verses fail to articulate a coherent set of meanings.¹⁹⁸

Similarly, Öztürk lists the several problems of inconsistency, exaggeration, incoherence, repetition, and contradictions in Quran as examples of problems that were brought into being by collecting the verses into book format.¹⁹⁹ According to him, there are even single verses that reflect several of these problems.²⁰⁰ Addressing similar issues, Güler does not think the text of Quran to be systematic in general.²⁰¹ And Azimli finds several consecutive passages that are unrelated to one another.²⁰² Kırbaşoğlu detects that some *qissas* are not told in the same way in several passages.²⁰³

Özsoy and Öztürk remind that they, the contemporary historicists, are not the first to detect such problems. Even the Sunni literature itself acknowledges many of them. As proof, they show *mushkilat al Quran*—the difficult issues in Quran—for which the Sunni scholars provide explanations of the various verses that contain linguistic or other problems.²⁰⁴ Of course, for Sunni authors of such explanations, what might seem to us to be problems are in fact examples of Quran's *i'jaz*, the inimitability of Quran, which is its miraculous linguistic property.²⁰⁵ In addition, historicists show the Sunni theory of *nash* (the abrogation of a verse by a later verse) more proof that the Sunni literature is aware of structural problems in Quran.²⁰⁶ *Nash* aims to solve the contradiction among the verses by proclaiming the older verse as abrogated, which is effectively to recognize, and admit to, the presence of contradiction in the text. Another perception of historicists is that *nash* demonstrates also how Sunni scholars fail to realize that what they are seeing as contradicting verses are in fact speech acts that belong to different social contexts.²⁰⁷ Accordingly, the verses in Quran that appear to be contradictory might have had different meanings in their different historical contexts. But, once written, they took on an apparently contradictory property because they lost their contextual uniqueness. Logically, historicists reject as *nash* what appears to them as contradictory verses in Quran when they are in fact about different subjects in their original contexts.²⁰⁸

We encounter examples in the works of historicists of the structural problems in Quran that have their origin in the compilation of the verses into a book. Typical examples can be read in Öztürk. Accordingly, for example, verse 2:220 has word order problems, creating serious obstacles to comprehension.²⁰⁹ In another example, Öztürk points to several verses that contradict one another. While verse 55:39 says, "on that Day neither mankind nor jinn will be asked about their sins," verse 37:24 reads as [God] "halted them for questioning." And verse 7:6 says, "We shall certainly question those to whom messengers were sent, and We shall question the messengers themselves." To Öztürk, there are also verses that give different information on the same subject: While verse 6:21 reads, "who fabricates a lie against God or denies His revelation" are doing the "greater wrong," verse 18:57 stresses that "who could be more wrong than the person who is reminded of his Lord's messages and turns his back on them."²¹⁰ Or, while verse 58:12 says, "when you come to speak privately with the Messenger, offer something in charity before your conversation." The very next verse, 58:13, declares that no such obligation is impose.²¹¹ As an example of the wrong placement of verses, Öztürk points to 2:226-241, the divorce verses. Two verses, 2:238-239, in this paragraph are irrelevant, for they are about how to perform *salah* (prayer) in dangerous situations.²¹² Verse 6:119 is another example of a misplacement in Quran that illustrates how seriously incongruent with its historical-chronological context a misplacement can be: This verse—"God has already fully explained what He has forbidden you"—is about why Muslims should not eat some animals. But the crux of that prohibition comes twenty-six verses later, at verse 6:145.²¹³ On the historicist perspective, the chronological mislocation of verses 6:119 and 6:145 is a typical problem that the book form Quran created.

Not seeing Quran as a book, historicists logically do not suggest that people who are without the expertise to apply the required method should read it. Güler, for example, argues that the average person who reads Quran in translation invites chaos.²¹⁴ Similarly, Öztürk is against the idea that all people can read and understand Quran.²¹⁵ Arguing that the book form Quran is only a collection of notes on the revelations, which were speech acts to be understood in their historical context, historicists warn the average person against reading it.²¹⁶

Historicists Interpreting Quran

Commending their method for the interpretation of Quran, historicist ground their rationale on the historical fact that the verses are speech acts that deliver their messages in the language and life conditions of the seventh-century Arab mindset.

This meaning-making mindset was lost when Quran was given a book format.²¹⁷ The solution for historicists is to interpret the verses in reference to their authentic meaning. This entails acquiring a familiarity with how early Muslims understood the verses in terms of their purpose, context, and social impact.²¹⁸ The reading of the verses in their authentic meaning is comparable with Searle's formulation: "X counts as Y in context C."²¹⁹ If X is the verse as written in Quran, Y is the authentic meaning. As Güler explains, this is done to salvage the nonlinguistic elements of meanings that are now lost in the written form of Quran.²²⁰ As we understand it, historicists expect their method to establish "authentic meaning" as the general norm of reading Quran. This is confirmed by Öztürk, who defines "authentic meaning" as God's purpose in revealing a verse.²²¹ His metaphorical explanation is that the authentic meanings of the verses are the "stem cells" of Islam.²²²

Basically, historicists project the hermeneutics method into the interpretation of Quran. Historicists, inspired by various scholars, such as Fazlur Rahman, Nasser Abu-Zayd, Paul Ricoeur, Friedrich Schleiermacher, Wilhelm Dilthey, and others, believe that it is possible to construct an imagined replica of the historical context in which the early Muslims understood the verses.²²³ In a nutshell, what matter for them is the principle of hermeneutic analysis, which Ricoeur defines as the interpretation of a speech act with reference to the analysis of the relationship of the event and its meaning.²²⁴ Thus, as Searle explained, a speech act is never a "zero context" that can be read literally. Instead, it must always be understood with reference to the "background," the historical context, in which it was acted out.²²⁵ Similarly, given that the noninstitutional elements of meaning are left in the past, and we are no longer part of that social setting, historicists assert that the best available method is to read the verses in their historical context.²²⁶ The only solution is to employ historical and hermeneutic analyses when interpreting the verses. Özsoy commends this as the reliable process for developing empathy with the first Muslims.²²⁷

There is also another rationale in the historicist method. Historicist worry that interpreting Quran without an objective framework could result in ultra-subjectivism.²²⁸ Like Abu-Zayd, they are concerned that transferring the verses into the present, thereby disregarding the relationship of the verses and their original contexts, can lead to incalculable misinterpretations.²²⁹ So the historicist position amounts to rejecting the Islamic reasoning of the verses as they are read in Quran (X). Öztürk complains that without an objective framework, the inevitable method is a freewheeling process of reasoning that legitimates "frameless interpretation."²³⁰ And Güler likens the interpreting of Quran without reference to the historical context to undisciplined phantasy.²³¹ For historicists, the danger of frameless interpretation is in the unleashing of anachronic conclusions, or attitudes of fixated presentism.²³² On this account, the historicist method is put to work to search for an objective framework for interpreting Quran. Accordingly, if there is any context that we can assume to be an objective framework in interpreting Quran, it is the seventh-century Arab society.²³³ Özsoy thus holds that the historicist method is a realistic way of interpreting Quran.²³⁴ For Öztürk, too, the historicist method provides a comparatively objective framework for interpreting the verses,²³⁵ and it contains the means of fixing the interpretation of the verses inside the boundaries of the historical context.[236] Logically, as Güler writes, this would mean that nobody has the authority to impose meanings on Quran. That cannot be done when there is an objective framework that determines the legitimate parameters of extrapolating the meanings of the verses.[237]

When it comes to the practice of their method, historicists, inspired by Fazlur Rahman, suggest a two-level interpretation. On the first level, the authentic meaning of a verse is defined when it is gleaned from a scrutiny of its historical setting.[238] "Authentic meaning," according to Rahman, is in the general moral-social objectives of the verses, "distilled" in the light of their sociohistorical background.[239] On the next level, the task is to work out how the authentic meaning of the verse under scrutiny is relevant today.[240] Having identified the general moral-social objective of the verse on the first level, reasoning in the second level pursues the terrain of its applicability in the present-day context. Thus, reasoning on the second level is expected to end with a new ruling. Logically, compared to the first level, the second level is more subjective.[241] Reason is given strong autonomy at the second level to discover how the authentic meaning is relevant now. That is tantamount to the enacting of a new ruling.[242] For Güler and Eliaçık, the objective here is to find out "what God would say to us today," or to "introduce new laws like God."[243] For Özsoy, this is like being a contemporary of Muhammad.[244]

Özsoy explains that this method does not treat a verse either as a finished or a dead text.[245] Accordingly, when historicists look at verse (X) in retrospect, they imagine it (Y) as a living phenomenon still knitted together with events, emotions, and speeches (C). This is what historicists mean by arguing that Quran is not a book. Instead, they imagine each verse as a living phenomenon in its historical context, along with all its contextual elements. The verse is then imagined similarly in the present, based on authentic meaning.[246] In consequence, the verse for historicists is not the written form in Quran (X), but a speech act along with all its contextual elements, past and present (C, C1). This is what Abu-Zayd dubbed the "humanistic hermeneutics," which treats the verses as living phenomena, and "stops reducing the Quran to the status of a text only."[247] Also, this is what Rahman saw as the abandoning of the traditional method of reading verses in isolation, without reference to the speech acts they were on delivery.[248]

In historicist method, reason does indeed have the authority to interpret Quran beyond the literal meaning by gathering references from the outer world. As Güler reminds, there is no difference between reason and revelation in the historicist view.[249] However, as I underlined in the Introduction, though human reason is the main agent, it does not preach the moral-social objectives that are used as the framework for interpreting the verses. Reasoning organizes the knowledge acquired from the past and in the present. That is, reasoning in this context is the pursuit of the authentic meanings of the verses and the quest to discover how they are relevant now. Thus, there is no doubt that historicist reasoning is rationalism, since it goes beyond the text.[250] However, it is also empiricist reasoning, since it is rooted in the knowledge acquired from external spaces.

Going back to the grand polarization of Islamic thought along the lines of traditionalism and rationalism, it becomes obvious that the historicist method is the opposite of the Shafi'i methodology. As a matter of fact, historicists criticize traditional methods like the Shafi'i, for the latter fails to differentiate the message and the text.[251] Accordingly, the major Shafi'i problem is that it treats Quran as if it were a metahistorical text revealed as a theoretical book. This is the misunderstanding that gave rise to the traditional text-based methods.[252] Öztürk likens those methods to the archaeological efforts to decipher inscriptions on old tablets that are frozen within the boundaries of language, logic, theology, and law, and never able to yield the truths that drive the dynamic relationship of Quran and its historical setting.[253]

Universalists on the Nature of Quran

Universalism is the method according to which human reason is assigned an absolute authority to interpret the verses according to the general principles of Quran. The concept "general/universal" principles entails the various norms like justice, freedom, and equality. The emphasis in universalism is therefore on human reason, and on Quran. Unlike historicism, universalism refuses to be guided by any historical context in the determination of the meanings of the verses. Universalism has a strong "holy book" concept. In universalism, Quran is the sole religious reference in Islamic reasoning. It requires a deeply skeptical approach to any other resource, including the traditions.[254] Universalism in the Turkish context is therefore like the Ahl-i Quran movement that emerged in colonial India. M. Abdullah Chakralawi (d. 1916), a prominent name of the movement, proclaimed that Quran is the sole authentic guide in Islamic reasoning.[255] Accordingly, Quran completed the full course of basic inoculations for Muslims, and "left them free in other matters to exercise their own judgement."[256] Similarly, the universalists propose that all Muslims' problems can be solved merely and only by their appeal to Quran.[257] Atay writes that the center of Islamic reasoning is Quran.[258]

Universalists' emphasis on Quran is a reflection of their methodology, which operates on the principle of full authority of human reason to interpret the verses. Therefore, for universalists, Quran is essentially an instrumental phenomenon through which they justify their reasoning. But this approach often leaves universalists none too worried about the methodological details, so long as their expectations are met. Like historicism's, universalism's method is possible, thanks to their arguments on the nature of Quran, which I present in the following text.

Quran's Divinity   Yaşar Nuri is closed to the soft Sunni approach on the nature of Quran. He suggests that there is a heavenly Quran that is other than the one we have in this world.[259] Before 2019, Atay also used to adopt the same approach. However, in his book published in 2019, he adopted the thesis of the created Quran. In this book, Atay criticizes the "divine Quran" as a contradiction of God's eternal nature. Employing the Mu'tazili thesis, Atay writes also that it is illogical to believe that the details of Muhammad's life, such as the wars, are told as if they happened before their creation. He joins the discussion that proclaims the idea that the "divine Quran" is like Christianity's attribution of the divine nature to Jesus.[260] But, for both Atay and Yaşar Nuri, Quran is still under divine protection.[261] According to both, no human intervention played a role in the formation of the verses.[262] For Yaşar Nuri, Quran's linguistic features are above human capacity.[263] Atay finds no contradiction in Quran.[264] Thus, neither Yaşar Nuri's embracement of soft theory nor Atay's adoption of the Muʿtazili thesis signals a shift toward a historicist conceptualization of Quran. They do not express their ideas about the nature of Quran in a way that weakens their universalist stance, which always requires a strong concept of Quran.

Quran Is Both Historical and Ahistorical Universalists have a categorical understanding of Quran's relations with history. Accordingly, Quran is in principle ahistorical, so independent of any historical context. No historical dynamic has had the capacity to affect the revelation. Being above history, Quran is read in each age as it is revealed in that age.[265] However, universalists exclude verses on shariʿa; hence, they are not above history, and are therefore historical.[266] Thus, for historicists, as Yaşar Nuri explains, Quran is "partially historical."[267] Reflecting this, universalists accept that while Quran is ahistorical in regard of its various higher principles and norms, its content incorporates historical passages on the subject of law, which constitutes the lower norms.[268] This is formulated by Eliaçık to mean that the historical elements in Quran are never about its essentials.[269] However, it is not clear how essential and secondary verses are differentiated. Yaşar Nuri writes only that what matters is how much historicism is required. Rejecting or accepting it totally is not a requirement.[270] But again, he states also that in principle there is no historicism of the verses; it can be invoked only for the secondary issues.[271]

Their partial historicism never leads universalists to a full-blown historicism. For example, Yaşar Nuri pays attention to the "raw meaning" of a verse.[272] Atay, too, counts the original meanings of the verses, which he defines in terms of how they were understood by early Muslims, as an important element in understanding Quran.[273] However, neither for Atay nor for Yaşar Nuri does the original meaning or the historical context determine the interpretation of a verse.[274] On principle, historicists are against historical, hermeneutical, or linguistic facts that emerge as monopolistic variables to limit the interpretation of the verses. Yaşar Nuri reminds of the principle of the "divine flexibility in Quran," which entails that, except for a few, the verses are open to endless interpretation, irrespective of any historical context.[275] The categorical view of Quran is a reflection of the universalists' instrumental approach to Quran. On the one hand, they decree that reasoning must be based only on the Quran, for the Quran is ahistorical. On the other hand, they retain the capacity to interpret the various verses differently, particularly those inextricably entwined with the law, for those verses are historical.[276]

Quran Is Universal For universalists, Quran is not a speech act performed for the seventh-century Arabs. It is a universal book. Atay writes that Quran is not limited to any period.[277] Yaşar Nuri describes Quran as speaking to all ages.[278]

Therefore, universalists suggest that contemporary Muslims should read Quran as if it is being revealed to them.[279] In Yaşar Nuri's view, no argument can be proposed against the universality of Quran.[280] To prove that Quran is a universal book, Atay asserts that there are verses with zero connection to any spatial or historical context.[281] Elsewhere, he asserts that only a few verses are historical.[282] So, unlike historicists, universalists accept that there are "null context" verses (to paraphrase Searle) in Quran.[283] Indeed, this is to argue that Quran has verses designed as theoretical propositions with universal meaning, without any connection to their historical or geographical context. Recalling the aforementioned comparison by Güler of Quran and *Capital*, for universalists Quran is therefore more like Aristotle's *Metaphysics* or Spinoza's *Etica*, books that give their messages through abstract and general principles. Quran as a universal book is a substantial axiom of universalism, since its method operates mainly on reason, and on Quran, exclusive of historical context.

Quran's Content Positing that Quran is the sole religious reference on Islamic reasoning requires that universalists accept that it contains all knowledge. So they define Quran as a book of sophisticated knowledge that humanity cannot grasp, or complex knowledge that can be understood only with the help of expertise.[284] Logically, for universalists, the content of Quran was beyond the knowledge of the Arabs who were subjected to the revelation in the seventh century. Atay accepts that verses have deep meanings.[285] In Yaşar Nuri's view, verses are polysemic.[286] He even argues that some verses have meanings hidden at the highly advanced levels of the sciences, such as astronomy, psychology or geology, that will become discoverable by future generations' advanced technologies.[287] Particularly, *muteshabih*,[288] the allegorical verses in Quran, have such deep meanings.[289]

Since they understand the verses as having deep meanings discoverable only with advanced levels of knowledge, the idea of progress becomes a subject with which the universalists must engage. Accordingly, they note that at different years of age, people have different levels of intellectual ability to interpret Quran. Thus, what previous Muslims understood from various verses might be irrelevant for later generations highly advanced in science.[290] Universalists thus believe in the idea of progress. Yaşar Nuri argues that the accumulation and progress of human knowledge will give a better understanding of Quran.[291] Similarly, Atay suggests interpreting the verses according to modern scientific data and findings.[292] A logical consequence of the universalist view is to accept that, as we read in Atay, there are always some verses in Quran that people cannot fully understand, since their knowledge level does not allow it.[293] The solution is to await the advancement of humanity. A case to prove this thesis, Yaşar Nuri submits, is the verse that informs about fingerprints, or microbes, that can be understood only once humanity has advanced in those fields.[294] Such a conclusion would be unacceptable for historicists, for whom human reason enables the understanding of the verses. Also, for historicists, the universalist argument that the verses have deeper meanings that were beyond the intellectual capacity of its seventh-century addressees is illogical to the point that it inhibits successful dialogue.

Their position on the content of Quran has two important methodological outcomes for universalists. Firstly, they justify rejecting previous scholars' reasonings on the assumption that their capacity to understand Quran was limited by their unadvanced knowledge capacity. Secondly, they justify interpreting Quran according to modern norms and practices, given that modern society represents the most advanced level in the sciences.

The Nature of Revelation   Universalists define revelation as an external message received by Muhammad via an angel.[295] The transmission of the divine message through an angel is a proof for Atay: It demonstrates that the message is from God.[296] The revelation has thus an external form: Muhammad received the revelations both in meaning and in style.[297] And the prophet had no affection for the whole process of the revelation.[298] Thus, for Yaşar Nuri, the idea that Muhammad put the revelation given to him into a human frame is wrong.[299]

Though they repeat the Sunni theory of revelation in terms of its nature, universalists have a radically different position on another aspect: The revelation that was received by the prophets is institutional revelation. Logically, there are other forms of revelation, since human nature has the capacity to receive messages from God at any time. Seen in this way, the institutional revelations ended with the death of Muhammad, but other forms continue. People can therefore receive noninstitutional revelations. For example, Yaşar Nuri speculates that people like Buddha, Socrates, and Confucius could have received noninstitutional revelations. Though the institutional revelation—that is, the revelations to prophethood—has ended, other forms, like intuition, still survive. Simply, the dialogue between man and God is a natural result of creation which cannot cease completely.[300] Atay believes similarly that God always reveals to human beings. But, since prophethood ended with Muhammad, the message is received through other ways, like intuition (*ilham*).[301] But for him, the ongoing dialogue between man and God in intuition-like forms should also be seen as a form of revelation.[302] He argues even that the knowledge that scientists and philosophers acquire contains such forms of revelation.[303]

As I discussed earlier, historicists challenge the Sunni theory of revelation by proposing that the revelation is historical. The historicist method is in harmony with their empiricist characteristic. Differently, universalists challenge the Sunni theory by introducing noninstitutional revelation in line with their classical rationalist manner. In so doing, universalists assign to human reason as powerful an authority as revelation.[304]

Quran Is a Book   Quran is a book for universalists. Yaşar Nuri states that Quran presents itself as a book.[305] So, as we read in Atay, it is the written form of the revelation.[306] To reinforce "book Quran," Atay and Yaşar Nuri reject any contradiction in Quran, for it is by nature miraculous. According to them, no human being played a role in Quran's formation.[307] Since on their method reason has the absolute ability to interpret Quran, universalists are not much interested in hermeneutical problems caused by the compilation of the verses as a book. Instead, "book Quran" is helpful to them.

While historicists challenge Sunnism mainly by deconstructing Quran, universalists challenge Sunnism by proposing a strong rationalism where Quran is transformed into an instrument to legitimize their reasonings. Logically, the universalist method requires a strong concept of Quran. Thus, they always emphasize that Quran is the sole reference book of Islam. For example, Atay calls for a method where Islamic reasoning focuses only on Quran and reason. Accordingly, the main explanation of problems in Muslim societies is that they no longer treat Quran as the central reference in religious reasoning.[308] Naturally, the method requires the defense of "book Quran," along with reason. As expected, the universalists' strategy in emphasizing "book Quran" for their rationalist method is criticized by historicists. Öztürk, for example, criticizes the universalist method for lacking an objective framework.[309]

Defining Quran as a book, universalists logically advice the average Muslims to read it. Atay believes that everyone can read and understand Quran.[310] For him, everyone would understand Quran according to his intellectual or professional level.[311] Similarly, Yaşar Nuri suggests that all people should read translations of Quran.[312] Indeed, this is also a reflection of the universalist argument about Quran's content, according to which the verses have layers with different meanings that can be understood differently by people with different degrees of knowledge. Not imagining "book Quran" should be interpreted in its historical context, universalists do not shy away from suggesting that people read Quran.

Universalists Interpreting Quran

Universalists believe that Quran has the purpose of realizing a society based on universal norms. To realize that purpose today, universalism suggests interpreting the verses according to what they name as the general principles of Quran.[313] "General principles" is to universalists what "authentic meaning" is to historicists. The crux of the universalist method is to accept that human reason is able to interpret verses via the general principles of Quran, without any need to take other factors, such as historical context, into consideration. So, the method aims to discover the universal message of the verses, for they are always independent of historical context.[314] Universalists do not provide a standard list of the universal principles of Quran, but they are usually concepts such as justice, equality, and freedom.[315] In principle, universalists are not categorically against other methods like history, etymology, and grammar.[316] However, they reject that methods are the main framework of the understanding of the verses.[317] Instead, as Atay writes, Quran is enough for Islamic reasoning.[318] Yaşar Nuri describes this method as "parenthesizing everything but Quran."[319] For him, what matters in Quran are the general principles about people and society, not the detailed discussions on grammar or other methods.[320]

As another key point, universalism's belief in the idea of progress requires a break for Islamic reasoning from tradition. Atay underlines that the past is dead, and Islamic revival is only possible with the interpretation of Quran within the present context.[321] As stated earlier, for universalists Quran is not historical. Instead, it is a book that speaks to all ages. Reminding of this point, Atay suggests that each generation interprets Quran in its context. How the verses were interpreted in the previous historical contexts are no longer relevant for Atay. He warns that Islam in Quran and Islam in history should not be confused.[322] The focus of universalists is the present.[323] Atay also warns that historical context, or its dynamics, should not limit how one understands the verses today.[324] Similarly, though Yaşar Nuri thinks that how Islam was understood by early Muslims is important. But for him, this should not be exaggerated, since any message naturally generates a contextual example in history. Thus, that framework should not be taken as a main framework for understanding Quran. Yaşar Nuri is firm on the point that reading Quran in historical context is the mistake of the "particularization" of its message.[325]

When it comes to the practice of the universalist method, there can be two stages of study. In the first stage, of the relevant general principle(s), one is selected for use in interpreting the verse under scrutiny. As stated before, universal principles are usually listed as justice, equality, freedom, private property, and human life. However, one encounters modern concepts such as human rights, gender equality, rule of law, and freedom of thought.[326] (The recognition of modern concepts like human rights as general principles is observed also in Fazlur Rahman.[327]) For example, Eliaçık counts as a general purpose of Quran the favoring of the oppressed against the oppressor.[328] Yaşar Nuri even takes the Universal Declaration of Human Rights as a reference in interpreting Quran.[329] For him, documents like the 1789 French Declaration of Human Rights have the same purposes that Quran also wants to introduce.[330]

To justify the expansion of the general principles of Quran so far as to incorporate modern concepts, universalists propose several explanations. First, it is argued that human reason has the authority to decide on them. For Atay, *ijtihad* (new reasoning) is reason updating itself to provide a new reading of Quran.[331] Accordingly, reason has also the authority to update the boundaries of universal principles of Quran, and thereby go beyond the literal content of Quran.[332] For Atay, this is natural, since there is no other authority for interpreting Quran.[333] As a second justification, universalists bring back *ma'ruf*, the Islamic method of incorporating common good practices from other cultures.[334] The theory traces back to the practice of Prophet Muhammad, who is reported to have incorporated the good customs of pre-Islamic Arabs.[335] For example, for Yaşar Nuri, human rights are a typical example of *ma'ruf*.[336] Thirdly, universalists believe in the existence of universal norms shared by humanity independently of any religious context. Inspired by Friedrich Schleiermacher (d. 1834), Yaşar Nuri speaks of a shared human ground upon which universal norms, such as justice and human rights, flourish. And he concludes that Islam cannot be imagined as standing separate on this ground.[337] For Schleiermacher, religion is a result of the natural dynamics of human nature, which, however, is reflected differently in the various cultural contexts.[338] Similarly, Yaşar Nuri asserts that no matter how various religions are reflected in their social contexts, there is also a universal religion beyond such particularities.[339] The narrative that frequently reminds that the Old Testament, the New Testament, and Quran have the same essential message in different contexts is a typical reflection of this perspective.[340] Finally, comparisons spring up about modern concepts and Islamic terms. For example, democracy is read as the contemporary equivalent of the *shura* in Quran.[341] As a method known since the late nineteenth century, it is argued that universal norms and practices are somehow embedded in Quran.

In the second stage, the verse under scrutiny is interpreted according to the selected general principle(s).[342] So human reason, having the verse and the general principle in mind, develops a new interpretation of the present conditions. As underlined earlier, the present is another important reference of interpreting a verse. Universalists pay enormous attention to modern practices while proposing solutions. But again, it is human reason that has absolute authority to make the final decision. At this stage, reason operates with absolute license to propose how the verse should be understood today. This is explained by Yaşar Nuri as that the meaning of the verse determined by both God and man.[343] Atay formulates the method as "submitting the verse to human reason" to illustrate the central role of human reason in the method.[344] He thus concludes that "anything that reason endorses is also compatible with shari'a."[345]

Universalists imagine reason as the mechanical process in their method that can work independently of any context, and always arrive at a correct and objective conclusion. For Atay, what is rational is Islamic. He describes reason as infallible, citing Aristotle. Quoting al-Jahiz (d. 869), Atay also describes reason as the vicar of God.[346] It is the "other revelation" of God.[347] To clarify his opinions, Atay also borrows from the Greek philosopher Anaxagoras. Accordingly, reason has the absolute authority over everything, and it is the autonomous mechanism that is able to find the truth without the need of any contextual reference.[348] Atay's "reason" is therefore like Anaxagoras' "cosmic mind," which is infinite in a temporal sense, and not limited by time, or by any other construct.[349] He repeats Anaxagoras' immaterial monism where the purpose is to search for "the deeper meaning of the whole construction."[350] Similarly, Yaşar Nuri defines reason as a divine gift that always conveys people to the truth.[351] He calls reason the "messenger of God" in a different format. But reason is indeed the dominant entity: "Reason is the commander; religion is the soldier." Thus, to him, reason is the sublime one, outranking even the revelation. It is the prime messenger.[352] Reminding that God gave reason to every society, even though many were not given prophets, Yaşar Nuri opines that reason dominates revelation, given that the latter is prone to contradicting itself. Quoting Qadi Abd al-Jabbar, Yaşar Nuri concludes that reason is the main revealer of meaning in Islamic thought.[353] Thus, as I noted in the Introduction, universalism is comparable to classical rationalism, where human reason is the prime agent of knowing and explaining that can work independently of any context, for it always arrives at a correct conclusion.

Logically, the universalist method is little restricted in terms of the methodological procedures of interpreting a verse. To move the debate along with an example: Interpreting relevant verses of Quran, Yaşar Nuri explains that the word *'asa* (baton) symbolizes "rebellion," given the etymological root of the word. In so doing, he reads the verse—where *'asa* is used—on the relationship of Moses and the Pharaoh as meaning that Quran justifies rebellion against an authoritarian regime.[354] Undoubtedly, such a reading is rejected by historicists as frameless interpretation. For example, Özsoy criticizes universalists for deriving modernity-friendly conclusions from Quran by using linguistic and similar methods.[355] In response, the universalists remind of the failure of traditional methods to provide a solution to many prolonged problems, like the survival of slavery, the various practices concerning the status of women, and the various methods of punishments in the Islamic law.[356] In this regard, universalism in Turkey is a response to the failure of attempts to overcome problems in the Islamic tradition. Universalists want to propose quick and concrete solutions to overcome those problems. As Atay writes, problems in Islamic thinking are best solved by proposing new solutions to those problems. His motto is simple: "Correcting a mistake is possible by presenting a solution."[357] Universalists are practical people who are critical of spending too much effort on methodology. Thus, they are not chary of borrowing modern practices, even when they appear to be updating Islamic law according to modern Western practices. For Yaşar Nuri, no contradiction is possible between modern universal values and Islam.[358] Such thinking has its origin in the idea of progress that is observed among universalists who believe in humanity's progress with the forward movement of chronological time.[359] Eliaçık also justifies this method by reminding that the opposite of religion is not modernity but faithlessness.[360]

Like historicists, universalists make frequent positive references to previous rationalists, such as Abu Hanifa, Umar, and various Mu'tazili scholars.[361] Particularly, Abu Hanifa's *istihsan* is quoted as a method that justifies the universalist method. Yaşar Nuri explains *istihsan* as a historical example where Quran is interpreted on universal principles rather than on the contextual elements of the early Muslim Arabs.[362] Eliaçık shares this point of view. In his opinion, Abu Hanifa distinguished the difference between local and universal departure from Arab culture.[363] We frequently read in the works of universalists that Abu Hanifa and Umar are presented as prominent actors in the introduction of the view that reasoning beyond Quran by means of new methods, such as *istihsan* and *ma'ruf*, is legitimate.[364] Like historicists, universalists are critical of al-Shafi'i for his hadith-restricted reasoning. His method is criticized for weakening the rationalist trait in the Islamic tradition.[365]

Universalists naturally remind of the *maqasid al-shari'a*, an Islamic legal doctrine understood by scholars like al-Juwayni (d. 1085), al-Ghazali, and al-Shatibi.[366] Both Atay and Yaşar Nuri refer to the various purposes of Islam, as in the *maqasid* doctrine, like the protecting of life, and protecting reason.[367] In literature, *maqasid* (the purposes) refer to the wisdom, divine interest, and moral concerns that underpin Islamic rulings.[368] They are categorized on the three worthy levels of human pursuit: necessities, needs, and luxuries. Necessities preserves one's faith, soul, wealth, mind, and offspring. Preservation of them is recognized as the basic objective of any Islamic law.[369] More importantly, the *maqasid* doctrine helps us develop new Islamic reasoning. For example, al-Ghazali, after listing the safeguarding of faith, of the human self, of intellect, of posterity, and of wealth, concludes that whatever ensures the safeguarding of these five assets serves the public interest, and is therefore desirable.[370] But, it is al-Shatibi who is usually credited with the *maqasid* doctrine, due to his studies according to which he systematized the doctrine. Like the previous scholars, al-Shatibi listed five essentials as the universal goals of Islamic law: the preservation of religion, human life, progeny, wealth, reason, and honor.[371] Basically, al-Shatibi's theory provides flexibility in Islamic law with the hierarchy of pursuits and hardship.[372] Al-Shatibi's theory later became a focus of interest, particularly in the modernist literature, where the focus is on the establishment of connections with Islam, and on modern norms like democracy.[373] Thus, as Rumee Ahmed put it, his theory is used to conclude that "new laws can be called Islamic when they are better at achieving the original objectives of shari'a."[374] In this vein, the universalists can be imagined as interpreting al-Shatibi in a reformist way, such as in Ahmed's "better at achieving . . ." way, for they often use terms such as "the public good," and "justice," which terms are usually regarded as part of the *maqasid* terminology. But universalists radically expand the scope of the general objectives of Islam so far as to recognize even contemporary norms. They are also less interested in the methodological details of *maqasid*. They prefer providing new solutions quickly, arguing that their proposals have already achieved the original objectives of Quran. Unlike al-Shatibi, who developed his doctrine on various concepts like pursuits and hardship, reasoning about the verses on universal principles is the *a priori* method of the universalists.[375]

The Rationalists on Hadith

Hadith (traditions) transmitted on the authority of the Prophet (including his deeds, speeches, and tacit approvals) are the second most important resources after Quran. Traditions are canonical elements of Islamic reasoning and practice, along with Quran, with the capacity to determine Muslim behavior in daily life, from adherence to Islamic law to dress code.[376] As expected, *hadith* occupies an important space in rationalist literature, for it is another pillar of Sunnism that they are critical of.[377] From the rationalist perspective, hadith is a tactically used traditionalist instrument.[378] Atay writes that the mainstream Islamic methodology is to interpret Quran by using hadiths; this is how Sunnism reproduces itself.[379] Kırbaşoğlu thus defines what is known as Sunnism as a paradigm created mostly by *ahl hadith*.[380] For rationalists, a *hadith*-based interpretation of Quran is therefore another major explanation of the stagnation in the Islamic thought that secures a text-based religious reasoning at the expense of rational thought.[381] Aware of how traditions shape average Muslims' understanding of Islam, rationalists are naturally in a position to propose an alternative interpretation of traditions, as well as to challenge the Sunni understanding of traditions.[382] As rationalists, they are primarily against the traditional status of traditions in Islamic reasoning, enjoying as they do a canonical status. Logically, the ultimate goal of the rationalists is to destroy that canonical status of the traditions.

The Status of Traditions

The rationalists' approach on hadith is mostly shaped by their critique of al-Shafi'i's legacy, which they see as the basis of what is known as the Sunni hadith methodology.³⁸³ Kırbaşoğlu's argument that the problems of the hadith literature can be solved only if it is rescued from al-Shafi'i dominance can serve as a summary of the complete works of the rationalists.³⁸⁴ As is known, al-Shafi'i institutionalized in Sunnism the doctrine of the duality of the divine revelation. According to this doctrine, what was transmitted through Muhammad, apart from Quran, is the nonrecited revelation (*wahyun ghayr matluw*). On this account, hadith is naturally recognized as a secondary canonical resource of Islam.³⁸⁵

To summarize: The critique of al-Shafi'i by rationalists—including both the historicists and the universalists—is firstly that they do not see traditions as a source of Islamic legislation with a capacity to introduce religious norms. Al-Shafi'i's method is rejected because it destroys Muhammad's human side by defining everything he uttered as divine. Unlike al-Shafi'i, the rationalists emphasize the human nature of Muhammad. Güler portrays Muhammad as a regular person who can make mistakes. Hence, things he did as a man cannot be sources of religion.³⁸⁶ Similarly, Atay writes that some of Muhammad's personal opinions might have been valid only in his age, but they are irrelevant in different times.³⁸⁷ Thus, for Atay, with al-Shafi'i, it becomes impossible to differentiate "local" and "universal" in Islam if everything about Muhammad is deemed an essential part of Islam.³⁸⁸ Rationalists are aware that, on al-Shafi'i's interpretation, Islam inevitably becomes the interpretation of the early Muslims, where even the smallest details are held to be indispensable rituals. On the contrary, rationalists understand the early practices as examples from which norms can be abstracted, but they do not accept those practices as the ultimate models to imitate.³⁸⁹

Secondly, as stated before, another legacy of al-Shafi'i is the tenet that Quran and the Sunnah are the sole material sources of Islamic law.³⁹⁰ For the rationalists, this is to confine Islamic reasoning to seeking solutions only in Islamic texts. Differently, the rationalists propose new reasoning that takes account of the new realities beyond the texts. Güler accuses al-Shafi'i of reducing Islam to a tradition of adherence to books disassociated from life.³⁹¹

Thirdly, the rationalists criticize al-Shafi'i for his method that presents traditions as canonical resources above human reason. Thus, they reprove al-Shafi'i for being a fully made-out present-day case to justify the rationalists' resistance to traditionalism. Logically, the rationalists see as a negative development the historical role of al-Shafi'i in the decline of rationalists scholars such as Abu Hanifa or the Mu'tazilis.³⁹² In this vein, the rationalists are particularly critical of al-Shafi'i for his stance on *istihsan*, the use of personal judgment or reasoning.³⁹³ To put it briefly, in *Risala*, al-Shafi'i denigrates as *istihsan* any initiative that is not based upon a parallel action in traditions. Thus, al-Shafi'i, sure that the ideal solution is the one that is derived from traditions, tolerates an initiative only if it is modeled on the closest alternative to a previous case.³⁹⁴ This is utterly unacceptable for rationalists.³⁹⁵ Atay criticizes al-Shafi'i for mistakenly equating *istihsan* with enacting a fake sharia.³⁹⁶

Having summarized the rationalist critique of al-Shafi'i, the next topic is the nature and the status of traditions as the historicists and universalists see them. To begin with historicists: They reject the divine nature of the traditions.[397] For they already reject external revelation, and define it as Muhammad's inner thoughts, historicists logically conclude that the difference between Quran and traditions is not very big.[398] We can see this in Kırbaşoğlu, who likens Quran and the traditions to concentric circles of which the functions are same.[399] Accordingly, traditions are Muhammad's *ijtihad* of the verses that make practical life examples of them. To explain his arguments, Kırbaşoğlu points to the example of Hassan ibn Atiyyah al-Andalusi (d. 1147), who offered a concept of hadith as dependent on revelation. Similarly, Kırbaşoğlu searches for a grand strategy in which the division of Islamic thought between hadith and Quran is negligible. He gives another example in this vein: Al-Amidi (d. 1233), who studied Islamic disciplines on a holistic perspective, avoided categoricals such as "hadith" and "Quran."[400] We see in these discussions Kırbaşoğlu's opinion that revelation and hadith are close in the strongest possible sense of proximity. Güler also endorses the holistic method where the distinction between Quran and hadith is no longer valid.[401] The rationale of bringing Quran and traditions closer is to incorporate the traditions into the historicist method.[402] In fact, this is like al-Shafi'i's method where revelation and traditions are approached as similar phenomena: However, unlike al-Shafi'i, who equalized revelation and traditions by canonizing the latter, historicists bring revelation and traditions closer by defining both as historical phenomena. In so doing, historicist expect to invalidate the Sunni method of using traditions one-by-one way to justify their arguments on any issue.[403] In this usage, which Kırbaşoğlu calls "the atomist reading of traditions," each tradition is treated as if it were a universal divine axiom independent of its historical context.[404] The historicist proposal is to interpret traditions in their historical context. In this line of thinking, traditions should be understood in a larger framework, with the purpose of abstracting some general norms from them.[405] In so doing, universalists reject the Sunni method of imitating the literal meanings of the traditions. The method is also expected to end the recognition of the traditions as an independent resource of Islamic reasoning.[406]

The universalists' position on the nature and the status of the traditions is comparatively clear. Universalism is very skeptical about the hadith literature, and deems Quran the only divine source of religious guidance for Muslims.[407] Logically, universalists do not see an ontological relationship between revelations and traditions. Yaşar Nuri holds that not recognizing traditions as an independent source of Islam is a symbol of rationalism.[408] Thus, for him, presenting hadith as a different form of revelation is wrong.[409] Traditions are not the equals of Quran, writes Atay.[410] Reminding that Muhammad was both prophet and man, Atay warns that his opinions as a man can be wrong, so putting his words on par with the verses is a mistake.[411] Yaşar Nuri states that prophets have no authority to legislate or prohibit. In the same way, traditions have no authority to abrogate a verse:[412] He holds that the traditions emerged in Islam only in the Umayyad period as if they were a "second Islam."[413] Thus, for universalists, traditions can at best be auxiliary resources for interpreting Quran, but they have no canonical status.[414]

Criticizing the Hadith Literature

The rationalists' opposition on hadith literature is not limited to taking issue with al-Shafi'i. As a typical rationalist conduct, their general strategy is to weaken the impact of hadith scholars upon Muslims. So, on the one hand, while they propose their alternative hadith methodology, on the other hand they provide systematic arguments to persuade Muslims that the hadith literature has serious flaws.

To begin with, rationalists criticize hadith scholars for being populists, which led them to deliberately incorporate weak traditions. Kırbaşoğlu writes that hadith scholars always had a motivation of narrate as many hadith as possible.[415] However, for rationalists, this populist approach is the structural problem of the hadith literature. Accordingly, having restricted Islamic reasoning to Quran and the traditions, traditionists effectively have no choice but to increase the number of traditions to fulfill the needs of Muslims. Yaşar Nuri accused that the traditionists increased the hadiths for their benefit.[416] In consequence, they tried all available tactics to achieve their goal. For example, they enlarged the definition of "companionship" to narrate more traditions. Unlike the traditional rationalists like the Mu'tazila, for whom only those who had a close relationship with Muhammad are the companions, hadith scholars define "companion" as any person who saw Muhammad even once.[417] Yaşar Nuri notes that this expansion of the definition led scholars to narrate hadith from various early Muslims, on subjects on which they had no expertise; this created the problem of giving the status of canons of religion to many problematic opinions.[418] For historicists, the carelessness of hadith scholars, caused by their eagerness to write as many hadith as possible, is evident even in major books. Kırbaşoğlu counts that *al-Ihya*, al-Ghazali's magnum opus, has more than 1,000 traditions without *isnad*. (*Isnad* is the list of authorities who have transmitted that hadith which determines also its validity.) Kırbaşoğlu wrote satirically that al-Ghazali attempted to revive religious sciences by using traditions with no *isnad*. The number of traditions with no *isnad* in al-Bukhari's *Sahih*, the most important hadith book of Sunnism, is more than 1,400. Kırbaşoğlu counts that the number of weak traditions in the *Al-Jami' al-Saghir* of al-Suyuti, and he again reminds satirically that al-Suyuti had in fact promised not to do that.[419] Atay, too, criticizes al-Bukhari (d. 870) for including weak traditions in his magnum opus.[420] And Yaşar Nuri quotes some fabricated traditions narrated by al-Qurtubi, who, ironically, was known for warning that this should not be done.[421] Rationalists point also to how the unstoppable tendency to narrate traditions caused a worrying inflation of their number. Reminding that the number of traditions narrated by Muhammad is around 1.5 million, Kırbaşoğlu calculates that Muhammad would have had to produce 185 traditions on each day of his twenty-three years of prophethood. There is also another problem with numbers: The number of traditions from al-Zuhri (d. 742) was around 4,000. The number is 4,400 for Ahmad ibn Hanbal (d. 855) and 7,000 in Ishaq Ibn Rahwayh (d. 853). Kırbaşoğlu finds their number reaching to 1.5 million within only two centuries.[422] Similarly, Yaşar Nuri writes that though the number of authentic traditions in the time of Abu Bakr and Umar was around 500, it later rose to millions.[423]

The rationalists criticize hadith scholars for infusing their scholarship with the Arab culture.[424] In view of that, they fail to correctly define the Arab culture vis-à-vis Islam.[425] Accordingly, hadith scholars, marginalizing rationalist scholars like Abu Hanifa, and tolerating only a text-based reasoning, incorporated Arabic motifs into Islam as if they were universal elements.[426] Instead, rationalists propose reading the traditions in term of their purposes, rather than seek to implement their literal message. For rationalists, efforts to implement the literal messages of traditions would only result in treating Arab practices as if they are religion.[427] In fact, as I shall explain in later chapters, a major critique of Sunnism by rationalists is its failure to grasp that "being Muslim" is not ipso facto "being Arab."[428]

The rationalists find that hadith scholars have a poor knowledge of scientific issues. This, they surmise, is due to their understanding that Islamic texts contain all knowledge. So the nonreligious sciences hold little interest for them. This affects their scholarship negatively, for they perform poorly in detecting mistakes as they narrate traditions with scientific and historical content. Kırbaşoğlu presents various examples: In Abu Davud's (d. 889) *Sunan*, there is a tradition of Muhammad on Basra city, which was, however, founded during the reign of Caliph Umar after several years of Muhammad's death. The case of al-Suyuti is more dramatic. He defended flat earth, despite the presence in his time of advanced Muslim scholars of the natural sciences. In his epistle on earthquakes, Al-Suyuti wrote also that God created Mountain Qaf, a mythological mountain that covers the whole universe and finally reaches the stone on which the earth stands. So, when God orders the mountain to move, there are earthquakes. For Kırbaşoğlu, such cases do not only show that the leading scholars of hadith had a poor knowledge of natural phenomena but also reveal that they could easily be mistaken on other points, too.[429] However, Kırbaşoğlu observes no alarm among hadith scholars when the complex problems of their literature are pointed out to them.[430] Referring to similar points, Güler finds hadith scholars intellectually weak, which, he opines, drives them to focus on simplistic subjects like the details of worship, rather than comparatively complicated and abstract concepts such as justice, equality, and peace.[431] The result, for Güler, is in the poor quality of the general discourse in hadith books, including *Kutub al-Sitta*—the six books, which contains collections of traditions which Sunni Muslims regard as the most authentic resource—which treats Muslims as infants who cannot contribute to their personal development.[432]

The rationalists slam hadith scholars for not developing a dynamic method to dismiss fabricated traditions.[433] Güler notes that traditionists behave as if there were no problem in the hadith literature.[434] For Atay and Öztürk, such an uncritical view causes the survival of absurd and irrational opinions in the literature.[435] Among the many examples that rationalists present in this vein, a summary by Kırbaşoğlu, selected from *Sahih*, is illustrative. This book contains traditions with strange content, such as the following: Muhammad's attempting suicide when the revelation ceased for a while, a view of women that presents them as lacking faith and reason, a portrait of Muhammad arresting a jinn and binding it to a tree, Moses crying for he has fewer followers than Muhammad, and Muhammad spitting into a meal for it would be healthy for Muslims.[436] Kırbaşoğlu adds that such traditions exist also in other key books of *Kutub al-Sitta*, as well as in many other prestigious books, such as al-Ghazali's *al-Ihya*. According to Kırbaşoğlu, although the study of hadith had been given credit in an earlier period for having a critical methodology, its existing traditions were declared canonical after Ibn al Salah (d. 1245) wrote *Ulum al-Hadith*. That brought on the transmission into the literature of many absurd traditions.[437]

Finally, the rationalists argue that the literature includes a lot of politically motivated traditions of which the authenticity is a matter of concern.[438] Particularly, rationalists see a systematic Umayyad impact on the early formation of hadith studies. Accordingly, the Umayyads were strategically interested in hadith studies to legitimize their rule. This led to their fabrication of traditions.[439] The rationalists in this vein criticize various early names in hadith studies for their connections with the Umayyads. Yaşar Nuri, for example, finds that al-Zuhri is under the Umayyad's influence.[440] In Öztürk's view, al-Zuhri was forced to incorporate various traditions, due to political pressure.[441] Many other names, Urwah ibn Zubayr (al-Zuhri's main resource), and Abu Hurayra were also criticized for their contacts with the Umayyads.[442] Yaşar Nuri even criticizes al-Bukhari for being under the influence of the Umayyads.[443] For example, he argues that the famous tradition in *Sahih* on the conquest of Istanbul, probably one of the most popular hadith among Turks, is a fabricated part of a political campaign during Caliph Yazid (reigned 680–3).[444] Supporting the political influence on al-Bukhari, Azimli highlights that various problematic traditions concerning women in *Sahih* were fabricated during the Civil War among early Muslims, mostly as a response to the role played by Aisha against Ali.[445] In this vein, rationalists are particularly critical of traditions presented in the *Kitab al-Fitan* chapters of key hadith books that contain traditions on the tribulations and political fights among Muslims, for they reflect systematic political motivations.[446]

The Debate on Methodology

A hadith is composed of two parts: *isnad*, the chain of transmitters (and information on them), and the *matn*, the text.[447] Traditional literature inclines heavily toward verifying the authenticity of a verse that is critical of *isnad* rather than toward evaluating its content.[448] This method has its origin in the belief that a tradition can be evaluated only by the scrutiny of its narrators, since its content comes from the Prophet, and is therefore necessarily flawless. Speculating on the sets of contradictory information from the Prophet, al-Shafi'i concluded that the case in point is a transmission problem, since no contradictory tradition is possible from the Prophet.[449] Even so, on the historical perspective, it is evident that the Sunni method evolved from the method of the verification of narrators.

Differently, the rationalists find the traditional *isnad*-style verification inefficient at preventing the transmission of irrational or absurd traditions, and they ask for a critique of the traditions' content.[450] As a second reservation, they do not find objective and reliable the criteria the Sunni method employs in evaluating narrators. Kırbaşoğlu thinks the traditional methods of hadith a Medieval approach.⁴⁵¹ Thus, for him, *'ilm al-rijal* (the science of studying narrators) is not a universal method.⁴⁵² Instead, the method is full of problems that are sometimes guilty of *ad hominem* fallacy. He gives an example where the narrator is dismissed because he stood while peeing, a conduct that is in conflict with the prophetic moral conduct.⁴⁵³ Or some people were not found reliable, for they were caught lying in their lifetimes. This is not a universal criterion for Kırbaşoğlu, since it cannot be argued that some people never lie, nor that a person who lied in some circumstances can never transmit correct information.⁴⁵⁴ Recalling such cases, Kırbaşoğlu concludes that the purpose of the *isnad* method is to verify traditions according to religious criteria. But wherein lies a guarantee of universal objectivity in someone's determination of what constitutes "religious criteria"?⁴⁵⁵

The rationalists dismiss the traditional method also for its lack of internal consistency, noting the contending opinions on the same narrators.⁴⁵⁶ They remind that the hadith literature has contradictory opinions even of key names such as Aisha and Abu Hurayra, who are among the *muqsirun* (the seven companions who narrated the most traditions).⁴⁵⁷ Such contradictory evaluations of key narrators prove, for rationalists, that the traditional method fails to provide a consistent and universalizable procedure. As Kırbaşoğlu underlines, *'ilm-i rijal*, a highly subjective method, was naturally open to other influences, like political considerations.⁴⁵⁸ To demonstrate how the *isnad* authentication lacks internal consistency, Kırbaşoğlu notes that al-Bukhari did not narrate from the 434 narrators who were found reliable by Muslim (d. 875). And Muslim did also not narrate hadith from 625 narrators who were found reliable by al-Bukhari.⁴⁵⁹ An equally important case in this vein is that various scholars like Yahya ibn Main (d. 847) did not deem al-Shafi'i, the architect of the Sunni hadith method, to be reliable to narrate traditions from.⁴⁶⁰

As expected, rationalists support the content-based evaluation of traditions to overcome endemic problems in the literature.⁴⁶¹ Basically, in content analysis, *matn* is analyzed on various criteria, such as whether the content is scientifically, logically, or historically correct or consistent.⁴⁶² Pragmatically, the key feature of the method is to assign to human reason the authority of evaluating the content of the traditions.⁴⁶³ As Kırbaşoğlu rightly sums up, this is to leave *ahl hadith* and to embrace *ahl ray*.⁴⁶⁴ A number of examples are illustrative in the effort to distill the criteria that rationalist apply to evaluate the content of a tradition. For example, traditions that contradict Quran are rejected.⁴⁶⁵ Yaşar Nuri asserts that though this method belongs to Abu Hanifa, it was dismissed tactically by the traditionalists.⁴⁶⁶ In principle, Muhammad cannot speak against Quran. Thus, for example, traditions that are critical of womanhood for Eve's disloyalty are rejected, for verse 20:121 informs on Adam as the person who erred first. Similarly, traditions that transmit tribal, sectarian or racial messages are also dismissed for not being authentic. Another criterion is a logical one: If a hadith was narrated by a few people, despite that it is by nature an event that takes place before a large audience, it is also proclaimed not authentic. For example, Kırbaşoğlu dismisses traditions that portray Muhammad stopping the sun, for they are narrated by only a few people.⁴⁶⁷ The applied criterion operates on the simple logic that such an event would have been narrated by many people, worldwide. A further criterion requires the dismissal of traditions that are in clear contradiction of scientific realities or reason.[468] For example, the hadith that reports Muhammad saying "recite 'God is great' when you see a fire. That will put it out" is not authentic.[469] Similarly, traditions that inform on people who lived hundreds of years before its narrator, or inform wrongly on geological matters, are dismissed.[470] Again, traditions where Muhammad is reported to have spoken of events that are to happen in 100 or 200 years are also not authentic, given that there was no calendar, nor a concept of century, in Muhammad's lifetime.[471]

Having discussed the rationalists' views on the nature and status of traditions, what can be concluded about their final position on hadith? In his *Muslim Tradition*, G. H. A. Juynboll defines his position on traditions as follows:

> I realize that it is difficult to accept that all those early reports are to be considered historically true, or that the details in each one of them should be taken as factually correct. But I maintain that, taken as a whole, they all converge on a description of the situation obtaining in the period of history under scrutiny which may be defined as pretty reliable.[472]

To a large extent, Juynboll's conclusion is valid to explain the position of the rationalists. As rationalists, they are critical of how traditionalists treat hadith in Islamic reasoning. However, they do not reject them. Instead, they want to redefine them as historical, sociological, or literary resources.[473] For example, Kırbaşoğlu writes that even if it does not belong to Muhammad, a hadith is important for observing how this teaching was understood by Muslims in the past.[474] Kırbaşoğlu simply treats traditions as instrument of social memory. Similarly, reminding that criticism of hadith is not to reject them categorically, Yaşar Nuri defines hadith as historical material.[475] Eliaçık suggests that hadith be seen as sociological material.[476] For Atay, even nonauthentic hadiths matter, for they can be read as mythological aspects of the Islamic tradition.[477] Echoing Atay, Güler proposes an approach to the traditions' authenticity problem that treats them a literary material.[478] On this account, hadith is no longer canonical, nor even a primary religious resource. Hadith is now treated as historical, sociological, literary, or even mythological material. Thus, in general, the rationalists, somewhat reminiscent of Herbert Berg, propose that traditions remain part of the Islamic tradition, but wield only a subjective influence, having vacated their canonical status.[479]

Conclusion

Aware that the Sunni paradigm survives on the premises of the fundamentals, that is, on Quran and the traditions, the rationalists are correctly of the opinion that a new approach to the fundamentals is required, lest it become impossible to propose new reasoning in the various fields, such as in Islamic law. Logically, the rationale of their new approach to the fundamentals is the justification of rationalist methods in Islamic reasoning. They therefore seek to reframe Quran and the traditions by lifting them out of the traditionalist paradigm.

Though their ultimate goal is the same, that is, to propose a rationalist view of the Islamic fundamentals, the strategies of historicists and universalists are different: Historicists defend a method of interpreting Quran on the norms discernable in the authentic meaning of the verses. The universalists defend a method where reason is deemed capable of interpreting Quran on universal principles that obviate the need to reference the historical context to find "authentic meaning." Though their methods differ, the universalists and the historicists use those methods against the Sunni paradigm in like manner, particularly in regard of Islamic law, with the result that their conclusions are identical. This is the subject of the next chapter.

Chapter 2

LAW

Demystifying Shari'a

Shari'a is the natural theme of any discussion on Islam. Several reasons account for this. The primary one is that shari'a is known as the actualization of Islam.[1] Many Muslims believe that Islam is not only about morality and theology but also about law. This forms their view that Islam and shari'a are similar concepts. Equating Islam with shari'a is thus an impact of Islamic tradition: As Mohammed Abed al-Jabri once stated, Islamic civilization can be defined as a civilization of law.[2] Secondly, Islamists, as well as many contemporary Islamic movements, hold that shari'a is the ultimate purpose of religious activism. Abul A'la Mawdudi decreed that a Muslim is not a Muslim unless he lives in an Islamic state.[3] Sayyid Qutb, too, interpreted Islam as a theory of governance.[4] The Islamic state in Iran, founded in 1979 and led by Ayatollah Khomeini, marks the zenith of contemporary Islamism.[5] Naturally, the Islamist turn consolidated among Muslims the view that Islam is not a concept that espouses a religion but also a theory of state with a body of law. Finally, the popularity of "shari'a" is about the negative reception of the term in the Western world. In both academic and nonacademic circles, many in the West find shari'a incompatible with Western values.[6] Particularly, Islamic law on penal regulations touches off an alarmed interest in the West when it seems to confront the various basic human rights and freedoms valued there.[7]

Aware that many problems in Islamic societies have their origins in how Muslims interpret Islamic law, the rationalists, too, give a large space to shari'a in their works. They not only try for a new perception of shari'a in regard of its nature and status but also propose their interpretations of key issues in Islamic law. Those are the practical reflections of their rationalist paradigm that I analyzed in the previous chapter. Their new reasoning about the key legal issues reflects the rationalist belief (which might be credited as another of their distinctive attributes) that perception of the need for change is not enough; what is required is initiatives that propose concrete changes in the interpretation of Islamic law.

The Nature and the Status of Shariʻa

The rationalists see shariʻa as the lowest, or the least important, layer in the hierarchy of Islamic norms. Reflecting this view, they regard Islamization or piety based on the primacy of shariʻa as wrong and harmful.[8] Reading their works, one quickly picks up that the main rationalist position is that values such as morality should rank in the higher layers of Islamic norms. There is a resistance in the rationalists' works to the traditional thinking that sees Islam as primarily a legal system.

We can study this rationalist approach by reading Kırbaşoğlu's analysis of shariʻa. Portraying Islamic norms as a pyramid, Kırbaşoğlu pictures shariʻa as the lowest layer (Figure 4). In that pyramid, metaphysical principles are the highest norms of Islam, followed by moral norms. Interpreting the pyramid, Kırbaşoğlu points out that what determines one's piety or Islamic identity is in the higher layers; shariʻa is not.[9] Promoting moral and ethical values to the normative higher layers, and demoting Islamic law, is a major determinant of the rationalists' approach to the interpretation of shariʻa, as well as to their understanding of the anatomy of piety. Adapting Ismail R. al-Faruqi's classification of Islamic values, Kırbaşoğlu separates them as two groups, higher and lower. The lower can be changed to reach the goals of the higher.[10] Al-Faruqi holds that moral values come before all other elemental values, since they presuppose them. Logically, moral values are the higher part of the divine will.[11] Similarly, in Kırbaşoğlu, the purpose of Islam is to realize the higher values.[12]

Kırbaşoğlu's pyramid reveals the rationalists' maxim on shariʻa. Equating shariʻa and Islam is wrong.[13] We observe this maxim in the works of other scholars, like Abdullahi An-Naʻim, who argues that shariʻa is not the whole of Islam, but only

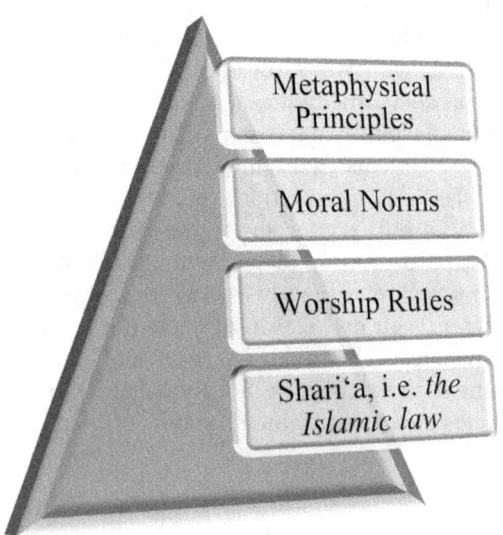

Figure 4 The hierarchy of Islamic norms according to Kırbaşoğlu.

an interpretation of its fundamental sources in particular historical contexts.[14] Similarly, for the rationalists, equating Islam with shari'a is a Sunni mistake.[15] For them, as we observe in the pyramid in Figure 4, shari'a is only one part of Islam, and its compatibility with the essence of Islam is more than a bit troubled. Güler clarifies this problem: While Islam is universal, shari'a is its historical local interpretation.[16] Thus, as Kırbaşoğlu explains, shari'a is only a parochial form of Quran's universal message.[17]

Logically, once the equation between Islam and shari'a is rejected, the latter is downgraded. Güler underlines that shari'a cannot represent the universal and unchanging content of Islamic norms, for those are metaphysical principles and moral values. Therefore, the shari'a rules in Quran are open to change.[18] Also, as we read in Öztürk, there is a widely held view that the laws in Quran can be applied as they are anywhere, and at any time. However, reflecting the conjectural tenet of shari'a, there are also Quranic laws that clearly cannot be applied universally or literally.[19] This insight reduces shari'a to a temporary and local form, whereas Islam is a universal religion.[20] Given this, and that the content of shari'a is collected mostly from seventh-century Arab laws and rituals, it is not universal form.[21] This is a natural conclusion, as a universal religion necessarily conveys its message in the context of a culture and a society.[22] It is illogical to imagine Muhammad as the Prophet who asked his community to practice a shari'a that is unknown to them.[23] As Azimli writes, Muhammad did not invent new laws; instead, he borrowed from the existing practices of his community, which of course changed and modified after his time.[24] Öztürk explains the formation of Islamic shari'a from Arab culture as an example of natural law where a legal system picks up from the various practices known to people.[25] He thus believes that all Quranic legal regulations have a pre-Islamic origin.[26] We get a better picture of this approach in Yaşar Nuri: Punishing the thief is a universal principle of Islam. However, the style of the punishment was formulated within the existing practices of the Arab society.[27] Naturally, Islamic methods, such as the chopping-off of hands, or the condoning of polygamy, are not authentic, since they were collected from pre-Islamic Arab culture.[28]

The *ma'ruf* principle is proposed as capable of explaining the relationship between shari'a and pre-Islamic Arab society.[29] As discussed in Chapter 1, this principle in Islamic law refers to the customary practices tolerated in Islamic law, mainly by Hanafi jurists.[30] As al-Nasafi (d. 1142) points out, practices that are rationally justified, and are not deemed repellent to good nature, can be adopted.[31] On this account, Güler defines shari'a as a general *ma'ruf* from Arab customs, not only in the fields of law but even in the field of worships, such as pilgrimage and prayer.[32] To illustrate his view, Güler likens shari'a to the *décor* in which Islam, the universal religion, became manifest. Simply, shari'a is a religion in a given milieu.[33] Similarly, Yaşar Nuri defines shari'a as a legalized Arab *ma'ruf* which naturally reflects the Arab culture and mentality.[34] This is completely normal. Öztürk reminds that any universal message actualizes itself in a spatial and temporal context by its reception into the context of existing customs.[35]

Reading their opinions on the subject, we understand that the rationalists regard Islam as the universal religion that God sent to humanity, in the interim between

Adam and Muhammad, via prophets such as David, Solomon, and Jesus.[36] In this regard, Islam represents universal continuity. So there is one universal religion in history. On this schema, Muhammad is the last prophet who preached that universal religion.[37] He did not bring a new religion. Rather, he brought a new shari'a, that is, the interpretation of the universal religion in the Arab context.[38] Logically, the rationalists' approach, which is built on the difference between Islam and shari'a, identifies Islamic law as formulated in Quran as a local, temporary law. In other words, that law is not universally binding for all times and societies.[39] This perceives shari'a as only a collection of first samples, not as the final model.[40] Thus, for the rationalists, equating Islam and shari'a is simply to treat the various practices of the Arab historical milieu as if they are universal norms.[41] In fact, shari'a was an ideal law only for the Muslims who lived in the seventh century.[42] A major implication of the rationalist view of shari'a is the right of succeeding generations to change shari'a rules according to their realities. Güler metaphorically likens Islam to milk, and shari'a to an Arab cheese. This figure of speech justifies the proposing of the evolutionary ways of shari'as.[43] Kırbaşoğlu accepts that the new realities of a time may even require new rules that might literally contradict the text of Quran.[44] The rationalist principle is clear: If the existing rules are not achieving the high and immutable principles of Islam, they can be changed.[45] Shari'a rules can be changed, since they are not per se the goals of Islam.[46]

Therefore, for the rationalists, the conjectural nature of shari'a requires permanent updates lest it become irrelevant.[47] Otherwise, stagnation in law would result in the continuous disruption of the Muslim society. As a matter of fact, the rationalist literature frequently reminds that the poor state of Muslim societies is due to their failure to update shari'a. For example, Güler asserts that treating shari'a as if it were fixed like the higher norms of Islam—which he presents as a Sunni misunderstanding—is a major cause of the stagnation of Islamic civilization.[48] Güler thus warns that people should not practice the law of past generations.[49] It is on this perspective that the rationalists criticize the contemporary Islamic movements from Pakistan to Turkey. They promise no change, but insist on the outdated Sunni law. In his *Introduction to the Critique of Sunnism*, Güler likens the contemporary Islamic revivalism to bringing Muslims back to the outdated form of Islamic law, which can lead only to corruption in society.[50] Similarly, Atay criticizes Islamic revivalism as "freezing Islam," for it calls for an Islamization based on an outdated interpretation of Islamic law.[51] For Yaşar Nuri, an Islamization agenda without an update of the law is always an attempt to bring Muslims back to a Medieval model.[52] That is why the failure of the Islamic movement in Turkey is not a surprise for the rationalists, as it is built on a theory that is false from the outset.

A Rationalist Interpretation of Shari'a

Having presented the rationalists' approach to shari'a, I shall now observe closely how their theoretical abstractions produce empirical manifestations in a number of selected issues and scenarios. As elaborated in previous chapters, two paradigms, historicism and universalism, prevail in the works of the rationalists. The paradigmatic procedure of each scholar is to analyze the various issues of Islamic law by studying the relevant verses in Quran, subjecting them to the scrutiny of the principles of the paradigm he espouses. The differences in their methodologies notwithstanding, both groups aim at finding the *ratio legis* of the verse under scrutiny: That is, each scholar seeks to discover *why a law is being enunciated*. That task isolates the subject of that law. The scholar is then ready to pronounce upon the contemporary applicability of that subject.[53] However, while the universalists take the general principles of Quran as the framework from which the *ratio legis* will emerge, the historicists take the sociohistorical context of the revelation as their framework. In other words, they address a different terrain of references as prime resource of the *ratio legis* of an Islamic law. But both groups accept that if a law—even when it is literally prescribed in Quran—fails to reveal its *ratio legis*, a new rule can be proposed. The justification of this method is twofold: First, both groups distinguish shari'a and Islam, and regard the former as inherently subject to change in different settings. Secondly, as I discussed in the previous chapter, both groups agree that the content of Quran in regard to shari'a is historical.

Corporal Punishment: Chopping

All the major schools of Islamic law, including those of the Shi'a, accept amputation as a punishment for theft.[54] The chopping-off of hands is practiced in several Muslim countries. The Brunei Penal Code, for example, stipulates the amputation of the right hand for a first offence and amputation of the left foot for the second offence.[55] Radical groups like ISIS practiced such methods. For example, *Ansar al-Shari'a* in Yemen chopped off the hands of those accused of stealing.[56] In countries where such methods are not practiced, scholars do not rule out corporal punishment. In Turkey, *Tefsir*—a five-volume exegesis of the Quran prepared for the general public by Diyanet—recognizes the chopping-off of hands as a legitimate method, and informs on details such as how the foot should be amputated.[57] Scholarly articles in Turkish that follow the Sunni law keep informing on the details of corporal punishment methods, including hand chopping.[58]

Corporal punishment in the form of hand chopping has its origin in verse 5:38, which lays down that Muslims "cut off the hands of thieves, whether they are man or woman, as punishment for what they have done." Treating shari'a as a divine and universal form, Muslims practice what they literally understand from the verse. In *Risala*, al-Shafi'i—whose view set the Sunni standard—ruled that the punishment as ordained in Quran and practiced by the Prophet is the final one.[59]

Not regarding hand chopping as the cast-in-iron Islamic method, the rationalists justify the advancing of alternate punishments.[60] Accordingly, alternate punishments are legitimate if they achieve Islam's higher principles of social order and morality.[61] The rationalists rest their reasoning on the principle that Islam makes no higher norm of amputating people's hands, but it does make such a norm of establishing a society where people are safe, and those who would breach the law are deterred by effective rules.[62] Indeed, this reasoning is a reflection of the rationalists' differentiation of Islam and shariʿa. Criticizing Sunni scholars for reducing shariʿa to a methodology of punishment, Güler reminds that the lesser norms like the shariʿa rules may change to realize higher norms.[63] The rationalists' stance on the subject reminds of Fazlur Rahman's approach, where the content of penal regulations are "variable," whereas "the universalized principles of good and bad are constant."[64]

Though both the historicists and the universalists justify new methods other than chopping, they explain themselves in different ways: The historicists propose new methods by reference to the authentic meaning of verse 5:38.[65] For Öztürk, the punishment verses in Quran are conjectural regulations that cannot be imagined as the fixed principles of Islam to be applied today. They should be understood with reference to their sociological setting. Presenting hand chopping as an Arab cultural method, Öztürk draws heavily from Abu Yusuf (d. 798), the leading Hanafite jurist, who spoke of this method as an Arab custom.[66] Similarly, Güler explains hand chopping as a constant in the economic infrastructure of the tribal Arab society. Theft was not primarily an economic crime in that tribal Arab society. It was first a crime against tribal honor. Regarding stealing as a direct attack on their tribal honor, the ancient Arabs developed radical punishments like chopping. For Güler, theft today is, however, primarily an economic crime that therefore requires different penal responses.[67] In the same line of thinking, Kırbaşoğlu sees chopping as the best available practice in the context of the seventh-century Arab society.[68] But he adds that chopping hands today proves that classical methods of Islamic reasoning—satisfactory in the Medieval Ages—are no longer effective.[69] Eliaçık's position is no different. Penal regulations in Quran as practical solutions derive from Arab culture. However, those methods, collected mainly from around Medina, a city with approximately 10,000 inhabitants, cannot be seen as universal rules.[70]

When it comes to the universalists, we see that they base their reasoning on the general principles of Quran differently. Noting that the universal norm in Quran is to prohibit stealing, Yaşar Nuri dismisses hand chopping because it cannot be a universal rule, but only a conjectural practice. It can be replaced by other practices that fit the universal norm.[71] Atay employs another universalist method: He determines the general purpose of Quran in verse 5:38 through an etymological analysis of it. As I discussed in Chapter 1, the origin of the method is the belief that the verses in Quran have many meanings. It is assumed therefore that God intended every meaning that can be drawn from a verse.[72] On this account, Atay, analyzing verse 5:38, argues that the verb *faqtaʿu*—cut off—means "remove the factors" that make stealing possible or inevitable in a society. The cutting off of the thief's hand is not necessarily the exclusive meaning of *faqtaʿu* in verse 5:38. So, when the verse commands "cut off their hands," it means to cut off the social, educational and economic reasons for theft. Consequently, Atay does not allow that hand chopping can be a universal principle, albeit written in Quran.[73] This explanation, which completely ignores how the verse was understood in its historical context, is naturally unacceptable for historicists. Güler argues that interpretations like that of Atay have no objective basis, and he reminds that the verse was understood as "chopping" in the past.⁷⁴ Responding to this criticism, Atay proposes that the first Muslims failed to understand the purpose of the verse, which is to *impede theft by various policies*, not to cut off the hands. Atay explains this misunderstanding as a lapse in the understanding of the early Muslims. He explains this lapse in terms of the impact of social understanding levels or of the impact of the Christian method of foisting Bible meanings on the Muslims. But in any case, for Atay, the first Muslims effectively misunderstood verse 5:38.⁷⁵

We observe the universalist method of etymological analysis also in Eliaçık, but in a different context: Explaining how "those who wage war against God and his messenger" should be punished, verse 5:33 calls for various ways of doing it, including the "amputation of an alternate hand and foot." Eliaçık interprets this part of the verse in quite novel way: To him, the verse does not ask for amputation. Instead, it informs metaphorically that those who wage war against God will perish, because they will face serious troubles in life.⁷⁶ Eliaçık here reads "amputating hand and food" allegorically as the loss of power, fortune, prestige, or health. Eliaçık's method, like Atay's, again implies that the early Muslims failed to correctly understand the verses.

The methodological debate on corporal punishment illustrates the difference between historicism and universalism: As we observed in Atay and Eliaçık, universalism may find the authentic meaning, that is, how the first Muslims understood the verse, as irrelevant, and even a misunderstanding. However, for historicists, arguing that the early Muslims failed to understand a verse is tantamount to breaking the foundations of historicism, which is that authentic meaning of a verse is seen as the objective framework in the interpretation of the verses.

Apostasy

Apostasy is another subject to observe when one is on a quest to collect all the various interpretations of Islamic law. Capital punishment is the due of apostates on the standard Islamic interpretation. There are states with apostasy laws: Afghanistan, Brunei, Mauritania, Qatar, Saudi Arabia, Sudan, and Yemen.⁷⁷ There are also Muslim countries where apostasy is punished in ways other than capital punishment. For example, in Malaysia and the Maldives, apostasy laws make those who are convicted liable to pay large fines and to serve prison sentences.⁷⁸ There is also an immense body of data showing that apostasy prevails in Islamic thought at different levels. A 2013 PEW Survey demonstrates that 76 percent of respondents in South Asia, and 56 percent in the Central North-East Africa region, support the death penalty for Muslims who renounce their faith.⁷⁹ These samples remind of the view of Rudolph Peters and Gert J. J. De Vries that even though the apostasy law is falling into desuetude, it is expressly abolished almost nowhere.⁸⁰ Naturally, we observe Muslim scholars or groups defending capital punishment for apostates. Yusuf al-Qaradawi and Abu 'Ala Mawdudi imagined Islamic law on apostasy as an important part of their narrative.⁸¹ Ebubekir Sifil, a Turkish academic and a public intellectual, said on a popular TV channel that he does not shy away from stating "proudly" that apostates are killed in Islam.[82] *Sorularlaislamiyet*, a popular web portal on Islamic issues, which is close to the Nurcu Movement, defends the capital punishment of apostates.[83] The various Nurcu groups' support of the apostasy law is not surprising, given that Said Nursi, who inspired them, justified capital punishment for apostates, arguing that they poison society.[84] Yet there is no evidence in the Diyanet of support for the capital punishment of apostates. In *Tefsir*, Islam does not ask for the capital punishment of apostates.[85] However, a *fatwa* by the Turkish Higher Council of Religious Affairs (THCRA), the highest authority under Diyanet as the issuer of religious decrees, rules that apostasy ends one's marriage.[86] Similarly, *İlmihal* lists apostasy as that which ends marriage.[87]

The rationalists are unanimously of the opinion that there is no capital punishment for apostates in Islam.[88] Defending this thesis, they propose two methods: As the main method, they attack the traditions that uphold apostasy. This is a kind of a structural method of which the purpose is to destroy the religious foundations of the apostasy law. In so doing, the rationalists show that the apostasy law is not an authentic principle in Islam. They prefer this method to engaging in historical or logical arguments. Kırbaşoğlu dismisses those traditions which are used to justify apostasy laws for being seriously flawed. He does not therefore hesitate to assert that previous examples in history where apostates were killed were wrong interpretations of shari'a.[89] Similarly, Azimli argues that neither in Muhammad's narrative nor in his practice was there anything that approved capital punishment for apostates.[90] Güler, too, dismisses as unauthentic the traditions that meted out capital punishment to apostates. He also asserts that even if they were accepted as authentic, they should have been rejected, for they are in clear contradiction of various verses like 18:29, which reads: "Let those who wish to believe in it do so, and let those who wish to reject it do so."[91] Taking these positions, the rationalists redefine the punishing of apostates as a historical invention of the later Muslims and emphasize that no major Islamic resource endorses it. Reminding that the punishment of apostates is not addressed in Quran, Kırbaşoğlu argues that previous scholars' opinions, which were based on traditions, are never enough to institute an Islamic law on such a critical subject.[92] We here observe how the rationalists' rejection of the canonical status of traditions, a subject we have already discussed in the previous chapter, play a key role in their reasoning.

As the second method, we come upon an argument in the works of the rationalists that locates the capital punishment of apostates in the context of the wars between Muslims and polytheists. Accordingly, there was no purpose to punish apostates in the early period of Islam. Rather, punishment was for war crimes, such as defecting to the enemy.[93] However, the later Muslims failed to see that difference, and read apostasy cases into the religious contexts.[94] The rationalists, however, keep such arguments short, and they carefully refrain from supplying detailed exemplification. On this account, apostasy is a rare subject in the works of the rationalists. They do not even care about methodological consistency when the subject is apostasy. Instead, they pay more attention to dismissing as unauthentic the traditions related to apostasy laws, and to challenging the historical practices that might be quoted to justify apostasy law as a correct interpretation of shari'a. But they are on thin ice here, for they do not provide accounts of historical practices, nor do they display the pertinent literature. Paradoxically, that might generate an effect that is the contrary of the one they seek. The rationalists do not want to leave a gray zone on apostasy; thus, they delegitimize the punishing of apostates in principle with three arguments: (i) There is no such practice in Quran and the traditions; (ii) the various traditions quoted to justify apostasy law are fabricated; (iii) later scholars' opinions, and Muslims' practices in the past which justify punishing apostates are wrong interpretations of shari'a.

Jihad

Though interpreted in different ways, jihad (holy war) is a subject that still prevails in contemporary Islamic thought.[95] In his *Milestones*, Sayyid Qutb criticizes those who argue that Islam prescribes only defensive wars. He believes that *jihad bil saif* (fighting with swords) is a legitimate method; thus, it is not correct to present Islam "as a defensive movement." To him, jihad is required for several reasons, such as "to establish Allah's authority on earth."[96] We encounter jihad in its military form also in the Diyanet narrative. That institution is quite moderate. But when the Turkish government ordered its troops to mount a military incursion into the Kurdish-dominated Syrian town, Idlib, in February 2020, the Diyanet asked imams to deliver a Friday sermon in which the incursion is saluted as jihad.[97] As events display, the intra-Islamic debate on jihad continues. Even the moderate actors are reluctant to give up the traditional military doctrine of jihad. The prevalence of the term in contemporary Islamic thought is critical also from another perspective: It affects seriously how Muslims govern their relations with other nations.[98]

The crux of the jihad subject is whether Islam has a doctrine of continuous war. Again, referring to Qutb, this doctrine can be defined as the rejection of the perception that jihad is a temporary obligation in transient conditions, or that it is concerned only with the defense of borders. Instead, it is a duty imposed by God on Muslims till the earth "be cleansed of corruption."[99] The rationalists reject the view that Islam has a doctrine of continuous jihad. For them, the central place of jihad in Islamic texts is a result of the wars in the early period of Islam, not a doctrinal requirement.[100] This is a thesis known since early authors like Montgomery Watt, who held that the Islamic concept of holy war developed gradually out of the circumstances in which the Muslims found themselves in their Arabian environment.[101] Similarly, the rationalists explain jihad with reference to the political aspect of Islamic history, rather than as a religious doctrine. For Güler, the jihad verses are specific regulations peculiar to the early period of Islam, when military fights were inevitable. However, since Quran was revealed as party to political and military struggles, many of the verses that reflect this were later confused about its universal message.[102] Öztürk, too, explains the war verses as references to the bellicose atmosphere, particularly in Medina, in the early years of Islam. Accordingly, the tense situation between Muslims and non-Muslims in Medina was the historical context that gave rise to the verses on war.

Besides, Muslims in Medina were in a process of establishing an Islamic polity, and this required some comparatively strict regulations concerning non-Muslims. However, as Öztürk argues, the war verses were later mistakenly coded as universal norms, even though they belong to a specific political setting in seventh-century Medina.[103] Reminding of several verses like 9:29—"fight those of the people of the Book who do not believe in God and the Last Day"—and verse 9:5 (aka the sword verse)—"wherever you encounter the idolaters, kill them, seize them, besiege them, wait for them at every look out post"—Öztürk warns that Muslims would understand them as a license to an open-ended state of war with non-Muslims if they fail to read them as conjectural regulations laid out when Muslim were at war with non-Muslims.[104]

As Güler and Öztürk both point out, the Islam of the early years was a period of long and intense battles. Al-Waqidi (d. 823) calculated that Prophet Muhammad participated in twenty-seven raids, fought in nine of them, and directed forty-seven expeditions.[105] The central place of wars in the formation period of Islam led even to the birth of an independent religious discipline on the wars of prophet: *Maghazi*. Seen in this way, for rationalists, the intense wars between Muslims and non-Muslims during the early period of Islam was a continuation of the Arab tradition that sees warring as a method of dealing with political issues. Güler reminds that the Arabs were organized as warring tribes. They had four months of pause from warring. Islam was naturally affected by the same culture.[106] On this account, for him, the central role of war in Islam is part of the Arab anthropological impact on the new religion.[107] The fact of the bellicose pre-Islamic Arab culture is mentioned since early Orientalists like Leone Caetani noted that pre-Islamic Arabs had no formal standing armies: "everyone was a warrior," and "the character of the Arabs was so warlike."[108] In like manner, Güler writes that Islam's conflict resolution methods were also derived from the existing Arab patterns through changes and modifications.[109] For example, the raiding of trade caravans, which was done tactically by the early Muslims, was a typical method that the Arab Bedouins practiced in desperate economic situation.[110] Reminding that such peculiar political dynamics caused Islam to survive Arab patterns of war, Güler laments that Islam could not express itself in pedagogical moral speeches. But his reaction is mainly to the Sunni scholars, for it is they who did not grasp that anthropological impact is not a universal norm.[111]

In this vein, the rationalists see al-Shafi'i as the architect of the Sunni doctrine of continuous jihad. In Güler's view, Sunnism is heavily under the impact of al-Shafi'i, who recognizes jihad as a legitimate method of expanding Islam, unlike Hanafi law, where jihad is legitimate only to end oppression.[112] In *Risala*, al-Shafi'i urges that jihad, particularly the rising up in arms, is obligatory for all able Muslims.[113] Commenting on how al-Shafi'i articulates his opinions in that book, Balcı criticizes him for proposing a wrong interpretation of the war verses because he ignores the fact that they were originally contextual regulations.[114] For Güler, al-Shafi'i's conclusion about jihad was thus a mistake, for it theologizes something that is no more than the early tribal violence in the Muslim society.[115]

However, though they reject the persistent jihad doctrine, the rationalists do not promote Islam as a pacifist religion. Güler thus finds meaningless the oft-repeated slogan "Islam is a religion of peace." Instead, he asserts that Islam has a conditional theory of war.[116] Accordingly, peace is the major principle of Quran. However, it allows war under some conditions.[117] For Güler, war is treated as a human condition in Islam, despite its negative consequences.[118] Kırbaşoğlu calls this a rational approach: Though war is unwelcome, Islam introduced some conditions for its waging, because war is inevitable.[119] So, as Balcı writes, Islam attempted to minimize the negative impact of war.[120] Yaşar Nuri, for instance, specifies that Islam justifies only wars that defy oppression.[121] As a logical upshot of their view of jihad, for the rationalists, war is not a legitimate method of religious expansion.[122] Once, the rationalists defined Islam as having a conditional theory of war. Now the central question is whether the early Muslims, including the companions, obeyed such a law of war.[123] As I will elaborate in next chapter, the rationalists take a revisionist perspective even on the many wars that occurred during the reign of the first four caliphs. Here, they do not shy away from criticizing key names like Abu Bakr and Umar for their leading of wars that were not compatible with Islamic standards.[124] In this context, the rationalists do not hesitate to criticize the early Muslims for sometimes returning to tribal Arab warfare after the Prophet's death and mistakenly making war a main strategy of expanding Islam.[125]

Slavery

The rationalists include slavery in their works to demonstrate the limits of Sunnism. According to them, a Sunni perspective is never able to abolish slavery, since it is part of Quran, and it was practiced by Muhammad.[126] For the rationalists, Sunnism can at best appeal to linguistic games, or to apologetics, to argue that Muslims treated their slaves humanely. But they do not reject it categorically.[127] The rationalists assert that the solid foundations of slavery in the fundamental Islamic resources are so adamant that they could only be overcome by new interpretations beyond Sunnism.[128]

To show how Sunnism has failed to abolish slavery, Öztürk reminds that the Ottomans abolished slavery due to Western pressure. This was resisted by the ulema as a deviation from shari'a.[129] Confirming Öztürk, for example, Ehud Toledano writes that the decision to prohibit the slave trade from Africa was extracted from the Ottoman government as a result of sustained pressure through diplomatic channels. The Ottomans had refused to yield to British pressure regarding the slave trafficking from various regions like the Caucuses.[130] For the rationalists, the survival of slavery in the Muslim world over centuries, and its abolishment only after the expansion of Western legal regulations (i.e., not through domestic dynamics in the form of new reasoning in Islamic law), is embarrassing, as well as a proof to demonstrate the ethical poverty of Sunnism.

On the rationalist perspective, it is the limitations of Sunnism that prevent the categorical rejection of slavery. Those limits also give way to anachronic conclusions about slavery. Not clearly abolishing slavery on a religious basis,

Öztürk argues that Sunnism can do no more than develop an apologetic narrative, for Islamic history is presented as a benign example of slavery of Muslims behaving fairly with their slaves. However, Öztürk criticizes such narratives for not being historically correct. He reports how highly deprecatory ideas on slaves were uttered by important names like Umar, Ibn Abas, Said ibn Jubayr, and Mucahid.[131] But more importantly, as Özsoy notes, this benevolent-masters narrative insinuates paradoxically that there can be ideal times when the Quranic regime of ideal slavery was applied.[132] This is what W. G. Clarence-Smith says of Sunnism: Its intellectual paralysis springs from the incompatible desire to condemn slavery and spare Islam.[133] An example that fits the picture of that paralysis is how Hayreddin Karaman, who is widely held to be the prominent leader in Islamic scholarship for his impact on the Islamist elites, including Turkish President Recep Tayyip Erdoğan, approaches the subject.[134] According to Karaman, there is no longer any form of slavery that Islam condones, given the recent developments at global level. But again, there is no acceptance on Karaman's part that slavery is abolished in Islam. Karaman merely repeats the typical Sunni conclusion that the Islamic form of slavery is still part of shari'a, albeit that there is no fitting social context in which to practice it.[135]

So, why does Sunnism fail to categorically reject slavery? For Öztürk, it is simply because it is justified by a doctrine of the divine Quran.[136] Accordingly, if Quran is literally divine, and the Word of God, the best service that human reason can offer is to reinterpret the verses on slavery as flexibly as possible, but never to conclude that slavery is abolished in principle. Thus, for the rationalists, slavery is a prominent display of the limitations of the Sunni concept of revelation. It displays also the Sunni propensity to generate anachronic religious conclusions.

The rationalists deem the Sunni approach dangerous, for it keeps slavery in the Islamic literature as if it were a harmless term which is to condone, even normalize, slavery.[137] Kırbaşoğlu complains that the Medieval narrative of slavery is still influential in contemporary books, as attested by the frequent uses of words like "slaves," and "concubines." Even worse, in Kırbaşoğlu's estimate, is that the preservation of slavery-linked vocabulary in the Islamic narrative still weighs negatively on other issues, such as freedom, by perpetuating a Medieval mentality.[138] In the same vein, Yaşar Nuri spots that the major classification of Islamic law still has three categories: men, women, and slaves. He thinks it problematic that key contemporary books on Islam continue the Medieval tradition that recognizes slavery as a normal state.[139] All the rationalists who engage with the "slaves" subject lament that open and unequivocal references to slavery keep it embedded in Islamic thought as if it were a normal institution. Confirming their worries is that many pages of *İlmihal* inform that freeing a slave is an expiation (*kaffarah*) of various wrongdoings. We read in *İlmihal* that those who make an oath should free one slave.[140] The rationalists are unnerved by the fact that such concepts remain in Islamic narrative, for their presence encumbers religious reasoning by inhibiting the development in it of a full-blown, individualistic, modern theory of freedom.

The rationalists' own approach to slavery is that they explain it in terms of the principle of gradualism and conclude that it is now abolished by religion. On this perspective, revelation is imagined as having a gradual strategy of realizing ultimate goals.[141] Fazlur Rahman formulates this as long-range objectives of Quran.[142] So it is presumed that Quran did not abolish various practices, but put up rules in a way calculated to bring Muslims to a "moral ideal towards which the society was expected to move."[143] This method asks those who interpret a verse to imagine the ultimate goal of Quran. It is supposed that Quran had the final goal of abolishing slavery, but this was late coming into practice for social and economic reasons. For Özsoy, given the central role of slavery in economics, Islam could introduce only some reformists principles in the favor of slaves, but had to postpone its outright abolishing.[144] Reminding that slavery was practiced also by the Romans and Persians, Öztürk explains it as the economic normalcy of the age.[145] However, for the rationalists, keeping up the practice of slavery was a historical phenomenon, and totally inconsistent with Quran's final goal. Therefore, Quran is correctly interpreted as having abolished slavery in principle, even though the revelations ended with the death of Muhammad without officially abrogating it. Kırbaşoğlu underlines that there is no doubt that Quran prohibited slavery.[146] Güler calls the revelations on slavery "half steps" with the ultimate purpose of abolishing slavery. That left its unequivocal abolishing a mission to be fulfilled by the later Muslims. This unwritten purpose is entailed in that abolishment was not realized during the lifetime of Muhammad.[147] Similarly, for Eliaçık, the logic of the revelation had a purpose of abolishing slavery even though it was not realized due to social and economic conditions. But he is confident that Islam abolished slavery.[148] As one would expect, the rationalists are also vehemently against keeping references to slavery-linked words in contemporary Islamic books.[149]

But again, we observe, particularly in historicists, an unhappiness, for Islam did not abrogate slavery openly. Öztürk writes that one wishes that Quran had explicitly prohibited slavery.[150] Given that the revelations introduced radical changes (such as forbidding the worship of idols, prohibiting the consumption of alcohol, and the forbidding of interest on loans), Güler finds that it is difficult to grasp why Islam did not abrogate slavery. He reminds of another controversial case in this vein: The revelations did not stay clear of introducing truly shocking regulations, such as the one (the verse 33:37) demanding that Prophet Muhammad's foster son, Zayd, divorce his wife Zaynab so that she could marry Muhammad. Güler is startled by the lack of a similar radical regulation on slavery, which for him would be a compatible with human honor. The case is made more difficult for Güler to grasp, for abolishing slavery would have been sociologically normal, given that many early Muslims were poor and slaves.[151] Güler's frustration suggests that the case of slavery in Quran is more than a case of conjectural dynamics. Supporting this, Öztürk, too, emphasizes the complicated status of slavery in Islam by referring to a critical debate in Islamic law: Shari'a justifies even the bending of the rules on veiling—a topic on which Islam is rigid—when the veil is invoked to distinguish free and slave women.[152] As historicists, Güler's and Öztürk's discussions are bold ideas, for they actually admit the limits of historicism on the subject of slavery. As a solution, Öztürk appeals directly to the rationalist axiom on the nature of Quran: What Quran offers with regard to slavery is by far not enough offer to enable the recommended practices that achieve the principles of human honor and freedom. Thus, the one solution regarding slavery is to go beyond Quran.[153]

The Status and Rights of Women in Islamic Law

The debate on the status of women in Islam is largely about how gender is handled in shari'a, why it is handled thus and whether Islamic law is gender-based beyond biological differences, such as women's pregnancy.[154] As one would expect, the subject occupies a large space in the works of the rationalists. Again, while interpreting "shari'a on women," the rationalists exercise the method of distinguishing the historical from the universal, which is a reflection of their understanding of shari'a.[155] However, before going through their proposals on the status and rights of women, a brief note on how the rationalists reference patriarchy to explain "the women question" in Muslim societies is necessary. The rationalists accept that a patriarchal view of women has survived within Islam since the beginning, causing many problems in the past and today. For this reason, their prime goal is a new religious reasoning on women that is not affected by patriarchalism.

For the rationalists, shari'a emerged historically with a patriarchal view of women. This is due to the complex relationship between the revelations and the Arab historical context.[156] The fact that the original Islam sought solutions to women's problems in a patriarchal society has left behind footprints such as the inegalitarian discourse on man and woman in Quran. Güler calls this as "the patriarchal shadow on Islam."[157] He emphasizes that it is therefore methodologically essential to keep in mind that the purpose of Islam was to solve the acute problems women experience in the Arab society, not to erect an egalitarian theory of gender that we know today.[158] Thus, we are warned that both Quran and the traditions contain passages where woman is approached from a patriarchal perspective. For example, Özsoy draws attention to verses 53:21-22, where God criticizes Arabs for committing "a most unjust distribution" when they image angels as the daughters of God, but keep the boys for themselves.[159] God here reacts with an Arab mentality, according to Özsoy. As we read in the works of Balcı and Atay, having boys rather than girls was, for Arabs, the prestigious achievement.[160] Quoting Izzat Darwaza, Öztürk writes that in these verses God speaks with an Arab mindset that sees having sons as better than having daughters.[161] Öztürk has another example to explicate the patriarchal mindset in Quran: In verse 4:3, God advices men to consider slave women if they fear that they cannot be fair to their wives. This verse reflects a patriarchal mentality, for it is not chary of taking the "slave women are utilities" view. The other problem with this verse is that it justifies the keeping of slave women.[162] For Atay, verse 33:33, which asks women to "stay at home," also reflects the patriarchal Arab culture.[163] And for Güler, verse 2:223 shows the patriarchal footprint in Quran when God tells men that "your wives are your fields."[164] Such cases are inevitable for the rationalists, given the nature of the dialogue between the Arabs and the revelation. The rationalists warn that such patriarchal elements should not be read as if they are essentials of the revelation.

The rationalist solution for overcoming the problems that the patriarchic primacy poses to the modern reader is not to focus on the laws per se, but, instead, to understand of the orientation or/and the general purposes that those laws had in the early Muslim society.

However, more problematic for the rationalists is the preservation by Muslims of the patriarchal mentality during the Middle Ages, as if it were essential to Islam.[165] Kırbaşoğlu criticizes Medieval Islamic scholarship for its endorsement of the patriarchal mindset.[166] As a result, the leading Muslim scholars continued the inegalitarian discourse on women as if it were part of the divine framework.[167] One major legacy of this trajectory, Öztürk writes, was that Islamic law on woman evolved mostly with regard to free women only, and this inserted a deep defect into the Islamic legal corpus. Thus, as he reports, leading Muslim scholars of the time, like al-Razi, approached nonfree women as no more that someone's property. Öztürk reports that al-Razi was of the opinion that the veiling of slave girls is illogical, since the logic of trade requires close inspection of their bodies.[168] His general view of women beyond the slaves is also not heartening: The purpose of women's creation was to serve men like animals and fruits.[169] The case is no different with many other scholars. Öztürk counts names such as al-Qurtubi and Ibn Kathir (d. 1373) among those who fed the unequal discourse on women.[170] We find on his list even al-Ghazali, who popularized several problematic perceptions of women. Quoting passages from al-Ghazali's magnum opus, *The Revival of Religious Sciences*, as well as from other of his books like *The Alchemy of Happiness*, Öztürk concludes that how he treated women is worse even than the pre-Islamic Arabs' ways. He is particularly shocked by al-Ghazali's view that women are the source of evil, and that they are toys men play with when they want. For Öztürk, al-Shafi'i, too, contributed to the patriarchal view of woman, for he saw women as the subjects of prohibitions (i.e., what women should not do) not freedoms in Islamic law.[171]

The rationalists observe that the patriarchal shadow on Islam survives today.[172] Atay and Yaşar Nuri regret that Muslims are not updating Islamic law rather than adapting the patriarchal interpretation of Islam to modern life.[173] Contemporary reflections of the patriarchal mentality are evident in the various anachronic behaviors, such as practicing a quarantine-like incarceration of women as if that were a religious virtue. Öztürk calls this "patriarchal victimization," where men emerge as the beneficiaries of modern life, while women are advised to stay at home. Neo-patriarchy views modernity as a threat to women, while it is regarded as opportunities for men. Thereby, a contemporary Islamic patriarchalism is reproduced as an unequal division of labor, where women are the objects of men, who are the subjects of modern life.[174]

As this brief note explains, for the rationalists, the major problem in the interpretation of religion in regard of the status of women is Islam's failure to unleash itself from the patriarchal mentality that survives in the Sunni tradition. Keeping this in mind, the rationalists seek a new religious interpretation free of the negative impact of the patriarchal mentality. We shall examine this in the following text.

Divorce Divorce is an all-time controversial topic, as several verses appear to give sole authority to husbands to decide upon a separation. The Muslim practice of divorce in various countries is criticized for not giving equal rights in this matter to women.[175]

Not interested in the different forms of divorce that Islamic law stipulates, the universalists propose equality between men and women in all the relevant affairs of divorce. They base their proposal on the universal Quranic principle of the equality of men and women. In keeping with this method, they treat the verses as if they were abstract axioms without reference to previous interpretations, including those of the first Muslims. Atay underlines that a holistic reading of the relevant verses would reveal that the revelation instructs equality between men and women in divorce.[176] To justify their conclusion, the universalists do not refrain from criticizing the previous Muslims, including the companions, for their misunderstanding that the revelation on divorce endow men with full rights of decision and execution in this matter.[177] Atay thinks the previous divorce practices in Islamic law chaotic and full of contradictions. It is no longer possible to rely on them to achieve the purpose of Quran on divorce. The solution for Atay is to embrace modern court procedures that presume the equal rights of women and men. Muslims should simply dispense with the previous legal opinions that are inconsistent with the modern model.[178] Eliaçık, too, defends the equal rights of both sexes as the correct interpretation of the relevant verses that mean to achieve Islam's general purpose in family matters.[179] Sharing those perspectives, Yaşar Nuri plies another typical universalist argument. He interprets the first part of verse 2:229, "Divorce can happen twice, with wives either kept on in an acceptable manner, or released in a good way," as a laying down of the equal rights of the sexes.[180] To reach this conclusion, he reads the word "twice" to mean "the equal rights for men and women."[181] On the historicist view, Yaşar Nuri's line of reasoning would come over like overinterpretation. Neither the grammatical structure of the verse, nor its previous historical interpretation, is supportive of his linguistically derived conclusion. Yet Yaşar Nuri interprets "twice" (*Ar. marratani*) as giving equal rights to both genders.

As anticipated, the universalists propose the abolishment of all extrajudicial forms of divorce, such as (i) *illa* (the husband takes an oath to not have sexual intercourse with his wife, and this results in divorce); (ii) *talaq*[182] (where a husband divorces his wife unilaterally, giving no reason, by repudiating the marriage); and (iii) *zihar* (I shall explain this in detail in the following text). And the universalist scholars propose the recognition of the modern legal regime as the only divorce framework. Reading the universalists, one quickly grasps that for them the ideal Islamic model is a legal regime where men and women have equal rights in divorce. All their references to Quran simply justify their conclusions, be those references etymological discussion of verbs or their reading of different verses together according to what they call "the holistic approach." However, as I said earlier, doing this is to treat the verses as abstract axioms with little reference to historical context. As I underlined in Chapter 1, this is a typical instance of the universalists using Quran to justify their reasonings on their pure rationalism trajectory.

The historicists have a different method of justifying their reasoning on divorce. For them, the literal reading of Quran gives more rights and privileges to men in divorce.[183] But, they see this as normal, given that the verses on divorce are historical, reflecting the social setting in which the revelation occurred. Admitting that the literal reading of Quran yields an unequal approach to divorce, the historicists have only one option: to develop solutions by giving reference to the authentic meaning of the relevant verses.

It is possible to analyze the historicist approach to divorce in various ways; however, I limit the discussion to *zihar*, for it alone is sufficient to demonstrate the gist of the historicist reasoning. *Zihar* is a pre-Islamic form of separation whereby the woman was deprived of sexual intimacy, yet she remained a wife. This happened when man likened his wife to the back of his mother.[184] Verse 58:3 rules *zihar*:

> Those of you who say such a thing to their wives, then go back on what they have said, must free a slave before the couple may touch one another again—this is what you are commanded to do, and God is fully aware of what you do--but anyone who does not have the means should fast continuously for two months before they touch each other, and anyone unable to do this should feed sixty needy people.

The practice is still part of Islamic law in various countries. The 168th article of the Qatar family law provides that "*zihar* occurs when a husband compares his wife and/or her body parts to that of another woman forbidden to him to marry."[185] The *Dissolution of Muslim Marriage Act* in India also recognizes extrajudicial divorces like *zihar* and *talaq*.[186] Though not recognized by state law, it is still part of Sunni law in Turkey, too, as *İlmihal* informs people of extrajudicial forms of divorce, including *zihar* and *talaq*.[187] As such cases display, Sunni law is adamant about continuing the extrajudicial forms of divorce. Thus, even in countries where the law does not recognize it, relevant rules on *zihar* are practiced by customary methods.

The historicists contend that the *zihar* verses are meaningful only in their historical contexts. Accordingly, the Arabs had many forms of divorce before Islam, and *zihar* was the worst of them.[188] Finding itself with the acute problems that stem from *zihar*, Islam was in a position to respond by introducing various rules to protect women. Özsoy explains the regulations on *zihar* in Quran as responses to severe problems that women faced in the Meccan society, where *zihar* was practiced excessively.[189] Thus, the historical context of the verse was the urgent need to respond to problems that had their origins in *zihar* by introducing heavy penances, such as the freeing a slave, or fasting for two consecutive months.[190] So, the authentic connotation of the *zihar* verses was not to do with introduction or justification. It had to do with the laying out of strict rules to protect women from its negative consequences. This being the case, Öztürk opines that Quran abolished *zihar* as a legal form of divorce. Thus, today, a man who wants to divorce his wife should appeal only to the legal forms of divorce procedure.[191]

To justify their thesis, historicists remind of the beginning of the Quran passage 58:1 on *zihar*: "God has heard the words of the woman who disputed with you about her husband." This refers to a woman who approach Muhammad to complain about her husband for his practicing of *zihar*.[192] On the historicist view, the first Muslims understood those verses—that is, in their authentic meaning—as new Islamic rules to end the previous practices where husbands had near-absolute rights, and practiced them at the expense of their wives. Reading those verses literally today, without reference to their historical context, however, misleads Muslims to think that Quran recognizes *zihar* as a universal divorce model.[193] For the historicists, therefore, the *zihar* case is a typical example that demonstrates how formalizing (i.e., writing) of a speech act is problematic and insufficient. The written form of the *zihar* verses in Quran have no capacity to transmit the nontextual elements of the revelation. This gives way to the serious problem of approaching those verses as if they were universal rules. If we visualize the historicist approach to *zihar* according to Searle's framework (discussed in Chapter 1), we get the illustration in Figure 5.

The problem of Sunnism, according to the historicists, is that it treats the *zihar* verses as if they had introduced universal rules. Thus, as noted earlier with reference to various states, in Qatar, Turkey, and India, *zihar* is today recognized by their Muslim societies as a universal Islamic regulation. For the historicists, such cases illustrate how a verse that was revealed to fight *zihar* became, ironically, a verse to justify it. The root of this problematic situation, according to the historicists, is the reading of these verses, revealed in response to various problems in the seventh century, as if they were abstract universal principles. As a consequence, the practice of *zihar* as a universal model in other cases, for example, in Turkey, where the social setting is completely different, is wrong for the historicists.[194]

The historicist approach to extrajudicial forms of divorce, like *talaq*, is same. Understanding them as historical practices, they justify their annulment, or propose their displacement by completely new forms, in terms of the needs of the various social contexts, and their times. So, for the historicists, if the society has the relevant setting, like a Western legal regime of divorce, then that might be the model for achieving the Islamic purpose. Öztürk reminds that the historicist principle is to consider the models in Quran as the best historical practices derived from Arab customs. They are not universal regulations, but responses to local problems.[195] Sharing that view, Güler adds that the reason for the authority given to men in the Islamic divorce mode was to do with the social and economic dynamics that prevailed in the early Muslim society. That is, the revelation searched for solutions within the realities of the contemporary society. Güler notes that egalitarian models would have had no effect in that society, where women had almost no economic independence.[196] On that reasoning, the historicists justify

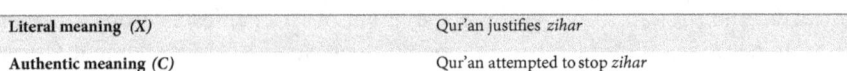

| Literal meaning (X) | Qur'an justifies *zihar* |
| Authentic meaning (C) | Qur'an attempted to stop *zihar* |

Figure 5 The literal and the historicist readings of the *zihar* verses.

new divorce rules that reflect the contemporary needs of women, so long as those rules pursue the authentic meanings of the verses.

The Law of Inheritance The traditional interpretation of shari'a on women's right of inheritance is resolved by verse 4:11, which stipulates that "a son should have the equivalent of two daughters' share." The THCRA restates that a daughter takes the half of the brother's share.[197] Sharing this perspective, *İlmihal* is satisfied to remind that men, who get the bigger share of inheritance, should not forget that their responsibilities are also bigger.[198] We read also articles by Turkish scholars who disseminate the same perspective on inheritance.[199] Those who defend the traditional view usually argue that equality is not simply a matter of mathematical distribution. Instead, the proposal in Quran is an advanced form of equality, given its social benefits.[200]

In contrast to the traditional view, the rationalists justify new ratios in inheritance law that go beyond the literal message of verse 4:11. Reading the verse in its historical context, the historicists deem that its purpose is to solve the various injustices that women face.[201] Their focus is on how the verse was understood by the first Muslims and how it changed their orientation as a community. The ratios designated by the verse are regarded as secondary elements that are historical rules devised in the seventh-century Arab society.[202] As Eliaçık writes, the model introduced in verse 4:11 is seen by the rationalists as a conjectural practice in a given historical setting.[203] Öztürk reminds that the Islamic regime of inheritance, though it introduced some new rules, was mostly a modified version of Arabic customary rules. Accordingly, Islam had attempted to resolve women's problems in a retro-vision mode that focused on the seventh-century Arabian setting.[204] Thus, a literal reading of inheritance verses in Quran today is pure anachronism, which inevitably results in the unequal regime for women. The historicist view here again emphasizes that the verses cannot be read as theoretical axioms (or like the provisions of modern civil law codes) independent of their social and historical setting. So, beyond the literal content of the verses, the purpose of Islam is to take the *direction* shown by the revelation. This introduced an invigorating change in the early Muslim society's perception of women's rights of inheritance. Such change, therefore, is legitimate in the contemporary Muslim society.[205] Logically, the historicist argument implies that to apply verse 4:11 today as it is written in Quran is to defeat the purpose of Islam.

The universalist approach is different: According to Yaşar Nuri, one general principle of Quran is the absolute equality of men and women. This presupposes the present-day interpretation that verse 4:11 gives equal inheritance shares to men and women because the contemporary socioeconomic scene is such that the unequivocal dependence of woman on man is rarely an observable condition.[206] Yaşar Nuri adds that the regulation that arose from verse 4:11 in the dynamics of the seventh-century Arab society could have arisen only in the economic and social conditions of a time when women were totally dependent on men. So revelation proposed the solution that took account of the social and economic realities of the time. That proposal would not be the ideal proposal for another society in which quite different socioeconomic conditions obtain.[207] Yaşar Nuri's point of departure is that the principle of the absolute equality of men and women is independent of how verse 4:11 was understood and practiced in the past. So, no matter that verses were linked to previous social settings, Quran extends the higher principle that enables Muslims to interpret this verse by leading with the premise that man and woman are absolutely equal. We observe another universalist method in Atay. He employs an etymological method to justify the introduction of alternate proposals into the law of inheritance: In his interpretation of Quran, he reads the word *yuşikumu* in verse 4:11 as "God advises."[208] To compare: Diyanet's translation, like other standard translations, puts it as "God commands."[209] So Atay redefines the model in Quran as conjectural advice rather than as divine order. Atay's approach denies any quarter to the historical interpretation of the verse by the previous Muslims.

Though the historicists and the universalists both justify the equal distribution of inheritance between men and women, we again observe a difference among them in method. By referring to the general principle of equality between men and women, the universalists have a tendency to recognize the equal distribution of inheritance as an ideal solution. Differently, for the historicists there is no ideal solution. Instead, there are proper solutions that can achieve the higher norms of Quran in any given contexts. Özsoy and Öztürk warn that the Western model of equal distribution of inheritance cannot be seen as the ultimate solution. Though their proposal is very much like the Western practice, they admit that alternative models could work under other conditions.[210] The historicists thus criticize the universalists for imagining an Islamic paradigm attuned to modern times.[211] They see the universalist method as being without an objective framework with which to interpret the verses, so they yield unconditionally to modern customs.

Women's Testimony On women's testimony, verse 2:282 rules on the need to "call in two men as witnesses. If two men are not there, then call one man and two women out of those you approve as witnesses, so that if one of the two women should forget, the other can remind her." This verse—called *ayat al-dayn* (the verse of debt)—is traditionally interpreted as equating the witness in testimony of two women with that of one man. This is so also in matters of evidence.[212] In various Muslim countries like Iran, penal or civil codes state that two male witnesses are needed to defend various types of evidences.[213] THCRA underlines that Hanafi jurists required one man and two women as a minimum precondition for testimony in marriage, whereas jurists from other Islamic legal schools required two men as the minimum precondition.[214] In *Woman from Jahiliya to Islam*, Öztürk analyzes the Islamic literature on women's testimony to provide a synoptic view of the Sunni approach. Studying various key scholars from different times, such as al-Baydawi (d. 1286), Ibn Kathir, and al-Alusi (d. 1854), Öztürk concludes that the standard view in Islamic law is that women cannot be the equals of men in testimony. And he sees the Shafi'i tradition as inherently critical of women's testimony. Though the Hanafi tradition recognizes the testimony of women in principle, it nevertheless excludes them when the subject of enquiry centers on technical topics, such as the penal rules.[215]

The rationalists, critical of the traditional Sunni view, propose an alternate narrative where men and women are equal in testimony. So I shall turn to the universalists. Atay and Yaşar Nuri propose that if the rationale of verse 2:282 in asking for two women is to provide against the "forgetting" problem (a human situation, not a gender one), then two men are also required. For the universalists, expertise, the second requirement of the verse, should be treated similarly. If a male is required to give testimony when the subject requires expertise, then again two male witnesses are required to compensate for lapses in each other's levels of expertise.[216] As we observe in this debate, the verse is read by the universalists as presumptions about forgetting and expertise not gender. So in no way does this verse confine itself to gender when it requires two women witnesses; it wades deeply into properties-of-gender assumptions. For that reason, no legal reasoning can be abstracted from this verse that addresses gender. At the core, the universalists' point of departure is again the general principle of equality among genders: The principle requires that presumed gender-based differences cannot be supposed to generate results in favor or disfavor of a gender.[217] Defending this perspective, Atay argues that the use of the gender noun in Quran is a natural result of the Arabic language *siga* (patterns) and is without a legal or religious purpose. He continues in this vein, pointing out that by nature, words in Arabic inform broadly about their function or meaning, as does their gender. He says that any word in Arabic occurs either in a male or female *siga*. This aspect of the revelations is misunderstood as if the gender-word always identifies a gender. He illustrates his point with reference to other rules in Quran with a male *siga*, like almsgiving, which is never limited to men. In so doing, Atay hints that the grammatical *siga* is usually considered when the verses are interpreted in disfavor of women. Since Arabic has a gender system, the use of one gender, for Atay is a grammatical necessity that should not be abused to legitimize the interpreting of Quran as disparaging women's suitability to serve as testifiers.[218] Approaching the debt verse also from a universalist perspective, Eliaçık suggests that it should be interpreted through the lens of another general principle: the common good. In his view, the common good today requires the equal status of genders in testimony.[219] Thus, he thinks the traditional practice in the Sunni interpretation no longer able to achieve the purpose of revelation.

On the historicist argument—shared by most of the universalists—the regulations of the debt verse stemmed from the economic and social realities when women had limited, if any, expertise or legal rights to act as economic subjects. The economy was dominated by men in the early period of Islam. Therefore, the revelation tried to achieve a moral economic order through the existing social and economic codes and balances.[220] Öztürk asserts that the equal status of the sexes in testimony was not realistic in the seventh-century Arab society, as women were not even economic subjects at the time.[221] Seen in this way, the reflection on gender in the verse is a historical necessity that has its origin in social conditions rather than directly gender-linked concerns. For the historicists, the revelation approached gender as the Arabs knew of it. However, today, alternate regulations on testimony, ones that are in line with the realities of the time, is religiously justifiable. Kırbaşoğlu holds that the *ratio legis* of the verse is not achieved today by the literal verse of Quran. So the only alternative is to adopt new practices.[222]

Beating Women Beating women, which is literally advised in verse 4:34, is another controversial topic. The case is coded as yet another cultural difference between Islam and modern values. Yet the literal reading of the verse is still endorsed by various influential Muslim scholars.[223] Importantly, there is scientific data, collected in various Muslim societies, that demonstrates a correlation between the social acceptance of violence against women and a religious thinking that considers wife battering a legitimate action.[224] As expected, proposing alternate interpretations of this verse is a key feature of reformist studies on Islam.[225] The rationalists are vehemently opposed to the literal reading of this verse.

For the universalists, there is no verse in Quran that advises violence toward women. Giving no credit to how the verse has been interpreted in the past, they read even the literal verse as free of any encouragement to beat. They argue their case on etymological and grammatical grounds. Analyzing the etymology of the word "*wa adribuhunna*" in verse 4:34, which is historically read as "beat them (i.e., the women)," they point out that God does not advise beating. Universalists claim that the word has meanings other than hitting. Atay, for example, reads the word to mean "do not have sex with women."[226] Applying the same method, Eliaçık finds seventeen different meanings of "*wa adribuhunna*," and concludes that the most suitable meaning is, "send your wife away from the house."[227] Yaşar Nuri shares Eliaçık's interpretation.[228] As stated earlier, the etymological method is the universalist approach that interprets a verse as an abstract principle, a zero-context one that references no historical context or action. Read this way, verse 4:34 does not ask for wife beating. Of course, this universalist exposition brings the usual rebuttal that the previous interpretations, including those of the first Muslims, leave the universalists' opinion untenable. How is it that the previous Muslims failed to see the universalists' interpretation? The answer is simple for the universalists. The previous Muslims either failed to understand the verse or their knowledge capacity could absorb only the traditional understandings that are redundant today. As I discussed in Chapter 1, the universalists are usually skeptical of the previous interpretations of the verses. Old religious reasonings are likely to be wrong or outdated. The best way is to reinterpret them in the present setting.[229]

Naturally, the historicists are critical of how the universalists interpret the verse on beating. They find it frameless and arbitrary. Özsoy counters that interpretation based on etymological argumentation, which we observe in Atay and Yaşar Nuri, is tantamount to inventing a new Quran. According to him, the universalists are not interpreting the verse; they would rather introduce completely a new rule.[230] Öztürk, too, rejects the etymological method, and reminds that the Islamic literature is full of examples to prove that the verse was understood as "beating women."[231] He emphasizes that the Islamic literature, even including the later works, is unanimous on the reading of *wa adribuhunna* as "beating" or "hitting."[232] Öztürk likens the universalists' etymological argumentation to an attempt to adapt Quran to modern norms, even to transform it into a contemporary text.[233] In his view, the universalists' dream about a Quran that has no verses with a "beating women" text.[234] In fact, this little mockery of Öztürk's reflects the paradigmatic difference between the historicists, whose rationalist trajectory is more empiricist, and the universalists, who are classical rationalists. As classical rationalists, the universalists simply make the verses endorse their opinions by grabbing any proper method that helps, no matter how the verse to hand was understood in its historical context.

For the historicists, there is a "beating of women" license in Quran. Its historical setting is the patriarchal Arab culture.[235] So no etymological or other grammatical method can help overcome this problem. It needs a historicist solution. And, as we read in Özsoy, that solution is to study the verse carefully to understand what it means to our generation. That understanding is possible only after its authentic meaning is properly understood.[236] Putting this into practice, Öztürk first reminds of the social conditions, that is, of the general state of early Arab society, in which verse 4:34 was revealed. As he depicts, that was a society where men were quick to beat their wives. There was nothing remarkable in that. Assessing that society realistically, the revelation introduced new rules to be observed before beating, expecting that it might avoid beating.[237] However, Prophet Muhammad never practiced or endorsed beating, despite that the verse literally commands it. This is critical support for the rationalist thesis. Öztürk concludes that whereas the verse had uptake on the general social level, Muhammad's practice was different, for his was well above the early Arabs' evolutionary condition. The Prophet's case displays that the revelation resounded with people in accordance with their social and intellectual capacities. Accordingly, how Muhammad understood verse 4:34 was unlike the way of the rest of his society. His social sensibility was far more advanced than the model anticipated by the revelation.[238] The yawning gap between Muhammad's and his society's understanding of the verse proves that what matters is not the verse literally but the purpose of the revelation. On this reading, the literal verse is the best practice that could be achieved in the early Muslim society. However, what should inspire Muslims who no longer live in that society is the purpose of verse 4:34. For the historicists, thus, the verse 4:34 cannot be proposed as a universal rule that justifies the beating of women.[239]

Hijab The *hijab* (the covering of the hair by women) issue is exponentially important in Turkey beyond its usual religious meaning. It was a major contention between Islamists and seculars, and shaped the trajectory of Turkish politics till the mid-2000s.[240] The intense political tension between the secular Kemalists and the traditional Muslims on the wearing/not wearing of the headscarf turned into the classic burning issue on which everyone had a vehement opinion. *Hijab* is, for the global Muslim community too, a subject that determines not only the status of women but also the general state of Muslims, taking in its tow into the public sphere the relations between the state and religion.[241] The *hijab* is among the few issues that associates uniquely with Islam.[242] The Sunni perspective unequivocally defines headscarf as an obligation. Women's bodies may not be seen in public except for their face, hands, and feet.[243] In a decree, THCRA declared that the covering of hair is for women a clear obligation imposed by Quran and the traditions.[244] Naturally, a woman's declining to observe the cover-obligation is seen by the large part of Sunni Muslims as a heretic argument. Again, the rationalists do not refrain from challenging Sunnism on this highly sensitive subject.

The rationalists are against the covering all of women's bodies by the *peçe* and *çarşaf*, which hide even their faces. Güler, for example, abhors such forms of cover for separating women from social life, as well as for humiliating their honor.[245] As expected, the controversy centers on the covering of the hair, the *hijab*. To start with the universalists, they appeal to their standard methods to argue that covering the hair is not a religious obligation for women in Islam. The universalist argument focuses mainly on the reinterpretation of verse 24:31, which was historically interpreted by the Islamic tradition as the obligation of women to practice *hijab*. Differently, the universalists claim that the meaning of the word, *khumur* (singular *khimar*)—which constitutes the backbone of the verse since women are asked to wear it—is not safely interpreted as an order to cover the hair. They reject the Sunni reading that understands *khumur* to be a hair-covering garment. Yaşar Nuri argues that the verse does not define *khumur* clearly.[246] Eliaçık asserts also that the verse can be read in different ways, for example as the covering of shoulders.[247] By proposing such arguments, the universalists remind of the principle that an Islamic obligation (*fard*) can be established only by a clear statement in Quran.[248] On this basis, how verse 24:31 informs on cover does not irrefutably establish a religious obligation for women to cover their hair. In this line of thinking, Atay and Yaşar Nuri conclude that covering hair is not a religious obligation, as there is no command in Quran that demands it.[249] To defend this thesis, Yaşar Nuri also quotes previous scholars like al-Jassas (d. 981) and Said ibn Jubayr (d. 714), who held the same views.[250]

The historicists' stance on *hijab* is a bit complicated. Given the highly sensitive nature of the subject, all the historicists except Güler conduct a cautious discourse on the *hijab*. For example, Öztürk, who deserves to be the seen as the champion of historicism on many other issues, takes a somewhat reluctant position on the *hijab*. He seems to have moved close to the traditional Sunni view of it in his recent public speeches. Also he does not want the subject to become another divisive debate among Muslims.[251] However, his books, including the most recent ones, have passages with highly provocative historicist arguments on the *hijab*.

Commenting on the early revealed verses like 33:59, where God asks Muhammad to tell women "to make their outer garments hang low over them so as to be recognized and not insulted," Öztürk entertains the argument that the rationale of such regulations was to protect free women in public.[252] Accordingly, the rationale of the verse is about the social status of women, and not primarily about gender or morality. To support this argument, Öztürk reminds that Caliph Umar prohibited slave women's covering up like free women. In a more controversial move, Öztürk narrates a tradition where Prophet Muhammad did not find disturbing his daughter being seen by a male slave when she was wearing a cloth that did not cover her body perfectly.[253] To emphasize the link between social status and cover, Öztürk also provides a summary of classical literature, and concludes that a large group of Muslim scholars, including several companions such as Ibn Abbas and Malik ibn Anas, were of the opinion that the cover regulations do not prohibit women being seen by male slaves.[254] Öztürk notes that later scholars such as al-Hawwari (d. 894) and Ibn Abi Zamanin (d. 1008) also explained the *hijab* as a marker of the social status of women, and they concluded that the covering of hair was meant to distinguish free women from the slaves. As another case to prove that veiling had no ab initio, nor a primary, religious rationale, Öztürk cites al-Jassas, who underlined that Muslim slave women were also exempt from this obligation. Meanwhile, for Öztürk, the debate on cover has landed on the side of those who are of the view that the revelation proposed the *hijab* solution only for free women, which amounts to an unequal treatment. Öztürk explains this in terms of the general state of Arab society in the seventh century. Nonfree women, even the Muslims, had virtually no protection in that society.[255] This fact, he adds, clarifies that the regulations of that period had a social rationale, not a religious one. The boundary recognized by the revelation was the one between free and nonfree women, not between Muslim and non-Muslim women. To confirm this, Öztürk notes that the early verses like 33:59 proposed solutions within the Arab social framework, and the unequal treatment of nonfree women is the unremarkable product of the moral timbre of that framework.[256]

When it comes to the verse 24:31, which is the most critical verse in shaping the current practice of women's covering their hair, Öztürk takes a cautious approach. In *Woman from Jahiliyyah to Islam*, he first notes that the word *khimar* is described in many classical exegeses as a garment that also covers the hair. However, he reminds that, even in the various early exegeses like the *Tafsir* of al-Hawwari and the *Tafsir* of Ibn Abi Zamanin, it was argued that the rationale of verse 24:31 was the differentiation of free women and slave women. It was not a regulation about hair. Reflecting this point of view, Öztürk summarizes various previous scholars such as al-Qurtubi, who argued that verse 24:31 does not prohibit a slave man's seeing his lady's hair. Öztürk even reports that the scholars Ibn al-Arabi (d. 1148), in *Ahkam al-Quran*, and Ibn 'Adil (d. 1475), in *Al-Lubab fi 'Ulum al-Kitab*, wrote that a woman can be totally naked before her male slave. He also informs that there have always been different interpretations of the word *khimar* by citing the contending views of various names such as Ibn Abbas, Ibn Mas'ud, and Hasan al-Basri.[257] However, Öztürk does not share his opinions on the covering of women's hair. He is instead satisfied to merely remind that there have been contending views on the *hijab* ever since the classical ages of Islam. But his emphasis is on the verse on hair covering and the social status of women, logically anticipating the historicist argument that new dynamics in a society might well invalidate the rationale that the verse 24:31 on hair covering for women marked their status as free women in the seventh-century Arab setting.

As stated earlier, the case of Güler is different: Reacting to those who interpret verse 24:31 as the ruling on covering hair, Güler thinks it to be the continuation of the Medieval perception of women and sexuality. Such thinking is no longer valid, given the radical differentness of today's society. Besides, there is no longer any connection between women's hair and their status. On his interpretation, women' hair in the contemporary world is a subject of beauty, not of sexuality or social status. Güler asks Muslims to realize that honor, sexuality, and other concepts change in time, and are different from society to society. Thus, the traditional interpretations of verse 24:31 are irrelevant today. And, since there is no difference between men's and women's hair today, no regulation on women's hair can be proposed with a rationale of honor, morality, or social status. Social changes have nulled the *ratio legis* of the verse.[258] So for Güler, covering hair is an anachronic religiosity.[259]

Polygamy Another complicated topic is polygamy. It is recognized by Quran, and it was practiced by Muhammad. Verse 4:3 reads thus: "if you fear that you will not deal fairly with orphan girls, you may marry whichever [other] women seem good to you: two, three, or four." Polygamy is legal in various countries, including Saudi Arabia, Jordan, Egypt, and Indonesia.[260] Though polygamy is outlawed in Turkey, *İlmihal* keeps it part of the Sunni view by pointing out that a man can have more than one wife under some conditions.[261] In the Turkish case, the recognition of polygamy by Sunni law reflects itself pragmatically in informal marriages with second or third wives.[262] Again, the mainstream scholarly articles keep disseminating the traditional Sunni view that justifies polygamy.[263]

In principle, the rationalists understand polygamy in Quran as the model that was exercised as a reflection of the special conditions of the early times of Islam. And they submit a number of arguments to prove why it is no longer timely. The universalists employ the same arguments on polygamy as do the historicists. As I discussed in Chapter 1, the universalists also see Quran as historical, but only in reference to the shari'a rules, and that authorizes them to employ historicist methods selectively. The foremost rationalist argument in this vein is that the verse on polygamy cannot be read literally today, since it was a regulation governing the women of the seventh-century Arab society, not contemporary women. A literal reading of the verses would only generate anachronic practices.[264] They emphasize that the *ratio legis* of the polygamy verse was to solve several acute problems in the Meccan society, not to introduce polygamy. Eliaçık explains these problems as the status of widows and orphan girls caused by endless wars.[265] Thus, for the rationalists, polygamy was justified by social and economic reasons, not by religious rationale.[266] In other words, as Yaşar Nuri puts it, the verse is not about polygamy, but about the various conjectural principles according to which polygamy can be legitimate.[267] Öztürk, too, writes that the emphasis of the verse is on moral concerns about not promoting polygamy.[268] And, to achieve those moral goals, the revelation attempted to solve problems by introducing rules and limitations on existing practices like polygamy, which are in fact borrowed from Arab culture and have no universal application.[269] Thus, the rationalists' examination discovers that verse 4:3 sets limits and rules on polygamy in a society where men have near-absolute authority to enjoy all sorts of dominance over women.[270] The limits and rules that this verse sets reframe polygamy by introducing new norms in favor of women. So the purpose of this verse is not to introduce the propriety of polygamy but to limit and formalize marital relations by introducing sharp limits in favor of women.[271] Eliaçık writes that the early Muslims understood the verse as an agenda to limit the traditional methods rather than to introduce an institution that was unknown to them.[272] For this reason, a verse that was introduced to limit polygamy cannot be interpreted today as if it had been revealed as a universal principle to justify polygamy. The rationalists reframe the polygamy verses in Quran as conjectural rules with a social rationale rather than as an authentic universal model proposed to Muslims.

However, it should be reminded that historicists like Öztürk—even though his interpretation of polygamy is similar to those of the other rationalists—remind that it is unsafe to conclude that the purpose of the revelation is to completely abolish polygamy. For Öztürk, that reading of Quran emerged in the nineteenth century among modernist Muslim scholars, whom he described as "traumatized" by the advancements in Western civilization. Thus, though he accepts that the purpose of the verse is to limit polygamy, arguing that polygamy is outlawed by Quran is an apologetic reasoning.[273] His is a typical historicist mentality that tends to refrain from voicing final verdicts on a subject. For historicists, the rule is the *ratio legis* of the verses; thus, how a verse is interpreted in a given setting is not to be recognized as the ultimate conclusion about it. This principle is succinctly summarized by Eliaçık: "Islam has no finalized and perfected law; it has only purposes and principles."[274]

Muslim Women Marrying Non-Muslim Men The conventional interpretation of Quran does not allow Muslim women to marry non-Muslim men.[275] In many countries like Afghanistan, Algeria, Bahrain, Bangladesh, Brunei, and Egypt a Muslim woman cannot marry a non-Muslim man.[276] The THCRA, too, ruled that interfaith marriage for Muslim women is not allowed.[277] Turkish scholars who follow the traditional Sunni view today disseminate the same traditional perspective.[278] The case is important, not only in regard of the gender-equality question but also in regard of the Islam-modernity debate, for the ban is in conflict with modern citizenship. The verse that comes closest to defining the Islamic norm on the subject is verse 2:221: "do not give your women in marriage to idolaters." There is also another verse, 60:10: "you who believe, test the believing women when they come to you as emigrants, and if you are sure of their belief, do not send them back to the disbelievers: they are not lawful wives for them, nor are the disbelievers their lawful husbands." Reading the verses as universal directives, Sunni scholars interpret them as prohibiting Muslim women's marriage to non-Muslims, including Christians and Jews.

Differently, for the rationalists, the *ratio legis* of the aforementioned verses was a political one. Accordingly, the ban in Quran was a conjectural decision arising from the political situation during the early years of Islam. By those verses, the revelation aimed at achieving various political goals, not religious ones. Atay writes that the ban was a strategic decision to protect Muslims' interests in the midst of prolonged wars with non-Muslims.[279] Muslims marrying non-Muslims in the midst of political and military tensions had the potential of creating demographic and strategic changes, as well as of breaking the fragile relations between tribes. For example, Güler notes that the early Muslim community had a severe demography problem. Quoting Ata Ibn Abi Rabah (d. 732), a famous transmitter of traditions whose work is particularly used in family matters,[280] Güler writes that the verses that prohibited interfaith marriage were revealed when Muslims faced serious demographic problems.[281] Reflecting on these political concerns, for rationalists, the rationale of the ban was the state of the early Muslim community, which was a comparatively small group fighting for survival, and in need of a strict demographic policy. Güler, too, asserts that the ban's purpose was political, not religious. In other words, the target of the ban was not Christians or Jews, but the tribes the Muslims were fighting.[282] Yaşar Nuri thus concludes that the ban cannot be imagined as a universal rule that affects negatively Muslims' peaceful relations with Christians and Jews forever.[283] However, he laments that the ban was later practiced as if it were a universal principle by Medieval Muslim scholars, who interpreted Quran under the influence of the Medieval patriarchal mentality. But, today, Muslim women can marry non-Muslim men so long as no political threat exists to put Muslims' security at risk.[284]

Another method to challenge the Sunni traditional view on interfaith marriage is to remind that the verses that rule out marriage to non-Muslims do not mention Christians and Jews. This view gives rise to the argument that the religious prohibition regarding Muslim women marrying Christians and Jews has no clear Quranic foundation. Therefore, the existing ban in the tradition is explained by reference to extra-Quranic sources, such as the consensus of scholars.[285] Arguing that the ban in verse 2:221 addresses "the idolatresses" (*mushrik*), Eliaçık concludes that it cannot be extended to Jews and Christians. Then, interfaith marriage is possible in Islam as long as the marriage does not constrain the Muslim woman's religious freedom.[286] Similarly, Öztürk points to the same discussion in the Islamic literature, where scholars argued that the ban in Quran targeted only the polytheists who lived around Arabia. Accordingly, the verse does not rule out Muslim women's marrying Christian and Jewish men.[287] Öztürk is also of the opinion that there is no clear rule, that is, *nass*, in Quran on the marriage of Muslim women to Christian and Jewish men. Referring to Ibn Ashur, he notes that the existing ban on Muslim women's marrying Christian and Jewish men relies on *ijma* (a consensus of Muslims and scholars) that was certainly shaped by the patriarchal mentality of Medieval times.[288]

Who Is a Good Muslim? A Moralistic Theory of Piety

Piety is another theme for the rationalists, for they understand it as the daily practice of shari'a. They see the proposing of an alternate piety as a necessity that goes beyond the proposing of new reasonings on selected issues in shari'a. Knowing that Sunnism prevails mostly because of the daily piety in Muslims' lives, they know also that their rationalist agenda will remain only an intellectual endeavor if it cannot permeate daily life sufficiently to effect changes there. Consequently, the rationalists' critique of Sunni-ritualistic piety is an endeavor to bring their ideas to the attention of the average Muslim. However, challenging traditional piety is not only very difficult but also risky, for any deviation from the standard piety is regarded by Muslims as proof of poor Islamic credentials.[289] As Fred M. Donner writes, piety has been seen throughout the Islamic history as external evidence of the claimants' inner moral quality.[290] Usually, the interpretation of Islam that innovators present to people is received as legitimate only if they, too, are recognized as pious. And piety is mostly accredited on visible criteria such as dress code, worship habits, and eating preferences.[291] On this count, the rationalists' critique of traditional piety makes them the natural targets of not only of traditional scholars but also of pious Muslims. Such risks notwithstanding, the rationalists are eager to renegotiate the perception of piety because the whole of the debate on Islam boils down to how religion is practiced in daily life. And that practice is the bedrock of piety.

İlmihal underlines that Quran does not inform on the formal details of worship. Worship is inherent in what Muhammad did.[292] Thus, in Sunnism, the interpretation of Muhammad's practices by scholars defines worship as very like the actions of the clergy in Christian liturgy.[293] But there is again a debate in the literature. Piety there is categorized in slots: juridical, Sufi, learned, devotional, socially oriented, ulema, popular, ascetic, and mass.[294] This is clear indication that "piety" has been a contested term throughout Islamic history. In this vein, the rationalists' view of piety is a reflection of their hierarchy of Islamic norms, which I discussed in the beginning of this chapter. As I noted there, for the rationalists moral principles are among the higher norms of Islam, while worship rules are among the lower norms. Reflecting that hierarchy, the core of the rationalist approach to piety is the ambition to insert the understanding that piety becomes manifest primarily through moral deeds, not in formal worship or rituals. Their main criticism of Sunni piety is that it is reduced to the religiosity of formal worship, and is made thereby to miss the complex meaning of the relationship between God and man.[295] As we read in Güler, for the rationalists ritualistic piety fails to ensure the moral property of man's approach to religion.[296] Atay, for example, asserts that the traditional ritualistic piety has a weak connection with moral concerns.[297]

Differently, the rationalists see piety in the upholding of morality, for that is the social role of religion. For them, the Sunni-ritualistic piety is reductionists, for it values rituals as the essential element of man's participation in religion, albeit only a secondary element of Islam.[298] But such ritualistic piety neglects the pursuit of Islam's social purposes, such as equality, justice, and freedom.[299] Atay likens the Sunni-ritualistic piety to a deadlock, for it has strangled "being religious" with the trappings of formal worship. He laments that in many countries nothing is taught to Muslims other than rituals such as fasting and prayer.[300] The problem for rationalists with the traditional approach is its promotion of the illusion that rituals are more significant than are the norms and good deeds of the morally and ethically enlightened Muslim.[301] The rationalists therefore redefine piety in terms of religion's role in society by challenging the Sunni perspective, where piety is primarily man's personal relations with God. They want Islamic piety to be responsive to the needs and expectations of society, rather than languish under a collection of rituals.³⁰² Moving in on this perspective, the rationalists propose that piety is not defined only in terms of worshipping. They develop their thesis particularly by engaging verse 51:56 differently. It says that God created men for *ya'buduni*. This word is commonly translated as "worshipping God" and usually translated into Turkish as *ibadet* (formal worship). But the rationalists interpret the word as "all the positive deeds of human beings" (*kulluk*). Reducing to mean "worship" is a wrong interpretation of the verse. The rationalists say that it is a Sunni reading.³⁰³ For the rationalists, as Atay notes, the word instead denotes all sorts of formal and informal good deeds.³⁰⁴ Özsoy and Eliaçık spot that the meaning of the term *ya'buduni* is not explicated adequately with the "worship" concept, since it entails other "good deeds" concepts.³⁰⁵ Echoing a typical universalist method, Yaşar Nuri displays that the Hebrew origin of *ya'buduni* is "to work," and rejects the traditional interpretation of it as "worship" only.³⁰⁶ Basically, the rationalists expand the scope of piety beyond the formal rituals.

Among the rationalists' many reasons for wanting to expand the scope of piety, one is that they deem the ritualistic expression of piety a mediocre understanding of religiosity, with only a limited capacity to edify Muslims. Basically, for them, ritualistic piety is a populist activity that cannot generate satisfactory intellectual and moral results in the interplay of men and religion. Eliaçık thinks that ritualistic piety has only a negligible capacity to contribute to society.³⁰⁷ Assessing ritualistic piety as a kind of imitation or repetition, Kırbaşoğlu does not see in it an effective contribution to Muslims' intellectual and moral advancement. Worse, its adherents nurture the illusion that there is a correlation between ritualistic piety and integrity.³⁰⁸ Bereft of intellectual and moral ambition, popular worship, a religiously meaningless activities, according to Güler, occupied center stage. Güler likens the five-times prayer to body exercises, and pilgrimage to traveling.³⁰⁹ He sees this sort of popular worship as a robotic pastime incapable of bringing moral or intellectual stimulus to Muslim communities. Proposing the actuality of a correlation between ritualistic piety and moral or intellectual advancement is therefore illogical for Yaşar Nuri.³¹⁰ Atay, too, thinks that ritualistic piety is without the capacity to contribute to Muslims' efforts to solve their complex problems.³¹¹ For Güler, ritualistic piety is intellectually a poor form of religiosity. He thinks it childish. For him, the popularity of ritualistic piety among average Muslims is due to their indifference to intellectual content: The imitative nature of rituals appeals to Muslims. Güler equates that style of piety and the having of no religion.³¹² Similarly, Atay explains that for the mediocre, whose religious knowledge is shallow, ritualistic piety, being both easy and simplistic, is preferred to the complexity of intellectual inquiry.³¹³ In Atay's view, the elevated position of this ritualistic piety is due to Islam's transition to becoming the religion of *avam* (laypeople) in which only rituals and pilgrimages dominate.³¹⁴ In this narrative, the rationalists see ritualistic piety as a historical construct that came into being as a result of the various social and economic changes in Muslim societies such as the decline of intellectual dynamism.³¹⁵ Such developments left a huge space for an imitative religiosity that demands neither reflection nor examination.

In this vein, despite the high sensitivity of the subject, we read in the works of the rationalists even a critique of the Sunni understanding prayer (*Ar.* Salah, *Tur.* Namaz). Prayer in the Sunni context is the formal worship that requires praying at five set times every day. The rationalists do not see prayer as the most important form or expression of worship.³¹⁶ For example, to symbolically challenge the Sunni concept of seeing prayer as the pillar of Islam, Eliaçık has one book with the title of *Social Islam: The Pillar of Religion Is Sharing*.³¹⁷ Indeed, this is a major deviation from Sunnism, in which prayer is *the* pillar of Islam. To remind, *İlmihal* informs that prayer is the major visible indicator of being Muslim. *İlmihal* quotes a tradition where Prophet Muhammad warns that the first question that people will face in the hereafter is about prayer.³¹⁸ The *Encyclopedia of Islam*—commissioned by Diyanet—defines prayer as the most important deed after faith.³¹⁹

Alternately, the rationalists urge the defining of piety in terms of Islamic norms such as justice and freedom.³²⁰ With that definition given high profile, piety becomes the performance of any deed done in keeping with the Islamic norms.³²¹ From here on, formal worship and rituals are no longer the sole, or even the prime, criteria of piety.³²² One's piety is not only about whether one performs prayers or wears a headscarf.³²³ Instead, piety is the dedicated attention to the social aspects of religion.³²⁴ Seen in this way, the rationalists incorporate contemporary norms into the field of piety deeds. Güler for example sees fighting against torture, or defending human rights, as piety deeds.³²⁵ Moralistic piety deeds properly dislodge rituals and formal worship from their present role as the measures of piety. Complaining that while Turkey has serious problems such as child marriage and violence toward women, Güler abhors the popularity of issues like the dress code.³²⁶ As we see through these examples, the rationalists expand the scope of piety, beyond rituals and formal worship, by suffusing acts of religious and worldly character.³²⁷ Eliaçık explains this form of expanded piety as comprehensive, for it is based directly on performing good deeds.³²⁸ Put simply, for the rationalists, moral behavior is piety.³²⁹ Seen in this way, the rationalists' definition of piety can be summarized as follows: A person who is moral is pious.³³⁰

A key point in the rationalist approach is to define piety in its social context.³³¹ The rationalists are critical of imagining piety as the ritualistic relationship between man and God. Instead, they emphasize that Islam's focus is this world, and that requires a comprehensive piety that incorporates the social norms, such as fighting for justice and against corruption. Güler condemns as narrow in perspective the piety that is focused on salvation in the afterlife.³³² The rationalists want piety to affect this life, rather than remain a ritualistic preparation for the hereafter. Reflecting this perspective, they are critical also of the habit of using ritualistic piety as the measure of personal quality. Finding ritualistic piety detached from moral concerns, Yaşar Nuri prefers that it stay in the private realm, and not be treated as a positive social etiquette³³³ This is indeed quite radical, given that rituals and formal worship are firmly set as the etiquette of being religious in Muslim societies. Güler, too, thinks that the etiquette status of ritualistic piety is not satisfactory, for it consists of nothing more than repeating of various rituals at fixed times. He sarcastically calls ritualistic piety a part-time piety. For Güler, a more comprehensive criteria-set is required, one that covers all of the requirements of living a good life.[334]

The intention of bringing piety to the social field has a logic: The rationalists are aware of the impulse of religion, but they believe that ritualistic piety wastes that impulse by generating a static relationship between Islam and Muslims. Ritualistic piety does not transform Islam into a positive social force that confronts and ameliorates the problems that persist in the Muslim society. Güler laments that ritualistic piety consumes the potential of religious Muslims to be differently motivated by Islam, such that they are more aware of social, intellectual, and artistic issues. Instead, the performance of rituals falsely persuades Muslims that they have fulfilled their religious duties.[335] Like Güler, Eliaçık writes that, satisfied by formalized ritual worship, Muslims are no longer mindful of the social aspect of Islam.[336] This is, for Güler, a moral decay imbibed through religion. Ritualistic piety inhibits Muslims' seeking out of a new reasoning, one that spurs them to activism in the defense of sound political and social norms in the quest for justice. Instead, they settle for the continuous expansion of the scope of rituals. Muslims are in an endless process of increasing or inventing forms of ritualistic worship. Güler calls this a "pragmatic *fiqh*" that secures piety through risk-free rituals, ignoring the political and social purposes of Islam.[337] The logic of this sort of Islamic law, Yaşar Nuri suggests, is a kind of contract between the state and the Sunni ulema. Accordingly, the ulema have promoted ritualistic piety in exchange for their gains from governments. In exchange, the state actors have benefited from ritualistic piety, since it helps them control Muslims.[338] Thus, historically, as Eliaçık notes, ritualistic piety has been a useful instrument for the state. It has blocked the path of religiosity toward the dynamic that fights social and political problems such as economic and social inequality, and authoritarianism.[339] In this vein, Eliaçık sees Diyanet as a typical reflection of this historical contract between the Sunni ulema and the state. Promoting ritualistic piety, Diyanet deals only with trivial issues such as the exact time to begin fasting, and whether chewing gum is proper while fasting, rather than with serious problems like the exploitation of the poor or the onset of authoritarianism.[340] For Yaşar Nuri, this model is in itself explanation of why Muslims are indifferent to severe problems such as authoritarian and corrupt governments.[341] Thus, for the rationalists, ritualistic piety has gradually transformed historic Islam into a religion of passive-piety with automat-like rituals that block Muslims' interest in political and social concerns such as justice and freedom.[342] Even for Güler, the rise of ritualistic piety is one of the explanations of the failure of Islamic civilization. It is the forger of the historical mentality that breeds "a piety minded and conformist Muslim typology."[343] This makes him call ritualistic piety a "dead religiosity" where Islam is practiced by automats without a moral dimension. He likens their demeanor to the shaman's dance.[344]

The rationalists demonstrate what they call "the paradox of ritualistic piety" in the Turkish case. Though Turkey has recently became visibly more religious, this did not stop the moral decay of society in regard of freedom, justice, and transparency. Kırbaşoğlu likens the Turkish traditional piety to a Medieval mentality where people hope that rituals solve their problems. However, rituals and worship have no direct ability to generate systematic effects in social morality.[345] Supporting this thesis, Yaşar Nuri adds that the rise in the number of mosques in Turkey has not brought any change in the crime statistics.[346] Similarly, Güler asserts that the mosques in Turkey no longer achieve impact in the ethical domain.[347] However, this is not a condition peculiar to Turkey. Eliaçık speaks of the same paradox in other Muslim societies, particularly Saudi Arabia and Iran. In none of these states does ritualistic piety make a positive change toward the improvement of awareness of the various norms, notably justice and freedom.[348] In fact, for Güler, the general state of Muslim societies clearly demonstrates how ritualistic piety, which has no engagement with moral or intellectual concerns, contributes to those societies' failure.[349] In this line of thinking, Eliaçık reminds that what is meant by the Islamization of societies is increase in how many people pray, or in the rate of women's adoption of the headscarf. To him, such criteria have nothing to do with making progress in more significant fields, such as justice and freedom.[350] The rationalists therefore propose that progress in awareness of the various norms (such as justice, freedom, and economic equality) should define what is meant by Islamization.[351] In this vein, Kırbaşoğlu links the unlikelihood of ritualistic piety contributing to society to individualistic mentality of its pious adherents. He believes that Muslims need a modern and systematic approach to the relationship between religion and society. He believes also that the traditional motto "good individuals make the moral society" is irrelevant in modern times. Instead, Islamic piety and morality should be updated systematically until it is geared to see the erection of the modern checks and balances that protect the Islamic norms. Kırbaşoğlu demands that piety focus systematically on society rather than on the individual.[352] The logical upshot of this proposal is to redefine piety in terms of the collective norms, including economic equality, justice, and freedom. Individual virtues, such as the zealous participation in ritualistic piety, are stand-alone, self-defined virtues.

Having theoretically challenged the traditional ritualistic piety, the rationalists defy another mainstream Sunni idea according to which Islam is supposed to have five pillars, a belief that shapes the average Muslim's understanding not only of piety but also of Islam in general.[353] In view of this, Islam is presented as having five pillars: Profession of God's Unity and Muhammad's Prophecy, Five-Times-a-Day at Pray, Fasting, Almsgiving, and Making Pilgrimage. These are considered to be the entire ritual structure of Islam because they are the obligatory practices.[354] Naturally, challenging the "Islam's five pillars" credo is another radical proposal, for it is to criticize what people know as Islam.

The rationalists' critique of the five pillars of Islam narrative has a dual rationale. Firstly, it is wrong in principle to call the five rituals "Islam's pillars." Formal worship by individuals cannot be a pillar of Islam. If there is anything to be recognized as the pillar of Islam, it is the Islamic norms and values (such as honesty and the supporting of the poor).[355] Secondly, "The five pillars of Islam" understanding breeds ritualistic piety. To look closer at the rationalists on this subject: Kırbaşoğlu sees the narrative of Islam's five pillars as composed only of rituals and as including no abstract principles such as justice or freedom. To him, the narrative reduces Islam to a set of wrong items. Thus, the Sunni mantra that "Islam has five pillars" is simply wrong.[356] As we observe also in Eliaçık, the rationalists are vehemently against defining rituals as pillars of Islam.[357] Güler, too, believes that the narrative is highly reductionist, since it reduces Islam into "one slogan and four rituals."[358] Similarly, Yaşar Nuri finds the narrative wrong, for its content constitutes only a small part of Islam, and excludes the more important norms, for instance, the norm "justice." Furthermore, the narrative has no reference in Quran.[359] To demonstrate how the five-pillars approach gives way to a problematic interpretation of Islam, Kırbaşoğlu gives *Büyük İslam İlmihali*, an all-time popular didactic religious work (i.e., catechist book) written by Ö. Nasuhi Bilmen, as an example of problematic interpretation: That writer allocates 250 pages to the five-times-daily prayer, but only 30 pages to moral issues.[360] He adds that most didactic religious works in Turkey are written on the same "Islam's five pillars" approach.[361] In his *Ahirzaman İlmihali* (The Catechist Book of Later Days), which he wrote as a reaction to the conventional didactic religious works, Kırbaşoğlu posits that equating Islam with what is called "the five pillars" is wrong.[362] For Kırbaşoğlu, the Mu'tazili formulation of the five pillars of Islam is the better didactic framework for its emphasis on the social norms like justice, and for its commending of what is good, and for its prohibiting of what is evil.[363] By giving reference to the Mu'tazila view, Kırbaşoğlu here explains the subject in the usual context of the rationalists-versus-traditionalists competition in the explication of Islamic thought. Supporting this thesis, Güler, too, explains that the consolidation of ritualistic piety as the standard framework of the nature of Islam is the legacy of traditionalists scholars such as al-Shafi'i and al-Ghazali.[364] Atay has similar views. He sees al-Ghazali's work as the turning point in Islamic history in the transition from active worship to passive worship.[365] Yaşar Nuri, too, explains the rise of the Sunni concept of the five pillars of Islam in terms of the Sunni ulema's relationship with the state.[366] There is no doubt that, for the rationalists, ritualistic piety is a result of the decline of rationalism in the Islamic history.

The Comprehensive Sunnah

Sunna is the legitimate practice of Islam, based on Muhammad's deeds and ideas.[367] Muslims naturally regard the sunnah of Muhammad as the best practice of shari'a. Thus, it shapes any discussion on shari'a for it is directly about actual religious practice.[368] This has its origin in the belief that sunnah is the practical exegesis of Quran.[369] In *Risala*, al-Shafi'i held that it is sunnah that makes evident what God meant in Quran, for it explicates his general and particular commands.[370] On this account, the Sunni concept of sunnah is basically the last word on how a Muslim is obliged to imitate Muhammad's deeds. For the rationalists, however, this concept not only keeps ritualistic piety alive but also impedes the possibility of an intellectual relationship between Islam and Muslims. Aware of the authority of sunnah among Muslims, thus, the rationalists' goal is to propose an alternate concept of sunnah that is in line with their rationalist framework.

The rationalists dismiss the Sunni concept of sunnah because it demands an atomist interpretation of the repeating of Muhammad's deeds. Kırbaşoğlu lampoons the atomist approach: "eat as Muhammad ate; sleep as he slept."[371] The rationale of atomism is the belief that how Muhammad acted in any given case, such as sitting, speaking, or walking, is the ideal way of fulfilling the purpose of Islam. This is formulated in al-Shafi'i as "whatever the prophet has decreed that is not based on any command from God, he has done it on God's command."[372] So, Muhammad was not only the agent who transmitted the divine message but also "the one who embodies divine wisdom in his acts, words, and deeds."[373] However, as Fazlur Rahman put it, this perspective requires sunnah to be not only a general directive but also absolutely literal and specific.[374] With imitation made obligatory, the atomist approach sees each deed of Muhammad as divine and universal, not a mere contextual example. As a matter of fact, Muslims are invited to eat, sleep, or walk as Muhammad did. For example, sunnah requires Muslims to sleep on their right side, and to begin the paring of nails on the right hand. This is why the beard is a symbol of religiosity.

According to the rationalists, the atomist view of sunnah, which imagines any deed of Muhammad as a divine instruction, creates anachronic conclusions. Kırbaşoğlu therefore criticizes the Sunni concept of sunnah for lacking a systematic methodology, and therefore generating only imitation without any moral purpose. He likens such an interpretation of sunnah to "powdering the face of the dead."[375] The consequence of this "powdering," for Kırbaşoğlu, is volumes of books full of endless details on dressing, ablution, and eating like the Prophet.[376] Interpreting sunnah in this way is, for Yaşar Nuri, to make a fetish of Muhammad, not a universal religious model.[377] Rejecting the view that the daily preferences of Muhammad in clothing and eating are universal norms, the rationalists also remind that this imitation-fetish is to treat Arab culture as religion.[378] They emphasize that Muhammad's dress habits and so on were cultural patterns known by the Arabs before Islam.[379] And Yaşar Nuri reminds that Muhammad's archenemy, Abu Jahl, had a similar dress code.[380] Güler, too, writes that the various clothes regarded today by Muslims as sunnah are originally Arab cultural elements.[381] Reminding that there was no textile or fashion industry in Mecca and Medina, Kırbaşoğlu notes that all clothing fabrics used by Arabs, including Muhammad, were brought from other regions, where non-Muslims had produced them.[382] Thus, the rationalists warn that promoting Muhammad's choices in daily life as sunnah is simply to promote a collection of Arabic elements, including Arabic cultural norms, which cannot be imagined as universal.[383] The Sunni "universals" gaff is not limited to clothing preferences; there is also the beard. Azimli points out that the beard was an all-time popular choice among Arabs. It was only later coded a religious norm.[384] Similarly, Güler notes that the beard was purely an Arab cultural phenomenon, and it had no religious connotation.[385] For the rationalists, the self-presentation styles of the early Muslims are certainly not universal norms to be imposed on Muslims in all climates and cultural settings, nor are they religious models.[386] This is indeed a prominent departure from Sunnism by the rationalist.[387]

Alternatively, the rationalists propose that sunnah should be understood as principle rather than a practice.[388] That is, its purpose should not be to imitate Muhammad but to understand why he acted as he did. Sunnah is now a paradigm, or a worldview, rather than the imitation of various registered acts.[389] On this point, Yaşar Nuri criticizes the Sunni method of imitation as a "photographic view" of Muhammad's life, where his deeds are recognized as universal rituals. This fails to understand the moral purpose of his deeds.[390] The rationalists thus ask for an understanding of the sunnah in terms of the moral purposes of Muhammad's deeds.[391] As a typical rationalist trait, we again observe here the demand for a religion differentiated from Arab culture.[392] A better approach is to leave beyond the literal reading of Muhammad's deeds, and to put forward the principles, or ethico-religious values, of his deeds.[393] For Kırbaşoğlu, this proposal is, however, impossible to implement in the traditional Islamic methodology. He thus suggests the incorporating of new methods from that relies on the social sciences.[394]

The rationalists again link the Sunni view of sunnah to the legacy of al-Shafi'i, whom they report to have claimed that Muhammad's deeds have a divine nature.[395] For example, Güler notes that whereas Muhamad's aim was to teach fishing, al-Shafi'i prohibited fishing, arguing that the fishes already collected in the nets are enough for Muslims.[396] As the foregoing metaphor displays, the rationalists are epistemologically for catching more fish, and throwing from the nets as unpalatable the "Muhammad's deeds as divine and universal to be repeated in every context" variety of inedible fish.

One major, if not shocking, consequence of the rationalist view of sunnah, which Sunnism would never yield to, is to accept that imitating Muhammad's deeds might be useless, or even wrong in other contexts. To elaborate this case with an example: The rationalists are against the practice of various medical methods under the banner of *al-tıbb al-nabawi*, the prophetic medicine, as sunnah. *Al-tıbb al-nabawi* is a system of medical therapeutics that flourished from the thirteenth century onward, and was mostly a continuation of ancient Greek medicine.[397] Muslims believe that it has its origins in Muhammad's sayings and practices.[398] Names such as al-Jawziyya (d. 1350) and al-Dhahabi (d. 1348) played key roles in turning *al-tıbb al-nabawi* into a systematic work. As Irmeli Perho puts it correctly, this is a creation of Muslim traditionists/traditionalist scholars.[399] However, as we read in Kırbaşoğlu, the rationalists see the knowledge of medicine narrated in traditions as the standard Arab practices known and practiced in Muhammad's time.[400] So they are not divine instructions. Azimli even warns that what Muhammad advised on health issues might have included some mistakes that modern medicine has never accepted.[401] Öztürk thus notes that reports from Muhammad on medicine should be seen as cultural practices.[402] However, this issue is not limited to medicine: Kırbaşoğlu explains various methods of calculating *zakat* (obligatory almsgiving) by using wheat or other local products as culturally formed practices.[403] For the rationalists, logically, such culturally formed practices are no longer relevant in modern times.

The rationalist approach is, however, unacceptable for Sunnism, which relies on the argument that "in every walk of life, the Prophet gave practical lessons in excellence."[404] In a Friday sermon delivered in Turkish mosques, Muslims were warned that all Muhammad's deeds were supervised by God. They were all perfect, since Muhammad was warned by God whenever he made the smallest mistake. As Quran and the Sunnah are complementary, it is underlined that Muhammad did not speak as he wishes.[405] Thus, the agents of Sunni Islam continue advising Muslims to act as Muhammad acted in daily life, from eating to walking.

A Religious Theory of Political Opposition

Politics and government are regarded by Muslims as the "other fields" where Islamic law guides people. The strong references to governance and state in Islamic law suggest that politics is a department of Islam.[406] Key books that shaped the main Sunni schools such as al-Ash'ari's *al-Ibanah* include sections on government and political events, like the election of Abu Bakr as Caliph.[407] As a result, a narrative emerged in the Islamic tradition according to which religion and politics are taken together.[408] Reflecting this historical tradition, Islam is either *the* or *a* source of law in various Muslim states, and this sees Islamic law incorporated into the legal system.[409] Additionally, the mindset that reads Islam also as a blueprint for politics has increased, thanks to Islamism. Major Islamist ideologues, from Qutb to Khomeini, define Islam a state ideology that requires certain types of government, along with specific laws.[410] But, as various PEW surveys demonstrate, there is also the general demand among Muslims for Islamic law to be the official law of the land.[411] Consequently, we still do not encounter a clear separation of Islam and politics, neither in Islamic literature nor among the global Muslim public. Obviously, the extant interest in juxtaposing Islam and politics is a continuous dynamic among Muslims that aims to Islamize politics.

On the complicated subject of Islam and politics, the rationalists' top claim is that Islam does not propose any political form or regime. Instead, the universal norms of good governance are justice, meritocracy, and consultation.[412] The ultimate political purpose of Islam is merely to erect a practical morality in state and society.[413] For the rationalists, even these norms are not aptly called Islamic. Rather, any decent political regime that respects the universal norms is Islamic.[414] In other words, the rationalists are not interested in the famous "Islamic government" discourse. There is a strict division between *institutions* and *norms* in the rationalist narrative. Thus, to them, the Islamness of a political system is about the quality of its norms, not about the formal appearance of its institutions.[415] Güler declares that there is no institutional or formal procedure that registers a political system as Islamic; working for a moral society does that.[416]

The rationalist approach to politics, working as it does on the promotion of the norms, is indeed different from the traditional approach, which defines the Islamness of a state in terms of various institutional and legal requirements. As we read in Muhammad Asad, the traditional approach requires a particular form of Islamic state with certain institutional and legal frameworks.[417] We see this also in Islamists like Qutb and Maududi. Thus, the upholding of the various norms such as justice is not deemed enough from an Islamic government. The rationalists reject this traditional approach. They do not respect the requirement for specific institutional and legal requirements; they welcome any political system as compatible with Islam, so long as it respects the universal norms of good governance.[418] The rationalists see no Islamic virtue in special procedural, constitutional, or institutional political constructs. Such constructs do not register a political model "Islamic."[419] So the rationalists would find pointless political constructs like those of Iran, which are styled as Islamic, unless those constructs achieve democracy, and are based on the rule of law. For sure, the rationalists are not impressed by the state that enforces Islamic rules and rites.[420] Basically, the rationalist approach to the state is fueled by standard political theory, not by religious fervor. They are more interested in the ideal-type state that reminds of Max Weber, according to whom the state is first a historical construct. An Islamic essence is not a feature of that historical construct.[421] Thus, for rationalists, the need for a state manifests in the quest for a normative order. Special condition of a political or religious kind are not a part of that quest.[422] Equally, the Islamic interest in the existence of the state is also manifest in the same quest for normative order. But the practice of ritualistic or procedural formats is, for the rationalists, not part of that order. Given this tenet, the rationalists are seen to have shifted radically from the classical Islamic legal theories usually attributed to names like al-Mawardi (d. 1058).[423]

To justify their approach, the rationalists explain that Islam does not propose any political model. Kırbaşoğlu points out that Quran has no information on government forms.[424] Atay, too, criticizes those who approach Quran as if it were a constitution.[425] The traditions, too, are analyzed in the same vein. Azimli dismisses the various famous traditions that are usually quoted to justify certain forms of government for being politically motivated to pursue Islamic ends.[426] In the same way, the historical discourse that presents Muhammad as a head of state is off course for the rationalists. Kırbaşoğlu maintains that what seems to be the political aspects of Muhammad's life are in fact historical cases that cannot be submitted as religious edicts.[427] Thus, he defies those who narrate Muhammad's life in Medina as a period where he preached a specific form of government.[428]

Interpreting the Medina period as the first model of the Islamic government is a popular argumentation among those who accept that Islam and the state are inseparable. In fact, what has been observed in this vein is a reflection of the grand debate on the political meaning of Muhammad's life. On the first view, Muhammad is presented as a kind of statesman. W. Montgomery Watt's *Muhammad Prophet and Statesman* is a typical example of the determination to make a political leader of Muhammad. That view is derived from the complexity of his duties concerning taxation, the organizing of military activities, and his correspondence with people whom he appointed to various executive roles.[429] Muhammad Hamidullah, whose studies also inspired Muslims, approached Muhammad as a stateman who established a state.[430] On the other hand, as we observe, for example, in Mohammed Abed al-Jabri, it is held that Muhammad's mission was to promulgate a new religion, not to set up a state. And there is nothing in Quran to clearly indicate that the Islamic mission was to establish a state, or a kingship, or an empire.[431] The rationalists stand with al-Jabri in this grand debate.

More interestingly, having rejected the idea that Islam proposes a specific form of government, the rationalists want to develop a moralistic theory of politics. Not being anarchists, they regard the state as necessary for maintaining public order. Their radical quest is quite other than anarchistic. They want Islam to be the inspiration of a theory of political opposition. In fact, this is the structural consequence of their approach to Islam and the state. Rejecting an Islamic form of government, but regarding the state a necessity, they urge that Islam become the moral contract between Muslims and the state. This is how the rationalists conceive of an Islamic opposition to any political authority that violates the norms of justice, and so on. It performs a religious moral duty. Indeed, such a position puts the rationalists into a completely different position compared to that of the historically state-friendly Sunni paradigm. Sunnism has survived as an orthodoxy thanks to the staunch power-sharing of the clergy and the state. This artificial collaboration interprets, institutionalizes, and propagates religion.[432] Consequently, Sunnism has historically failed to generate a strong and systematic religious theory of opposition. In contrast, the rationalists, who ironically come from a Sunni sociological background, ask Muslims to challenge corrupt political systems and leaders, arguing that the core of the relationship between Islam and politics is the search for public morality.[433] Actually, the rationalist approach to politics in this regard is a reflection of their moralistic piety. They again remind that religiosity is not limited to rituals and formalized worships. Inherently, it is the promoter of virtuous norms like justice in the political realm.[434] On this count, Islam is essentially a political religion in the normative terms for the rationalists.[435]

In this line of thinking, opposition to corrupt governments is an Islamic duty.[436] To remind: The obligation of loyalty to the ruler, even if he is not a just ruler, was a big topic in all Medieval Islamic discussions. A large number of influential Sunni scholars interpreted Quran and the traditions as requiring loyalty even to a corrupt ruler, for the sake of political stability.[437] The rationalists, however, harshly condemn Sunnism for legitimizing loyalty to corrupt leaders. They see the Sunni principle of political loyalty as the historical reason that transformed Islam into a religion of rituals, never again to rise to its duty to flourish as a religion of moral virtues.[438] For Kırbaşoğlu, the reluctance of Sunnism to generate a moral activism in politics is due mainly to the impact of the Medieval political understandings that formed the Sunni paradigm that demands unconditional loyalty to political rulers as a virtue, even if they are corrupt.[439] The rationalists instead incorporate a moral opposition into the realm of genuine piety. Defining Quran as a book of protest against unjust rulers, Yaşar Nuri underlines that the violations of norms like justice by rulers is also a major sin in Islam.[440] Similarly, Güler reminds that religion is practiced also when the Muslim declines to commit social and political sins such as violating human rights.[441] Eliaçık lists corruption, social inequality, and fraud committed against public assets as major sins in Islam.[442] He thus likens Sunnism to a "temple religion," according to which religiosity is defined through rituals, not through moral norms.[443] Kırbaşoğlu underlines that political opposition is the most ignored aspect of religion. For him, opposition to immorality is the *à priori* ontological justification of the existence of any religion. Indeed, Islam is itself to be understood as inherently an oppositional force that sets itself against immorality.[444] As these positions argue, Islam requires its adherents' engagement with politics as fighters of corruption and authoritarianism, all be the latter two wrongs the practices of political leaders.[445] The rationalists therefore urge repeatedly that opposing corrupt or authoritarian rulers is an Islamic duty.[446] They want to displace "loyalty" in Islamic political theory with "disobedience." This is an ambitious agenda, but a preeminently moral one. As Kırbaşoğlu intones: "Disobedience will rescue the world!"[447] Indeed, this perspective is the opposite of the Sunni political theory, where norms like obedience and stability are more important.

In this context, we also encounter a revisionist history of Islamic origins where Islam is narrated as the conveyor of protest to those who exploit the Meccan society by political and economic means.[448] Eliaçık reminds that Muhammad's adversaries were not members of a clergy, but those who exploited the Meccan society.[449] Similarly, Güler shows the Meccan bourgeoisie as the preeminent targets of the revelation.[450] Yaşar Nuri agrees that Muhammad's enemies were the members of the Meccan oligarchy.[451] Kırbaşoğlu makes the same point, and presents Muhammad as a leader of protest movements against the Meccan oligarchy.[452] Read in this context, as we see in Güler, Muhammad is presented as "the great master of the critical tradition" in human history.[453] And Kırbaşoğlu deems Muhammad the "last opponent."[454] This an attempt to reframe Islamic history, exactly as Fazlur Rahman had done, as a historical reaction to polytheism, and to gross socioeconomic disparities.[455] Accordingly, it is stated that Islam at its outset was primarily interested in social virtues, not ritualistic details.[456] Thus, the rationalists repeat Rahman's approach, according to which the goal of Islam is to establish an ethical, egalitarian social order, which is possible only by the severe denunciation of economic disequilibrium and social inequalities.[457]

Another argument in the works of the rationalists is to present Abu Hanifa as a symbol of political opposition in Islamic history. Yaşar Nuri penned a book on Abu Hanifa, *The Greatest Imam*, in which he presents him as a man of opposition who stands against corrupt rule.[458] For Yaşar Nuri, resisting an oppressive ruler is a major act of worship in Abu Hanifa's thought.[459] In this vein, Atay narrates in close detail Abu Hanifa's opposition to Caliph Abu Ja'far al-Mansur.[460] Abu Hanifa's opposition to the Caliph is for Güler a brilliant example that proves how questioning the legitimacy of an incumbent corrupt ruler is an Islamic deed.[461] We observe the same narrative on Abu Hanifa in Kırbaşoğlu, who presents him as a towering Islamic figure of opposition in a corrupt political regime whose legacy has nevertheless not become a tradition.[462]

The rationalist attempt to interpret Islam as a theory of political opposition has probably the most radical consequence on another major subject. Unlike Sunnism, which has the Muslim versus non-Muslim (or believer and nonbeliever) as its main antagonism, the rationalists propose that Islam has an oppressed versus oppressor, or a just versus the unjust, as the main polar oppositions[463] (Figure 6).

What is the Prime Antagonism?	
Sunnism	Muslim *versus* non-Muslim, faithful *versus* faithless
The Rationalists	Just *versus* unjust, oppressor *versus* oppressed

Figure 6 Comparing the "prime antagonism" for Sunnis and the rationalists.

Thus, the rationalist narrative puts fighting *zulm* (oppression), the general term for all sorts of unjust rule, as the sublime Islamic norm.[464] *Zulm* may, in contemporary context, include forms like "violation of human rights."[465]

Defending this perspective, Güler argues that the category "believers" in the early revealed verses does not refer exclusively to Muslims, or to being Muslim, but to all people who were critical of the Meccan exploiters.[466] This is a radical expanding of term, so far as to destroy the traditional conceptualization of Islam as merely a state/condition with a religious mindset. It effectively problematizes the fact that the sets of faith and political morality might not always overlap perfectly, and prefers the second set as the paramount one. Demonstrating this choice, Yaşar Nuri states that the sole antagonist in Quran is not the faithless but the oppressor. Güler concludes similarly that reducing Islam to the matter of faith, rituals, and worship is simply wrong.[467] On Eliaçık' view, norms like justice are more important than Islamic law and rituals, since norms operate as Islam's nerve center.[468] Logically, this is to demand that sociopolitical norms, not any other factor, be the primary determinants of the state of being Islamic. To emphasize this, Yaşar Nuri asks whether it is correct to remember Muhammad as primarily a symbol of the fight for freedom and justice, or as a symbol of praying for long hours, and wearing a turban. In the same line of thinking, he asserts that countries known as Islamic, like Iraq under Saddam Hussain or Turkey under R. Tayyip Erdoğan, are not Islamic. His criterion is neat: A just non-Muslim is better than a Muslim oppressor.[469]

Basically, the rationalists want Islam to be a morality-first religion, unlike the Sunnis, who live by a law-first religion. If we define the classical Sunni ulema as legalist, then the rationalists are moralist. In fact, they frequently criticize Sunnism for being a law-centered paradigm that ignores the moral dimension of religion.[470] As a matter of fact, for the rationalists, countries like Turkey, where problems like corruption devastate social and political life, prove that this paradigm is a failed one.[471]

Conclusion

This chapter has tried to reveal the rationalists' ambitious agenda on Islamic law. They demand new reasoning in the key fields of Islamic law. This ambitious agenda has its origin in the rationalist belief that an Islamic revival is not possible without a radical split from the traditional Sunni law-centeredness. A final point to be highlighted in my final note in this chapter is that the rationalists—as we observed in this chapter—do not refer to traditions at all to justify their opinions. Instead, they rely on reasoning, and do not appeal to the traditional methods of justification in the manner of the existing Islamic texts. They do not hesitate to benefit from previous Muslim scholars, but this never tempts them to give up their conviction that they are now the virile agents in the reformation of Islamic reasoning.

Chapter 3

HISTORY

DE-ISLAMIZING ISLAMIC HISTORY

Though law and theology, as two pillars of Sunnism, are enough to explain and regulate human affairs from marriage to politics, neither can provide intellectual instruments to frame the past in line with Sunni premises. Any paradigm requires a meaningful narrative of time and history. And this need is fulfilled in Sunni history by selected materials, and a history narrative from a Sunni perspective.[1] Seen in this way, history is the third pillar of Sunnism, with law being the first and theology the second. The critical role of history for Sunnism, as H. A. R. Gibb writes, is maintaining its universalism against internal and external challenges. History is required for the realizing of religious, cultural, and social unity in the Islamic world.[2] Hence, Islamic civilization has produced a profuse body of writing on history.[3] Since the early ages, the biographical works on Muhammad emerged as key Islamic discipline.[4] History quickly became a semi-canonic discipline, its content always affecting the legal and theological literature in Islam. Registered as another religious discipline, alternate views on historical events might be refused as heresy, a case that Azimli depicts as a history as faith.[5] Öztürk reminds that the very early formulations of basic theological concepts—such as free will, destiny, and grave sins—came out in connection with the various political crises in the early Muslim community, such as the Camel War (656), and the Civil War (657), creating a complicated relationship between the faith and the history of Islam.[6] As an example of how this complicated relationship reflects itself in historical writings, Güler gives a list of scholars: Ibn Taymiyya (d. 1328), al-Ash'ari, al-Shafi'i, and al-Tahawi (d. 933), who explain the war between Ali and Muawiya in purely theological terms.[7]

In parallel with the central role of history in the Islamic tradition, historiography—including the early *hadith* scholarship—evolved in a complex web of political and social relations since Abd al-Malik ibn Marwan's reign (685–705) when the Umayyads used the traditions to consolidate the religious basis of their rule. A "proto-historical consciousness" was always relevant in the collection and systematizing of the traditions.[8] The Abbasids later developed a similar relationship this time with historical writings, the new trend. Came to power in 750 after a revolution, the Abbasids faced severe doubts about their credibility among the various sections of society.⁹ As a revolution usually ends with the violent elimination of political opponents and their regimes, the same happened between the Abbasids and their rivals.¹⁰ The transition from the Umayyads to the Abbasids opened the doors to the complex changes in the configuration of the political elites, as well as to the social bases of political authority.¹¹ Naturally, the ideological split unleashed by the revolution forced the Abbasids to look for new configurations of legitimacy.¹² One method that appealed to them was historical writing: Caliph al-Mansur (d. 775) commissioned works such as Ibn Ishaq's universal history. Historical writing was helpful in providing the Abbasids with Islamic credentials by way of a body of supportive narrative.¹³ The Abbasids' expectation from historiography was its contribution to their social legitimacy, including the support of the *ulama*, which was key to maintaining their rule within the larger sociopolitical area.¹⁴ To attain their expectation, they patronized historical writing to establish their cultural credentials, and even to legitimize the violence that brought them to power.¹⁵ Azimli reminds that the Umayyads were in general treated by the Abbasid-period historians as the *ancien regime*.¹⁶ Logically, there are many opportunities in historical writing—in comparison with *hadith* writing—to devise commentary on past events that bears upon political concerns.¹⁷ Chase Robinson explains this as "history had taken a decisive turn," after the Abbasid revolution, "the Abbasids' claim to rule was naturally expressed in terms that made men instruments of God's plan." The mission of historiography was there to fit events "into an epochal scheme laid out in the Quran."¹⁸ Naturally, the impact of the Abbasid patronage on historical writing is noted by many scholars. Reading al-Tabari's account of the civil wars (the Battles of Camel and Siffin) in the formative years of Islam, Abdelkader I. Tayob concludes that what we encounter is a narrative according to Abbasid views.¹⁹ Or, according to Rizwi Faizer and Andrew Rippin, al-Waqidi's description of al-'Abbas (the eponym of the Abbasids) as the caring uncle of Prophet Muhammad—even though he did not convert in the first years of Islam—is a typical case illustrating the impact of politics on historical writing.²⁰

As the aforementioned introduction illustrates, the complex relationship of historical scholarship and the politico-social setting in which the historian happens to be naturally resulted in different historical narratives, such as those of the Abbasid and the Umayyad, even when they use almost the same documentary evidence.²¹ Balcı writes that in both the Umayyads' and the Abbasids' works it was the "imagination of the narrator"—which is always under certain political and social impacts—that constructed the portrait of the past. This is inevitable in any historiography.²² The case of the rationalists in this context is no different. The thrust of their interest in history is to confront Sunni history, for their paradigm is possible only by means of an alternate historical narrative. The rationalists see Sunni history as a self-expression of Sunni law and theology.²³ Their opinions on many subjects, such as their treatment of shari'a as a conjectural framework rather than a universal one, are viable only with a new historical narrative. Yaşar Nuri characterizes this reasoning strategy about Islam as a requirement of its liberation from the "sacred tutelage," that is, the dominance of previous people's opinions, such as those of scholars and of the companions. This is possible only with a new historical narrative.[24]

In this regard, the rationalists are revisionists of Islamic history, for their aim is to dismantle Sunni historiography (the dominant narrative of Islamic history) of its truth value.[25] To elaborate on their revisionism at practical level, we observe in the rationalists two types of revisionism. We can distinguish them as a "significance-driven revisionism" (which results from changes in what historians consider significant in history) and "value-driven revisionism" (which is to reevaluate the historical events historians describe and explain). We do not observe in the rationalists an "evidence-driven revisionism," which overturns the old with new evidence (one that discovers new manuscripts or archeological findings).[26] But then, we should remember that they are not historians. So in effect, the rationalists reevaluate Islamic history according to what they consider significant, for they believe that the dominant Sunni narrative is a misleading historiography. Rationalist revisionism positions itself against the teleological assumptions and political biases of Sunni history, which are as follows:

1. Incorporating supernatural dynamics into the historical narrative;
2. Appealing to exceptionalism as a method in Islamic historiography, while ignoring the impact of social and economic dynamics,
3. Crediting of the politically motivated accounts of various events;
4. Entertaining propagandist and pedagogical accounts of Islamic history, and ignoring or underrating various events and factors—all done in the name of not damaging the Muslim faith.

The result of rationalist revisionism naturally submits a completely different picture of Islamic history than that displayed by the Sunni narrative. But, beyond how the rationalist historical narrative differs from Sunni history, there is the more important ultimate purpose of rationalist revisionism. That is to put an end to the treatment of the Islamic past as if it were adequately captured in religious history. The rationalists' prime goal is to reject the study of religion in its specific sphere and to study the Islamic past on a secular (or humanist) perspective, like other events in history.[27]

The Rationalists on Causation in History

The fundamental of rationalist history is to explain the Islamic past in the nexus of historical and natural causes.[28] The rationalists do not see Sunni history as completely yielding to causality in the explanation of historical events.[29] This creates typical problems in Sunni history, such as with the recognition of the supernatural in history, and with the reduction of complicated social events to the single dynamic of the religious factor by underrating economic and social factors.

For the rationalists, the shortfalls of Sunni history on causality originate in its reliance on Ash'ari occasionalism. To revisit Ash'ari occasionalism: God's omnipotence is the main principle in explaining nature.[30] Accordingly, causality is repudiated, as there is nothing that God does not will:[31] No being or event in the world causes another, as God creates each event.[32] Thus, what is known as causality among people is merely the sequence of events created by God. In *Kitab al-Lum'a*, al-Ash'ari defines all things that proceed from others as acts of God.[33] No causal chain exists among things and events. This was later explained by al-Ghazali, an influential interpreter of Ash'arism, as God creating events independently of natural causes. Therefore, proposing that natural law has the capacity to cause events is to deny God's omnipotence. That denial is in the implication that something is action in its own right.[34] Ash'ari theology regards God not only as the creator, but also as the agent of all events in nature and history. This automatically repudiates human agency. God's creation, which includes all things, even intentions, leaves no space for a human autonomy with a capacity to act, nor yet to will. In *Al-Ibanah*, al-Ash'ari wrote that there is no acquisition on the part of human beings that God does not will.[35] Since no person has a role in His creative activity, attributing agency to man is simply wrong in Ash'arism.

According to the rationalists, the Sunni historical narrative, which is based on Ash'ari occasionalism, inevitably sacrifices causation and free will to divine agency. In Güler's view, Ash'arism regards history as simply the collection of God's acts, and leaves no space for human agency. However, this is to reject history, which is made only by human agency. Thus, he sees Sunni history as essentially theological and demands that its narrative be regarded as having a "cosmic status."[36] Kırbaşoğlu sees this Ash'ari foundation as the main cavity in Sunni history, for it does not recognize the human being as a full-blown agent in history.[37] Differently, as we read in Özsoy, the rationalists regard the human being as having the full capacity of agency in history.[38] When it comes to how Ash'ari foundation inhibits a consistent view of causality in history, the rationalists see Sunni history as committed to the strange idea of a continuum in history that is oblivious to the standard view of the nature of causation. Accordingly, arbitrary leaps and changes are possible in Sunni history, as it operates through Ash'arism, which regards God—who is indeed above any causal law—as an agent of history.[39] But, as Azimli explains, bringing God into history as sole agent is inevitably to repudiate natural and historical causation. Doing this, they have it that only God makes human history, and that divine interventions are naturally the subjects of history, for they are its supreme causes.[40] Güler reminds that unlike the Mu'tazila's God, the al-Ash'ari's God does not accept natural rules, and thus acts arbitrarily in the universe.[41] Eliaçık thus finds Sunni history ineluctably focused on the belief that the prime cause of history is God's intervention.[42] For Öztürk, this is the result of the Sunni view of history and nature as the "mirrors of God's acts." This requires that theology explain nature as well as history.[43] As a result, the Ash'ari elements that Sunni history takes on are, for the rationalists, what Güler explains as the habit of ignoring sociological and economic aspects in constructing a historical narrative.[44] Islamic history is never seen through the lens of the material dynamics of social and economic factors. Eliaçık calls this as an established skepticism in Sunni history about material factors.[45] Instead, an idealistic narrative prevails in

Sunni history to explain complex events in terms of the religious dynamic. For Yaşar Nuri, treating material elements as secondary factors makes Sunni history full of exceptional ruptures explainable in terms of the religious dynamic: God's intervention.[46] Thus, the rationalists simply do not think Sunni history realistic. They see it as a salvation history, the purpose of which is interpretative rather than informative.[47] Güler illustrates this point in the cases of several scholars like al-Ash'ari, al-Shafi'i, al-Tahawi, and al-Nasafi, for it is they who regard the religious factor as the major cause to be recognized in the narration of the complicated events in Islamic history.[48] The rationalists underline another negative consequence of the exceptionalism of that makes the prime cause a religious factor: This makes of Sunni history a collection of best samples, and creates a fatalism among Muslims that makes them imagine the past as a perfect age, and their own times as always worse. The rationalists see Sunnism as promoting the idea of decline in history and as oblivious to the modernist idea of progress.[49]

Differently, according to the rationalists, God does not intervene in history as an agent. Özsoy finds God's agential intervention into history incompatible with the principle of divine justice. It is more possible to understand history through a rational framework, for there is causation in nature and history.[50] Criticizing the Ash'ari concept of God as a Medieval imagination, Güler reminds that Quran's God is a God of causality.[51] Öztürk dismisses the Ash'ari concept of God as a "totalitarian deity" mostly derived from the political mentality of the Umayyads' age.[52] Logically, this perspective results in the rationalists' employment of a secular view of Islamic history, where events are caused only by earthly factors. As Azimli writes, there is no space for divine intervention here, for that would be to displace the universal principles upon which nature operates.[53] The rationalists do not formulate the relationship between God and nature/history in the framework of agency. Instead, it takes place within the framework of the natural laws.[54] On this model, God's *qudra* (transcendental power), not his agency, is in nature.

Not surprisingly, the rationalist view of the relationship between God and nature/history is similar to that of the classical Muslim rationalists. To revisit the classical rationalists' opinions here: According to Ibn Rushd, God's omnipotence renders an agency-like intervention into nature as impossible, for God is out of space and time. That requires no counterpart to God's will being in the empirical world. A superior view, according to Ibn Rushd, is that while God is the creator of everything, things depend on agencies such as the natural law and human will. Otherwise, for Ibn Rush, the repudiation of natural causes would render God a "tyrannical prince who has the highest power, for whom nobody in his dominion can deputize, of whom no standard or custom is known to which reference might be made."[55] Thus, for Ibn Rushd, there is a continuum of causality underlying the physical reality that can be discovered and studied by humans.[56] The Mu'tazila view is similar. There is an order in nature where God does not intervene as an agent, and man has the capacity to make his own choices freely and to act on them.[57] Similarly, al-Maturidi, whom the rationalists admire deeply, has a parallel view of free will and causality, though not as sharp as the Mu'tazilas'. Accordingly, "man is the doer of his acts." On agency, his ideas are reminiscent of those of Ibn

Rushd: Although agency belongs to God in terms of creating man's action, man does have agency when it comes to his own actions, and that agency does not contradict God's sovereignty. Thus, al-Maturidi, too, recognizes that God created things with various features and structural qualities, and that one can thus speak of rules governing the natural order. Al-Maturidi sees no problem with recognizing that the natural laws have causal efficacy. God's agency is not contradicted, since God created the laws, that is, the structure of nature, in the first place.[58]

Proceeding with similar views, the rationalists accept God's *qudra* as the source of creation, but they reject the tenet of God's intervention in nature as an agent. There is an order in nature.[59] Predictably, the rationalists are against interpreting verses in Quran as if they prove God's intervention in history as an agent.[60] To remind: Verses like 34:16 ("we let loose on them a flood") and 17:16 ("when we decide to destroy a town") are usually interpreted by Sunnis as affirming divine intervention in history. However, for Güler, interpreting such verses as if they prove the suspension of the natural order is an anachronic reading.[61] Özsoy contends that those verses should be understood as the usual historical causation, just as Quran warns that societies that do not respect moral norms will eventually collapse. For him, such verses simply remind of the natural law: The set of norms and laws that societies follow do indeed determine their material and nonmaterial states.[62] Therefore, those verses in Quran do not mean that the events referenced happened in supernatural ways. Instead, they are spoken for their symbolic meanings.[63] In fact, no contradiction is found between those verses and the natural law.[64]

To conclude: The rationalist view has three major principles that could be summarized as their philosophy of Islamic history:

1. Historical causation is limited to natural and historical causes and dynamics;
2. God is the creator and sustainer of the universe; however, he does not interfere in human history as an agent; and
3. The human-being is the only agent in history with a volition faculty.

Revisionism on the History of Quran

By "the history of Quran," I refer to the process in which the revelations ended up as a book format, that is, a codex/*Mushaf*. Sunni history presents the compilation of Quran as an effort achieved without the smallest flaw. The revelations were routinely scribed, and they were later perfectly compiled and copied.[65] In fact, the history of Quran is another typical subject to observe for how Islamic doctrines on the nature of Quran determine Muslims' ideas in other fields, including history. The doctrine of the "divine Quran" is interpreted by Sunnism as being under a miraculous protection, and thus immune from human intervention. On this interpretation, it is believed that God's divine words cannot be distorted by any historical factor. This interpretation is supported by verse 15:9, where God proclaims: "we have sent down Quran as ourself, and we ourself will guard it." *İlmihal* underlines that Quran was transmitted to us without change or distortion, and it will be transmitted just so.[66] In a related decision, THCRA opined that Quran has survived to this day "without change even to one of its letters, thanks to divine protection."[67]

The rationalists, however, find the Sunni history of Quran unconvincing. Without a systematic account of that history, there is only the Sunni history that appeals to dogmatic views and narrates Quran's history as a religious phenomenon for which supernatural and exceptional dynamics are responsible. In *History of Quran*, Öztürk criticizes the Sunni literature for presenting a problem-free propagandist account of Quran's history. On the contrary, the Sunni history is full of contradictions and dark spots. It appeals to various clichés instead of providing systematic arguments when it comes to critical problems.[68] By the same token, Güler sees the Sunni narrative of Quran's history as a tactical masking of various dubious subjects. To mask those subjects, Sunni history has forbidden zones on Quran, and protects them by dogmatic assertions. For Güler, the poverty of Sunni history on Quran is visible also in Sunni scholars' poor responses to Orientalists such as Theodor Nöldeke, Alphonse Mingana, John Burton, Richard Bell, Arthur Jeffrey, and John Wansbrough. The Sunni scholars do no more than repeat clichés, like accusing the Orientalists of not understanding Islamic culture.[69] Azimli joins Güler in criticizing the Sunni response to the Orientalists. They are mostly ad hominem arguments, devoid of any persuasive counterarguments.[70]

Differently, the rationalists hold that the compilation of Quran took place within history, in human conditions. All phases related to the compilation of Quran were human works.[71] They remind that the compilation happened after Muhammad's death, without even prophetic intervention.[72] The message of this argumentation is clear: If Quran is part of human history, everything related to Quran, including its protection, has to have happened within historical causation.[73] The compilation of Quran happened more than twenty years after the death of Muhammad (632), on the commission established by Caliph Uthman (c. 652). The compilation task was done by numerous people who relied on the information available to them in the context of the social and political dynamics of their time. The rationalists simply reject the Sunni assumption that such a long and complex procedure happened with zero human impact; the compilation of Quran was not a simple act of copying. Reminding that several verses had not been included in the Abu Bakr copy (c. 634), but were later added to the final copy by the Uthman's commission, Azimli concludes that the mission of the Uthman commission cannot have been limited to replicating only the Abu Bakr copy.[74] Advancing such arguments, the rationalists dismiss the Sunni argument that presents Quran as an exceptional phenomenon in history, and above human impact, thanks to divine protection. For the rationalists, the history of Quran is not a subject of theological inquiry. It is a historical event that happened in a process of historical causation where social and political factors played roles. The outcome of this argumentation is something that the Sunni view would never approve: Quran, that is, *Mushaf*, is what companions could remember and record of Muhammad's teachings. Though the rationalists never argue that there were deliberate additions to Quran, they do, however, accept that human effects played a role in its compilation, and that had some concrete results. What is meant by "concrete results"? We shall analyze this in detail in the following. But briefly, it might mean several things: change in a verse, loss of verses, disagreement on the reading or writing of verses, mistakes in the script, disagreement on whether a verse is really a revelation, and disagreement on the final forms of the verses. Logically, assuming that those situations might have happened is tantamount to accepting that not all verses that were revealed to Muhammad were perfectly compiled and transmitted.[75] Therefore, the gist of the rationalist revisionism of the history of Quran is their illustration of how historical factors caused concrete effects in the text of Quran. Quite definitely, the rationalists' divergent opinions on this subject are yet another factor in their split from traditional Sunnism.

Before the Compilation

In regard of this period, and, firstly, the rationalists pay attention to the uncertainties in the history of revelations, and they consider those a main reason for their skepticism about the historical accounts on the compilation of Quran. For the rationalists, any account of Quran's history inevitably has some gaps, due to the unavailability of the full body of information required for completeness, particularly on the history of the early revelations. The rationalists provide various examples to illustrate how historical information on the origins of Quran has dark spots that obstruct the Sunni claim about its flawless historical account. Öztürk asserts that, in general, no clear information is available on the verses revealed in the first ten years.[76] Azimli notes that there is no satisfactory information even on certain symbolic subjects, such as the first revealed *surah*/chapter. While for some it is al-Fatiha, others see it as al-Alaq.[77] The rationalists believe that such dark spots were later filled in by scholars to make then run in parallel with the Sunni narrative. More critically, the lack of historical data on the history of each verse would later become a serious problem in the compilation of Quran. Lacking that information, the order of verses in Quran was finalized independently of chronological order. This created huge interpretation problems.[78]

According to Öztürk, one reason for the lack of adequate information is the absence of a permanent secretariat to record revelations. For him, contrary to the Sunni narrative according to which a group of secretaries immediately scribed the revealed verses,[79] it is not known whether the secretaries were organized people with a permanent status, or they were volunteers. Öztürk is not convinced that there was a permanent secretariat to record the revelations.[80] His account here reminds of the thesis that the narrative on secretaries is likely to be a latter-day Sunni construction.[81] A rather abstract, or theoretical, revisionist argument in this vein is about the early Muslims' perceptions of the revelation. One of their premises is that it was not clear to people in the early years of Islam what is meant by "revelation." This would have registered on their decisions about what to preserve or abandon.[82] This argument has already been analyzed by scholars like William A. Graham, who held that the early Muslim understanding of the divine word and the prophetic word was primarily a unitive one. According to him, the distinctions between revelation and prophetic inspiration were "less absolute, and certainly less important" among the early Muslims. The "rigid bifurcation" of Muhammad's words and Quran happened only later.[83] Illustrating this problem, Azimli and Yaşar Nuri remind of the *codex* of Ubay ibn Ka'b, which had included verses that were excluded by other Muslims.[84] Ubay ibn Ka'b was one of the key names in the Sunni chain of Quran transmitters whose *codex* was used in various places almost as the standard form before the proclamation of the Uthman *codex* as the official copy.[85] Another example is the *codex* of Abdullah ibn Mas'ud, which did not incorporate three chapters, al-Fatiha among them, that are categorized being among the early revealed chapters.[86] Such cases, for the rationalists, demonstrate the differences among the early Muslims' perceptions of revelation. However, as Öztürk points out, Sunni history presents the early Muslims as having had a consensual understanding of the revelation, as if they had received the revelations as a finalized book that left no space for dispute.[87]

Secondly, the rationalists also argue that the historical information on the early attempts to compile Quran (i.e., those before the Uthman commission) are full of uncertainties. Öztürk writes that it is not even known who first attempted to compile the verses. The literature presents names like Abu Bakr, Ali ibn Abu Talib, Umar ibn Khattab, and Salim ibn Ubayd. He quotes various early scholars like Ibn Sirin (d. 729), who claimed even that Abu Bakr and Umar died without getting this job done.[88] To remind: For Sunni history, Abu Bakr's compilation of Quran is a major element, for it helps fix the collection of Quran just after Muhammad's death. Logically, it also requires that the final copy prepared during the caliphate of Uthman was identical to the Abu Bakr copy.[89] But Öztürk insists that even if one believes that the first attempt happened under Abu Bakr, many questions still lack satisfying answers. For example, was Abu Bakr the first actor to succeed to compile the verses? Or did he put the already-compiled verses into a better condition? Öztürk is not satisfied with the existing literature on the role played by Abu Bakr in the compilation of Quran. Further, he is not satisfied with the historical account that refers to the Yemame War during Abu Bakr's caliphate, when almost 700 *hafiz* (persons who memorized Quran) companions are reported to have been martyred, and seeks to use this event to explain the early Muslims' decision to compile Quran. Many controversial aspects aside, Öztürk does not find the number of martyred companions realistic.[90] He suspects that the Yemame narrative is a later construction, and part of the emerging Sunni historical narrative on Quran.[91] Azimli notes other problems on Abu Bakr's attempt. It is not clear that Abu Bakr succeeded to gather all the existing verses, losing none. There are reports that some of the verses could not be reached during the formation of the Abu Bakr copy. The companions noticed the missing verses.[92] And there were important disagreements among the companions over the authenticity of various verses. There is no historical information about how such disagreements were resolved at the time. As a matter of fact, the surge of the same disagreements during the compilation in Uthman's time displays that the Abu Bakr copy failed to reconcile the differences among the companions on the status of several verses.[93]

The Compilation

Caliph Uthman convened the *istinsah* commission (hereafter the Uthman Commission), believed to have worked *circa* 652, where the final copy (the *codex*) was declared the standard copy, and other copies or relevant materials were ordered to be burned. According to the Sunni narrative, the Uthman Commission developed its final copy based on the first copy made by Abu Bakr. The rationalists are, however, uncomfortable with the Sunni historical narrative on the Uthman commission. Moreover, according to them, the formation of Quran did not finish with the Uthman Commission. Changes were made right up until the Umayyad times, all be they minor orthographic ones.[94] Entertaining such opinions is tantamount to heresy in Sunnism. As we read in the earlier pages of al-Qurtubi's *Tafsir*, the Sunni view condemns as rejecters of Quran, and of Muhammad's transmitted deliveries, those who say that there was addition and retraction in Quran by the Uthman Commission.[95]

To begin analyzing the rationalists' critique: They first revisit the burning of the "other copies." According to various resources, once the Uthman Commission declared its copy the official *codex* to be distributed across the Muslim regions, the other surviving copies and materials were burnt. The case is narrated in al-Bukhari's *Sahih* as follows: "Uthman sent to every Muslim province one copy of what they copied, and ordered that all the other Quranic materials, whether written in fragmentary manuscripts or whole copies, be burnt."[96] For the rationalists, the burning of the "other materials" is proof of the human role in the compilation of Quran: (i) The final decision on the status of the various verses was made by humans, and (ii) there was yet no consensus on the authenticity of the various verses.[97] The rationalists highlight the "burning" as critical, for it proves that the debate among the companions on the authenticity of the various verses was never resolved. Thus, "burning" was a substantial political intervention by the caliphate to end the debate among the companions.[98] As Nicolai Sinai writes, there was "something inherently problematic about the burning of rival codices."[99] Öztürk reminds that there were still companions who were critical of the burning of the other material because they knew of the differences between the final copy and the previous copies.[100] Yaşar Nuri asserts that among the burnt *Mushafs* were ones compiled by Abu Bakr and Ali ibn Abi Talib.[101] Öztürk has a similar view: Among the burnt *Mushafs* were those that belonged to the various companions like Abdullah ibn Mas'ud, Ali ibn Abi Talib, and Abu Musa al-Ash'ari. These were different, in one way or another, from the final copy prepared by the Uthman Commission.[102] Azimli, too, says that there were at least dialectic differences between the final copy and the burnt *Mushafs*. Besides, the order of verses in Abu Bakr's compilation was different from that of the final copy of the Uthman Commission.[103] In addition to this, for Öztürk, it is not even clear how many copies were produced by the Uthman Commission, as no consensus exists among historians. As he reports, there were nine copies for Ya'qubi (d. 897), five for al-Suyuti, and only two for Ibn al-Jawzi (d. 1201). The lack of adequate information on such a sensitive topic is intriguing for Öztürk. More dramatically, the final copy is no longer extant. Reminding that many trivial things were protected, such as Muhammad's hair and broken teeth, Öztürk finds highly problematic the absence of any sample of the Uthman Commission's final copy.[104]

The compilation of Quran under Caliph Uthman happened in a period when the early Muslim society had tense political conflicts, and even hostilities. The early Muslim society was deeply divided, as were the key companions, along political and tribal lines.[105] Caliph Uthman was assassinated only a few years after the Commission, sparking a civil war. Given that the compilation of Quran did not occur in a vacuum free of social and political factors, the rationalists ruminate on whether those political and tribal dynamics played any role in the elevation of the "final copy," and earlier. In this regard, the rationalists see Caliph Uthman as preferring loyalists, and excluding oppositional figures from the Uthman Commission. This resulted in the exclusion of companions like Ali, who was to be next caliph, for holding oppositional opinions on various issues, including on the way Uthman formed the Commission.[106]

As expected, the Sunni view defends the manner of the Uthman Commission members' election, asserting that it was merit based. To validate their stance, Sunni scholars display reports on the credentials of Zayd ibn Thabit, the head of the Uthman Commission. These reports narrate how Zayd was fluent in various languages, and had mastered an exquisite calligraphy.[107] The Sunni view denies the presence of political problems in the formation of the Uthman Commission and its works. However, having studied the biographies of the Uthman Commission members, Öztürk dismisses the Sunni argument. To him, political allegiances certainly played important roles in the formation of the Uthman Commission.[108] The Sunni literature also contains long discussions on why some companions, like Abdullah ibn Mas'ud, who openly questioned the capacity and legitimacy of Zayd ibn Thabit, were not elected to the Uthman Commission, despite their recognized all-round merits. Öztürk is also not persuaded by those discussions. He spots that Caliph Uthman excluded Abdullah ibn Mas'ud, an oppositional figure who claimed publicly that the caliph is corrupt, and an unjust ruler.[109] We read details in Azimli on the relationship between Caliph Uthman and Abdullah ibn Mas'ud. When Abdullah called out Walid, the governor of Kufa, for corruption, the caliph punished Abdullah brutally.[110] He was beaten, and his bones were broken.[111] The rationalist narrative sees the political tension between Caliph Uthman and Abdullah ibn Mas'ud as the reason for his exclusion from the Uthman Commission. Notably, Abdullah ibn Mas'ud was always close to Muhammad, and as it is frequently underlined, he claimed to have already known many of the verses when Zayd ibn Thabit was still a boy.[112] He is known to have broadcast his opinions on religious matters even while Muhammad was alive.[113] Abdullah never endorsed Zayd ibn Thabit's eligibility for such critical work. Azimli notes that Abdullah had not endorsed the Uthman Commission's copy. Instead, he advised his followers to keep his copy.[114] As Yaşar Nuri discusses in detail, Abdullah's *codex* was different, for it did not include the three surahs—al-Fatiha, al-Nas, and al-Falaq—but he did include the Qunut prayers, which were left out of Quran by the Uthman Commission.[115] Some studies suggest that Abdullah ibn Mas'ud's *codex* survived into the tenth century.[116] Meanwhile, for Öztürk, the *codex* of Abdullah ibn Mas'ud is not the only example of surviving different copies. He narrates from al-Tabari that when Marwan I became a caliph (684), he burnt a surviving *codex* of Abu Bakr for its divergence from the now-official Uthman codex.[117]

The rationalists also submit a revisionist view on the work of the Uthman Commission. Not interested in the Sunni doctrine of the divine protection of Quran, the rationalists see the works of the Uthman Commission as a procedure where some sort of human factors, including mistakes, had played roles. To elaborate on this, the rationalists draw attention to the various cases where we read the companions' report that some verses were forgotten or lost. For example, Öztürk presents a list of cases from classical scholars (such as al-Shahrastani (d. 1158), al-Qurtubi, Abu Davud, Muslim, Ahmed ibn Hanbal, Ibn Majah (d. 887), al-Khattabi (d. 997), al-Tahawi, and al-Bukhari) where we read that the companions talked about how they forgot several verses, or they disagreed on some verses.[118] In more detail: Azimli reports that several companions talked about a number of verses that were lost during the Apostasy Wars under the rule of Abu Bakr.[119] Öztürk analyzes the reports narrated by Aisha, where she talks about how the Surah al-Ahzab verses were shortened by the Uthman Commission.[120] In this vein, Azimli reminds of the famous passage in *Sahih*, where Zayd ibn Thabit, the head of the Uthman Commission, said that he missed a verse from Surah al-Ahzab when they were copying the Quran, and they were later given that verse by Abu Khuzaima ibn Thabit for inclusion into Quran.[121] Öztürk contends that this passage from *Sahih* displays serious problems in the compilation of Quran. Accordingly, the account of Zayd ibn Thabit admits that the Uthman Commission violated the procedural principle of seeking out two witnesses to validate a verse proposed for inclusion in Quran. The passage from *Sahih* also displays that many companions had not kept that verse and that it was strangely available only to Abu Khuzaima ibn Thabit. Öztürk is uncomfortable also about who Abu Khuzaima ibn Thabit actually was, given that even key authorities (such as al-Bukhari, Ahmad ibn Hanbal, al-Tirmidhi (d. 892), and al-Bayhaqi (d. 1066)) had contending views of him.[122] We observe here how the rationalists probe a verse that is now part of Quran and how they articulate their various discomforts with the historical account that justifies the inclusion of a verse in Quran. Reminding that the history of Quran was open to human factors, the rationalists think such cases normal. What is problematic for them is the Sunni history method that retrospectively interpreted the problematic exclusions of verses as divine intervention. God made the companions forget or lose several verses.[123]

Another controversial case in this vein is an event, again narrated in *Sahih*, where Alqama narrates the case of Abdullah ibn Mas'ud and Abu ad-Darda on how to read the third verse of Surah al-Layl. Their advice is to read it without the two words, *wa ma khalaqa*, in Quran. More interestingly, Abu ad-Darda laments that though they heard it in this way from Muhammad, "these people" do not consider it the correct recitation.[124] Given that Abu ad-Darda was also a member of the Uthman Commission, it is strange to observe him lamenting the final copy of the Quran as having two additional words in a verse which he also finds incompatible with Muhammad's recitation. Azimli clarifies that the change was made by the Umayyads, Abu ad-Darda's "these people."[125]

We encounter other examples in the works of the rationalists. We read in Öztürk that the Uthman Commission faced difficulties in its effort to confirm the authenticity of various verses, such as the 33:23 and 9:128-129. Finally, the former verse was authenticated only by Khuzaima ibn Thabit, and the latter was authenticated by another companion whose name was, strangely, also Khuzaima. Öztürk finds this explanation unsatisfactory, for there is no reliable information on the two names. The Uthman Commission also failed to agree on how to write the word *at-tabutu* in verse 2:248. This was resolved only after Caliph Uthman's intervention, who ordered its inscription in the Quraysh dialect. This case again shows how political intervention was an essential factor in the compilation of Quran.[126]

The Uthman Commission also failed to provide against the many misspellings in the final copy, which, for Öztürk, proves that the finalization of Quran was not free of human mistakes. To present several samples: A word in 27:20 has one redundant *alif*, and a word in 51:47 has one redundant *ye*. Öztürk says that such misspellings were later interpreted by Sunni scholars as having several purposes. For example, the second *ye* in 51:47 is interpreted as symbolizing the power of God. However, even the companions who played a role in the history of Quran, like Aisha and Uthman, were aware of those misspellings.[127] In fact, grammatical mistakes had already been a problem well before the Uthman Commission, as we have reports in al-Bukhari and Muslim where Aisha informs people of a number of *lahn* (grammatical mistakes) in Quran caused by secretaries.[128] But Azimli writes that the Uthman Commission made new mistakes that survive today.[129] Öztürk points out examples of them in verses 5:69, 4:162, and 20:63.[130]

A relevant subject in this vein is the confusion in gender forms, which is usually a *lahn*. Öztürk counts tens of examples where there is no standard usage of the male and female gender forms in Quran. However, he attributes the *lahn* errors to the lack of an established grammar at that time.[131] Then again, for Öztürk, this case is very important in the challenge of the Sunni view, for it presents such cases as being indicative of a divine wisdom rather than explain them in a realistic manner.[132] For example, even when an act is that of women, the verb is rendered in the male form in verse 12:30: "*Wa qala niswatun fi al-madinati* (some women of the city said)." Grammatically, the verb should have been *qalat*, the female form." (In line with the Sunni method, scholars like Said Nursi explain this grammatical error as a most proper example of eloquence, for with this apparent error Quran indicates that "an association of weak, meek and soft woman gains strength, toughness, and force, and even acquires a certain kind of virility."[133]) *Lahn* is particularly important for the rationalists' illustration of how the history of Quran was determined also by the limits of human capacity and the condition of the not-yet-perfected Arabic language of the time.[134] Illustrating this, Öztürk writes that influential actors, including Caliph Uthman, agreed to keep the text that way, with several mistakes, hoping that time will resolve those mistakes.[135] The impossibility of solving this problem was due to the lack of a developed set of Arabic grammar rules, a long-term problem. It was as late as the time of the Umayyad governor, al-Hajjaj ibn Yusuf (d. 714), when a final incursion into Quran made small changes via a commission.[136]

The issue of dialect is covered similarly by the rationalists. In the original, several verses were written in Quraysh dialect. Others were written in Hudhayl (Huzail), and there are some verses in the Harith ibn Ka'b dialect. The issue of dialect was a matter of disagreement also among the companions during the compilation of Quran. For example, Abdullah ibn Mas'ud preferred the Mudar dialect in his copy.[137] The dialect issue is important, for it displays how human dynamics played a role in the linguistic expression of the revelation, as the verses were written in different dialects. However, reading and writing Quran in different dialects was later abrogated. Öztürk reminds that Muhammad permitted the recitation of the revelations in various dialects.[138] In a passage in *Sahih*, we read of a quarrel between Umar, who was to be the second caliph, and Hisham ibn Hakim on Surah al-Furqan, when the Prophet was still alive. They read some verses differently, claiming that they heard them so from the Prophet. Once, they brought the issue to the Prophet. He told them to read as they wish, given that the Quran was revealed in seven different ways.[139] There was also the tribal factor behind that license. Each tribe was permitted to read Quran in its dialect. Quoting Ibn Qutayba (d. 889), Öztürk writes that forcing tribes to read Quran in another dialect would have been a serious problem.[140] However, the Uthman Commission was asked to finalize the script of Quran in Quraysh dialect as much as possible, and Caliph Uthman prohibited the use of alternate dialects, and event burnt material written in them.[141]

For Öztürk, the early Muslims never imagined a *book* Quran, so paying prime attention to its meaning was not unknown to them. So, the early Muslims read it in different dialects. Accordingly, the purpose of the contact between Muslims and the revelation was its meaning.[142] This approach, which is usually affiliated with Abdullah ibn Mas'ud, privileged "the oral transmission of Quran based on meaning (*riwaya bi-l-ma'na*) rather than verbatim dictation (*riwaya bi-l-lafdz*)."[143] Öztürk reports that Muslims therefore read Quran by changing words with a synonym, or similar, so long as there was no change in the meaning. For example, "*hakimun 'alim*" was read as "*'alimun hakim*." What was regarded as wrong was to change meaning, not the *lafdz* (pronunciation and reading). However, Öztürk says, imagining Quran as a book elevated the significance of linguistic rules for Muslims: The smallest detail of linguistic rules redundantly became a huge theological principle. In a sense, the Uthmanic turn was the victory of verbatim dictation. But, Öztürk (recall that he is a historicist who is critical of the book Quran) underlines that this shift was made on political and social-conjectural reasons, not for any religious reason. Neither Quran nor Muhammad asked for it.[144]

Revisionism on Muhammad

Revisionism on the life of Muhammad is as difficult as the history of Quran. Sunni history narrates his life on the key principle that Muhammad was a perfect human, supported by miracles. As expected, the focus is on his extraordinary and various qualifications.[145] On Muhammad's life, the rationalist revisionism against aims to narrate his life within the context of historical causation, giving no credit to supernatural exceptionalism. The rationalists challenge Sunni history for portraying Muhammad as an infallible person supported by miracles.[146] Instead, they argue, every segment of his life happened within the context of natural and historical causation.[147] Muhammad was a normal human being who made mistakes, and he was not sinless.[148] The rationalist rest their quest for the historical Muhammad on this premise.[149] Meanwhile, the rationalists' reservations about the Sunni history of Muhammad are not merely about their concern for historical consistency and authenticity. They also do not see as helpful the narrative that presents Muhammad as a model personality for Muslims.[150] Eliaçık slams the Sunni brand of idealistic portrayal of Muhammad as surreal, like a children's story.[151]

But why is the Sunni narrative of Muhammad so surrealistic? The rationalists provide a number of explanations. As we read in Yaşar Nuri, the first reason is the Sunni method of justifying its premises through Muhammad's life. The canonical status of the *sunnah* and *hadith* automatically made the biography of Muhammad another resource to justify any religious or political argument. Sunni history gradually transformed Muhammad into an almost divine personality. This is helpful in the dissemination of any argument. Reference to his life trumps all doubt. It helps Sunnism declare a large part of its theoretical basis as undisputable.[152] In this vein, the rationalists refer to *al-nur al-Muhammedi* (the Muhammadan light)—a doctrine that accepts that the light of Muhammad had existed before creation, and that everything else was created from it—to illustrate how Sunnism defines Muhammad as a divine phenomenon. The doctrine also implies that the whole universe is created for Muhammad.[153] As Gerhard Böwering explains, this doctrine interprets "the Muhammadan light" as a primordial substance that exists in a special relationship with God.[154] The rationalists point out that the popular characterizations of Muhammad, such as *fahri alem* (the pride of the universe), *seyyid-i kainat* (the lord of the universe), and *efendimiz* (our lord) are examples of super-veneration.[155] According to Güler, "the deification of Muhammad" in Sunnism reached a peak after the fifth Islamic century, when key scholars like al-Suyuti developed the doctrine that Muhammad is still alive in body and soul.[156] Güler concludes that the reframing of Muhammad as a sacred divine essence naturally distorted the Sunni scholarship on his life.[157] Put differently, the life of the Prophet was transformed into an ahistorical or canonical field.

A second factor is linked to the nature of early Islamic scholarship. As we read in Azimli, the early Muslim scholars gathered much unverified information on Muhammad's life, making no serious effort to assess it. Accordingly, the prime motive of those scholars was to gather as much documentation as they can about Muhammad. They were collectors rather than historians. However, the negative consequence of such a method is the immense volume of unverified material on Muhammad.[158] The Azimli critique is very like the arguments of Western scholars that question the way-and-the-how of the early Muslim scholars' collection of their information. For example, Harold Motzki writes that "the authors of the historical biographies have been allowed to choose from the sources the information which they personally liked best."[159]

Thirdly, the rationalists refer to the Sunni habit of a caring public psychology while narrating various dramatic events that happened in the early years of Islam. Accordingly, Muslim scholars skip several complicated issues in the name of protecting Muslims. Azimli, for example, writes that Ibn Hisham did not use some material from Ibn Ishaq lest it be harmful to average people.[160] However, for Güler, this pedagogical perspective ended up with an ascetic portrayal of Muhammad that falls short of picturing his life realistically. Moreover, such a pedagogical attitude became a habit, and many events in Muhammad's life were narrated as if they were theological by nature. Then, any case that was difficult to narrate in "secular" terms was increasingly explained in terms of theological dynamics such as the divine wisdom behind events.[161]

A final point that rationalists make about the formation of Sunni history is about the early scholars' interest in the most exceptional narrative. Muslim scholars usually prefer the narrative that incorporates supernatural elements, even when other narratives are available. Azimli explains this with an example. In an oft-quoted case, Muhammad left a meeting early after he was informed about a plot against his life. Despite the fact that there is a second narrative that has it that a Medinan women warned Muhammad, Azimli finds that scholars mostly preferred the narrative where an angel is reported to have notified him of the plot against him.[162] The rationalists' exceptional-narrative thesis is in fact important to observe for how they diverge from the Medieval Islamic narrative to promote a modern view. As modern scholars, the narrative that they prefer is the one that presents historical events as standard historical causation that stays clear of supernatural elements. However, the Medieval Muslim society, like the European, believed that "so many ungovernable forces" affect nature and their lives.[163] People often saw invisible dynamics as more important than the deeds of people.[164] Particularly when it comes to purely religious affairs, the Medieval mentally accepted that "the chronological and causal aspects determining the destiny of an individual" were only secondary.[165] Öztürk writes that the early Islamic historical writing, too, imagined history as being subject to the impact of both material and metaphysical causes.[166] Confirming him, the early Muslim chronicles are too full of miracles, devils, omens, *jinn*, spirits, and other ungovernable forces. In al-Tabari, we read that the devil appeared in a meeting of Meccan notables, "in the form of a venerable old man wearing a coarse garment," to persuade them to kill Muhammad, but the angel came to Muhammad and informed him of the plot.[167] Ibn Ishaq reports that people witnessed angels protecting Muhammad with their wings from the sun's rays.[168] In al-Waqidi, Satan appears in the shape of a man before critical wars like the Badr, trying to change the course of events against Muslims.[169]

Questioning Basic Factual Data on Muhammad

The purportedly basic facts about Muhammad's life are given special attention by the rationalists, for they regard them as critical details that serve Sunni history.

Regarding them as later-produced historical information, the rationalists question their authenticity.[170] A typical case in this vein is Muhammad's illiteracy. Unlike Sunni history, the rationalists claim that Muhammad was not illiterate.[171] The illiteracy of Muhammad relates to the idea that he was not influenced by any knowledge that "he could possibly have gained through reading" from any other source.[172] Based on the analyses of distinguished figures such as Abu al-Walid al-Baji (d. 1081) and Abu Fath al-Nishaburi (d. 1086), and considering Muhammad's experience in trade, Öztürk thinks it is illogical to believe that Muhammad was illiterate.[173] Eliaçık interprets "illiterate" as a social-status distinguisher for having rejected elitism and as a protester against the Meccan elites.[174] We encounter similar inquiries in the works of the rationalists on other factual data, such as numbers, dates, ages, and names in Muhammad's life. Azimli rejects the standard account that Khadija was forty years old when she married Muhammad. He argues that this would have meant that Khadija had her first child when she was fifty-five years old, and this is not realistic. Based on al-Baladhuri (d. 892) and Ibn Sa'd (d. 845), Azimli argues that Khadija would have been around twenty-eight when she married Muhammad.[175] As another example, Balcı proposes that Muhammad was born in 569 rather than in 571.[176] Engaging with such topics, the rationalists seek to emphasize that Muhammad's life between the ages of twenty-five and forty. is not documented clearly.[177]

The rationalists challenge the Sunni account of the basic facts in Muhammad's life, suspecting that account of being mostly later productions constructed on Sunni premises. To them, Sunnism justifies itself by referring to "basic facts" about Muhammad. A relevant second concern is to minimize the impact of traditions on Islamic reasoning by emphasizing that Muhammad's biography is not clear, nor was it important for Quran and the early Muslims. Instead, the rationalists want to emphasize that what mattered for the early Muslims was the Islamic norms. They draw attention to the fact that the exaggeration of Muhammad is a later phenomenon. To support this, Balcı points out that the first biographical study of Muhammad's life was written almost 120 years after his death.[178]

Humanizing Muhammad

The strategy of portraying Muhammad as a perfect man is a key feature of Sunni Islam. However, the rationalists believe that this strategy gradually evolved into a surreal narrative full of exaggerations. Yaşar Nuri thinks that the Sunni Muhammad narrative transforms him into a superhuman who is above history.[179] Eliaçık even contends that the hyper-veneration of the Prophet reached the level of "idolizing Muhammad."[180] Güler explains the Sunni view in general as a "monumental history" of Muhammad, a term he borrows from Nietzsche.[181] In contrast to the Sunni view, the rationalists portray Muhammad as a regular man of his time and society. Balcı presents him as a man who listened to the poets of his age, and spent time in the market.[182] Thus, the key element of the rationalist revisionism on Sunni history in regard of Muhammad's biography is to criticize it for replacing the historical Muhammad with a superhuman.[183]

As a response to the Sunni discourse, the rationalists' intention in their works is to humanize Muhammad. To achieve this, they provide an alternate narrative of Muhammad's life where he errs and fails, no supernatural event occurs, and social, political, and economic dynamics affect him like other people. We read therefore vivid presentations of rarely discussed issues in his personal life to emphasize his human nature. To present a number of examples in this vein, we see the rationalists discuss events where Muhammad failed. Balcı, for example, writes that he failed to persuade his uncle, Abu Talib, to accept Islam.[184] Azimli elaborates on how Khadija's father did not endorse the marriage to Muhammad, due to his reservations about the latter's social and economic status. Khadija was able to persuade her father only by getting him drunk.[185] Azimli gives another example: Abu Talib, his uncle, also did not endorse Muhammad's proposal to marry his daughter, Ummu Hani, for Muhammad did not have the required social rank for the marriage.[186] As these samples show, the rationalists challenge the Sunni narrative of Muhammad's life as perfect. For example, the Sunni history that narrates Muhammad's marriage specifies that Khadija made insightful observations about Muhammad, and received information from angels (and monks) that persuaded her that he will be the next prophet.[187] Rejecting these sorts of historical account, the rationalists portray Muhammad as an ordinary man of his society. Azimli points out that there are times when he was angry or happy, as well as defeated or mistaken.[188] Balcı portrays Muhammad as "an average man in the *jahilliya* society."[189] For Atay, Muhammad was a normal man in deeds and opinions, but for the revelations.[190] To emphasize the human aspect of Muhammad, the rationalists do not even refrain from discussing some highly personal matters. Azimli incorporates into his books various reports from classical historians, such as the one from al-Waqidi, about Muhammad's snoring while sleeping.[191] Such quite interesting details, which might even be seen as redundant, are in fact carefully quoted by the rationalists, for they have huge potential for humanizing Muhammad.

Another method in this vein is to illustrate how Muhammad was a man of his time and society.[192] The purpose here is to emphasize that the developments in Muhammad's life were not exceptional incidents, but the natural experiences of the society in which he lived. We read a long list of examples under this title. The rise of Muhammad as a leader in his society is not a surprise for Balcı, as the Prophet was a member of a noble family in Mecca. His grandfather, Abdulmuttalib, was already a prestigious tribal leader who presided over the *hajj* affairs.[193] We similarly read a human account of Muhammad's marriage to Zaynab. Unlike the Sunni view, which presents the case as a divine intervention, Öztürk—based on various classical sources such as Qatadah, Ibn Zayd, Muqatil ibn Sulayman (d. 767), and al-Tabari—explains the case by incorporating emotions, and writes that Muhammad personally wanted Zaynab's quick divorce from Zayd.[194] In the same context, while criticizing the ascetic portrayal of Muhammad, Eliaçık notes that he was fond of women, and he enjoyed a dynamic life.[195]

Indeed, the "cost" of such a deconstructive perspective is to extract or minimize the religious aspect from/in Muhammad's life. Take, for example, the case of Muhammad's confinement in the cave where he received the revelation. The confinement in a cave is etherealized by Sunnism. Many Sunnis today never think of it as a habit in Arab culture. But the rationalists deconstruct that narrative, and remind that confinement in caves was a cultural tradition among Arabs. Azimli writes that spending time in caves during Ramadan was a tradition of the Meccan polytheists.[196] As we read in Balcı, Abdulmuttalib, the Prophet's grandfather, also made a habit of spending time in a cave on Arafat during Ramadan, in the place and time of Muhammad's received the first revelation.[197] Öztürk lists some others, such as Zayd ibn Amr, and Nufayl from Quraysh who were known for spending time in that cave.[198] The Hira cave, where Muhammad received the first revelation, was a popular place of sojourn for Mecca people. It was also a place for poor people to seek aid from the rich Meccans who came there for confinement.[199] Revisiting the cave detail in Muhammad's life is methodologically important. As Nasr Abu-Zayd writes, it helps display that what Muhammad did was not exceptional; it was what the people of his society did.[200] Like Abu-Zayd, the rationalists believe that social patterns are key to understanding Muhammad. Only by understanding the social patterns of his age, Azimli writes, can one grasp why Muhammed ordered the attack on a trade caravan before the Badr War. That order has the feel of an indecent action. Yet it was a completely normal act, for it was atypical military tactic in the Arab tradition.[201]

Another example of the rationalists' humanization quest is the narrative of Muhammad's stay in his early childhood as a foster child with a family. This event is a key subject of Muhammad's life in any Sunni biography. Muhammad was given to a family to acquire some benefits, such as learning better Arabic among nomads, or spending time in a healthier environment.[202] However, Balcı is not satisfied with those explanations. The sending of a small child away from the family must have been occasioned by a *force major*, such as that Amina, the Prophet's mother, had no breast milk.[203] However, Balcı asserts that the case was later covered by alternate narratives that cast it as a negative situation, an unbecoming event in the Prophet's life.[204] Also not satisfied with the Sunni narrative, Azimli suggests that the plague could have been the *force major* that forced the decision to send him away from home.[205]

The rationalists do not refrain from humanizing Muhammad highly provocatively. One typical example is the reference to Muhammad's beliefs before Islam. Sunnism casts Muhammad and his family members (i.e., parents and ancestors) as *hanif* who were far from idolatry.[206] Azimli dismisses *hanif* as a later-developed theory by Sunni scholars to explain Muhammad's status before Islam.[207] Accordingly, the purpose of the *hanif* discourse is the Sunni goal to narrate Muhammad and his family members as if they lived like Muslims before Islam.[208] The narrative on Abdulmuttalib is a typical case, as he is presented as a *hanif*. However, conversely, Azimli and Balcı remind that Abdulmuttalib was a worshipper of idols like Hubel, and even named his two sons after idols: Abd Manaf and Abd al-'Uzza.[209] Balcı thus concludes that Muhammad's family and ancestors were average Arab people sharing others' faiths and customs. He notes that one of Muhammad's grandfathers had the name Abdulshams, meaning "slave of the Sun," and one uncle of his name was named Abd al-'Uzza.[210] As a matter of fact, Quraysh,

Muhammad's tribe, has 'Uzza as its idol.[211] Azimli reminds that it was Qusai ibn Kilab (d. c. 480), Muhammad's ancestor, who established the systemic relations between tribes and idols in Mecca.[212] On this account, Azimli and Balcı find that the Sunni narrative that depicts Muhammad as always angry with idols is an anachronic interpretation. Azimli narrates also reports of Muhammad eating the meat of an animal sacrificed in the name of an idol.[213] Balcı, too, recounts the same event, adding that Muhammad's boys from Khadija were given the names Abdul-'Uzza and Abd Manaf, typical pagan names. Reminding that Quran informs how Prophet Abraham once worshipped the sun and stars, Balcı finds Mohammed's case sociologically normal.[214] Unsurprisingly, we also encounter in the works of rationalists the account of Ibn al-Kalbi (d. 819), who says in *The Book of Idols*: "We have been told that the Apostle of God once reported 'Uzza saying, 'I offered a white sheep to 'Uzza while I was a follower of the religion of my people.'"[215]

Rejecting Miracles

The final topic in this section is the rejection of miracles, which occupies a large space in the Muhammad biographies.[216] Prophethood and miracles are regarded in Sunni Islam as substantially linked.[217] Sunnism therefore sees miracles as the privileges given to Muhammad, as they were to the previous prophets. Reflecting mainstream Sunnism, *İlmihal* defines miracles as proof of Muhammad's prophethood.[218]

The rationalists do not accept miracles because they see them as incompatible with natural law.[219] As a result, they categorically dismiss the miracles of Muhammad, such as the splitting of the moon into two pieces, feeding the poor in miraculous ways, informing about the future, speaking with the dead, and healing the sick. For the rationalists, Muhammad was a man who acted in history, and was therefore subject to natural law.[220] Beyond its incompatibility with natural law, the rationalists also provide some other explanations for rejecting the supernatural element in Muhammad's life. To begin with, the rationalists see miracles as reincarnations of pre-Islamic Arab beliefs that are alien to Islam. Yaşar Nuri explains the attributing of miracles to Muhammad as a return to the pre-Islamic customs where people were thought to have divine attributes.[221] For example, Balcı calls a typical reincarnation of pre-Islamic beliefs the frequently narrated miracle where Muhammad was given the choice of dying or staying alive for as long as he wished.[222] In the same way, Atay dismisses the famous *Miraj* miracle (Muhammad's ascent to heaven to meet God) for its being the resurrection by Islam of a pagan tradition.[223]

A second argument is that miracles are inconsistent with Quran, and that requires their refutation. Öztürk repudiates the miracle of Muhammad's ability to inform about future events, for it is incompatible with verse 46:9, where God asks Muhammad to respond by saying that "I do not know what will be done with me or you."[224] Similarly, Azimli dismisses one of the most famous miracles, in which Bahira, a Christian monk, told young Muhammad that he would become a prophet: This is incompatible with verse 28:86, which reads: "You yourself could not have expected the Scripture to be sent to you."²²⁵ According to Kırbaşoğlu, traditions that miraculously inform of future events are unauthentic, even when they are transmitted by major books.²²⁶ Balcı, too, dismisses the foretelling of future events, for they are fabricated.²²⁷ Beyond its incompatibility with Quran, miracles of foretelling are rejected by rationalists also for their incompatibility with natural law. Accordingly, human beings cannot inform of future events, and Muhammad, as a man without supernatural powers, had no power to see the future.²²⁸

A third method of rejecting miracles is to demonstrate how they are illogical. Balcı studied a number of traditions recorded in prestigious books such as *Sahih* and *Sunan*, according to which the Prophet gave out in advance the list of the names of people who would be killed in future civil wars. Balcı wonders why the companions who died could not protect themselves from death in civil wars despite the key information the Prophet gave them. In another tradition, allegedly reported by the key names Ahmad ibn Hanbal and Abu Davud, Muhammad gives details on how Hussain, his grandson, would be killed in Karbala. Balcı also thinks these traditions illogical, and wonders why Hussein did not to protect himself despite clear warnings from the Prophet.²²⁹ According to the rationalists, the miraculous traditions that center on various political events, such as civil wars or the assassinations of early caliphs, were fabricated later, to cover shocking events with religious arguments such as "destiny."²³⁰ The goal is to persuade Muslims that those events were foreseen by the Prophet. It was a tactic to normalize such horrible events in the eyes of Muslims. Another goal of the tactic is to help political actors who played roles in those shocking events.²³¹

Another method is to reject miracles as simply wrong or contradictory. Miracles in which Muhammad informs about the invasion of Ka'ba by Abyssinians or he declares that there would be no living person after a hundred years are dismissed. The first never happened, and the second was already refuted.²³² The rationalists also use this method to dismiss the *Miraj* miracle. Accordingly, the information on *Miraj*, even those provided by key scholars like al-Bukhari, al-Baladhuri, Ibn Kathir, and Ibn Sa'd, fails to provide a consistent historical account. There are even reports in al-Bukhari's *Sahih* claiming that *Miraj* happened before Muhammad's prophethood. This makes the whole narrative more complicated.²³³ Finally, the rationalists reject some miracles because they are borrowed from other cultures, such as Persian and Indian. The Muslims encountered those miracle narratives during the expansion of Islam, particularly after the second Islamic century.²³⁴ For example, the rationalists engage this argument to reject *Miraj*, pointing out that it is regarded as mostly Zoroastrian and Christian inspired.²³⁵ Yaşar Nuri regards *Miraj* as an attempt to mythologize Muhammad in the manner of other cultures.²³⁶ Balcı notes that no account of *Miraj* exists even in the earlier resources (those written before Muslims' complex interaction with other cultures) like the works of Muqatil ibn Suleiman or Abdullah ibn Mubarak (d. 797).²³⁷ Thus, Güler does not hesitate to dismiss the whole *Miraj* account as a "collection of lies."²³⁸

To the question of why previous key scholars such as Ibn Sa'd, Ibn Ishaq, Ibn Kathir, al-Bukhari, al-Baladhuri, Ibn Mace, and many others incorporated so many miracles into their works that the rationalists find illogical, fabricated, and wrong, we are again referred to the Medieval mentality of those scholars, a subject I elaborated in the beginning of this chapter. Simply, the Medieval mentality of those scholars had a different approach to miracles than that of modern man. Atay asserts that many natural events were easily interpreted as supernatural events because of the attributing scholars' limited knowledge of the natural sciences. Atay opines that Medieval Muslim scholars had two interconnected problems: Their cosmological knowledge was limited and this created the second problem, that is, the propensity to declare natural events as supernatural because they failed to explain them.[239] Atay's critique is very much like that of Charles Taylor, who writes that it was easier to believe in the supernatural in Medieval times because of people's shallow ideas of "the natural world they lived in," and "its place in the cosmos they imagined."[240] The evolution of Islamic thought has also always been linked to the evolution of Islamic cosmological ideas.[241] Echoing this debate, the rationalists believe that some problems in Sunni history obviously have their causes in the failure of Muslims to shift from the Medieval to the modern paradigm.[242] In this regard, the rationalists' revisionism in history is an attempt to update Islamic thought such that it comes in line with modern cosmology, where there is no space for miracles.

Revisionism on Early Islamic History

The works of the rationalists include revisionist opinions on early Islamic history, a period that extends from the beginning of Muhammad's prophethood to the end of Ali's caliphate. Sunni history presents this period as a golden age of Muslims.[243] The period is called *asr-ı saadet* in Sunni-Turkish literature, which literally means "the century of felicity."[244] The rationalists find the Sunni narrative of this period to be another example of unrealistic history. Öztürk declares the Sunni account of this period yet another "romantic discourse" on the Islamic past. He notes that the idea that Muhammad transformed a very primitive society into a civilized community is a romantic account.[245] For Balcı, the Sunni history, rather than providing a realistic account of the past, narrates this period as a "collection of best practices."[246] Güler explains the main tactic of Sunni historiography on this period as the underrating of the impact of social and economic factors, and the reliance on religious factors. He thus describes the Sunni discourse on early Islamic history as a religious account of events.[247] Given that the rationalists spare large portions to the early Islamic period in their works, I shall limit my inquiry to four subjects when I analyze the rationalist revisionism on this period.

The Companions

For understandable reasons, there is special attention among the rationalists to the critique of the Sunni concept of companionship. The Islamic tradition on which Sunnism relies is mainly transmitted through the knowledge attributed to the companions.[248] Illustrating the central role of the companions in Sunnism, *İlmihal* emphasizes that "the words of companions" have special status in Islamic law.[249] Logically, dispensing with the Sunni tradition requires a revisionist view of the companions, whom Sunnism treats almost as infallible people. The rationalist aim is to challenge the treatment of all knowledge transmitted through the companions as if it were ipso facto authentic.[250] To achieve this goal, they conduct a highly critical discourse on the companions, which is deliberately designed to persuade that the companions were people who made many mistakes.

For this purpose, the rationalists first propose a narrow definition of "companionship." In fact, as discussed in Chapter 1, the rationalists' narrowing of the definition reminds of the classical Islamic schools like the Mu'tazila, which aimed to minimize the impact of traditions by reducing the number of companions through a definition so strict as to seriously reduce their number.[251] As we observe in Kırbaşoğlu, the rationalist find problematic the classical definition that casts a wide net: "whoever as a Muslim has seen the Prophet is a companion." A better definition is to include only Muslims who spent a satisfactory amount of time with Muhammad.[252] The rationalist reject also the regarding of the status of companionship as essentially a positive category.[253] They dismiss the traditional idea of companionship, for it mistakenly presents them as if they were infallible persons.[254] Güler points to the various tragic events like the civil wars, where thousands of companions killed each other brutally.[255] For Eliaçık, tragic events like the civil wars not only proved that the companions made serious mistakes but left a problematic political legacy to future generations from which Muslims still suffer.[256] Atay, too, underlines that what is called "the legacy of the companions" also includes negative elements for later generations.[257] As their third step, the rationalists narrow the category "Companion" by putting it vis-à-vis with "knowledge." On this view, being a companion is not always a qualification for transmitting religious knowledge. As we read in Yaşar Nuri, this point warns that narrating traditions from various early Muslims, on subjects on which they had no expertise, created the problem of giving a religious status to many awkward opinions.[258] As an example: Atay writes that there are many cases where "the shallow understanding of some companions" caused serious problems in Islamic law, such as the misunderstanding of Quran on punishment.[259]

Next, we read the rationalists submitting a seriously critical discourse on the companions by citing vivid details of their lives. Obviously, the purpose here is to prove their revisionist approach by pointing out how the idealistic portrayal of the companions in Sunnism is wrong. Under this rubric, we read many details where the companions are portrayed as normal people subject to various human conditions. To present an indictive list of examples: We read that Khalid ibn Walid killed many people during the conquest of Mecca, despite Muhammad's warning;[260] Talha ibn Ubeydallah and Zubayr ibn Avvam acted politically to gain their appointments as governors in Basra and Kufa. Aisha, Muhammad's favorite wife, behaved pragmatically in political fights.[261] Hassan, Muhammad's grandson, abused his social status by marrying more than ninety women.[262] Abd al-Rahman ibn Awf chased booty during the war rather than fight the enemy.[263] Umar thought of Sa'd ibn Ubade, a leading companion, as a hypocrite and also believed that Amr ibn al-As was, another important companion, involved in graft.²⁶⁴ Abdullah ibn Mas'ud believed that it was legitimate to kill Uthman.²⁶⁵ Companions like Abu Jandal ibn Suhayl, Dhiraar ibn Al-Azwar, and Kudame ibn Maz'un continued drinking alcohol, not believing that it is prohibited in Quran.²⁶⁶ Khalid ibn Walid had the habit of marrying the women or daughters of men he killed, a behavior even criticized by Abu Bakr in the letter quoted in al-Ya'qubi, al-Waqidi, and al-Tabari, where the caliph condemned Khalid for being obsessed with women.²⁶⁷ Again, Khalid ibn Walid killed people in the most brutal ways that are not seen proper in Islamic law.²⁶⁸ The companions accused one another of various serious crimes, such as adultery, robbery, and murder.²⁶⁹ Some companions drank so much on the night before the Uhud War that they were responsible for the loss of the battle. This demonstrates how the companions behaved even in critical times, though the event happened before the alcohol ban.²⁷⁰

The rationalists also submit a revisionist approach to Abu Bakr, Umar, Uthman, and Ali, who are venerated in Sunnism as the Rightly Guided Caliphs (*al-Khulafa al-Rashidun*) whose opinions and practices are reliable guides on Islam.²⁷¹ To begin with the fourth, Ali: Azimli and Balcı criticize him for appointing his relatives to key positions and consulting on government affairs with only a small group.²⁷² According to Atay, Ali practiced one-man rule, which resulted in wrong decisions during his reign.²⁷³ On Azimli's account, Ali engaged in tribal politics, creating anger among tribes other than his own, who were unsatisfied with that.²⁷⁴ Atay also challenges the Sunni mythological discourse that presents Ali as a great military commander. There are cases that contradict this narrative, such as Ali's failure to control the troops in the Siffin War.²⁷⁵ The revisionist narrative on Ali offers personal details on him too. We read that when he was sent to Yemen as a tax collector, he kept a concubine who was given by local tribes as a part of their local taxes.²⁷⁶

Revisionism on Umar is especially interesting, for he is known as "the saga of law and conquest" in Sunni Islam.²⁷⁷ The rationalists provide a revisionist history of Umar that attends to both these excellences. To begin with law: Atay faults Umar for centralizing power instead of delegating it to sophisticated councils.²⁷⁸ A second criticism is about tribalism. Umar's tribalism was evident in that he appointed many Hashimids. And he saw the Quraysh tribe as the inevitable pillar of statehood.²⁷⁹ Tribalism, Öztürk notes, created moral problems such as his relatives' rapid accumulation of wealth.²⁸⁰ However, for the rationalists, Umar's institutionalizing of tribalism to the point that it became almost a state principle was more outrageous. According to Azimli, Umar actually incorporated tribalism as a principle in the distribution of state revenues, giving higher incomes to several tribes.²⁸¹ Thus, for Yaşar Nuri, Umar's identity politics sowed the seeds of later Umayyad political ideology.²⁸² In view of this, Eliaçık does not hesitate to distrust Umar on ground of his failure to fulfill Islam's goal of establishing a Muslim brotherhood beyond tribal loyalty.²⁸³ For Yaşar Nuri, identity politics under Umar also caused problems in Muslims' relations with non-Muslims: His radical policies of sending Jews to Damascus, and Christians to Iraq, weakened the social balance of the early Islamic polity.²⁸⁴

When it comes to conquests, Umar is criticized by rationalists for his wrong strategic decisions during the expansion of Islam. Azimli asserts that when Roman Emperor Heraclius strategically left Syria to the Arabs, Umar was trapped by the Roman strategy, and, subsequently, he was satisfied to stay focused on the lands toward Iran rather than go beyond the Tauris mountains.[285] Balcı argues that this strategic mistake delayed the expansion of Islam in deep Anatolia. Besides, it gave the Romans the necessary time for military recovery.[286] For Güler, another strategic mistake of Umar, which is rather indirectly linked to the Muslim conquests, was his failure to sustain a balance between the economy and wars. This caused a legacy of skepticism in Islam about private property.[287] (Umar stopped distributing newly conquered lands and, instead, kept them as state-run resources. Logically, this brought a change to the power of the state in the economy.[288]) Other rationalists take up Güler's point by reminding that Umar did not refrain from confiscating private properties. This happened to Amr ibn As, Abu Hurayra, and Sad ibn Abu Vakkas, as well the properties of exiled Christians and Jews. One major legacy of such decisions was the onset of problematic relations between the state and private property.[289] Umar is criticized also for his military promotions. Abu Ubayd's knowledge of the Sassanids was limited.[290] So Azimli deems it a strategic mistake for Umar to have appointed him as Commander of the War of Jisr (634) against the Sassanids. This act displaced Musenna ibn Haris, who had been appointed by Abu Bakr. Similarly, Atay criticizes Umar for dismissing Khalid ibn al-Walid, the undisputed military hero of the whole history of early Islamic expansion.[291]

We observe also a revisionist approach to Abu Bakr, who is undisputedly the most important name in Sunni Islam after Muhammad. Again, we encounter criticisms such as tribalism, and of the pursuing of a one-man regime. According to Atay, the one-man rule mentality has its origin in Abu Bakr's political legacy.[292] What we observe in the case of Abu Bakr we shall observe (in the following text) also in the case of Uthman: the rationalists' criticism of the first four caliphs' failure to create a sophisticated administrative body. This is about their frustration with the general performance of the early caliphate as an institution. Reading about civil wars and sectarian conflicts, the rationalists—unlike the Sunni narrative—see the early caliphate as an ineffective political model. (This reminds of Ibn al-Muqaffa' (d. 756), who suggested adaptations of the Sassanid model, given that the early caliphate was inefficient at sustaining political stability.[293]) However, a more radical critique of Abu Bakr is linked to the various punishments he carried out during the Apostasy Wars, such as the burning and smashing bodies. The rationalists regarded this as the origin of radicalism in the Islamic tradition. As we read in Azimli, such inhuman practices were reincarnations of the pre-Islamic military customs.[294] But more critical is the political legacy that such practices left. Güler finds fault with Abu Bakr for his having left a legacy that is today referenced by radical groups like the ISIS.[295] Confirming Güler, ISIS mostly "centers its references on Abu Bakr," and sees his policies as "the guiding light for their strategy and legitimacy."[296] It should be pointed out that the self-proclaimed "Caliph of ISIS" gave himself the name "Abu Bakr." It is in the same vein that Atay sees Abu Bakr responsible for starting the problematic practice of killing Muslims for political reasons. To him, Abu Bakr started this practice during the Apostasy Wars, against the various tribes who refused to pay their *zakat* (alms) to the central caliphate in Medina.[297] Abu Bakr is here accused of treating those tribes as enemies, despite that they were Muslims who rebelled against the hegemony of Medina on political and financial, not religious, grounds.[298] Similarly, Azimli portrays Abu Bakr as the first Muslim ruler who ordered the execution of political rebels.[299]

Uthman occupies the largest space in the rationalist literature. In a certain sense, the rationalists understand the rule of Uthman as the case that provides all sorts of grounds for the revisionist critique of Sunni history. To begin with, the rationalists present Uthman's rule as the age of nepotism and corruption.[300] Even rationalists like Azimli and Yaşar Nuri do not hesitate to rank Uthman a few scales lower than the other three caliphs.[301] According to them, Uthman, occupied only by his clan's (the Umayyads') priorities, was not in full charge of political affairs.[302] However, this made tribes like Banu Bakr and Azd, who had played beneficial roles in the early wars of Islam, become dissatisfied with him.[303] Uthman was harsh also to his critics, and given to torturing and exiling them.[304] The rationalists provide many examples of nepotism and corruption under Uthman. Yaşar Nuri and Eliaçık give a list of governors appointed by Uthman, who had some personal connection with the caliph. The list has several names, such as Abdullah ibn Amir ibn Qurayz and Walid ibn Ukba, Uthman's closest relatives.[305] Uthman's relatives had the lion's share of public revenue. Marwan ibn Hakam, Uthman's cousin and son-in-law, was given the revenue of Medina market, as well as a large share of the revenue from Africa.[306] A large part of the Basra revenue was given to Abdullah ibn Khalid ibn Husayn, another relative.[307] Worse, as we read in the works of the rationalists, the caliph was never alarmed by the wrongdoings of his relatives and friends. He virtually let the budget become a private matter of the Umayyads.[308] When his chancellor, Abdullah ibn al-Arqam, attempted to stop funding Uthman's relatives from the budget, he was replaced by Zayd ibn Thabit, whom Azimli blames for "opening the doors of the Treasury to Uthman's relatives."[309] Zayd ibn Thabit, the head of the Uthman Commission, whom I analyzed earlier under the title "Revisionism on Quran," was a close friend of Uthman; he, too, became rich during the latter's rule.[310]

However, we encounter the most graphic illustrations when it comes to the assassination of Uthman. The details provided by the rationalists about Uthman's death have the capacity to shake the Sunni discourse on early Islam, teeming as it is with romanticized and idealized elements. Here is a short summary of the works of the rationalists on Uthman's death. Caliph Uthman was killed inhumanly. Not even the leading companions defended him, for they were upset by the caliph's nepotism and corruption. There were fewer than ten people at his funeral. The Caliph of Islam could be buried only at night, in a Jewish cemetery, due to the protests of an enraged people.[311] Talha, a leading companion, did not participate in Uthman's funeral.[312] People were not even mildly saddened by Uthman's killing.[313] Aisha, the Prophet's surviving and most beloved wife, thanked God when she was informed of Uthman's assassination. Other leading companions, like Talha, Zubayr, and even Ali, stayed silent, preferring to focus on their political strategies during the critical hours of Uthman's killing.³¹⁴ It was Abu Bakr's son Muhammad, who struck the last blow that killed Uthman. Caliph Uthman was eighty-six years old. He reportedly asked his killer whether his father, Abu Bakr, would have been happy to learn of what his son is doing. Muhammad, however, did not stop, and joined in the cutting of the caliph's throat. In the meantime, the accomplices were digging their knives into Uthman's throat, and hitting his head. Though acting horrendously, they were relatively calm, and some of them were even singing. Shocked and helpless, Naile, Uthman's wife, made a hopeless attempt to save her husband by offering herself to the assassins. But they were not interested in the offer, for she was not young.³¹⁵ The caliph's body was left in different places for several days before the funeral. Quoting al-Tabari, Azimli says that one leg of the body was eaten by dogs.³¹⁶

Bringing Material Causes Back In

The early Islamic history, which we read from the rationalists, unlike Sunni history, which concerns itself primarily with the religious factor, is a history of material dynamics like economic and political factors.³¹⁷ We do not see in the rationalists what Aziz al-Azmeh describes as the belief that nonmaterial elements distinguish Islamic history from the histories of other societies.³¹⁸ Take, for example, how the rationalists approach the expansion of Islam: Sunni history is per se a history of religious motivation and sacrifice. In diametric opposition, Güler writes that tribalism was a dynamic of early Islamic expansion, which Sunni history later intentionally ignored.³¹⁹ Balcı expands the impact of identity by introducing another factor: Arabic identity. He reminds how non-Muslim Arabs fought Arab Muslims in many wars. As expected, the involvement of non-Arab Muslims in the expansion of Islam breaks down the standard narration, which sees everything in this period through religious lenses. For example, the Arab identity emerged as an important dynamic, particularly in the wars against the Sassanids. Caliphs Abu Bakr and Umar benefited enormously from an Arabist agenda against the Sassanids and the Romans, so much so that the strategy, even for Balcı, later backfired by giving way to Umayyad racism, as well as in the angering of non-Arab Muslims.³²⁰ As the case after the Buwayb War (635) during the caliphate of Umar, when Christian Arab tribes supported the Muslim armies against the Sassanids, political tensions rose among the local people, the rulers, and the non-Muslim populations.³²¹

The rationalists also incorporate economic motivation into their accounts of the expansion of Islam. Balcı cites economic expectations as a major factor behind the motivation of Arabs during the expansion of Islam. It was so persuasive that even non-Muslim Arab tribes fought with Muslims. Given that Hijaz was a poor region, for Balcı, war quickly transformed into a mechanism to generate revenue for the emerging Muslim society. Even some expeditions, like the ones to Egypt and Rhodes, were undertaken primarily to raise revenue, not to promote religious expansion.³²² Similarly, the expansion of Islam toward Syria and Palestine during Abu Bakr's reign was motivated mainly by economic concerns. To persuade tribes to participate in the military expeditions, Caliph Abu Bakr mentioned the richness of the northern lands, for there were obviously various tribes whose prime interest in war was booty.[323] The complex relationship between wars and the economy transformed the Islamic polity. Yaşar Nuri spots that wars had already become a means of raising revenue for Umar's caliphate.[324]

Seeing the wars during the expansion of Islam mostly as fought for political and financial motives, the rationalists accuse that they were therefore deviations from the Islamic theory of *jihad*. Güler argues that Muslims expanded the idea of *jihad* by incorporating new elements, like economic factors, and the result was the new doctrine of *fath* (conquest) that was to justify wars that acquire new lands and financial resources.[325] Yaşar Nuri thus considers only a few wars after Muhammad to be legitimate on religious grounds. For him, many wars were fought for economic benefit, mainly land acquisition.[326] Balcı says that it was the Sunni scholars who later framed military activism as religious wars.[327] However, for Güler, such later Sunni corrections are nonsense. He lampoons them harshly, likening the corrections to "raping a woman, calling the feat a conquest, then marrying her in the name of *jihad*, and finally, arguing that all this was done to protect her."[328] He does not even hesitate to call the various wars after the death of Muhammad "occupations."[329]

Beyond the complex relations of economic factors and wars, the rationalists present how the early Muslims—whom Sunni history depicts as heroic personalities above worldly aspirations—paid serious attention to booty. We read, for example, that the companions had frequent quarrels over the distribution of the booty. After the Taif Incursion, Azimli reports, the companions cornered Muhammad, for they were not happy about the distribution of booty.[330] A similar case happened, as Balcı narrates, after the Hayber War, when the Prophet gave the Abyssinian Muslims a share of the booty.[331] According to Azimli, such intra-Muslim quarrels happened after almost every expedition.[332] The rationalists simply tell us that the expansion of Islamic society naturally provided a lot of financial opportunities for the early Muslims. Eliaçık reminds of the fortunes of the various members of the *Ashara Mubashara* (the ten companions promised paradise), and noted that some of them were so rich that they had hundreds of villages paying taxes to them. Eliaçık finds no poor companion among them.[333] Similarly, Azimli notes that some of those ten companions had hundreds of slave women.[334] In this, Azimli spots a conflation of religious reasoning and economic factors in the early Islamic period. He points to the quickly fabricated traditions like "no religions will survive in the Arab peninsula" after Umar exiled the Christians and Jews in Hejaz, and distributed their lands to his people.[335]

The Myth of Islamic Republicanism

Many Muslims interpret the period of the Four Rightly Guided Caliphs as a republic.[336] The idea became popular among Islamist intellectuals in Turkey, particularly in the late Ottoman and early Republican periods.[337] Since then, imagining the early caliphate as a republic has survived as a popular and charming idea, particularly in Turkey.[338] According to this imagination, it is claimed that the first four caliphs were elected by the people. The rationalists dismiss this discourse as another Sunni construction. According to them, the early caliphate was not a successful political regime to be regarded as democracy or republic, for several reasons. It had many deficits and weak points.[339] However, I shall not detail here how the rationalists elaborate the failures of the early caliphate, since I have already done this in the previous sections, particularly under the subheading "The Companions." I shall instead limit my discussion to the general problems of the early caliphate, as analyzed in the works of the rationalists:[340] Firstly, the system had no clear rule to govern the transition of power. Secondly, there was no legitimate framework for the opposition.[341] Thirdly, the system had no checks-and-balances mechanism to control the caliph. Fourthly, women had virtually no role in the whole procedure.[342] Fifthly, tribalism was always essential to the caliphate.[343]

Beyond institutional shortcomings, the rationalists describe the early caliphate as a model derived from Arab tribal customs, which cannot be likened to a democracy or a republic. For the rationalists, the veneration of the early caliphate as an ideal Islamic administrative model is also wrong, since it was not derived from Quran, nor is it the legacy of the Prophet.[344] The point the rationalists make is that the "ideal Islamic administrative model" is a thorough misunderstanding of the nature of the caliphate. Elsewhere, al-Azmeh notes that the misunderstanding is that "God in Islam mandates a blueprint for the system of governance called the caliphate."[345] For the rationalists, too, the early caliphate is a model derived from Arab customs. Öztürk writes that the debates after the death of Muhammad prove that there was no known Quranic principle to govern the leadership issue.[346] Abu Bakr was elected mainly in line with the previous *jahilliya* methods by a comparatively small group composed of leading tribal elites, not of all Muslims.[347] In this context, the support of the Aws tribe given to Abu Bakr had the motive of preventing someone from the Khazraj becoming the next leader. This was a typical tribal pattern.[348] Similarly, the election of Umar was by no means a republican method; it was heavily affected by traditional tribal factors. Reminding that Umar was elected because of Abu Bakr's nomination of him, Atay claims that this method sacrificed Islamic principles to Arab traditional patterns. For him, Abu Bakr's nomination of Umar later became a source of inspiration to the Muawiya engaged in establishing a dynastic monarchy.[349] In the same way, Umar's setting up of a small council to elect the new caliph after himself was a reflection of tribal balances. The council was composed of Quraysh representatives.[350] The council, for Azimli, therefore opened the gate for a Quraysh aristocratic hegemony that would gradually lead to the Umayyad monarchy.[351] However, for Atay, the central role of tribal and traditional factors later generated wrong political positions, such as accepting Quraysh as the center of Islamic polity.[352] Thus, the problem is, as Balcı writes, the incorporation by Sunni scholars of the whole experience of the early caliphate as if it were a religious framework.[353] The rationalists' opinions are in harmony with other scholars, such as al-Jabri, who reminded that the Sunni thinking failed to conceptualize the question of the caliphate until al-Shafi'i, after whom the issues linked to the caliphate became a religious doctrine.[354]

Redefining Jahiliya

The rationalists are against the strong negative emphasis on *jahilliya* in Sunni history that presents Islam as a radical rupture from the previous age. They interpret the Sunni concept of *jahilliya* is an "official history" according to which the pre-Islamic Arab society is purposefully presented as violent, ignorant, and immoral.[355] Öztürk writes that the Sunni view of *jahilliya* gives a wrong picture of pre-Islamic Arabs, who had many cultural and institutional merits.[356] Yaşar Nuri underlines that history did not begin with Quran.[357] Unlike Sunnism, the rationalists therefore do not regard pre-Islamic Arab society in negative terms such as imagining Islam as the continuation of the Arab customs and culture.[358] To reemphasize: Imagining Islam as the continuity of Arab culture is a main premise of rationalist thought. As we analyzed in Chapter 2, many rationalist opinions, such as treating shari'a as a framework derived from Arab customs, are based on the assumption that Islamic law is a continuation of the pre-Islamic Arab culture.

The rationalists are particularly interested in how Islamic rituals are connected to pre-Islamic Arabic practices. According to them, the Sunni view of *jahilliya*, which reads Islam as a radical break from the past, creates the delusion that approaching rituals and laws as if they were divine directives is to be imitated forever. Logically, rationalist revisionism aims to illustrating how Islamic rules and rituals are the updated or modified versions of pre-Islamic Arab customs.[359] As a result, we read detailed accounts in rationalist works of how Islamic beliefs, rules, and rituals are updated versions of the pre-Islamic Arab society.[360] Öztürk writes that the pre-Islamic Arabs had the idea of destiny, afterlife, resurrection, angels, ablution, prayer, almsgiving, fasting, and sacrificing animals.[361] The Arabs even knew Allah as the creator of earth and sky.[362] Thus, for Balcı, Islam did not introduce a totally unknown God but corrected Arabs' opinions of Allah, reminding that Quran recognizes that most *jahilliya* Arabs had faith in Allah but corrects their joining of idols to him.[363] Referring to such similarities, Eliaçık explains Islam as a selective reorganization of the previous cultural patterns.[364] Öztürk illustrates this by asserting that Muhammad kept up almost 90 percent of the pre-Islamic practices.[365] The rationalists emphasize especially that many rituals of Islam, such as prayer and *hajj* (pilgrimage), were practiced also by pre-Islamic Arabs.[366] Azimli reminds that the Arabs were not surprised when they were asked to perform prayers, since it was already known by them.[367] Balcı writes that Quran (8:35) itself informs of how pre-Islamic Arabs performed prayer in front of Ka'ba.[368] Similarly, Öztürk sees no major difference between the Islamic and pre-Islamic *hajj* rituals.[369] Supporting Öztürk, Balcı, and Azimli give many details to illustrate that what is known as the Islamic rites of *hajj* were mostly initiated by Qusay ibn Qilab, who reorganized the tribes and social life of Mecca in the late fifth century.[370] The similarities can be observed even in small detail, such as the rite of shaving, which was also practiced by pre-Islamic Arabs during the visit to their tribal idol.[371]

As one would imagine, the continuity thesis about rituals is a strong one that Sunnism takes into serious consideration. Thus, even though Sunni history narrates Islamic history as a rupture from the past, when it comes to some hard facts such as *hajj* and Ka'ba—the roles of which even Sunnism cannot deny among the pre-Islamic Arabs—Sunni scholars appeal to an alternate discourse according to which those pre-Islamic customs are reinterpreted as the remnants of Abraham's monotheism.[372] So, what Islam continued is not *jahilliya* customs, but the remnants of Abraham's religion.[373] We read in *İlmihal* that Ka'ba was constructed by Abraham and his son. The angel then taught them how to perform prayers, such as circumambulating the Ka'ba.[374]

Conclusion

The goal of rationalist revisionism in the early Islamic society is to illustrate how this period was a failure—contrary to what the Sunni accounts portrays—in terms of fulfilling the various grand promises of Islam, such as solving economic disparities among the social classes, or establishing a just society.[375] While analyzing the protests during the Caliph Ali period, Atay notes that the majority of rebels were the young people who happened to have been born during the times of previous caliphs. This indicates the frustration of the new generation at that point of the early Islamic society.[376] Basically, the rationalists give the message that Islamic norms should be the prime sources of religious reasoning, not the practices of the early Muslims, who had already failed to address those norms.

On the other hand, rationalist revisionism has the pragmatic goal of putting an end to a major element of the Sunni idea of history. Franz Rosenthal wrote that Muslims believe that all crucial developments in Islam had their source in the early ideal periods.[377] Accordingly, Muslims look to the practices of the early Islamic period to justify various issues, or to solve the problems they encounter in the present.[378] However, as Konrad Hirschler notes, by drawing such parallels with past, later generations discover genetic interconnections with the previous founding fathers, and, in so doing, history has become organized around the notion of endless repetition, not change.[379] This is an approach that can be summarized as with the motto "the future is in the past."[380] The rationalists do not rate this view as a consistent and helpful paradigm. For them, the present should not model the future on the precepts of the distant past. Özsoy writes that there is no idea of decline in Islam that rates the Islamic past as a better epoch than the present. Instead, causal dynamics determine the flow of history, and those dynamics throw up both better and worse situations.[381] The ultimate goal of rationalist revisionism is to direct the attention of Muslims away from the past to the present.

Chapter 4

POLITICS AND SOCIETY

WHAT WENT WRONG?

There is a widely shared understanding that posits a causal link between how Islam is interpreted and the problems that plague various Muslim societies. Accordingly, the interpretation and the concomitant practice of Islam are identified as the causes of the various problems that beset Muslim societies in regard of democracy, law, and scientific and technological issues.[1] This is not, of course, to explain all problems in Muslim societies in terms of Islam alone. Instead, it is to mean to point out that how Muslims interpret Islam is a major problem along with others. As we have already highlighted several times in previous chapters, the rationalists, too, see how Islam is today interpreted and practiced as a major reason behind many problems that we encounter in Muslim societies.

In this regard, the notorious question "what went wrong?" steers the querist to a mainstream perspective in contemporary Muslim thought that explains the poor state of Muslim societies as a result of various historical developments. Accordingly, a decline happened in Islamic history that damaged leading Muslim societies, once at the forefront of advanced civilization. W. Cantwell Smith glosses this approach critically as imagining that "something has gone wrong with Islamic history," then concluding that Muslims' mission is "to rehabilitate that history" so that Muslims may once again flourish.[2] The rationalists are interested in this grand debate, as they too accept that various developments in history gave way to a problematic interpretation of Islam that is still causing many problems among Muslims.[3] As one would expect, answering the question "what went wrong?" is, for the rationalists, to tell which political and social events, as well as intellectual trends, worked in Islamic history to give way to the consolidation of the Sunni political and intellectual *status quo*. So they address the Sunni interpretation of Islam as the historical and paradigmatic source of the problems of Muslims. In previous parts of this book, I have directly or indirectly touched upon many of the factors that the rationalists see as the historical origins of the decline of Islamic societies. Therefore, in the following text, I shall now only reemphasize them under their various headings, and analyze how the rationalists join the "what went wrong" debate by providing their historical perspective.

The Mainstream Theory of Decay

The rationalists adhere to what could be called "the mainstream theory of decay" (aka the Sunni revival theory), a grand narrative that argues that it was the various developments between the eleventh and thirteenth centuries that marked a major break from the previous age (dubbed "the golden age of Islam") that created the dynamics that later caused the decay in Islamic societies. Accordingly, the decline of Muslim societies has its origins in developments such as the rise of the Ghazalian paradigm, which is believed to have destroyed rationalist thought in the Islamic tradition, and the rise of a new statehood inspired by the Sassanid tradition, which is believed to have weakened the trade-oriented mentality of Islamic societies.[4] More critically, the aforementioned changes later developed a religious orthodoxy in the post-Abbasid period, mainly through new actors like the Saljuqis, where governments and religion formed an alliance of perfect cooperation. This affected religious reasoning. On this account, administrative ideas and practices borrowed from the Sassanids were incorporated into the Islamic tradition, creating a radical break with the previous egalitarian models, and they subsequently transformed Islamic societies into a different model, where a government enjoys a veritably transcendental quality.[5] The Saljuqi madrasas, seen as the reflection of the new alliance between Islam and political authority, played a special role in this transformation that promoted and consolidated a new religious thinking in line with political changes.[6] The doctrinal uniformity required by the new political configuration of the post-Abbasid period was forged by those madrasas, in return for political and financial support.[7] The ongoing tensions between the Saljuqis and the Ismailis of the period, often erupting as military fights as well as stoking shocking events like the assassination of the Seljuqi Grand Vizier Nizam Mulk, were indeed another factor that pushed Sunni scholars and Seljuqi statesmen closer.[8] Such complex developments resulted in the Sunni Islamic orthodoxy, which is addressed by the mainstream theory of decay as mainly responsible for the decline of Islamic civilization.[9]

Adhering to the mainstream paradigm, the rationalist brand of the "what went wrong?" narrative also recognizes the period between the eleventh and thirteenth centuries as relevant in the understanding of the historical roots of the many problems that Muslims societies encounter today.[10] Thus, the rationalists approach critically the new concept of statehood, which came into being as result of external receptions, mainly from the Sassanid culture. For the rationalists, the Sassanid impact introduced a new type of rulership, where rulers assume some sort of religious nature, which inevitably resulted in a hierarchical relationship of the state, the people, and religion.[11] Rulers, who acquired some sort of transcendental characteristics, are now above both religion and society. Atay writes that the Sassanid elements transformed rulership into a quite unprecedented transcendental or sacred mission.[12] Subsequently, the rise of a new concept of statehood, as well as a new type of relationship between state and religion, allowed the Islamic society to acquire the capacity to develop a religious orthodoxy. The model where society and religion are organized under the control of an absolute statehood later became the organizing principle of Muslim societies.¹³ In Güler's view, Sunnism has since then survived as a state-friendly "rightist" perspective.¹⁴

Again, in parallel with the Sunni revival thesis, the rationalists see the Saljuqi *madrasa* as a key institution in this historical transformation, for the role it played in the consolidation of the nascent Sunni orthodoxy. Güler presents the *madrasa* as designed to serve the new relationship between state and religion, where a traditionalists and state-friendly interpretation of religion was promoted.¹⁵ Thus, for Atay, the *madrasa* is a symbol of political authority over religion at the expense of the autonomy of scholars, a model which ended all intellectual anarchism in the Muslim world.¹⁶ After the advent of the *madrasa*, the Islamic intellectual tradition became inward looking, and was no longer interested in Greek philosophy.¹⁷ Now, as a religious orthodoxy supported by the state, the new model left no chance for alternate religious interpretations to survive.¹⁸ Thus, for the rationalists, the new relationship between rulers and religious scholars, which is the backbone of the Sunni orthodoxy, is a key factor in the stagnancy of Islamic thought. According to Yaşar Nuri, Islam is, since the birth of Sunni orthodoxy, a religion of power politics. This was not so in the previous ages, where scholars dominated.¹⁹ Thus, for Atay, Islam as taught in the *madrasa* quickly responded to the new alliance between religion and state. Islamic education, particularly in the law, became a disciplining instrument in the hands of traditionalist scholars, as well as of the political rulers.²⁰ The inevitable consequence of this new model is Islam's becoming a religion of law, having lost its previous friendly and fruitful relationship with theology and philosophy.²¹

One major consequence of the birth of Sunni orthodoxy is the decline of rationalist thought in the Islamic tradition. The rationalists analyze this decline in terms of the legacy of al-Ghazali, again in line with the mainstream theory of decay. They repeat the known critique of al-Ghazali, which depicts him as the symbol of the traditionalists' triumph over the rationalists in the Islamic tradition.²² In this regard, al-Ghazali is accused of institutionalizing an enmity toward rationalist philosophy in the Muslim world. Yet, his legacy, that is the ongoing dichotomy in Islamic societies of reason and the revelation, still affects Islamic thought and Muslim societies negatively.²³ Again in parallel with the Sunni revival thesis, the rationalists see al-Ghazali's incorporation of Sufism into mainstream Islamic thought as another negative element of his anti-rationalist legacy.²⁴ As we read in Öztürk, the critical point here is the recognition by al-Ghazali of "inner knowledge" as another form of revelation.²⁵ Inner knowledge is an esoteric type of knowledge acquired without sensory perception or reasoning, through a self-realization that transcends all spatiotemporal dimensions. Al-Ghazali defined this knowledge as not coming about "by systematic demonstration or marshalled argument, but by a light that God most high cast into my breast. That light is the key to the greater part of knowledge."²⁶ Of course, bestowed by God's grace, inner knowledge is the supreme knowledge.²⁷ For Atay, the inner-knowledge concept developed a new understanding in which reason is only a secondary authority.²⁸ Equally critically, Öztürk writes that al-Ghazali incorporated esoteric methods like *i'tibar*—a method where the verses are taken introspectively as symbols of complex esoteric meanings in the background—into the interpretation of Quran, which lead to completely frameless and arbitrary conclusions about the meaning of the verses.[29] In consequence, the incorporation of Sufism into the Sunnism is condemned by the rationalists for it left anti-rationalist legacies, such as seeing revelation and inner knowledge as always superior to reason, and a strong foundation for an esoteric interpretation of Quran.[30]

A second subject in the rationalist critique of al-Ghazali is political theory. The rationalists censure al-Ghazali for justifying a new political model, that is, the post-Abbasid Seljuqi order, which subjugates religion to political authority.[31] Eliaçık writes that the model that al-Ghazali legitimized imitates the Sassanid tradition, where religion and state are seen as twins.[32] In this regard, Eliaçık likens al-Ghazali's legacy to St. Augustine's *City of God* inasmuch as both propose a theory of religion-state relations.[33] In a sense, the rationalists interpret the works of al-Ghazali as reflecting the new hierarchical society maintained in part by the cooperation of state and religion. However, doing this, al-Ghazali made two mistakes. Firstly, by incorporating loyalty to the sultan into the Islamic paradigm, al-Ghazali destroyed the idea of social contract in the Islamic tradition, replacing it with a pure theory of subjugation.[34] Secondly, al-Ghazali justified the political rulers' destruction of the autonomy of scholars, and their being put under strict control and patronage, a key feature of the nascent Sunni orthodoxy, which prioritizes raison d'etat.[35] Yaşar Nuri illustrates the new relationship between scholars and rulers as "never writing anything that could anger Nizam al-Mulk," the Grand Vizier of the Saljuqs who was behind the Saljuqi madrasas where al-Ghazali worked.[36] In the matter of cooperation between scholars and rulers, Öztürk critically reminds how al-Ghazali tried to prove why obedience to Caliph Al-Mustazhir (reigned 1094–1118) was an Islamic obligation.[37]

On the other hand, beyond specific critical points on the legacy of al-Ghazali, the rationalists are especially furious with him, for his legacy still affects Muslims.[38] Güler repeats the famous aphorism starring al-Ghazali, where his influence is graded as the strongest on Muslims after Muhammad's.[39] The rationalists find it necessary to challenge al-Ghazali today. Their works have many direct and indirect attacks on him, not sparring even the quality of his scholarship. For example, not finding him an original scholar, Güler depicts al-Ghazali as a populist author whose magnum opus, *Ihya*, contains too many quotations from other scholars.[40] Echoing the same criticism of this sort of populism, Atay repeats that al-Ghazali's works include many echoes of previous scholars, so his is not an original contribution to Islamic thought, for he effectively taught people to be satisfied with previous works.[41] Reading the rationalists, we detect a special aversion to *Ihya*. It is faulted for its many deficits, such as not being original but populist, promoting patriarchal ideas against women, promoting imitation rather than intellectual inquiry, resting arguments on fabricated traditions, not quoting previously written books accurately, narrating untrue stories under the rubric of miracles, and for many other shortcomings.[42] Öztürk categorizes *Ihya* as an example of the "popular religious fiction book."[43] Such critiques are probably due to the ongoing impact of this book on average Muslims across the Muslim world. Like in many other countries, *Ihya* has succeeded to be the standard book in Turkish households.

Ash'arism: The Paradigmatic Obstacle

The rise of Ash'arism is the convenient reason for rationalists to explain the many problems that have their origins in the interpretation of Islam. Accordingly, the consolidation of the Ash'ari school of theology as a dominant paradigm in the Muslim world—which was possible thanks to the Sunni orthodoxy based on the alliance between the state and religion in the post-Abbasid period[44]—virtually destroyed the rationalist elements in the Islamic tradition and reframed Islamic thought in line with the traditionalist tenets. On this account, the rationalists simply see Ash'arism as a paradigm that is unable to generate rational and effective solutions to Muslims' problems.[45] In this regard, the poverty of Sunnism for the rationalists is essentially a reflection of the poverty of Ash'arism.[46] As a matter of fact, the rationalist critique of Sunnism—as we observed many times throughout this book—is the collection of their critiques of various Ash'ari scholars. Thus, it is no wonder that the scholars frequently criticized by the rationalists, such as al-Shafi'i and al-Ghazali, are renowned Ash'aris.[47]

In some other chapters, I discussed in detail how Ash'arism, through key representatives like al-Shafi'i and al-Ghazali, consolidated an anti-rationalist stance in Islam. Not repeating those arguments here, I shall present only how the rationalists interpret the legacy of Ash'arism in regard of the "what went wrong" debate. For the rationalists, Ash'arism is the theological framework behind Sunnism and its deficiencies, such as the repudiating of causality and free will, all of which have prohibited Muslims' development of a consistent approach to nature, or of an effective theory of freedom. The Ash'ari view successfully convinced Muslims that God is the agent of everything in nature.[48] One natural consequence of this mindset is the identification of Islamic law (rules) as the main, if not the sole, framework to rule human life.[49] However, the mindset caused by Ash'arism leads Muslims to fatalism, and for the rationalists; that is why there is an inertia among Muslims: If Islamic rules provide answer to all questions, and if God is the agent of all events in nature, as the Ash'ari mindset asserts, then there is not much space for human agency.[50] Along this line of thinking, Atay writes that Ash'arism promotes a fatalism that leads to Muslims' self-destruction of their thinking and reasoning faculties.[51] For Güler, it breeds nihilism in Islamic thought.[52] To conclude: Ash'arism, for it prohibits Muslims' development of a successful religious paradigm in terms of science, nature, and society, is seen by the rationalists as a major obstacle in the way of progress in social and technological fields.[53]

al-Shafi'i: "The Villain"

The global reformist literature usually faults the Islamic tradition by focusing on al-Ghazali. He is regarded as the central figure of the grand debate between traditionalism and rationalism about Islamic thought. Similarly, there is almost a consensus among the rationalists to read the failure of the rationalist trajectory in the Islamic tradition as al-Ghazali's anti-rationalist legacy. However, though they are also critical of al-Ghazali, the "villain" of the "what went wrong" debate is, for all nine rationalists, al-Shafi'i. So, intellectually, it is al-Shafi'i, not al-Ghazali, whom the rationalists blame as primarily responsible for the negative legacy of the problems pertaining to the interpretation of Islam. I have already pointed out the rationalists' critical stance on al-Shafi'i several times in previous chapters by reporting how they see the legacy of al-Shafi'i as the prime causer of the many problematic religious interpretations among Muslims. As all those discussions illustrate, the gist of the rationalist critique of al-Shafi'i is his scholastic method of reducing Islamic reasoning to a search for solutions only in religious texts, the Quran and the traditions.[54]

But, why is al-Shafi'i, not al-Ghazali or any other, the "villain" in the rationalist narrative of Islamic intellectual history? The answer lies in the impact of methodology. For the rationalists, it is al-Shafi'i's scholastic methodology that shaped Sunnism as we know it. In this regard, his impact is far greater than that of other scholars like al-Ghazali, who can be listed only for their intellectual influence. Put another way: al-Shafi'i is the scholar whose methodology defined, and even made, Sunnism.[55] Reflecting this, the rationalists attribute Sunnism to the Shafi'i methodology that determined how Islamic law is interpreted, and how the prophetic sunnah should be understood. Thus, the rationalists do not see al-Shafi'i as another influential scholar like al-Ghazali; they see him as the architect of Sunnism.

Indeed, the rise of the Shafi'i *madhab* as the dominant Islamic law school, particularly in the heartland of Islamic societies, including the Arab regions, played a key role in spreading the al-Shafi'i scholastic method. This point is also critical in regard of the contribution of al-Shafi'i to the survival of Ash'arism, as the Shafi'i legal school has been the historical transmitter of Ash'arism in the Muslim world. The Shafi'i-Ash'ari axis successfully become the dominant legal and theological paradigm in the Muslim world, as far afield as the regions where the competing Hanafi-Maturidi school is supposed to have been dominant, like in Turkey.[56] As a matter of fact, it was the impact and opportunities provided by the Shafi'i-Ash'ari axis that allowed al-Ghazali to emerge as a star.[57] To remind: al-Ghazali was a graduate of the Nishapur madrasa founded by Saljuqis. He became famous as a member of this madrasa system of Saljuqis, the embodiment of Sunni orthodoxy.[58] Kırbaşoğlu correctly spots that the purge of Mu'tazila—which was usually explained in the standard narrative of the mainstream theory of decay in reference to al-Ghazali versus the rationalists—was in fact made possible in large part by the rise of the Shafi'i school as the mainstream paradigm.[59] It is therefore al-Shafi'i who come before al-Ghazali in the works of the rationalists that narrate the triumph of traditionalism over rationalism within the context of the "what went wrong" grand debate.

The Umayyads: The Distortion of Islam

The Sunni revival thesis, as summarized earlier, centers on the consolidation of Sunnism in the post-Abbasid period. However, for the rationalists, the "what went wrong" debate refers also to developments that occurred well before the Sunni revival. So the Umayyads occupy a special place in their works, for they see the Umayyads as the stereotypical ultra-decay in Islamic history: Arabism, corruption, the politicization of religion, the distortion of religious theology, and the fabricating of traditions.[60] But, methodologically, the Umayyads grab the attention of the rationalists for two reasons. Firstly, they see the Umayyads as the originators of the various wrong religious opinions and practices, such as the Sunni view of destiny and its concept of ritualistic piety. The rationalist critique of Sunnism thus necessitates a revisionist view of the Umayyads, the sources of the problems in Islam. Secondly, the revisionist view of the Umayyads provides many opportunities for the rationalists to find fault in any actor or practice that they do not endorse. It should be noted that negative reference to the Umayyads is a rarely tolerated critical thinking in contemporary Muslim societies.[61] We frequently encounter the frame *Emevi İslam'ı* (the Umayyad Islam) in the rationalists' works. For example, Yaşar Nuri lambasts the JDP and the Gülen movement for their sympathetic approach to Umayyad Islam. According to him, the Islamist JDP's rule employs "the typical Umayyad policies," such as using religion as a political instrument, as well as for authoritarian purposes.[62]

When it comes to "what went wrong" during the Umayyads, the rationalists first underline that the Umayyads institutionalized hereditary rulership, a key deviation from the practice that had prevailed since Muhammad.[63] As is known, Muawiyya designated his son Yazid as his heir. For Güler, the Umayyad usurpation of political rule was one of the key historical developments that caused the "stillbirth" of Islamic political theory.[64] The rationalists see the Islamic tradition as being led astray from Quranic principles by the Umayyad hereditary monarchy.[65] Eliaçık calls this shift a "practical distortion" of Islam.[66] In fact, as we discussed in Chapter 3, the rationalists are aware of the institutional weakness of the early caliphate. Azimli thinks that the early caliphate was poised to end up as a kind of monarchy sooner or later, given its structural deficits.[67] However, they do not see the shift to hereditary rule as the Islamically correct adjustment of the early caliphate.

Secondly, the rationalists accuse the Umayyads of having started the politicizing of religion:[68] They adopted the various strategies of using religion for political purposes, such as using the *masjid* (a house of worship) to deliver their political messages.[69] In the view of Güler, whereas religion used to oversee politics, the Umayyads put religion under the control of politics.[70] For Yaşar Nuri, putting religion into the service of politics effectively transformed Islam into a political instrument insensitive to the moral norms, no longer a top priority.[71] Instead, religious reasoning became a function of political reasoning under the Umayyads. This reminds of Gibb's analysis of the Umayyads where he emphasizes that they developed a new statehood under which hereditary monarchy, along with many new functions, paved the way for the thinking that the interest of Islam comes second to the interest of the state/the Umayyads.[72] Such gaps in the Umayyad system made the use of power more appealing to the political elites than the traditional methods, such as consultation and persuasion in pursuit of social legitimacy.[73]

Consequently, the failure of traditional political norms such as consultation left the Umayyads with other instruments, such as centralized power, other ancillary instruments like tribalism, and the distribution of state revenues.[74] However, as we read in Eliaçık and Güler, the rise of sheer power as the central element of state-society relations transformed politics into a field of ultra-pragmatism that disconnected politics from ethics.[75] The upshot of this new power equation was the excessive exertion of power in state-society relations.[76] Moreover, for Güler, this state-society relations mentality initiated a new pattern in Islamic history that stretched from the Umayyads to the Ottomans. On that continuum, "politics" consisted of subjugation by power holders, legitimate or not.[77]

Of the negative legacy of the Umayyads regarding the interpretation of religion, the rationalists discuss various subjects. For example, ritualistic piety—which I discussed in Chapter 2—is attributed by the rationalists to the Umayyads. For the rationalists, this is another major historical dynamic that explains "what went wrong" in Islamic history. Yaşar Nuri calls ritualistic piety "a genetic change" in religion.[78] Ritualistic piety disconnected piety from morality in politics, economics, and society. The rationalists think that the Umayyads promoted ritualistic piety because it served their political interests.[79] Piety as the mere repetition of various formal rituals, rather than piety as social and political morality, later became convenient for the political elites.[80] However, as I have already discussed the rationalist critique of ritualistic piety in Chapter 2, in this section I shall elaborate another subject of the negative legacy of the Umayyads: destiny.

According to the rationalists, the Umayyads' politization of religion gave way to an innovation in theology which is as another historical reason that explains the poor state of Muslim societies. This innovation in theology was in practice a modification of the concept of *qadar* in Islam that turned it into what is today known as "destiny." The motive behind the Umayyad strategy to promote a new interpretation of *qadar* was to justify their policies by presenting them to the public as predestined by God.[81] The rationalists are in principle against predestination, for it contradicts the concept of free will, a core rationalist value.[82] For them, the term *qadar* in Quran refers to the order, or measure, in nature, and has nothing to do with the predestination of human deeds.[83] Thus, for the rationalists, the Umayyad concept of "destiny"—which later became a key Sunni principle—was developed on an overinterpretation of a term in Quran that destroyed its meaning. Sunni scholars mistakenly reinterpreted *qadar* to mean "predestination."[84] To support the rationalist thesis, we observe frequent references to al-Nasafi's *Tabsirat al-Adilla*, where "destiny" is not counted as a principle of Islamic faith.[85] Again, there are various references to other scholars, such as Hasan al-Basri, who were critical of the Umayyads on "destiny,"[86] or Ibn Taymiyya, who is reported to have argued that *qadar* in Quran is not about human deeds but about nature.[87]

The rationalists also devote long sections to persecuted scholars, for they reject the Umayyad concept of "destiny." In this vein, the famous cases of Ma'bad al-Juhani and Gaylan al-Dimashqi, who were killed by the Umayyad authorities,[88] are analyzed in detail.[89] Supporting free will, both scholars were critical of the Umayyad concept of "destiny." The rationalists take particular note of al-Awzai's fatwa supporting the execution of Gaylan al-Dimashki. For them, this case illustrates how traditionalist/traditionist-minded scholars took part in the consolidation of "destiny" in the Islamic tradition.[90] Al-Awzai (d. 774) was a typical traditionist/traditionalist who rejected rationalist methods in Islamic jurisprudence. He was known for his hostile approach to Abu Hanifa.[91] Indeed, for the rationalists, cases of the execution of opposing scholars prove that the Umayyad concept of "destiny" became institutionalized in Islam by means of sheer power. Güler here reminds that the Muʿtazila school even declared justice a pillar of Islam in response to the Umayyad policy of enforcing "destiny."[92] In this regard, the rationalists' discussions on "destiny" is a reflection of the historical tension between traditionalists and rationalists. Like the classical rationalists, the contemporary rationalists are against the Sunni concept of "destiny." Naturally, the rationalists' rejection of "destiny" is another serious departure from Sunnism, which counts "destiny" as one of the six axioms of the Islamic faith.[93]

The rationalists explain that the intention behind the Umayyad concept of "destiny" was to justify various Umayyad policies, as well as to develop a new political theory in which the caliph cannot be held accountable.[94] The new doctrine of "destiny" provides the Umayyads with a lot of religious arguments to defend their mistakes as predestined by God.[95] Balcı writes that when Hussain, Prophet Muhammad's grandson, was killed in Karbala during Caliph Yazid's reign, Kufa governor Ubayd-Allah ibn Ziyad declared that they did not kill him; God did.[96] For Güler and Balcı, the core dynamic of the Umayyad strategy of promoting "destiny" was the acute legitimacy crisis that forced them to such radical solutions to gain public support.[97] On the other hand, for Balcı, the ready acceptance by the Muslim public—already shocked by brutal events like the civil wars, and by mind-blogging events like the Umayyad soldiers' destruction of Kaʿba with catapults—explains how "destiny" easily became popular among Muslims.[98]

As I underlined earlier, more than with its theological aspects, the rationalists are unhappy with the negative outcomes of the new doctrine of "destiny." They count this as another factor in the grand debate about "what went wrong." Accordingly, the Sunni "destiny" turned into a historical dynamic of political and social pacifism that still affects Islamic societies. Muslims think of political and social events as the inevitable consequences of predestination.[99] Thus, "destiny" works as a major obstacle to individual emancipation.[100] Gradually, "destiny" transformed into a slogan of political pacifism, barring Muslims' reaction to the injustices of rulers and governments. Noting that "destiny" makes Islam a dogmatic religion, Güler sees it leaving Muslims unconcerned about serious problems like political and social corruption.[101] He notes that "destiny" in the hands of Sunnism was transformed into a narrative of "legitimizing immorality" on the pretext of divine predestination.[102] To illustrate how "destiny" has been abused, Balcı reminds of various traditions, which the rationalists regard as fabricated, where Muhammad is reported to advise Muslims that the best deed during the times of chaos is to escape to remote places.[103] This is theology for the sake of politicians. Kırbaşoğlu thus dismisses such traditions, as they were fabricated by the Umayyads, and warns that belief in "destiny" was declared an axiom of faith despite its not being mentioned in Quran.[104] Along with its negative consequences in politics, "destiny" also turned into another obstacle to economic and technological development, for it promotes fatalistic mindsets among Muslims.[105] Atay asserts that "destiny" transformed Muslims into robots, a metaphor he uses to illustrate how Muslims are fatalist, and not interested in personal progress.[106] Further, "destiny" is a structural cause that promotes various related problems in this vein, such as underrating scientific studies, economic poverty, laziness, a passive mentality, and professional immorality.[107] But, despite many problems prevailing in the Muslim world, for Güler, "destiny" prevents Muslims' learning from their mistakes, since everything, even serious failures, are regarded as divinely predestined developments.[108]

Sufism: The Popularization of Anti-Rationalism

As stated earlier, the rationalists see Sufism as another factor that explains "what went wrong" in Islamic history. It is part of the anti-rationalist legacy of al-Ghazali. However, apart from the Sunni revival thesis, the rationalists refer also to the failure of theology and law to grab the attention of Muslims. While the former failed to propose a charming narrative to Muslims, the latter could not save itself from turning into a dry and formalist jargon. Both provide a huge opportunity zone for Sufism.[109] Seeing Sufism as the popular paradigm that fills the gaps left by law and theology is, for the rationalists, the same delusion that bolstered anti-rationalist tendencies among Muslims throughout history. In this regard, the rationalist critique of Sufism should be seen as part of the modern critical narrative of the Sufism that emerged in the nineteenth century (in various countries like Egypt and Indonesia) to present it as the paradigm that blocks Muslim's social and technological progress.[110]

As I have already discussed why the rationalists reject Sufi methods, in this section I shall only summarize how the rationalists elaborate on Sufism in regard of its negative role in the decline of Islamic societies. To begin with, the rationalists are critical of Sufi mystical knowledge, deeming it the historical impediment to Islamic rationality.[111] Although rationalists like Kırbaşoğlu and Yaşar Nuri believe that Sufism was better, and indeed useful in its early times, they accept that it later became a factor in the decline of Islamic societies.[112] Güler—unlike Kırbaşoğlu and Yaşar Nuri—categorically rejects Sufism, no matter the role it played in the past, and sees Sufism as a parallel religion injected into mainstream Islam by scholars like al-Ghazali that has historically hindered the emergence of rationalist thought. Its negative impact is visible even in Turkey in people's interest in a mythological kind of religious thought.[113] This problematic thought, for the rationalists, gives way to absurd and outdated interpretations of Islam.[114] In this regard, the rationalists see Sufism as transmitting a mediocre interpretation of Islam. Even Yaşar Nuri suggests the renewal of Sufism by incorporating the modern arts into it, given that the Medieval formats are no longer effective.[115] To justify his suggestion, he reminds that Sufism in the past borrowed many elements from Indian and Iranian mysticism, so a similar interaction with modern art or other universal values is therefore an option.[116]

The second problem of Sufism is its contribution to political pacifism in Muslim societies.[117] The rationalists argue that the institutionalization of Sufi groups as organizational networks transformed them into interest-based structures, killing their ability to pursue a critical agenda against rulers.[118] They gradually transformed into ritualistic organizations that contribute nothing to society.[119] Güler explains this as the propensity of Sufism to be the agent of the popular Ash'arism that transmits a metaphysical view of nature that repudiates free will and causality.[120] The output of such messages is always to consolidate ritualistic piety at the expense of freedom and individualism.[121] On this account, the rationalists criticize Sufism for it promotes a piety drained of Islam's social messages, such as political opposition to authoritarian or corrupt regimes, which is in contradiction of Quran's callings of Muslims to action.[122]

Islamic Social Movements: A False Theory of Revival

Previously, I pointed out that the rationalists are substantive critics of contemporary Islamic movements (religious social movements, such as orders, groups, and communities like the Gülen movement, or the Naqshbandiyya order) for they repeat the Sunni paradigm. Seeing historical Sunnism as the paradigmatic reason for the failure of Muslim societies, the rationalists naturally find any revivalist agenda based on historical Sunnism a futile enterprise. Thus, the rationalists see Islamic movements as highly problematic organizations. We observe in Eliaçık's statement that it is vital to rescue Islam from the control of Islamic movements.[123]

Why are the rationalists against Islamic movements? To begin with, they see Islamic movements as obstacles to rationalism and individualism among Muslims.[124] And they see Islamic movements in Turkey as a continuation of the Islamic traditionalism.[125] Yaşar Nuri depicts those movements as collectivist and traditionalists organizations that inculcate strong anti-individualism and anti-rationalism attitudes on the pretext of group solidarity and heroic leadership. For him, the theory of leadership in Islamic movements is a particularly dangerous cultic treatment of group leaders as infallible persons.[126] Atay describes the cultic model that we observe in Turkish Islamic movements as leader-centered rather than God-centered, where people are encouraged to imitate the leader.[127] Eliaçık likens this cultic leadership of Islamic movements to the shamans of the old Turkish religious traditions.[128] Balcı's and Öztürk's analyses support this thesis, as they, too, find that Islamic movements do not shy away from crediting their leaders with supernatural abilities such as seeing future events.[129] The cultic profile of the leader in Islamic movements, for Yaşar Nuri, is more compatible with the Shi'a imamate theory, which incorporates the principle of divine selection.[130] Naturally, the rationalists are alarmed by the fact that the cultic and collectivist nature of Islamic movements glorify anti-individualistic norms such as discipline and subjugation.¹³¹ Öztürk calls this "the culture of allegiance."¹³² Another negative outcome of this model, for Güler, is its delegitimization modern values such as criticism and opposition. But then, continuing the traditional mindset, Islamic social movements approach such modern values as *fitnah*.¹³³

As the second critique, the rationalists see Islamic movements as agents of corruption.¹³⁴ Accordingly, those movements in Turkey are primarily organized networks pursuing various economic interests rather than focusing on Islamic activism. Thus, despite their religious outlook, they in fact operate as interest-seeking bodies.¹³⁵ Öztürk presents Islamic movements as primarily interested in their corporate welfare rather than in the Islamic norms that seek to maintain moral quality in society.¹³⁶ Güler criticizes them for transforming their followers into clients by creating complex financial networks.¹³⁷ He has in mind here the billion-dollar-worth companies, that is, Islamic capital, owned by various Islamic movements operating in fields such as health, banking, media, and tourism. The rationale of such companies is to convert the movement's social network into a financial power by creating various companies in different fields. Atay sees Islamic movements' ownership of such gigantic corporates as ironic, for they frequently preach social self-isolation and concentration on the hereafter to the average Muslims.¹³⁸ Though the rationalists do not refer to the leftist critique of Islamic movements, their opinions in this regard remind of the perspective where Islamic actors like the JDP are criticized for promoting neoliberal strategies.¹³⁹

Thirdly, Islamic movements' complex relationships with political parties and the state is another dynamic that the rationalists are critical of.¹⁴⁰ They see Islamic movements as promoting only their members to bureaucracies, which is a modern tribalism that weakens the ideal of meritocracy in society.¹⁴¹ Besides, cohabitation with politicians transforms Islamic movements into facilitators of authoritarian and corrupted rulers. So long as Islamic movements get their expectations from politics, such as recruitment to the bureaucracy, they are never critical of political mistakes, mindful of their corporate interests. Again, Islamic movements' propagation of ritualistic piety is welcomed by politicians in Turkey.¹⁴² The pragmatic relationship between Islamic movements and politics creates another serious problem, as spotted by Yaşar Nuri. Keeping their followers on political issues under the strict control of the group leader, Islamic movements inculcate the idea among Muslims that politics is a game among the elites where the average individual has only one option: to follower the leader, an understanding that weakens political individualism.¹⁴³

Conclusion

As contemporary rationalists, the nine scholars answer the question "what went wrong?" mainly by giving reference to the historical competition between traditionalism and rationalism in the Islamic history. In fact, as I wrote in the Introduction, this is a reflection of their general perspective, which sees the whole

Negative					Positive		
The Umayyads	Al-Shafiʻi	Al-Ghazali	Ashʻarism		Muʻtazila	Al-Maturidi	Abu Hanifa

Figure 7 The spectrum of Islamic history in the context of the "what went wrong" debate.

of Islamic history through the lens of the competition of traditionalism and rationalism.[144] Accordingly, certain developments that promoted traditionalism as anti-rationalism and anti-individualism are those that went wrong in the Islamic history. If we transfer this perspective to a chart (Figure 7), we get the spectrum of the rationalists narrating Islamic history in the grand debate about "what went wrong."

For the rationalists, the history of Muslim societies is on this chart (Figure 7) a journey from the rationalist side to the traditionalists. This is more or less like Fazlur Rahman's glossing of the transformation of Muslim societies as having dampened, three centuries later, the vibrant messages of Quran.[145] So, going back to the question "what went wrong?" the rationalist answer is neat: the consolidation of the traditionalist axis at the expense of rationalist dynamics, ideas, and actors in the Islamic tradition.

CONCLUSION

Commenting on how the content of his works radically differ from the Sunni interpretation of Islam, Kırbaşoğlu quotes Daniel de Foe, and asks: "It is hard for a man to say that all the world is mistaken but himself, but if it be so, who can help?" This aptly summarizes the state of the rationalists vis-à-vis Sunnism.[1] The rationalists' ambitious intellectual agenda requires a radical break with Sunnism, and a new reasoning in almost all major fields of theology, law, and history. Reading them, one feels that their works are a reaction to their fatigue bred by the decades-old literature of reformist Islamic studies and attempts. The rationalists are eager to provide concrete and neat solutions to old problems. Seeing Sunnism as either an outdated or a mistaken paradigm, they are not satisfied by criticizing it; they not only provide a complex alternate perspective on the interpretation of Islam but apply their method also to developing concrete solutions in theology, law, and history.

For the rationalists, though intellectual arguments that underline the need for change in the interpretation of Islam are important, they are not satisfactory; concrete, and sometimes even radical, solutions are required. Accordingly, the subject of change in Islamic thought is not primarily an intra-intellectual debate; instead, it should target the average Muslim directly. Confirming this are the long passages in their works on piety, worships, and the various subjects of Islamic law such as divorce. The search for balance in the intellectual articulation of Islam, and its practice by average Muslims, is a key dynamic in the works of the rationalists. While they pay enormous attention to new articulations in the interpretation of Islam in regard to theology and law, they pay equal attention to providing concrete solutions to the practice of Islam in daily life. Seen in this way, their works have strong theoretical and practical dimensions.

The Rationalists as Moderns

Various etiquettes, such as "Neo-Mu'tazila" or "Neo-Maturidi," are usually used to explain cases like that of the rationalists. However, such etiquettes can explain them only partially. The rationalists' interest in the Mu'tazila scholars, as well as in Maturidi thought, are more about their general interest in the classical rationalist Islamic scholars. Thus, it is not correct to understand the rationalists specifically as Neo-Mu'tazila or Neo-Maturidi. I do not detect in their works a clear strategy to revive Mu'tazila or Maturidi. Indeed, they frequently criticize the mainstream Sunni tradition for being under the impact of Ash'arism at the expense of other perspectives, including the Mu'tazila and Maturidi ones. However, it would be overinterpretation to present the rationalists as interested in reviving Mu'tazila. Equally importantly, there is no case to prove that the rationalists openly own such a mission by presenting themselves as Neo-Mu'tazila or Neo-Maturidi. Besides, neither Neo-Mu'tazila nor Neo-Maturidi can encompass the rationalists' intellectual point of view entirely. Imagining the trajectory of Islamic thought as the polarization of rationalism versus traditionalism, the rationalists are interested also in many other scholars whom they identify as rationalist, such as Ibn Rushd and Ibn Khaldun.

On the other hand, unlike the Ash'ari school, the classical rationalist schools of Islam (like the Mu'tazila, and even the Maturidi) have long ago lost their intellectual dynamism, and are not available today as if they were sophisticated and lively paradigms. Thus, references to various previous scholars, such as Qadi Abd al-Jabbar or al-Maturidi, do not amount to imagining that there are effective Neo-Mu'tazila and Neo-Maturidi paradigms. In my understanding, terms like "Neo-Mu'tazila" and "Neo-Maturidi" symbolize for Muslim intellectuals the search for a better religious paradigm than the existing ones. So, we know not only what the scholars of yore stand against but also that they lack a coherent content. Neither the Mu'tazila nor the Maturidi have the intellectual magnitude and influence of Ash'arism in contemporary Muslim societies. Islamic law and theology are determined mainly by the Ash'ari tenet in today's Muslim world, even in countries like Turkey, which is affiliated with Maturidism.

In this regard, it is better to see the rationalists as being in the context of the contemporary mainstream rationalist scholars. Applying a quantitative analysis, Fazlur Rahman would certainly be the most frequently quoted name in the works of the rationalists. But other names, such as Hassan Hanafi, Nasser Abu-Zayd, Muhammad Taha, Izzat Darwaza, and Abdullah al-Na'im, are also quoted. Thus, presenting the rationalists as connecting Turkish rationalist thought with the wider global reformist Islamic scholarship would not be wrong. Again, confirming this argument, we see only rare references to the late Ottoman scholarship on Islam. "Neo-Ottomanism," which prevails in Turkish thought on the full spectrum of politics to culture, is not detected in the rationalists. The rationalists' intellectual orientation is toward other rationalists, both historically and geographically, which gives them a globalist appearance rather than that of a national intellectual movement.

Positioning the rationalists on an intellectual scale, we find the crucial point is that they hold a modern concept of rationalism. This determines their intellectual identity. On this account, they want to break with the Medieval interpretations of Islam, particularly that of Sunnism. Their break from the Medieval, for the rationalists, means their embracing of modern views of science, knowledge, causality, and free will. Thus, fundamental in the works of rationalists is their modern view of nature while they study a subject be it the status of woman in Islamic law or the proper approach to the writing of the biography of Muhammad. In this regard, the rationalists are pushing Islamic scholarship from the traditional methods to a new position close to the modern social sciences. Their argumentations, as well as their texts, are typical examples of modern scholarship. As a major sign of their modern rationalist stance, we almost never see them relying on traditions in their argumentation. For them, scholarship is not in searching for proof in Islamic texts, nor in references to religious *dicta*. Rather, it is in line with the typical modern methods of argumentation. As I noted in the Introduction, one origin of this modernity among the rationalists is the modern education through which they acquired their attitudes to studying Islam. Seen in this way, the rationalists can be seen as the products of modern religious higher education in Turkey, which is, ironically, a legacy of Kemalism.

The Impact: The Crisis of Sunnism and the Rationalists

There is a visible increase in the public visibility of the rationalists. A growing number of followers are showing ever more interest in their ideas by engaging their works in the social media, conferences, and TV programs. The rationalists' most visible impact is observed among the urban population, and among the young people who have recently became critical of the traditional Sunni interpretation of Islam. Therefore, the rising interest in the rationalists should be seen as the rise of a critical approach to religion among young people, particularly in the last decade.[2] Similarly, the secular sections, readily critical of the Islamist politics in the country, pay close attention to the rationalists. However, on the opposite side, the historical machinery of Sunni orthodoxy—which depends on the cooperation of the state and the religious clergy—keeps propagating its interpretation of Islam by all sorts of means. Diyanet, the embodiment of Sunni orthodoxy, employs almost 120,000 officers and spends budget money to the tune of billions of dollars to promote its religious position. With so many means and opportunities for transmitting its interpretation as the official Islam, the Diyanet is a major actor in religious socialization.[3] The state, meanwhile, does not only finance the Diyanet. It is a constitutional requirement that students attend courses of religious instruction for eight consecutive years, during which they learn Sunnism, the official religion. Next come the Islamic social movements as important partners in the equation. A myriad of Islamic movement, including traditional orders like the Naqshbandiyya and Qadiriyya, as well as modern organizations like Süleymancılar, Işıkçılar, and Nurcular, disseminate Sunnism. Though not officially linked to the state, they again enjoy state-originated opportunities so long as they are on the loyalist track, which is mostly the case.

Logically, compared to the ability of the historical network of Sunni orthodoxy, the rationalists' impact is sociologically limited to the mainly new urban groups who are interested in alternate religious interpretations. But again, the rationalists exert considerable influence on such groups, for they rely on intellectual argumentation and persuasion, unlike Sunni orthodoxy, which is concerned mostly with socialization. Yet many who had been socialized in traditional Sunnism later become unsatisfied by the traditional narrative of Sunnism. Demonstrating the extent of the traditional Sunni actors' alarm that the rising influence of the rationalists arouses, they sometimes even mount verbal attacks on the rationalists. In a public sermon, Ahmet Ünlü, a popular religious figure and a prominent name in the Naqshbandiyya-İsmailağa order, has portrayed some of the rationalists as the "most dangerous group," citing their names, inter alia, Güler and Öztürk.[4]

At a more general level, two dynamics are likely to determine the long-term impact of the rationalists. One is that the Islamist movement in Turkey has in the last two decades generated a negative legacy that is problematic to the Sunni interpretation of Islam in this country. The failure of Sunni Islamic actors in regard of key issues, such as authoritarization and corruption, has seen Sunni Islam become a target of severe criticism. This is a unique case in modern history. The silence of leading Sunni religious actors on the important subjects of corruption, authoritarianism, violence against women and children, environmental issues, and labor rights has created a reaction against them among young and urban people. Visibly, Sunni Islam in Turkey is now on the defensive trajectory. A growing number of people, apart from the traditional seculars who had long been critical of Islamization, have become dissatisfied with Islamic politics. On this account, the Islamic movement in Turkey is likely to leave a legacy that will operate as a barrier, at least for a large sector of the young people. Logically, the negative legacy of the Sunni Islamic actors is simultaneously likely to become a long-term asset of the rationalists, particularly vis-à-vis those who are looking for alternate religious interpretations. In fact, aware of this new sociological dynamic, the rationalists position themselves in sharp opposition to Sunnism. They explain the problems that have their origin in the wrong, or anachronic, interpretations of Islam as the products of the Sunni paradigm. Accordingly, a major factor to explain why the Islamic movement in Turkey turned out to be a political and moral failure is the actors' interpretation of Islam in line with Sunnism. In this regard, as I noted in the Introduction, the rationalists are the first religious opposition to the Sunni revival in Turkey.

Secondly, Sunni Islam has lost its contact with many Muslims, particularly with the growing number of young people, simply because the Sunni actors show no signal of intellectual dynamism to reclaim them. Instead, Sunni religious actors are increasingly aggressive in response to alternate Islamic interpretations, for they are unable to engage them with counterarguments. Particularly, the rapprochement of Islam and state during the Islamist regime of the last two decades has, paradoxically, weakened the intellectual rigor of Sunnism. Unlike the Sunni Islamic thought that was prominent till the late 1990s, which was somewhat a vivid intellectual opposition to the Kemalist regime, the Sunni Islamic thought today is hampered by a mental laziness. In many cases, the Sunni Islamic actors' first resort is to the political authority, to request the silencing of their opponents. While the Sunni Islamic actors appeal for the jailing, lynching, and the banning from the media of their opponents, they propagate their own opinions through a dazzling network of institutions, thanks to their alliance with the Islamist regime.

Ironically, Sunni Islamic politics today relies heavily on the state rather than on intellectual strength.

Criticizing the state-led modernization in Turkey in 1978, Şerif Mardin wrote that one major fault of the secular modernizers is their belief that establishing "mega-structures" will help them achieve their goals. For Mardin, this belief inevitably weakened the "small structures," that is, those means that empower individual, social, and civil actors.[5] Proving Mardin right, the Kemalist regime was destroyed some decades later by Islamic actors, who in those times operated mostly through "simple structures." In this regard, the current Islamic movement is courting the fate of Kemalism. Despite its grandeur in narrative along with its mega-structures, the Islamic movement, which relies on Sunnism, is intellectually weak. It would not be an exaggeration to liken the whole network of Sunni Islam in Turkey today to a rentier mechanism that relies primarily on the external revenues and opportunities made available by the state. On the other hand, alternate religious paradigms, including the rationalists', might find a lot of opportunity spaces in this context, given that they rely solely on "simple structures."

The Rationalists and the Quandary of Change in Islamic Thought

Reading the works of the rationalists, one notices that the difficulty of any intellectual attempt to reform Islamic thought is always same. Islam has its fundamental corpus, the Quran and traditions, which literally endorses various understandings and practices, such as polygamy, slavery, and the chopping-off of hands, and has its historical experience where such practices were (and some of them still are) practiced by Muslims. And the rationalists always find themselves in a position to argue that the purpose of Islam is something different from, and many times the opposite of, what that corpus and the historical experience literally suggest. Islam, as it appears in the texts and in historical experience, is always different from Islam as presented by the rationalists. Thus, alternate Islamic perspectives are usually a tireless intellectual effort to explain that Muslims should interpret their religion in a way that does not justify acts such as the killing of apostates or the beating of women. The rationalists, too, participate in these efforts: They spare long sections in their works to persuade Muslims that the correct interpretation of Islam requires certain behaviors that are other than what we find in the texts, or in historical practice.

Beyond that traditional argumentations, the rationalists propose also a paradigmatic solution to the earlier quandary in Islamic thought: They propose the redefining of the relationship of God, nature, and history. In fact, reading the rationalists' opinions and solutions in the various fields of law or theology, one always notices that they emphasize this structural proposal carefully, to establish that it is the general philosophical framework of their arguments and opinions. Accordingly, to consolidate the autonomy and supremacy of human beings, the rationalists take God-as-agent out of history and nature. To do this, they define nature as dependent on God, but not an agent in its effects. Instead, it is God's transcendental power (*qudra*) that affects life, nature, and history. Thus, the relationship between God and nature takes place in a way that never contradicts natural law. For the rationalists, everything in this world is thus subject to the natural law. Not acting in history as agent, God affects nature through its rules. This is quite unlike the God of Ash'ari, where the deity acts arbitrarily in history as an agent, sometimes by suspending natural law.[6] Metaphorically, we can explain the rationalists' God as the world's Sun, thus, the cause of every form of life, including that of human beings. Like the Sun, God's transcendental power is the source of everything in nature, as well as in human history. However, God does not intervene as an agent who decides what human beings do.

The rationale of redefining of God's relations with nature and history is twofold. Firstly, the rationalists understand that no matter what the subject, the Sunni axiom always depends on the God's agential intervention in nature and history. Hence, the power of Sunnism originates in its capacity to present axiomatically that law, theology, and history are the works of God. Inevitably, Sunnism limits human autonomy by defining the "subject" under scrutiny as the work of God. Thus, licensed by its tenet of divine agency, Sunnism puts itself beyond rational inquiry. Observing the existential quandary in which this position leaves the human being, the rationalists conclude that so long as God is seen as part of human history as an agent, it is impossible to achieve a change in the interpretation of Islam, save by metaphorical or conjectural new interpretations. Secondly, bringing God into nature and history generates a two-level rationality: the human and the divine. And Sunnism resorts to both interchangeably, not caring about consistency. Imagining God as an agent of history and nature allows Sunnism's reductio ad absurdum method of positing the nonfalsifiability of the interchangeability of the human and the divine rationalities. Thus, for the rationalists, Sunnism claims the privilege of not caring about inconsistency, since divine intervention is always available to fill the gaps that reason questions. Things seen as illogical or wrong can easily be explained by Sunnism as divinely correct. Recall the account in the history chapter, where Sunnism, facing some rational arguments on the history of Quran, or of the early Muslim society, quickly appeals to the divine wisdom explanation. Even if the companions had lost some verses, the Sunni thesis is not weakened, for that act was the result of God's intervention. Or when there are grammatical mistakes in Quran, there is a divine wisdom in the background that gives a message more valuable than a grammatically correct text could have carried.

To overcome this logical quandary, the rationalists—echoing Nietzsche's "God is dead"—take God-as-agent out of history and nature. In so doing, the rationalists maintain that Islamic thought is no longer a game of persuasion; human reason has the authority to go beyond the religious axioms. Rejecting God's intervention in history as agent, the rationalists now assign to human beings the role of ultimate actors in history, leaving everything about religion subject to the natural law. That done, it is no longer required to engage with the inconsistent arguments of Sunni theology: It is simply wrong when it is inconsistent with reason and science.

NOTES

Introduction

1. Naser Ghobadzadeh, *Religious Secularity: A Theological Challenge to the Islamic State* (Oxford: Oxford University Press, 2005).
2. Nikki R. Keddie, *Response to Imperialism: Political and Religious Writings of Sayyid Jamal ad-Din "al-Afghani."* (Berkeley, Los Angeles: University of California Press, 1983), 30.
3. Stanford J. Shaw and Ezel Kural Shaw, *History of the Ottoman Empire and Modern Turkey Volume II Reform, Revolution, and Republic: The Rise of Modern Turkey, 1808–1975* (Cambridge: Cambridge University Press, 1977), 157.
4. Indira Falk Gesink, *Islamic Reform and Conservatism: Al-Azhar and the Evolution of Modern Sunni Islam* (London: I. B. Tauris, 2010), 24.
5. Falih Rıfkı Atay, *Baş Veren İnkılapçı* (Istanbul: Cumhuriyet, 1997), 65–8.
6. M. Hayri Kırbaşoğlu, *Alternatif Hadis Metodolojisi* (Istanbul: Otto, 2015), 15.
7. Masooda Bano, *The Revival of Islamic Rationalism: Logic, Metaphysics and Mysticism in Modern Muslim Societies* (Cambridge: Cambridge University Press, 2020), 119.
8. M. Hayri Kırbaşoğlu, *İslam Düşüncesinde Hadis Metodolojisi* (Ankara: Ankara Okulu, 2018), 29.
9. Yaşar Nuri Öztürk, *Kur'an Verilerine Göre Kötülük Toplumu* (Istanbul: Yeni Boyut, 2015), 34.
10. Uzay Bulut, "Turkey: Religious Backlash?" https://www.gatestoneinstitute.org/14815/turkey-religious-backlash (January 17, 2020).
11. Güler presents the Gülen movement as "a recent embodiment of Sunnism." İlhami Güler, *Vicdan Böyle Buyurdu* (Ankara: Ankara Okulu, 2018), 318.
12. Yaşar Nuri Öztürk, *Maun Suresi Böyle Buyurdu: Din Maskeli Zulme Tanrı'nın Vuruşu.* (Istanbul: Yeni Boyut, 2017), 281; İlhami Güler, *Sünniliğin Eleştirisine Giriş* (Ankara: Ankara Okulu, 2017), 165–8.
13. Güler, *Vicdan*, 318–26; Yaşar Nuri, *Maun*, 287; R. İhsan Eliaçık, *Demokratik Özgürlükçü İslam* (Istanbul: Tekin, 2014), 88. Hüseyin Atay, *Ben: Akıl ve Kuran Işığında 1400 Yıllık Süreçte İslam'ın Serüveni* (Istanbul: Destek, 2019), 124.
14. İlhami Güler, *Evrensel Ümmetçiliğe Doğru: Türkiye İslamcılığının Eleştirisi* (Ankara: Ankara Okulu, 2016), 112.
15. İlhami Güler, *Direniş Teolojisi* (Ankara: Ankara Okulu, 2015), 102.
16. İlhami Güler, *Realpolitik ve Muhafazakarlık* (Ankara: Ankara Okulu, 2016), 7.
17. Güler, *Evrensel Ümmetçiliğe*, 81.
18. Yaşar Nuri Öztürk, *Emevi Dinciliğine Karşı Mücadelenin Öncüsü: Ebu Zer* (Istanbul: Yeni Boyut, 2016), 9.
19. M. Hayri Kırbaşoğlu, *İslami İlimlerde Metot Sorunu* (Istanbul: Otto, 2015), 46.
20. Mustafa Öztürk, *Cumhuriyet Türkiyesi'nde Meal ve Tefsir'in Serencamı* (Ankara: Ankara Okulu, 2015), 219.

21. For example, Stefan Wild, "Islamic Enlightenment and the Paradox of Averroes," *Die Welt des Islam* 36, no. 3 (1996): 379–90.
22. Ömer Özsoy, *Kur'an ve Tarihsellik Yazıları* (Ankara: Kitabiyat, 2004), 91; Yaşar Nuri Öztürk, *Dinde Reform Değil İslam'da Tecdit: Peygamber'in Yüklediği Görev Volume I* (Istanbul: Yeni Boyut, 2018), 20; R. İhsan Eliaçık, *Bana Dinden Bahset* (Istanbul: İnşa, 2017), 161.
23. İlhami Güler, *Derin Ahlak: Teolojik Siyasi Ahlak Analizleri* (Ankara: Ankara Okulu, 2016), 83; Mustafa Öztürk, *Tefsirin Halleri* (Ankara: Ankara Okulu, 2016), 29; Kırbaşoğlu, *İslam Düşüncesinde Hadis*, 31.
24. A. J. Arberry, *Revelation and Reason in Islam* (London: Routledge, 2008), 17; George F. Hourani, *Reason and Tradition in Islamic Ethics* (Cambridge: Cambridge University Press, 1985), 24–5.
25. Hayreddin Karaman, Ali Bardakoğlu and İ. Kafi Dönmez, *İlmihal I* (Ankara: Diyanet, 1998), 33; George Makdisi, "The Significance of the Sunni Schools of Law in Islamic Religious History," *IJMES* 10, no. 1 (1979): 1–8.
26. Christopher Melchert, "Traditionists-Jurisprudents and the Framing of Islamic Law," *Islamic Law and Society* 8, no. 3 (2017): 383–406; Jonathan A. C. Brown, "Is the Devil in the Details? Tension Between Minimalism and Comprehensiveness in the Shariah," *Journal of Religious Ethics* 39, no. 3 (2011): 465.
27. Umar F. Abd-Allah Wymann-Landgraf, *Malik and Medina: Islamic Legal Reasoning in the Formative Period* (Leiden: Brill, 2003), 8–9; Patricia Crone, *Roman, Provincial, and Islamic Law: The Origins of the Islamic Patronate* (Cambridge: Cambridge University Press, 1987), 21–2.
28. Binyamin Abrahamov, *Islamic Theology: Traditionalism and Rationalism* (Edinburgh: Edinburgh University Press, 1998), 12.
29. Goldziher uses the taxonomy of "the orthodox and the rational" where the Mu'tazila is the latter. Ignaz Goldziher, *On the History of Grammar Among Arabs: An Essay in Literary History* (Philadelphia: John Benjamins, 1994), 40.
30. Georges Tamer, "Preface," in *Islam and Rationality: The Impact of al-Ghazali Papers Collected on His 900th Anniversary*, edited by Georges Tamer (London: Brill, 2015), xiv.
31. Bernard W. Geiss, *The Spirit of Islamic Law* (Athens: The University of Georgia Press, 1998), 37.
32. Muhsin Mahdi, "Rationalist Tradition in Islam," in *Intellectual Traditions in Islam*, edited by Farhad Daftary (London: I. B. Tauris, 2001), 62.
33. R. İhsan Eliaçık, *Devrimci İslam* (Istanbul: Doğu, 2013), 82.
34. Richard C. Martin, Mark R. Woodward and Dwi S. Atmaja, *Defenders of Reason in Islam: Mu'tazilism from Medieval School to Modern Symbol* (London: Oneworld, 1997), 11.
35. Richard C. Taylor, "Ibn Rushd/Averroes and "Islamic" Rationalism," *Medieval Encounters* 15, no. 1 (2009): 225–7.
36. al-Maturidi, *Kitabü't-Tevhid Açıklamalı Tercüme [Kitab al-Tawhid]*. Translated by Bekir Topaloğlu (Ankara: ISAM, 2018), 64.
37. Abu Hamid al-Ghazali, *The Just Balance [Al-Qistas Al-Mustaqim]*. Translated by D. P. Brewster (Lahore: Sh. M. Ashraf, 1978), 2–5.
38. Fiazuddin Shu'ayb, "Al-Ghazzali's Final Word on Kalam," *Islam & Science* 9, no. 2 (2011): 157.
39. Abu Hamid al-Ghazali, *Deliverance from Error [Al Munkidh min Ad Dallal]*. Translated by W. M. Watt (Lahore: Sh. M. Ashraf, 1963), 21–3.

40 Ibid., 25.
41 Mohd Fakhrudin Abdul Mukti, "Al-Ghazali and His Refutation of Philosophy," *Journal Usuluddin* 21, no. 1 (2005): 9.
42 Syed Muhammad Naquib Al-Attas, *Islam and Secularism* (Kuala Lumpur: ISTAC, 1993), 146.
43 Wilfred Madelung, "Al-Ghazali's Changing Attitude to Philosophy," in *Islam and Rationality: The Impact of al-Ghazali Papers Collected on His 900th Anniversary*, edited by Georges Tamer (London: Brill, 2015), 27.
44 Mohammed Abed al-Jabri, *The Formation of Arab Reason: Text, Tradition and the Construction of Modernity in the Arab World* (London: I. B. Tauris, 2011), 361.
45 Hunt Janin and Andre Kahlmeyer, *Islamic Law: The Sharia from Muhammad's Time to the Present* (London: McFarland and Company, 2007), 58.
46 George Makdisi, "The Juridical Theology of Shafi'i: Origins and Significance of Usul al-Fiqh," *Studia Islamica* 59, no. 1 (1984): 5–47.
47 John Kelsay, "Divine Command Ethics in Early Islam: Al-Shafi'i and the Problem of Guidance," *The Journal of Religious Ethics* 22, no. 1 (1994): 115.
48 al-Shafi'i, *al-Shafi'i's Risala Treatise on the Foundations of Islamic Jurisprudence*. Translated by Majid Khadduri (London: The Islamic Text Society, 1997), 182.
49 Massimo Campanini, "The Mu'tazila in Islamic History and Thought," *Religion Compass* 6, no. 1 (2012): 41.
50 Sabine Schmidtke, "Theological Rationalism in the Medieval World of Islam," *Al–'Usur al Wusta* 20, no. 1 (2008): 17.
51 İlhami Güler, *Aklın İçindeki İlhamlar* (Ankara: Ankara Okulu, 2018), 8.
52 Öztürk, *Tefsirin Halleri*, 332.
53 M. Hayri Kırbaşoğlu, *Üçüncü Yol Mukaddimesi* (Ankara: Otto, 2014), 26.
54 Güler, *Sünniliğin Eleştirisine*, 17; Mustafa Öztürk and Hadiye Ünsal, *Kur'an Tarihi* (Ankara: Ankara Okulu, 2018), 11; Noel J. Culson, *A History of Islamic Law* (Edinburg: Edinburg University Press, 2005), 60.
55 İlhami Güler, *Özgürlükçü Teoloji Yazıları* (Ankara: Ankara Okulu, 2011), 8; Hüseyin Atay, *Cehaletin Tahsili* (Ankara: Atay, 2018), 51. Kırbaşoğlu, *Üçüncü Yol*, 60.
56 Eliaçık, *Bana Dinden*, 290.
57 Güler, *Özgürlükçü Teoloji*, 8.
58 Atay, *Ben*, 40–3.
59 Alan Nelson, "The Rationalist Impulse," in *A Companion to Rationalism*, edited by Alan Nelson (Oxford: Blackwell, 2005), 4.
60 Hüseyin Atay, *Osmanlılarda Yüksek Din Eğitimi: Medrese Programları İcazetnameler Islahat Hareketleri* (Istanbul: Atay, 2018), 31; Yaşar Nuri Öztürk, *İnsanlığı Kemiren İhanet: Dincilik* (Istanbul: Yeni Boyut, 2015), 29.
61 Hüseyin Atay, *İslam'da İşçi-İşveren İlişkileri* (Ankara: Atay, 2015), 50.
62 Yaşar Nuri Öztürk, *Tanrı, Akıl ve Ahlaktan Başka Kutsal Tanımayan İnanç Deizm Teofilozofik Bir Tahlil* (Istanbul: Yeni Boyut, 2015), 160.
63 Atay, *Cehaletin*, 292–4 and 85; Yaşar Nuri, *İnsanlığı Kemiren*, 31.
64 Hüseyin Atay, *İslam'da Bilgi Teorisi* (Istanbul: Furkan, 1982), 42.
65 Atay, *Cehaletin*, 151.
66 Yaşar Nuri, *Tanrı, Akıl*, 166.
67 Yaşar Nuri Öztürk, *Kur'an Penceresinden Özgürlük ve İsyan: Teofilozofik Bir Tahlil* (Istanbul: Yeni Boyut, 2015), 243.
68 Hüseyin Atay, *Kur'an'a Göre Araştırmalar V* (Ankara: Atay, 2012), 27. Yaşar Nuri, *Tanrı, Akıl*, 160.

69 Yaşar Nuri, *Kur'an Penceresinden*, 243.
70 Thomas M. Lennon, "The Rationalist Conception of Substance," in *A Companion to Rationalism*, edited by Alan Nelson (Oxford: Blackwell, 2005), 12.
71 İlhami Güler, *İsimsiz İlhamlar* (Ankara: Ankara Okulu, 2017), 60 and 51.
72 Kırbaşoğlu, *Alternatif Hadis*, 77. Also see, Güler, *İsimsiz*, 12.
73 Mustafa Öztürk, *Kur'an ve Tarihsellik Üzerine Çerçeve Yazılar, Örnek Konular* (Ankara: Ankara Okulu, 2018), 86; Özsoy, *Kur'an ve Tarihsellik Yazıları*, 62.
74 Özsoy, *Kur'an ve Tarihsellik Yazıları*, 21.
75 George Makdisi, *The Rise of the Colleges: Institutions of Learning in Islam and the West* (Edinburgh: Edinburgh University Press, 1981).
76 Martin et al., *Defenders of Reason*, 11.
77 Roxanne L. Euben, *Enemy in the Mirror: Islamic Fundamentalism and the Limits of Modern Rationalism* (Princeton: Princeton University Press, 1999), 21; Wolfgang Schluchter, *The Rise of Western Rationalism: Max Weber's Developmental History* (Berkeley: University of California Press, 1991), 15.
78 Gertrude Himmelfarb, *The Roads to Modernity: The British, French and American Enlightenments* (New York: Vintage Books, 2004), 6 and 38; Joao Carlos Espada, "The Tradition of Liberty and Why It Does Matter," in *The Liberal Tradition in Focus Problems and New Perspectives*, edited by Joao Carlos Espada, Marc F. Plattner and Adam Wolfson (New York: Lexington Books, 2000), 10.
79 Eliaçık, *Bana Dinden*, 318; İlhami Güler, *Allah'ın Ahlakiliği Sorunu: Ehl-i Sünnet'in Allah Tasavvuruna Ahlaki Açıdan Eleştirel Bir Yaklaşım* (Ankara: Ankara Okulu, 2017), 83.
80 Ömer Özsoy, *Sünnetullah: Bir Kur'an İfadesinin Kavramsallaşması* (Ankara: Fecr, 2017), 134; R. İhsan Eliaçık, *Kur'an'a Giriş: Gerçeğe, Hayata ve Topluma Dönüş* (Istanbul: İnşa, 2017), 147; Atay, *Kur'an'a Göre V*, 78; Mehmet Azimli, Bedir Savaşı Çerçevesinde Bazı Mülahazalar," *Bilimname* 8, no. 1 (2010): 16; İsrafil Balcı, "Erken Dönem Arap Kültüründe Peygamberlik Tasavvuru," *Ekev Akademi Dergisi* 10, no. 29 (2006): 121.
81 Ibn Rushd, *The Incoherence of the Incoherence [Tahafut al-Tahafut]*. Translated by Simon Van Den Bergh (Cambridge: EJW Gibb Memorial Trust, 1987), 90; Ruth Glasner, *Averroes' Physics: A Turning Point in Medieval Natural Philosophy* (Oxford: Oxford University Press, 2009), 172.
82 al-Ash'ari, *Kitab al-Luma' [The Luminous Book]*. Translated by Richard J. McCarthy (Beirut: Imprimerie Catholique, 1953), 33–4; Abu Hamid al-Ghazali, *Tahafut al-Falasifa [The Incoherence of the Philosophers]*. Translated by Michael E. Marmura (Provo: Brigham Young University Press, 2000), 226.
83 Ayşe Öncü, "Becoming Secular Muslims: Yaşar Nuri Öztürk as a Super-Subject on Turkish Television," in *Religion, Media and the Public Sphere*, edited by Birgit Meyers and Annelis Moors (Bloomington: Indiana University Press, 2006), 228.
84 Similar attempts to synthesize traditional rationalism and empiricism are known also in the West. Erhard Scheibe, *Between Rationalism and Empiricism: Selected Papers in the Philosophy of Physics* (New York: Springer, 2001), 1.
85 Yaşar Nuri Öztürk, *Dinde Reform Değil İslam'da Tecdit: Peygamber'in Yüklediği Görev Volume II* (Istanbul: Yeni Boyut, 2018), 7; Özsoy, *Kur'an ve Tarihsellik Yazıları*, 68; Mustafa Öztürk, *Kur'an'ı Kendi Tarihinde Okumak: Tefsirde Anakronizme Ret Yazılar* (Ankara: Ankara Okulu, 2013), 26; Eliaçık, *Kur'an'a Giriş*, 123.
86 M. Hayri Kırbaşoğlu, *İslam Düşüncesinde Sünnet: Eleştirel Bir Yaklaşım* (Ankara: Ankara Okulu, 2018), 19.
87 İlhami Güler, *Dine Yeni Yaklaşımlar* (Ankara: Ankara Okulu, 2016), 204.

88 Güler, *Özgürlükçü Teoloji*, 11–12.
89 İlhami Güler, *Kur'an'ın Mahiyeti ve Yorumu* (Ankara: Ankara Okulu, 2018), 59.
90 Eliaçık, *Kur'an'a Giriş*, 98; Yaşar Nuri Öztürk, *Türkiye'ye Mektuplar* (Istanbul: Yeni Boyut, 2004), 70.
91 Özsoy, *Kur'an ve Tarihsellik Yazıları*, 61.
92 Kırbaşoğlu, *Alternatif Hadis*, 51.
93 İsmail Hakkı İzmirli, *'Ilm-i Kelam: Birinci Kitab* (Istanbul: Şehzadebaşı Evkaf-ı İslamiyye Matbaası, 1925), 3.
94 Hüseyin Atay, *İslam'ı Yeniden Anlama* (Ankara: Atay, 2017), 19.
95 Eliaçık, *Bana Dinden*, 138.
96 Ergun Özbudun, "State Elites and Democratic Political Culture in Turkey," in *Political Culture and Democracy in Developing Countries, Larry Diamond* (Boulder: Lynne Rienner, 1993), 191.
97 Nilüfer Göle, "Secularism and Islamism in Turkey: The Making of Elites and Counter-Elites," *The Middle East Journal* 51, no. 1 (1997): 46–8.
98 Özbudun, "State Elites," 194.
99 Sinan Ciddi, *Kemalism in Turkish Politics: The Republican People's Party, Secularism and Nationalism* (New York: Routledge, 2009), 8.
100 Kemal Karpat, "Some Historical and Methodological Considerations Concerning Social Stratification in the Middle East," in *Commoners, Climbers and Notables A Sampler of Studies on Social Ranking in the Middle East*, edited by C. A. O. Van Nieuwenhuijze (Leiden: E. J. Brill, 1977), 100.
101 Kemal Karpat, *Studies on Ottoman Social and Political History: Selected Articles and Essays* (Leiden: Brill, 2002), 16.
102 The case was similar during the Ottoman period as Mardin wrote, "entrance to the modern sector of education was much easier for children with fathers who were already part of the class of reformist officials, or even any part of the bureaucracy." Şerif Mardin, "Center-Periphery Relations: A Key to Turkish Politics?" *Daedalus* 102, no. 1 (1973): 179.
103 Ibrahim Kaya, *Social Theory and Later Modernities: The Turkish Experience* (Liverpool: Liverpool University Press, 2004), 81.
104 Ciddi, *Kemalism*, 113.
105 For definition see, Pitirim Sorokin, *Social Mobility Vol. 3* (London: Routledge, 1998), 134.
106 Carol Delaney, *The Seed and the Soil: Gender and Cosmology in Turkish Village Society* (Berkeley: University of California Press, 1991), 25.
107 Sabrina Kayıkça, "'Cumhuriyet'in Kuruluşundan Günümüze Kadar Köye ve Köylüye Yönelik Olarak İzlenen Politikalar," *Türk İdare Dergisi* 448, no. 1 (2005): 14.
108 Mustafa Mutluer, "Gelişimi, yapısı ve sorunlarıyla Türkiye'de enerji sektörü," *Ege Coğrafya Dergisi* 5, no. 1 (1990): 203.
109 Mustafa Öztürk, *Söyleşiler Polemikler* (Ankara: Ankara Okulu, 2015), 40–1.
110 İlhami Güler, *Kuş Bakışı* (Ankara: Ankara Okulu, 2016), 171.
111 Hakan Yavuz, "Political Islam and the Welfare (Refah) Party in Turkey," *Comparative Politics* 30, no. 1 (1997): 78. Also, see, A. Dubetsky, "Class and Community in Urban Turkey," in *Commoners, Climbers and Notables A Sampler of Studies on Social Ranking in the Middle East*, edited by C. A. O. Van Nieuwenhuijze (Leiden: E. J. Brill, 1971), 361.
112 İpek Gencel Sezgin, "Islamist Party Identity in Right-Wing Milieus: The Case of the National Outlook Movement in Kayseri (1960–1980)," in *Contemporary Turkey at*

a Glance Interdisciplinary Perspectives on Local and Translocal Dynamics, edited by Kristina Kamp, Ayhan Kaya, E. Fuat Keyman and Özge Onursal Beşgül (Wiesbaden: Springer, 2014), 95.

113 Soon-Yong Pak, "Articulating the Boundary Between Secularism and Islamism: The Imam-Hatip Schools of Turkey," *Anthropology and Education Quarterly* 35, no. 3 (2004): 327; Howard A. Reed, "Turkey's New Imam-Hatip Schools," *Die Welt des Islams* 4, no. 2/3 (1955): 152.

114 François Georgeon, "La formation des élites à la fin de l'Empire ottoman : le cas de Galatasaray," *Revue des mondes musulmans et de la Méditerranée* 72, no. 1 (1994): 15–25; Carter Vaughn Findley, *Ottoman Civil Officialdom: A Social History* (Princeton: Princeton University Press, 1989), 155.

115 İbrahim Aşlamacı and Recep Kaymakcan, "A Model for Islamic Education from Turkey: The Imam-Hatip Schools," *British Journal of Religious Education* 39, no. 3 (2017): 279–80.

116 İsmail Kara, "Diyanet İşleri Başkanlığı," in *İslamcılık*, edited by Yasin Aktay, Tanıl Bora and Murat Gültekingil (Istanbul: İletişim: 2005), 183.

117 Şinasi Gündüz, "From Apology to Phenomenology: The Contemporary State of the Studies of History of Religions in Turkey," in *Change and Essence: Dialectic Relations Between Change and Continuity in the Turkish Intellectual Tradition*, edited by Şinasi Gündüz and Cafer S. Yaran (Washington: The Council for Research in Values and Philosophy, 2005), 39.

118 Bayramali Nazıroğlu, "İlahiyat Fakültelerinde Din Eğitimi ve Sorunları," in *Türkiye'de Din Eğitimi ve Sorunları*, edited by Mustafa Köylü (Istanbul: Dem, 2018), 195.

119 Siyami Akyel, "Batıcılar ve Dinde Reformcular," *Milli Gazete*, November 7, 2016.

120 Jenny B. White, "The End of Islamism? Turkey's Muslimhood Model," in *Remaking Muslim Politics Pluralism, Contestation, Democratization*, edited by Robert W. Hefner (Princeton: Princeton University Press, 2005), 97.

121 İsmail Narin and Abdulnasir Süt, "Prof. Dr. M. Hayri Kırbaşoğlu ile Problemlerimiz ve Çıkış Yolu Üzerine Söyleşi," *Bingöl Universitesi İlahiyat Fakültesi Dergisi* 3, no. (2014): 221.

122 Yunus Cengiz, "Türkiye'de Mu'tezile Hakkında Yapılan Çalışmaların Değerlendirilmesi," *İslami İlimler Dergisi* 12, no. 12 (2017): 107.

123 Born to an aristocratic family in Burdur, where his father was a leading Muslim scholar, Hatiboğlu, along with several other scholars, symbolizes a break in Turkey of the traditional Sunni paradigm and the nascent rationalist paradigm. See, Mehmed S. Hatiboğlu, "İslam'da İlk Siyasi Kavmiyetçilik Hilafetin Kureyşiliği," *AÜİFD* 23, no. 1 (1979): 121–223; Mehmed S. Hatiboğlu, *İslami Tenkid Zihniyeti ve Hadis Tenkidinin Doğuşu* (Ankara: Otto, 2016), 1–15.

124 Güler, *Dine Yeni*, 204.

125 Münir Koştaş, "Ankara Üniversitesi İlahiyat Fakültesi," *AÜİFD* 31, no. 1 (1989): 1–27.

126 *TBMM Tutanak Dergisi*, 8 (20). June 6, 1949, 278. Also available at https://www.tbmm.gov.tr/tutanaklar/TUTANAK/TBMM/d08/c020/tbmm08020101.pdf (22 January 2020).

127 Güler, *Aklın İçindeki*, 116.

128 İhsan Çapçıoğlu, "Türkiye'deki İlahiyat Fakültelerinde Din Sosyolojisi Alanında Tamamlanmış Lisansüstü Tezler Üzerine Bir Araştırma," *AÜİFD* 45, no. 1 (2004): 203–24.

129 Hüseyin Atay, *Kur'an'da İman Esasları ve Kader* (Ankara: Atay, 2018), 9.

130 Fazlur Rahman, *Islam and Modernity Transformation of an Intellectual Tradition* (Chicago: The University of Chicago Press, 1982), 95–7.
131 Fazlur Rahman, *Islam* (Ankara: Selcuk, 1981), xxxvi.

Chapter 1

1   In the translations of Quranic verses, I use M. A. S. Abdel Haleem, *The Quran* (Oxford: Oxford University Press, 2005).
2   Özsoy, *Kur'an ve Tarihsellik Yazıları*, 75.
3   Öztürk, *Kur'an ve Tarihsellik*, 43.
4   Paul Hamilton, *Historicism* (London: Routledge, 1996), 2.
5   Öztürk, *Kur'an ve Tarihsellik*, 10.
6   Öztürk, *Kur'an'ı Kendi*, 41. Güler, *İsimsiz*, 87.
7   Mustafa Öztürk, *Kur'an'ın Mu'tezili Yorumu: Ebu Muslim el-İsfehani Örneği* (Ankara: Ankara Okulu, 2015), 35. Another example is the verse 18:83. Öztürk, *Söyleşiler*, 70.
8   Güler, *Sünniliğin Eleştirisine*, 28.
9   Mustafa Öztürk, *Kur'an, Vahiy Nüzul* (Ankara: Ankara Okulu, 2018), 31. For Ibn Hanbal, even the voice of a man who recites Quran is uncreated. M. Hayri Kırbaşoğlu, *İslam'ın Kurucu Metni: Kur'an Araştırmaları* (İstanbul: Otto, 2015), 11–17; Christopher Melchert, "Ahmad Ibn Hanbal and the Quran," *Journal of Quranic Studies* 6, no. 2 (2004): 22–34.
10 Karaman et al., *İlmihal I*, 103.
11 al-Ash'ari. *Al-Ibanah. 'An Usul Ad-Diyanah [The Elucidation of Islam's Foundation]*. Translated by Walter C. Klein (New Haven: American Oriental Society, 1940), 88; al-Maturidi, *Kitab al-Tawhid*, 98.
12 İlhami Güler, *Sabit Din Dinamik Şeriat* (Ankara: Ankara Okulu, 2017), 106; Öztürk, *Kur'an'ı Kendi*, 11–12; M. Hayri Kırbaşoğlu, *Ehl-i Sünnet'in Kurucu Ataları* (İstanbul: Otto, 2011), 233–44.
13 Mustafa Öztürk, *Tefsir Tarihi Araştırmaları* (Ankara: Ankara Okulu, 2014), 80; Kırbaşoğlu, *İslam'ın Kurucu*, 9; Sophia Vasalau, *Moral Agents and Their Deserts: The Character of Mu'tazilite Ethics* (Princeton: Princeton University Press, 2008), 123; Martin et al., *Defenders of Reason*, 77.
14 Margaret Larkin, "The Inimitability of the Quran: Two Perspectives," *Religion and Literature* 20, no. 1 (1998): 32.
15 See Christopher Melchert, *The Formation of Sunni Schools of Law, 9th–10th Centuries. C.E.* (Leiden: Brill, 1997), 76. Ibn Kullab's theory is the practice of rationalist methods, and the promulgation of traditionalist doctrines. J. R. T. M. Peters, *God's Created Speech: A Study in the Speculative Theology of the Mu'tazili Qadi al-Qudat Abu l-Hasan 'Abd al-Jabbar bn Ahmad al-Hamadani* (Leiden: Brill, 1976), 21.
16 John A. Nawas, "The Miḥna of 218 A. H./833 A. D. Revisited: An Empirical Study," *Journal of the American Oriental Society* 116, no. 4 (1996): 698–9.
17 Öztürk, *Kur'an ve Tarihsellik*, 60–1; Kırbaşoğlu, *İslam'ın Kurucu*, 20.
18 Öztürk, *Kur'an'ı Kendi*, 14; Kırbaşoğlu, *İslam'ın Kurucu*, 8; Güler, *Sabit Din*, 150.
19 Öztürk, *Tefsirin Halleri*, 299–302.

20. Wilfred Cantwell Smith, "Can Believers Share the Quran and the Bible as the Word of God?" In *On Sharing Religious Experience: Possibilities for Interfaith Mutuality*, edited by J. D. Gort, H. M. Vroom, R. Fernhout, and A. Wessels (Amsterdam: Rodopi, 1992), 56.
21. Güler, *Sabit Din*, 8.
22. Öztürk, *Tefsirin Halleri*, 318.
23. Güler, *Sabit Din*, 149.
24. Öztürk, *Tefsirin Halleri*, 299.
25. Güler, *Özgürlükçü Teoloji*, 37.
26. Özsoy, *Kur'an ve Tarihsellik Yazıları*, 150; Öztürk, *Kur'an ve Tarihsellik*, 85; Angelika Neuwirth, "Quran and History—A Disputed Relationship. Some Reflections on Quranic History and History in the Quran," *Journal of Quranic Studies* 5, no. 1 (2010): 1–5.
27. Öztürk and Ünsal, *Kur'an Tarihi*, 11; Güler, *Kur'an'ın Mahiyeti*, 13.
28. Öztürk, *Kur'an'ı Kendi*, 11–17; Güler, *Sabit Din*, 156; M. Hayri Kırbaşoğlu, *Müslüman Kalarak Yenilenmek* (Istanbul: Otto, 2019), 37.
29. Özsoy, *Kur'an ve Tarihsellik Yazıları*, 77 and 93. Also, see Mehmet Azimli, *Dört Halifeyi Farklı Okumak-1: Hz. Ebu Bekir* (Ankara: Ankara Okulu, 2018), 136.
30. Cf. Nasr Abu-Zayd, *Rethinking the Quran: Towards a Humanistic Hermeneutics* (Utrecht: Humanistic University Press, 2004), 30.
31. Öztürk, *Kur'an ve Tarihsellik*, 113. The meaning of *hanif* remains in dispute. It is usually defined as "a person linked to monotheism in the pre-Islamic period." Fred M. Donner, *Muhammed and the Believers at the Origins of Islam* (Cambridge, MA: The Belknap Press of Harvard University Press, 2010), 71. Also, see Mahmoud M. Ayoub, *The Quran and Its Interpreters Vol. I* (Albany: State University of New York Press, 1984), 164.
32. Öztürk, *Siyaset İtikad*, 193–208.
33. Öztürk, *Kur'an ve Tarihsellik*, 191–2.
34. Güler, *Kur'an'ın Mahiyeti*, 87.
35. Özsoy, *Kur'an ve Tarihsellik Yazıları*, 17.
36. Güler, *Kur'an'ın Mahiyeti*, 79. "Piracy and war gave place to trade, politics and letters; the war lord to the law lord; the law-lord to the merchant; and the mill-owner . . .." Ralph Waldo Emerson, *English Traits* (Boston and New York: H. Mifflin Company, 1903), 174.
37. Güler, *Vicdan*, 181.
38. Öztürk, *Kur'an'ın Kendi*, 211.
39. Güler, *İsimsiz*, 49.
40. İlhami Güler, *Kur'an'ın Ahlak Metafiziği* (Ankara: Ankara Okulu, 2015), 35.
41. Güler, *Kuş Bakışı*, 246.
42. Mustafa Öztürk, *Siyaset İtikad, Din* (Ankara: Ankara Okulu, 2018), 241.
43. Kırbaşoğlu, *Müslüman Kalarak*, 166.
44. Tazeem Haider, "Universality in the Message of Quran," *Journal of South Asian Studies* 4, no. 2 (2016): 61.
45. Güler, *Kuş Bakışı*, 241; R. İhsan Eliaçık, *Daru's-Selam: Evrensel Adalet ve Barış Yurdu* (Istanbul: İnşa, 2015), 45.
46. Güler, *Kur'an'ın Mahiyeti*, 15; Mustafa Öztürk, *Meal Kültürümüz* (Ankara: Ankara Okulu, 2016), 68; Özsoy, *Sünnetullah*, 16.
47. Güler, *İsimsiz*, 99; Özsoy, *Kur'an ve Tarihsellik Yazıları*, 74.
48. Güler, *İsimsiz*, 88.

49 Özsoy, *Kur'an ve Tarihsellik Yazıları*, 75; Öztürk, *Kur'an'ı Kendi*, 62. We observe the impact of Abu-Zayd, here. Nasr Abu-Zayd, "The Others in the Quran: A Hermeneutical Approach," *Philosophy and Social Criticism* 36, no. ¾ (2010): 282.
50 Güler, *Sünniliğin Eleştirisine*, 27. Also, see Özsoy, *Kur'an ve Tarihsellik Yazıları*, 12. Kırbaşoğlu, *Müslüman Kalarak*, 43.
51 Öztürk, *Kur'an'ı Kendi*, 62.
52 Öztürk, *Tefsirin Halleri*, 17; Özsoy, *Sünnetullah*, 17.
53 Paul Ricoeur, *The Interpretation Theory: Discourse and the Surplus of Meaning* (Texas: The Texas Christian University Press, 1976), 13 and 31.
54 Öztürk, *Kur'an'ı Kendi*, 74.
55 Kırbaşoğlu, *Müslüman Kalarak*, 43. Searle writes, "contextually dependent elements of the sentence, which are only with a background." John R. Searle, *Expression and Meaning: Studies in the Theory of Speech Acts* (Cambridge: Cambridge University Press, 1979), 79.
56 Özsoy, *Kuran ve Tarihsellik Yazıları*, 14; Mustafa Öztürk, *Kur'an ve Tefsir Kültürümüz* (Ankara: Ankara Okulu, 2017), 21.
57 Kırbaşoğlu, *Üçüncü Yol*, 147.
58 Mustafa Öztürk, *Kur'an, Tefsir ve Usul Üzerine Problemler, Tespitler, Teklifler* (Ankara: Ankara Okulu, 2017), 81.
59 Öztürk, *Siyaset İtikad*, 185 and 270–1; Güler, *Kur'an'ın Mahiyeti*, 58.
60 Güler, *Sabit Din*, 108.
61 Güler, *Realpolitik*, 88.
62 Öztürk, *Kur'an'ı Kendi*, 219–22. Also, see Kırbaşoğlu, *Müslüman Kalarak*, 346. Mehmet Azimli, *Cahiliyye'yi Farklı Okumak* (Ankara: Ankara Okulu, 2017), 83.
63 Azimli, *Cahiliyye'yi Farklı*, 18–23.
64 Öztürk, *Kur'an'ı Kendi*, 211–20; İsrafil Balcı, *Tartışmalı Siyer Meseleleri* (Istanbul: Düşün, 2018), 108. Umayyah presented himself "as a simple religious teacher, expecting a reward only from the God he serves, in the life to come." His poems are important historical evidence of the comparative study of religious terminology in the seventh century. E. S. J. Power, *Umayya Ibn Abi-s Salt* (Beyrouth: Imprimerie Catholique, 1906), 2–3 and 21.
65 Ibn Ishaq, *Sirat Rasul Allah [The Life of Muhammad: A Translation of Ibn Ishaq's Sirat Rasul Allah]*. Translated by. A. Guillaume (Oxford: Oxford University Press, 1955), 28–9 and 180.
66 Öztürk, *Kur'an'ı Kendi*, 219–22; Kırbaşoğlu, *Müslüman Kalarak*, 347.
67 Balcı, *Tartışmalı Siyer*, 120.
68 Güler, *Realpolitik*, 89; Öztürk, *Tefsirin Halleri*, 305.
69 Öztürk, *Kur'an'ı Kendi*, 151. "If the Quran is the sum total and seal of divine revelation then it must contain all that humankind needs." Sumaiya A. Hamdani, *Between Revolution and State: The Path to Fatimid Statehood* (London: I. B. Tauris, 2006), 85.
70 Abu Hamid al-Ghazali, *The Jewels of the Quran: Al-Ghazali's Theory [Kitab Jawahir al-Quran]*. Translated by Muhammad Abul Quasem (Kuala Lumpur: University of Malaya Press, 1977), 19–20.
71 Karaman et al., *İlmihal I*, 105–-6.
72 Güler, *Kur'an'ın Mahiyeti*, 66.
73 Mustafa Öztürk, "Kur'an Vahyinin Anlaşılması ve Yorumlanması," in *Tefsir Geleneğinde Anlam-Yorum Nüzul-Siret İlişkisi*, edited by Mustafa Öztürk (Ankara: Ankara Okulu, 2017), 31.

74 Öztürk, *Tefsir Tarihi*, 251.
75 For al-Suyuti, Quran's "knowledge cannot be computed." Imam Jalal-al-Din 'Abd al-Rahman, *The Perfect Guide to the Sciences of the Quran Volume I [Al-Itqan fi 'Ulum al-Quran]*. Translated by Hamid Algar, Michael Schub and Ayman Abdel Haleem (Reading: Garnet, 2011), xx.
76 Öztürk, *Söyleşiler*, 7; Güler, *Kur'an'ın Mahiyeti*, 27.
77 Güler, *Kuş Bakışı*, 237.
78 Öztürk, *Kur'an ve Tarihsellik*, 84; Kırbaşoğlu, *Üçüncü Yol*, 26; Janin and Kahlmeyer, *Islamic Law*, 58.
79 Öztürk and Ünsal, *Kur'an Tarihi*, 11. Culson, *A History of Islamic Law*, 60. Traditionalists saw al-Shafi'i's work as corrections of the "subjective trend" of Abu Hanifa's methodology. Ignaz Goldziher, *The Zahiris Their Doctrine and Their History: A Contribution to the History of Islamic Thought* (Leiden: E. J. Brill, 1971), 20.
80 Güler, *Kur'an'ın Mahiyeti*, 75.
81 Öztürk, *Kur'an'ın Mu'tezili*, 80.
82 Öztürk, *Kur'an'ı Kendi*, 29.
83 Rahman, *Islam and Modernity*, 26.
84 Güler, *Kuş Bakışı*, 232; İsrafil Balcı, *Hz. Peygamber ve Mucize* (Ankara: Ankara Okulu, 2013), 18–24; Kırbaşoğlu, *Müslüman Kalarak*, 354.
85 Güler, *Kur'an'ın Mahiyeti*, 10; Kırbaşoğlu, *Müslüman Kalarak*, 354.
86 Özsoy, *Sünnetullah*, 25 and 70; Öztürk, *Kur'an, Tefsir ve Usul*, 57; R. İhsan Eliaçık, *İslam'ın Üç Çağı: İnşa Çağında Yeni-İslamcılık Söylemleri* (Istanbul: Çıra, 2004), 60.
87 Kırbaşoğlu, *Müslüman Kalarak*, 41 and 157.
88 Güler, *Vicdan*, 119.
89 Kırbaşoğlu, *İslam Düşüncesinde Sünnet*, 93.
90 Öztürk, *Kur'an'ın Mu'tezili*, 41; Öztürk, *Tefsir Tarihi*, 82.
91 Öztürk, *Kur'an'ı Kendi*, 50–4.
92 Güler, *Kur'an'ın Mahiyeti*, 120.
93 Öztürk, *Siyaset İtikad*, 129.
94 Öztürk, *Kur'an, Vahiy Nüzul*, 51.
95 Öztürk, *Kur'an'ı Kendi*, 50–4; Güler, *Dine Yeni*, 107.
96 R. İhsan Eliaçık, *İslam'da Sosyal Değişim ve Devrimler* (Istanbul: Doğu, 2013), 47; İsrafil Balcı, *Peygamberlik Öncesi Hz. Muhammed* (Ankara: Ankara Okulu, 2014), 140; Özsoy, *Kur'an ve Tarihsellik Yazıları*, 18.
97 Öztürk, *Tefsir Tarihi*, 20.
98 Nasr Muhammad Abu-Zayd, "The Dilemma of the Literary Approach to the Quran," *Alif: Journal of Comparative Poetics* 23, no. 1 (2003): 8–47. Khalafallah inspired contemporary reformists like Abu-Zayd. Massimo Campanini, "Quranic Hermeneutics and Political Hegemony: Reformation of Islamic Thought," *The Muslim World* 99, no. 1 (2009): 126.
99 Güler, *Dine Yeni*, 219.
100 Özsoy, *Kuran ve Tarihsellik Yazıları*, 111–2.
101 Öztürk, *Söyleşiler*, 65. Al-Qaffal was interested in the Mu'tazili School in his early years. His approach to Islamic law played a role in the consolidation of the *maqasid* theory. Cengiz Kallek, "Kaffal, Muhammed bin Ali," in *İslam Ansiklopedisi Vol. 24*, edited by commission (Ankara: TDV, 2001), 146–8; Wael B. Hallaq, *The Origins and Evolution of Islamic Law* (Cambridge: Cambridge University Press, 2005), 177.
102 Eliaçık, *Sosyal İslam*, 66. Öztürk, *Meal Kültürümüz*, 93.
103 Öztürk, *Söyleşiler*, 184.

104   Güler, *Sünniliğin Eleştirisine*, 28. For Öztürk, exegeses written in Turkish are under the impact of the "deep meaning" doctrine. Öztürk, *Cumhuriyet Türkiye'sinde*, 118-9.
105   R. İhsan Eliaçık, *İhyadan İnşaya İslam Düşüncesi* (Istanbul: İnşa, 2015), 16.
106   Öztürk, *Meal Kültürümüz*, 94. For Öztürk, this is also a response to the harsh Western intellectual assaults, such as Ernest Renan's argument that Islam is against development. Öztürk, *Kur'an, Tefsir ve Usul*, 69.
107   Eliaçık, *Bana Dinden*, 101.
108   Güler, *Özgürlükçü Teoloji*, 3; Güler, *Kur'an'ın Mahiyeti*, 81.
109   Öztürk, *Kur'an, Tefsir ve Usul*, 45. See R. E. Witt, "The Plotinian Logos and the Stoic Basis," *The Classical Quarterly* 25, no. 2 (1931): 103-11. However, compared with myth, logos in Plotinus is supported by argument and evidence. Stephen R. L. Clark, *Plotinus Myth, Metaphor, and Philosophical Practice* (Chicago: The Chicago University Press, 2016), 151.
110   Eliaçık, *İslam'ın Üç*, 48.
111   Özsoy, *Kur'an ve Tarihsellik Yazıları*, 19.
112   Öztürk, *Kur'an, Tefsir ve Usul*, 54.
113   Kırbaşoğlu, *Müslüman Kalarak*, 350.
114   Mahmoud Ayoub, "Uzayr in the Quran and Muslim Tradition," in *Studies in Islamic and Judaic Traditions*, edited by W. M. Brinner and S. D. Ricks (Atlanta, GA: Scholars Press, 1986), 15.
115   Özsoy, *Kur'an ve Tarihsellik Yazıları*, 111-12; Mustafa Öztürk, *Kur'an'a Çağdaş Yaklaşımlar* (Ankara: Ankara Okulu, 2019), 204.
116   Azimli, *Cahiliyye'yi Farklı*, 22.
117   Öztürk, *Kur'an, Vahiy Nüzul*, 172.
118   Öztürk, *Meal Kültürümüz*, 98.
119   Özsoy, *Kur'an ve Tarihsellik Yazıları*, 114.
120   Öztürk, *Meal Kültürümüz*, 94-8. Al-Baghdadi incorporated what scholars thought about natural events when deciding whether they are heretic or not. He wrote about al-Nazzam (d. 835) that "in his fifth heresy he contended that all animals are of one species." Al-Baghdadi, 'Abd Qahir ibn-Tahir, *Moslim Schism and Sects [Al-Fark Bain al-Firak]*. Translated by K. Chambers Seelye (New York: New York University Press, 1920), 122.
121   Öztürk, *Kur'an, Tefsir ve Usul*, 53.
122   Özsoy, *Sünnetullah*, 29.
123   Özsoy, *Kur'an ve Tarihsellik Yazıları*, 15-16.
124   Özsoy, *Sünnetullah*, 64.
125   Charles Taylor, *A Secular Age* (New York: Belknap, 2007), 25.
126   Öztürk, *Kur'an, Tefsir ve Usul*, 237.
127   Öztürk, *Kur'an, Vahiy Nüzul*, 56-7; Karaman et al., *İlmihal I*, 103.
128   Öztürk, *Tefsirin Halleri*, 298.
129   Öztürk, *Kur'an, Vahiy Nüzul*, 8-9 and 187.
130   Öztürk, *Kur'an, Vahiy Nüzul*, 55-7. According to *Islam Ansiklopedisi*, there is a consensus of resources that Gabriel appeared to Muhammad in the appearance of Dihyah. Ali Yardım, "Dihye bin Halife," in *İslam Ansiklopedisi Vol. IX*, edited by commission (Ankara: TDV, 1999) 249. Dihya was the companion sent by Muhammad to Emperor Heraclius with a letter on Islam. Nadia Maria El-Cheikh, "Muhammad and Heraclius: A Study in Legitimacy," *Studuia Islamica* 89, no. 1 (1999): 5-21.

131 Kırbaşoğlu, *Alternatif Hadis*, 375.
132 Rahman, *Major Themes*, 67.
133 Öztürk, *Kur'an, Vahiy Nüzul*, 56–61.
134 Ibid., 145. "Kuran metnindeki ayetler Hz. Peygambere lafız ve mana olarak vahyedilmemiştir."
135 Güler, *Realpolitik*, 87.
136 Eliaçık, *Kur'an'a Giriş*, 31.
137 Eliaçık, *Kur'an'a Giriş*, 29–30; R. İhsan Eliaçık, *Çağdaş Dünyada İslam* (Istanbul: İnşa, 2017), 290.
138 Rahman, *Major Themes*, 69; Rahman, *Islam and Modernity*, 5.
139 Öztürk, *Kur'an, Vahiy Nüzul*, 144–6.
140 Öztürk, *Kur'an'ın Mu'tezili*, 167; Özsoy, *Kur'an ve Tarihsellik Yazıları*, 94; Abu-Zayd, "The Others," 283; Toshihiko Izutsu, *God and Man in the Quran: Semantics of the Quranic Weltanschauung* (Tokyo: Keio University Press, 1964), 164.
141 Güler, *Kur'an'ın Mahiyeti*, 9–10.
142 Güler, *Realpolitik*, 87.
143 Öztürk, *Kur'an, Vahiy Nüzul*, 147; Öztürk and Ünsal, *Kur'an Tarihi*, 10.
144 Güler, *Kur'an'ın Mahiyeti*, 13–15.
145 Güler, *Sabit Din*, 201.
146 Özsoy, *Sünnetullah* 25; Mustafa Öztürk, *Kur'an Dili ve Retoriği* (Ankara: Ankara Okulu, 2015), 16; Güler, *İsimsiz*, 92.
147 Eliaçık, *İslam'ın Üç*, 20 ; Özsoy, *Kur'an ve Tarihsellik Yazıları*, 57; Kırbaşoğlu, *Müslüman Kalarak*, 75–6. Cf. Abu-Zayd, *Rethinking the Quran*, 9. Muhammad Arkoun, *The Unthought in Contemporary Islamic Thought* (London: Saqi, 2002), 99.
148 Öztürk, *Söyleşiler*, 96; Kırbaşoğlu, *Müslüman Kalarak*, 144–60.
149 Kırbaşoğlu, *Müslüman Kalarak*, 69; Güler, *Kur'an'ın Mahiyeti*, 29.
150 Kırbaşoğlu, *İslam'ın Kurucu*, 69. However, Jeffrey defended the view that Muhammad was preparing a book for his community. Arthur Jeffrey, *Islam, Muhammad and His Religion* (New York: The Bobbs-Merrill, 1958), 47; Arthur Jeffrey, *Materials for the History of the Text of Quran: The Old Codices* (Leiden: Brill, 1937), 1–18.
151 Kırbaşoğlu, *Müslüman Kalarak*, 75 and 160.
152 İlhami Güler, *İtikaddan İmana* (Ankara: Ankara Okulu, 2017), 19.
153 Özsoy, *Kur'an ve Tarihsellik Yazıları*, 54.
154 Öztürk and Ünsal, *Kur'an Tarihi*, 23; Öztürk, *Siyaset İtikad*, 118.
155 William A. Graham, *Divine Word and Prophetic Word in Early Islam* (Paris: Mouton, 1977), 10.
156 Kırbaşoğlu, *İslam'ın Kurucu*, 207.
157 Güler, *Sabit Din*, 197–200.
158 Eliaçık, *Kur'an'a Giriş*, 185.
159 Eliaçık, *İslam'ın Üç*, 17–19; Güler, *Dine Yeni*, 213. Öztürk, *Kur'an'ı Kendi*, 17.
160 Öztürk, *Kur'an ve Tarihsellik*, 68–71.
161 Öztürk, *Siyaset İtikad*, 267.
162 Balcı, *Peygamber ve Mucize*, 42.
163 Öztürk, *Tefsir Tarihi*, 34.
164 Eliaçık, *İhyadan İnşaya*, 12–13.
165 Güler, *Kuş Bakışı*, 224.
166 Öztürk, *Kur'an Dili*, 14–15.
167 Searle, *Expression and Meaning*, 7.
168 Özsoy, *Kur'an ve Tarihsellik Yazıları*, 208.

169 Öztürk, *Kur'an ve Tefsir*, 12.
170 Ricoeur, *The Interpretation Theory*, 25–7.
171 Graham, *Divine Word*, 10.
172 Barry Smith, "John Searle: From Speech Acts to Social Reality," in *John Searle*, edited by Barry Smith (Cambridge: Cambridge University Press, 2003), 11.
173 Özsoy, *Kur'an ve Tarihsellik Yazıları*, 49–58.
174 Öztürk, *Kur'an Dili*, 13.
175 Özsoy, *Kur'an ve Tarihsellik Yazıları*, 49–58.
176 Özsoy, *Kur'an ve Tarihsellik Yazıları*, 110; Eliaçık, *Kur'an'a Giriş*, 32.
177 Öztürk, *Tefsir Tarihi*, 13.
178 Öztürk, *Kur'an Dili*, 29.
179 Özsoy, *Kur'an ve Tarihsellik Yazıları*, 57.
180 Öztürk, *Meal Kültürümüz*, 11.
181 Özsoy, *Kur'an ve Tarihsellik Yazıları*, 56.
182 Öztürk, *Kur'an ve Tarihsellik*, 81.
183 Özsoy, *Kur'an ve Tarihsellik Yazıları*, 46 and 109–10.
184 Öztürk, *Kur'an Dili*, 18.
185 R. İhsan Eliaçık, *Sosyal İslam: Dinin Direği Paylaşımdır* (Istanbul: Destek, 2011), 10.
186 R. İhsan Eliaçık, *Yaşayan Kur'an: İlk Mesajlar* (Istanbul: İnşa, 2012), 22–35.
187 Eliaçık, *Daru's-Selam*, 92.
188 Öztürk, *Tefsirin Halleri*, 96; İsrafil Balcı, *Hz. Peygamber ve Namaz* (Ankara: Ankara Okulu, 2018), 40.
189 Öztürk, *Tefsirin Halleri*, 95–100. See al-Bukhari, *Sahih al-Bukhari Vol. V*. (Riyadh: Darussalaam, 1997), 429.
190 Kırbaşoğlu, *İslam'ın Kurucu*, 173.
191 Özsoy, *Sünnetullah*, 25; Öztürk, *Kur'an Dili*, 29. To justify such arguments in the Islamic tradition, Öztürk, cite several previous scholars with similar arguments, such as Izz ad-Din ibn Abdul Salam (d. 1262) and Abu Hayyan (d. 1344). Öztürk, *Kur'an'ı Kendi*, 57--62.
192 Özsoy, *Kur'an ve Tarihsellik Yazıları*, 47.
193 Güler, *Kuş Bakışı*, 240.
194 Öztürk, *Kur'an'ı Kendi*, 18.
195 Öztürk, *Kur'an ve Tarihsellik*, 81.
196 Öztürk and Ünsal, *Kur'an Tarihi*, 196; Güler, *Kur'an'ın Mahiyeti*, 49; Özsoy, *Kur'an ve Tarihsellik Yazıları*, 47.
197 Said Nursi, *The Words* (Istanbul: Sözler, 2008), 378.
198 Özsoy, *Kur'an ve Tarihsellik Yazıları*, 47.
199 Öztürk, *Meal Kültürümüz*, 12. As an example of exaggeration in Quran, Öztürk gives the verse 12:31, which tells that when women saw Joseph "they were stunned by his beauty and cut their hands." Öztürk, *Kur'an'a Çağdaş*, 221.
200 Öztürk, *Kur'an Dili*, 29.
201 Güler, *Kuş Bakışı*, 220.
202 Azimli, *Ebu Bekir*, 126. Also: Öztürk, *Kur'an'ın Mu'tezili*, 107.
203 Kırbaşoğlu, *Müslüman Kalarak*, 160.
204 Öztürk and Ünsal, *Kur'an Tarihi*, 195–6; Özsoy, *Kur'an ve Tarihsellik Yazıları*, 55. For a Sunni approach to difficulties in Quran, see Abdulcelil Candan, *Kur'an-ı Kerim'de Anlaşılması Güç Ayetler* (Istanbul: Seyda, 2016)..
205 For the Ash'ari school, the inimitability of Quran is manifest in both message and language. Larkin, "The Inimitability," 39. For some scholars, the inimitability of

Quran is only about its message not language. For example, Rahman quotes Abu Hanifa, who supported this view. Fazlur Rahman, "Translating the Quran," *Religion & Literature* 20, no. 1 (1988): 25. Though Turks are known as Hanafi, *İlmihal* prefers the Ash'ari view on *i'jaz*. Karaman, et al., *İlmihal I*, 105. For traditionalists, what historicists define as linguistic problems, such as repetitions, are in fact examples of literary beauty. Hussein Abdul-Rauf, *Quran Translation: Discourse, Texture and Exegesis* (London: Routledge, 2001), 67. In general, for Sunni Islam the quality of language in Quran is miraculous, which is evidence of its divine origin. Bassam Saeh, *The Miraculous Language of the Quran: Evidence of Divine Origin* (London: International Institute of Islamic Thought, 2015), 1–5.

206 Öztürk, *Kur'an'ın Mu'tezili*, 88; Louay Fatoohi, *Abrogation in the Quran and Islamic Law: A Critical Study of the Concept of "Naskh" and Its Impact* (London and New York: Routledge, 2013), 13.
207 Öztürk, *Siyaset İtikad*, 187; Abu-Zayd, *Rethinking the Quran*, 15. Similarly, for historicists, what appear as repetition in Quran are in fact verses with different meanings in their contexts. Öztürk, *Kur'an Dili*, 45–53.
208 Kırbaşoğlu, *Müslüman Kalarak*, 39; Öztürk, *Siyaset İtikad*, 187.
209 Öztürk, *Söyleşiler*, 121. The verse: "On this world and the next. They ask you about [the property of] orphans . . ." Öztürk here refers to the first short sentence.
210 Öztürk, *Kur'an Dili*, 19–20.
211 Öztürk and Ünsal, *Kur'an Tarihi*, 65.
212 Öztürk, *Kur'an'ın Mu'tezili*, 107.
213 Öztürk and Ünsal, *Kur'an Tarihi*, 195.
214 Güler, *Kur'an'ın Mahiyeti*, 116.
215 Öztürk, *Tefsirin Halleri*, 15.
216 Öztürk, *Kur'an'ı Kendi*, 63.
217 Güler, *Kur'an'ın Ahlak*, 98–9; Öztürk, *Kur'an ve Tarihsellik*, 46; Özsoy, *Kur'an ve Tarihsellik Yazıları*, 14.
218 Özsoy, *Kur'an ve Tarihsellik Yazıları*, 97–102; Güler, *İsimsiz*, 88; Azimli, *Cahiliyye'yi Farklı*, 11.
219 John R. Searle, *Speech Acts: An Essay in the Philosophy of Language* (Cambridge: Cambridge University Press, 1969), 35.
220 Güler, *İsimsiz*, 94.
221 Öztürk, *Kur'an'ı Kendi*, 38.
222 Öztürk, *Kur'an ve Tarihsellik*, 10–15.
223 Öztürk, *Kur'an'ı Kendi*, 26; Güler, *İtikaddan İmana*, 22.
224 Ricoeur, *The Interpretation Theory*, 9.
225 Searle, *Expression and Meaning*, 117.
226 Öztürk, *Kur'an'ı Kendi*, 63; Özsoy, *Sünnetullah*, 37; Eliaçık, *İhyadan İnşaya*, 14. "Authentic meaning" is different from *asbab al-nuzul*. According to al-Wahidi (d. 1075), who authored the classical book on the subject, *asbab al-nuzul* is to know the story and occasion of a revelation. al-Wahidi, *Al-Wahidi's Asbab al-Nuzul*. Translated by Mokrane Guezzou (Louisville, KY: Fons Vitae, 2008), 1. Historicists find *asbab al-nuzul* simplistic for not reflecting successfully the interaction of the revelation and its social, political, and economic dynamics.
227 Özsoy, *Kur'an ve Tarihsellik Yazıları*, 23.
228 Ibid., 80–1.
229 Abu-Zayd, "The Others," 282.
230 Öztürk, *Kur'an ve Tarihsellik*, 86.

231 Güler, *Kuş Bakışı*, 247.
232 Öztürk, *Kur'an'ı Kendi*, 9; Özsoy, *Kur'an ve Tarihsellik Yazıları*, 20.
233 Güler, *İsimsiz*, 88; Öztürk, *Kur'an ve Tarihsellik*, 42.
234 Özsoy, *Kur'an ve Tarihsellik Yazıları*, 21.
235 Öztürk, *Kur'an ve Tarihsellik*, 13.
236 Özsoy, *Kur'an ve Tarihsellik Yazıları*, 61.
237 Güler, *İsimsiz*, 98.
238 Öztürk, *Kur'an'ı Kendi*, 59; Mehmet Azimli, "İsra Miraç Olayları Üzerine Bazı Mülahazalar," *Bilimname* 1, no. 1 (2009): 48.
239 Rahman, *Islam and Modernity*, 6.
240 İlhami Güler, *Politik Teoloji Yazıları* (Ankara: Ankara Okulu, 2018), 59.
241 Öztürk, *Kur'an ve Tarihsellik*, 10–11.
242 Güler, *Direniş Teolojisi*, 35.
243 Güler, *Sabit Din*, 200–1; Eliaçık, *İslam'ın Üç*, 24–5.
244 Özsoy, *Kur'an ve Tarihsellik Yazıları*, 103.
245 Güler, *Kur'an'ı Kendi*, 45.
246 Eliaçık, *İslam'ın Üç*, 95.
247 For Abu-Zayd, Quran is a living phenomenon "like the music played by the orchestra," whereas the Mushaf, the written text, is analogous to the musical score; it is silent." Abu-Zayd, *Rethinking the Quran*, 13.
248 Rahman, *Islam and Modernity*, 2.
249 Güler, *Özgürlükçü Teoloji*, 37–9.
250 Özsoy, *Kur'an ve Tarihsellik Yazıları*, 50–1; Güler, *Direniş Teolojisi*, 12.
251 Güler, *Kuş Bakışı*, 115.
252 Özsoy, *Kur'an ve Tarihsellik Yazıları*, 99; Öztürk, *Siyaset İtikad*, 185; Güler, *Allah'ın Ahlakiliği*, 7.
253 Öztürk, *Kur'an'ı Kendi*, 43–5.
254 Hüseyin Atay, *Kur'an'a Göre Araştırmalar IV* (Ankara: Atay, 2012), 36.
255 Ali Usman Qasmi, "Towards a New Prophetology: Maulwi 'Abdullah Cakralawi's Ahl al-Quran Movement," *The Muslim World* 99, no. 1 (2009): 155.
256 Aziz Ahmat, *Islamic Modernism in India and Pakistan, 1857–1964* (Bombay: Oxford University Press, 1967), 120.
257 Hüseyin Atay, *Kur'an'a Göre Araştırmalar I* (Ankara: Atay, 2012), 18.
258 Atay, *Kur'an'a Göre V*, 13–14.
259 Yaşar Nuri Öztürk, *Arapçılığa Karşı Akılcılığın Öncüsü İmam Azam Ebu Hanife: Esas Fikirleri Gölgelenen Önder* (Ankara: Yeni Boyut, 2009), 406.
260 Atay, *Ben*, 122.
261 Yaşar Nuri Öztürk, *Kur'an'daki İslam* (Istanbul: Yeni Boyut, 2018), 172; Atay, *Cehaletin*, 57.
262 Yaşar Nuri Öztürk, *Cevap Veriyorum: Gerçek Din Arayanlarla Baş Başa* (Istanbul: Yeni Boyut, 2001), 83; Atay, *Kur'an'a Göre V*, 62.
263 Yaşar Nuri Öztürk, *Merak Edilen Yönleriyle İslam* (Istanbul: Kaynak, 2018), 99.
264 Hüseyin Atay, *Kur'an'a Göre Araştırmalar II* (Ankara: Atay, 2012), 36–7.
265 Yaşar Nuri, *Dinde Reform II*, 11; Atay, *Kur'an'a Göre II*, 12–25.
266 Yaşar Nuri Öztürk, *400 Soruda İslam* (Istanbul: Yeni Boyut, 2016), 138.
267 Yaşar Nuri, *Cevap Veriyorum*, 85.
268 Yaşar Nuri Öztürk, *Cevap Veriyorum 3: Gerçek Din Arayanlarla Baş Başa* (Istanbul: Yeni Boyut, 2003), 16; Atay, *Cehaletin*, 78.
269 Eliaçık, *Kur'an'a Giriş*, 59–60.

270 Yaşar Nuri, *Dinde Reform II*, 7–24.
271 Yaşar Nuri, *Cevap Veriyorum* 3, 16.
272 Yaşar Nuri, *Dinde Reform II*, 13 and 47.
273 Atay, *Kur'an'da İman*, 40–2.
274 Atay, *Cehaletin*, 170; Yaşar Nuri, *Cevap Veriyorum*, 75.
275 Yaşar Nuri, *Dinde Reform I*, 275.
276 Atay, *Cehaletin*, 183.
277 Atay, *Kur'an'a Göre II*, 12–25.
278 Yaşar Nuri Öztürk, *Din ve Fıtrat* (Istanbul: Yeni Boyut, 1990), 217.
279 Yaşar Nuri Öztürk, *Konferanslarım: Bir İmanın Destanlaşması* (Istanbul: Yeni Boyut, 1996), 113.
280 Yaşar Nuri, *400 Soruda*, 159.
281 Atay, *Cehaletin*, 169–70.
282 Yaşar Nuri, *Cevap Veriyorum*, 85.
283 Searle, *Expression and Meaning*, 117.
284 Atay, *Kur'an'a Göre I*, 13.
285 Atay, *Kur'an'a Göre IV*, 36.
286 Yaşar Nuri, *Dinde Reform II*, 24–35.
287 Yaşar Nuri, *Konferanslarım*, 93; Atay, *Kur'an'a Göre I*, 18.
288 Leah Kingberg, "Muhkamat and Mutashabihat (Koran 3/7): Implications of a Koranic Pair of Terms in Medieval Exegesis," *Arabica* 35, no. 2 (1988): 144. The *muteshabih* are "subject to further explanation or interpretation, or they need proper clarification to transmit the truth and objective of the divine message." Thameem Ushama, "Issues in the Understanding of Muhkam and Muteshabih Passages of the Quran," *Al-Shajarah: Journal of the International Institute of Islamic Thought and Civilization* 16, no. 1 (2011): 85.
289 Yaşar Nuri, *400 Soruda*, 19.
290 Yaşar Nuri, *Konferanslarım*, 93.
291 Yaşar Nuri, *Merak*, 134.
292 Hüseyin Atay, *Kur'an'a Göre Araştırmalar III* (Ankara: Atay, 2012), 6.
293 Atay, *Kur'an'a Göre V*, 74.
294 Yaşar Nuri, *400 Soruda*, 125. For Yaşar Nuri, the verse 10:12 warns of poisonous gases in the atmosphere. Yaşar Nuri Öztürk, *Kur'an'ın Yarattığı Muci Devrimler* (Istanbul: Yeni Boyut, 2014), 260 and 295.
295 Yaşar Nuri, *Kur'an'daki İslam*, 26.
296 Atay, *Ben*, 61.
297 Yaşar Nuri Öztürk, *İslam Nasıl Yozlaştırıldı* (Istanbul: Yeni Boyut, 1988), 462–4.
298 Yaşar Nuri, *Cevap Veriyorum* 3, 169.
299 Yaşar Nuri, *İslam Nasıl*, 462–4.
300 Yaşar Nuri, *Merak*, 28–30.
301 Atay, *Cehaletin*, 289.
302 *İlham* is a form of a self-realized reality that does not rely on senses or reasoning. It happens in its original absoluteness, beyond all spatiotemporal determinants. Toshiko Izutsu, *Creation and the Timeless Order of Things: Essays in Islamic Mystical Philosophy* (Ashland: White Cloud Press, 1994), 1–37.
303 Atay, *Cehaletin*, 291.
304 Yaşar Nuri, *Dinde Reform I*, 20.
305 Yaşar Nuri, *Merak*, 83.
306 Atay, *Kur'an'a Göre II*, 33.

307 Atay, *Kur'an'a Göre V*, 62; Yaşar Nuri, *Merak*, 113-8.
308 Atay, *Kur'an'a Göre V*, 10.
309 Öztürk, *Siyaset İtikad*, 181.
310 Atay, *Kur'an'a Göre II*, 34.
311 Atay, *Cehaletin*, 237.
312 Yaşar Nuri, *Konferanslarım*, 21.
313 Atay, *Ben*, 44.
314 Atay, *İslam'ı Yeniden*, 143; Yaşar Nuri, *Cevap Veriyorum*, 79.
315 Yaşar Nuri, *Emevi*, 203.
316 Yaşar Nuri, *Merak*, 127; Eliaçık, *İslam'ın Üç*, 53; Atay, *Kur'an'da İman*, 10.
317 Yaşar Nuri Öztürk, *Din Maskeli Allah Düşmanlığı: Şirk ve Şirke Tepkinin Felsefeleşmesi: Deizm* (Istanbul: Yeni Boyut, 2013), 263. Cf. Rahman, *Islam and Modernity*, 17.
318 Atay, *Kur'an'a Göre V*, 15.
319 Yaşar Nuri, *Dinde Reform I*, 57.
320 Yaşar Nuri, *Konferanslarım*, 196.
321 Atay, *Kur'an'a Göre III*, 147.
322 Atay, *Kur'an'a Göre II*, 75.
323 Atay, *Kur'an'a Göre V*, 14.
324 Atay, *Kur'an'a Göre II*, 12-13.
325 Yaşar Nuri, *Din Maskeli*, 263.
326 Atay, *Ben*, 16; Yaşar Nuri, *Emevi*, 15.
327 Fazlur Rahman, *Major Themes of Quran* (Chicago: The University of Chicago Press, 2009), 31.
328 Eliaçık, *Kur'an'a Giriş*, 70.
329 Yaşar Nuri Öztürk, *Kur'an-i Kerim'de Lanetlenen Soy* (Istanbul: Yeni Boyut, 2017), 7.
330 Yaşar Nuri, *Kur'an Penceresinden*, 19. This book is dedicated to Che Guevara.
331 Atay, *Kur'an'a Göre V*, 155.
332 Atay, *Cehaletin*, 214-5. Atay also uses another Greek philosopher, Xenophanes, for his rationalist ideas of concept of God. Atay, *Ben*, 148.
333 Atay, *Cehaletin*, 64-78.
334 Muhammad Zain bin Haji Othman and Muhammad Bakhit al-Muti'i, "Urf as a Source of Islamic Law," *Islamic Studies* 20, no. 4 (1981): 343-55.
335 Mohamed El-Awa, "The Place of Custom (Urf) in Islamic Legal Theory," *Islamic Quarterly* 17, no. 3 (1973): 177.
336 Öztürk, *İslam Nasıl*, 294.
337 Yaşar Nuri, *Dinde Reform II*, 77.
338 Friedrich Schleiermacher, *On Religion: Speeches to Its Cultured Despisers* (Cambridge: Cambridge University Press, 1996), 51-5. Schleiermacher also "replaced the Bible with the church as sole authority," which makes it critical to study Yaşar Nuri and Atay, who similarly suggest a "Quran Islam." See Theodore Vial, "Friedrich Schleiermacher," in *Nineteenth-Century Philosophy of Religion*, edited by Graham Oppy and N. N. Trakakis, 31-47 (London: Routledge, 2013), 35.
339 Yaşar Nuri, *İnsanlığı Kemiren*, 42.
340 R. İhsan Eliaçık, *Mülk Yazıları 2* (Istanbul: İnşa, 2010), 7-8.
341 Yaşar Nuri, *İnsanlığı Kemiren*, 53. The comparison of *shura* and democracy is relatively old, affecting almost the whole of contemporary Islamic literature. Uriya Shavit, "Is Shura a Muslim Form of Democracy? Roots and Systemization of a Polemic," *Middle Eastern Studies* 46, no. 3 (2010): 349-74. Also, see Mishal Fahm

al-Sulami, *The West and Islam: Western Liberal Democracy versus the System of Shura* (London: Routledge, 2003), 5; Gudrun Kramer, "Islamists Notions of Democracy," *Middle East Report* 183, no. 1 (1992): 8.
342 Yaşar Nuri, *Konferanslarım*, 196.
343 Yaşar Nuri, *Dinde Reform II*, 71.
344 Atay, *Ben*, 29.
345 Atay, *Cehaletin*, 297.
346 Atay, *Ben*, 62–3.
347 Atay, *Kur'an'a Göre II*, 77.
348 Atay, *Cehaletin*, 286.
349 Adam Drozdek, "Anaxagoras' Cosmic Mind," *Estudios clásicos* 47, no. 127 (1971): 23.
350 Felix M Cleve, *The Philosophy of Anaxagoras* (New York: King's Crown Press, 1949), 156.
351 Yaşar Nuri, *Dinde Reform II*, 66.
352 Yaşar Nuri, *Kur'an'daki İslam*, 152–3.
353 Yaşar Nuri Öztürk, *Kur'an'ı Anlamaya Doğru* (Istanbul: Yeni Boyut, 1995), 8.
354 Yaşar Nuri, *Kur'an'ın Yarattığı*, 11.
355 Özsoy, *Kur'an ve Tarihsellik*, 91.
356 Eliaçık, *Kur'an'a Giriş*, 75; Yaşar Nuri, *Cevap Veriyorum 3*, 17.
357 Atay, *Kur'an'a Göre II*, 25–6.
358 Yaşar Nuri, *Din ve Fıtrat*, 199.
359 Yaşar Nuri, *Türkiye'ye Mektuplar*, 165.
360 Eliaçık, *İhyadan İnşaya*, 357.
361 Yaşar Nuri, *Din Maskeli*, 168.
362 Yaşar Nuri Öztürk, *İmamı Azam Savunması Şehit Bir Önder İçin Apolocya* (Istanbul: Yeni Boyut, 2017), 76.
363 Eliaçık, *İslam'ın Üç*, 89.
364 Yaşar Nuri, *Arapçılığa Karşı*, 234–55.
365 Yaşar Nuri, *Dinde Reform II*, 236.
366 Rahmi Yaran, "Karafi'den Şatibi'ye Makasıd/Maslahat Söylemi," *Marmara Universitesi İlahiyat Fakültesi Dergisi* 45, no. 1 (2013): 5–30.
367 Atay, *İslam'da İşçi*, 25; Yaşar Nuri, *Din ve Fıtrat*, 40; Eliaçık, *Kur'an'a Giriş*, 125.
368 Muhammad Hashim Kamali, "Maqasid al-Shari'ah: The Objectives of Islamic Law," *Islamic Studies* 38, no. 2 (1999): 193.
369 Auda Jasser, *Maqasid al-Sharia of Islamic Law: A Systems Approach* (London: The International Institute of Islamic Thought, 2008), 4–6.
370 Asyraf Wajdi Dusuki and Nurdianawati Irwani Abdullah, "Maqasid al-Shari'ah, Maslahah, and Corporate Social Responsibility," *American Journal of Islamic Social Sciences* 24, no. 1 (2007): 31.
371 Ahmad Al-Raysuni, *Imam al-Shatibi's Theory of the Higher Objectives and Intents of the Islamic Law* (London: The International Institute of Islamic Thought, 2005), 141–2.
372 Ibrahim Ibn Musa Abu Ishaq al-Shatibi, *Al-Muwafaqat fi Usul al-Shari'a Vol. II [The Reconciliation of the Fundamentals of the Islamic Law]*. Translated by Imran Ahsan Khan Nyazee (Reading: Garnett, 2014), 98.
373 See Muhammad bin Tahir Ibn Ashur, *Treatise on Maqasid al-Shari'a* (London: The International Institute of Islamic Thought, 2006), 223.
374 Rumee Ahmed, "Which Comes First, the *Maqasid* or the *Shari'a*?" in *The Objectives of Islamic Law: The Promises and Challenges of the Maqasid al-Shari'a*, edited by Idris Nassery, Rumee Ahmed, and Muna Tatari, 239–62 (London: Lexington, 2018), 241.

375 al-Shatibi is a source of inspiration for historicists, too. However, historicists are critical of the universalists' interpretation of al-Shatibi's *maqasid* doctrine. Özsoy, *Sünnetullah*, 24.
376 Jonathan A. C. Brown, *Hadith: Muhammad's Legacy in the Medieval and Muslim World* (Oxford: Oneworld, 2009), 3.
377 Kırbaşoğlu, *İslam Düşüncesinde Hadis*, 16–18.
378 Eliaçık, *Devrimci*, 58.
379 Atay, *Cehaletin*, 61.
380 Kırbaşoğlu, *Üçüncü Yol*, 26. See Eeric Dickinson, *The Development of Early Sunnite Hadith Criticism: The Taqdima of Ibn Abi Hatim al-Razi (240/854-327/938)* (Leiden: I. B. Tauris, 2001), 2–5.
381 Güler, *İsimsiz*, 111; Atay, *Kur'an'a Göre V*, 29.
382 Kırbaşoğlu, *İslam Düşüncesinde Sünnet*, 134; Atay, *Kur'an'a Göre V*, 47.
383 Kırbaşoğlu, *İslami İlimlerde Metot*, 234; M. Hayri Kırbaşoğlu, "İmam Şafi'i'nin Er-Risalesi'nin Hadis İlmindeki Etkileri," in *Sünni Paradigmanın Oluşumunda Şafi'i'nin Rolü*, edited by M. Hayri Kırbaşoğlu (Istanbul: Otto, 2016), 341.
384 Kırbaşoğlu, *İslam Düşüncesinde Hadis*, 32.
385 Aisha Y. Musa, *Hadith as Scripture: Discussions on the Authority of Prophetic Traditions in Islam* (New York: Palgrave Macmillan, 2008), 5 and 31; Öztürk, *Kur'an, Tefsir ve Usul*, 13.
386 Güler, *Sabit Din*, 185-4.
387 Atay, *Kur'an'a Göre IV*, 32-4.
388 Atay, *Kur'an'a Göre III*, 139–40.
389 Güler, *Politik Teoloji*, 276; Yaşar Nuri, *Merak*, 22.
390 Wael B. Hallaq, *A History of Islamic Legal Theories* (Cambridge: Cambridge University Press, 1997), 18.
391 Güler, *Özgürlükçü Teoloji*, 23–4.
392 Kırbaşoğlu, *İslam Düşüncesinde Hadis*, 55. Kırbaşoğlu argues that hadith scholars usually hate rationalists such as the Mu'tazili scholars, and even Abu Hanifa. Kırbaşoğlu, *Alternatif Hadis*, 45.
393 Güler, *Sabit Din*, 183–5.
394 al-Shafi'i, *al-Shafi'i's Risala*, 70–9 and 290.
395 Öztürk, *Kur'an'ı Kendi*, 85; Güler, *Kur'an'ın Ahlak*, 73.
396 Atay, *İslam'ı Yeniden*, 67.
397 Öztürk, *Kur'an'a Kendi*, 72–5.
398 Güler, *Kur'an'ın Mahiyeti*, 17. Also, Özsoy, *Kur'an ve Tarihsellik Yazıları*, 60.
399 Kırbaşoğlu, *İslam'ın Kurucu*, 325.
400 Kırbaşoğlu, *İslami İlimlerde Metot*, 15. On al-Amidi, see Bernard G. Weiss, *The Search for God's Law: Islamic Jurisprudence in the Writings of Sayf al-Din al-Amidi* (Salt Lake City: University of Utah Press, 2010), 678.
401 Güler, *Aklın İçindeki*, 7.
402 Kırbaşoğlu, *İslam Düşüncesinde Sünnet*, 18.
403 Kırbaşoğlu, *İslam'ın Kurucu*, 318–24; Öztürk, *Kur'an'a Çağdaş*, 133–5. Özsoy, *Kur'an ve Tarihsellik Yazıları*, 60.
404 Kırbaşoğlu, *Üçüncü Yol*, 158.
405 Öztürk, *Kur'an'a Göre*, 60–75; Güler, *Kur'an'ın Mahiyeti*, 35.
406 Güler, *Kuş Bakışı*, 138.
407 Qasmi, "Towards a New Prophetology," 156; Yaşar Nuri, *Türkiye'ye Mektuplar*, 34; Atay, *Kur'an'a Göre III*, 37.

408 Yaşar Nuri, *Arapçılığa Karşı*, 241.
409 Yaşar Nuri, *Din Maskeli*, 265.
410 Atay, *Kur'an'a Göre IV*, 32.
411 Atay, *Kur'an'a Göre III*, 137.
412 Yaşar Nuri, *Kur'an'ın Yarattığı*, 219.
413 Yaşar Nuri, *Tanrı, Akıl*, 292-3.
414 Yaşar Nuri, *400 Soruda*, 21.
415 M. Hayri Kırbaşoğlu, "Şaf'i'in Er-Risale'deki Hadisçiliği," in *Sünni Paradigmanın Oluşumunda Şafi'i'nin Rolü*, edited by M. Hayri Kırbaşoğlu (Istanbul: Otto, 2016), 371.
416 Yaşar Nuri, *İmamı Azam*, 80.
417 Kırbaşoğlu, *Üçüncü Yol*, 158.
418 Yaşar Nuri, *İmamı Azam*, 99.
419 Kırbaşoğlu, *Alternatif Hadis*, 155.
420 Atay, *Kur'an'a Göre I*, 15.
421 Yaşar Nuri Öztürk, *Fatiha Suresi Tefsiri* (Istanbul: Yeni Boyut, 1997), 21.
422 Kırbaşoğlu, *Alternatif Hadis*, 189. Ibn Rahwayh was a scholar who did not use al-Shafi'i's methodology, unlike other jurists. Such cases demonstrate that the rise of al-Shafi'i methodology as the mainstream approach in hadith is a later phenomenon. Susan Spectorsky, "Hadith in the Responses of Ishaq b. Rahwayh," *Islamic Law and Society* 8, no. 3 (2002): 429-30.
423 Yaşar Nuri Öztürk, *İslam Dünyasında Akıl ve Kur'an Nasıl Dışlandı?* (Istanbul: Yeni Boyut, 2016), 64.
424 Öztürk, *Kur'an, Tefsir ve Usul*, 158.
425 Yaşar Nuri Öztürk, *Kur'an'ın Temel Buyrukları Emirler ve Yasaklar* (Istanbul: Yeni Boyut, 2017), 176.
426 Eliaçık, *Demokratik*, 59.
427 Güler, *Kuş Bakışı*, 140.
428 Güler, *Kur'an'ın Mahiyeti*, 85.
429 Kırbaşoğlu, *Alternatif Hadis*, 31-5.
430 Kırbaşoğlu, *İslam Düşüncesinde Hadis*, 22-8.
431 Güler, *Kuş Bakışı*, 241.
432 Güler, *İsimsiz*, 96.
433 Kırbaşoğlu, *Alternatif Hadis*, 18.
434 Güler, *Dine Yeni*, 47.
435 Atay, *Ben*, 128; Yaşar Nuri, *İslam Nasıl*, 26.
436 Kırbaşoğlu, *İslam Düşüncesinde Hadis*, 268-97.
437 Ibid., 17-28. Ibn as-Salah found the use of previous key hadith books as reliable hadith transmissions that do not need the performing of the classical *isnad* methods. We observe the formation of general methodology on traditions with al-Salah, which is different from the classical *isnad*-based studies. Eeric Dickinson, "Ibn al-Salah al-Shahrazuri and the Isnad," *Journal of the American Oriental Society* 122, no. 3 (2002): 488.
438 Mehmet Azimli, *Tarih Okumaları* (Ankara: Ankara Okulu, 2018), 22. Atay, *Ben*, 117; R. İhsan Eliaçık, *Mülk Yazıları: Göklerde ve Yerde Mülkiyet Allah'a Aittir* (Istanbul: İnşa, 2016), 33; Yaşar Nuri, *Dinde Reform I*, 207.
439 Yaşar Nuri, *Lanetlenen*, 84; Kırbaşoğlu, *İslam Düşüncesinde Hadis*, 12.
440 Yaşar Nuri, *Kur'an'daki İslam*, 102.
441 Öztürk and Ünsal, *Kur'an Tarihi*, 22.
442 Yaşar Nuri, *İmamı Azam*, 88.
443 Yaşar Nuri, *Arapçılığa Karşı*, 290.

444 Yaşar Nuri, *İslam Dünyasında Akıl*, 74. Also, Mehmet Azimli, *Farklı Okumak: Hasan ve Muaviye* (Ankara: Ankara Okulu, 2016), 142.
445 Mehmet Azimli, *Halifelik Tarihine Giriş: Başlangıcından IX. Asra Kadar* (Istanbul: Cizgi, 2016), 40.
446 İsrafil Balcı, *Hz. Peygamber ve Gayb* (Ankara: Ankara Okulu, 2016), 171; Güler, *Vicdan*, 195.
447 John Burton, *An Introduction to Hadith* (Edinburgh: Edinburgh University Press, 2001), 29–30.
448 Mustafa Shah, "Introduction," in *The Hadith Critical Concepts in Islamic Studies*, edited by Mustafa Shah (London: Routledge, 2009) 4–7.
449 al-Shafi'i, *al-Shafi'T's Risala*, 182.
450 Kırbaşoğlu, *İslam Düşüncesinde Hadis*, 41; Özsoy, *Kur'an ve Tarihsellik Yazıları*, 68.
451 Kırbaşoğlu, *İslam Düşüncesinde Sünnet*, 91–2.
452 Kırbaşoğlu, *Alternatif Hadis*, 143–4. For Kırbaşoğlu, even hadith cannot normally be defined as a science. To him, it is rather a collection of data. Kırbaşoğlu, *İslami İlimlerde Metot*, 106.
453 Kırbaşoğlu, *İslami İlimlerde Metot*, 245–52.
454 Kırbaşoğlu, *Alternatif Hadis*, 144.
455 Kırbaşoğlu, *İslam Düşüncesinde Hadis*, 13.
456 Yaşar Nuri, *Arapçılığa Karşı*, 241; Kamaruddin Amin, "The Reliability of the Traditional Science of Hadith: A Critical Consideration," *Al-Jami'ah Journal of Islamic Studies* 43, no. 2 (2005): 269.
457 Atay, *Kur'an'a Göre I*, 113; Yaşar Nuri, *Dinde Reform I*, 223. The works of the rationalists have a lot of discussions on Abu Hurayra. See Atay, *Kur'an'a Göre I*, 113. Yaşar Nuri, *İmamı Azam*, 89.
458 Kırbaşoğlu, *İslami İlimlerde Metot*, 244.
459 Kırbaşoğlu, *Alternatif Hadis*, 47. For several scholars *isnad* was a unique Islamic methodology of scholarly authentication which worked successfully. Tarif Khalidi, *Arab Historical Thought in the Classical Period* (Cambridge: Cambridge University Press, 1994), 23–4.
460 Yaşar Nuri, *Kur'an'daki İslam*, 103. Also, see Kırbaşoğlu, "Şaf'i'in Er-Risale'deki Hadisçiliği," 371.
461 Güler, *Dine Yeni*, 47; Yaşar Nuri, *İslam Nasıl*, 409–10. The content-based analysis we observe in the works of the rationalists is a shared perspective globally among rationalist Muslim scholars. Khaled Abou El Fadl, *Speaking in God's Name: Islamic Law, Authority, and Women* (Oxford: One World, 2001), 211; Sami Catovic, "Finding a Principled Approach to *Matn* Analysis," in *Contemporary Approaches to the Quran and Sunnah*, edited by Mahmoud Ayoub (London: The International Institute of Islamic Thought, 2012), 165–6.
462 Kırbaşoğlu, *İslam Düşüncesinde Hadis*, 57.
463 Kırbaşoğlu, *İslami İlimlerde Metot*, 292; Atay, *Kur'an'a Göre V*, 46; R. İhsan Eliaçık, *Hangi Muhammed: Sihirbaz, Kahin, Ruhban Değil Arkadaş Peygamber* (Istanbul: İnşa, 2017), 74.
464 Kırbaşoğlu, *İslam Düşüncesinde Hadis*, 36.
465 Yaşar Nuri, *Arapçılığa Karşı*, 241.
466 Yaşar Nuri Yaşar Nuri, *Ses Birgün Yankılanır* (Istanbul: Yeni Boyut, 1998), 108. This method is proposed by other scholars, too. See Israr Ahmad Khan, *Authentication of Hadith: Redefining the Criteria* (London: The International Institute of Islamic Thought, 2010), 72–138.

467 Kırbaşoğlu, *Alternatif Hadis*, 297.
468 Ibid., 277. Eliaçık, *Hangi Muhammed*, 74
469 Kırbaşoğlu, *İslam Düşüncesinde Hadis*, 43.
470 Kırbaşoğlu, *Alternatif Hadis*, 273.
471 Ibid., 242–7. Yaşar Nuri, *Din Maskeli*, 280.
472 G. H. A. Juynboll, *Muslim Tradition: Studies in Chronology, Provenance and Authorship of Early Hadith* (Cambridge: Cambridge University Press, 1983), 70 and 6.
473 Kırbaşoğlu, *İslam Düşüncesinde Sünnet*, 317.
474 Kırbaşoğlu, *Alternatif Hadis*, 64.
475 Yaşar Nuri Öztürk, *Çıplak Uyarı* (Istanbul: Yeni Boyut, 1998), 8.
476 Eliaçık, *Çağdaş Dünyada*, 91.
477 Atay, *İslam'ı Yeniden*, 38.
478 Güler, *Kur'an'ın Ahlak*, 128.
479 Herbert Berg, "Competing Paradigms in Islamic Origins: Quran 15:89-91 and the Value of Isnads," in *Method and Theory in the Study of Islamic Origins*, edited by Herbert Berg (Leiden: Brill, 2003), 281; Güler, *Kuş Bakışı*, 138.

Chapter 2

1 Frank Griffel, "Introduction," in *Islamic Law in the Contemporary Context: Shari'a*, edited by Abbas Amanat and Frank Griffel (Stanford: Stanford University Press, 2002), 2.
2 al-Jabri, *The Formation of Arab Reason*, 96–106.
3 Roy Jakson, *Mawlana Mawdudi and Political Islam Authority and Islamic State* (London and New York: Routledge, 2011), 46–9.
4 Sayed Khatab, *The Power of Sovereignty: The Political and Ideological Philosophy of Sayyid Qutb* (London: Routledge, 2006), 7–46.
5 Vanessa Martin, *Creating an Islamic State: Khomeini and the Making of New Iran* (London and New York: I.B. Tauris, 2003), 100–28.
6 Andrew G. Bostom, *Sharia versus Freedom: The Legacy of Islamic Totalitarianism* (London: Prometheus, 2012).
7 Adel Omer Sharif, "Generalities on Criminal Procedure under Islamic Shari'a," in *Criminal Justice in Islam Judicial Procedure in the Shari'a*, edited by Muhammad Abdel Halim, Adel Omar Sharif and Kate Daniels (London: I.B. Tauris, 2003), 3; John R. Bowen, *Why the French Don't Like the Headscarf* (Princeton: Princeton University Press, 2010), 1–7.
8 M. Hayri Kırbaşoğlu, *Ahirzaman İlmihali* (Ankara: Otto, 2017), 23–4; Güler, *Sünniliğin Eleştirisine*, 13.
9 Kırbaşoğlu, *İslami İlimlerde Metot*, 63. Also, see Güler, *Sabit Din*, 104.
10 Kırbaşoğlu, *Müslüman Kalarak*, 150.
11 Ismail R. Al-Faruqi, *Al-Tawhid: Its Implications for Thought and Life* (London: The International Institute of Islamic Thought, 2000), 5; Ismail R. Al-Faruqi, *Selected Essays* (London: The International Institute of Islamic Thought, 2018), 1–35.
12 Kırbaşoğlu, *İslam'ın Kurucu*, 64. While elaborating on the higher norms of Islam, the rationalists excessively quote al-Shatibi. Öztürk, *Kur'an'ı Kendi*, 46.
13 Kırbaşoğlu, *Ahirzaman*, 367; Güler, *Kur'an'ın Mahiyeti*, 11; Yaşar Nuri, *Dinde Reform Değil II*, 244.

14 Abdullahi Ahmed An-Na'im, *Toward an Islamic Reformation Civil Liberties Human Rights, and International Law* (New York: Syracuse University Press, 1990), xiv. Abdullahi Ahmed An-Na'im, "Islamic Law, International Relations, and Human Rights: Challenge and Response," *Cornell International Law Journal* 20, no. 2 (1987): 320. Kırbaşoğlu quotes An-Nai'im's *Towards an Islamic Reformation* as an important contribution that could help in solving problems of Muslim societies. Kırbaşoğlu, *İslami İlimlerde Metot*, 59.
15 Mustafa Öztürk, *Cahiliyeden İslamiyet'e Kadın* (Ankara: Ankara Okulu, 2017), 191.
16 Güler, *Kur'an'ın Mahiyeti*, 7.
17 Kırbaşoğlu, *Müslüman Kalarak*, 153.
18 Güler, *Sabit Din*, 103–4. Also, Yaşar Nuri, *Ses Birgün*, 194.
19 Öztürk, *Kur'an ve Tarihsellik*, 11.
20 Güler, *Aklın İçindeki*, 92; Kırbaşoğlu, *Ahirzaman*, 70.
21 Yaşar Nuri, *Kur'an'daki İslam*, 205.
22 Güler, *Kur'an'ın Mahiyeti*, 103; Atay, *Cehaletin*, 91. Cf. Abdullahi Ahmed An-Na'im, "What Do We Mean by Universal?" *Index on Censorship* 4/5, no. 1 (1994): 126.
23 Eliaçık, *İslam'ın Üç*, 19–20; Güler, *Realpolitik*, 88.
24 Azimli, *Halifelik Tarihine*, 58.
25 Öztürk, *Kur'an'a Çağdaş*, 145.
26 Öztürk, *Kur'an, Tefsir ve Usul*, 98.
27 Yaşar Nuri, *400 Soruda*, 139.
28 Eliaçık, *Devrimci*, 33; Öztürk, *Kur'an ve Tefsir*, 187.
29 Öztürk, *Kur'an, Tefsir ve Usul*, 98–9.
30 Othman, "Urf as a Source," 345. *Ma'ruf* implies that reason can also establish what is good along with revelation. Muhammad Abu Rida, "Abd al-Hadi. 'Norms and Values,'" in *The Different Aspects of Islamic Culture: The Individual and Society in Islam*, edited by A. Bouhdiba and M. M. al-Dawalibi (Paris: UNESCO, 1998), 20.
31 Ayman Shabana, "Custom in the Islamic Legal Tradition," in *The Oxford Handbook of Islamic Law*, edited by Anver R. Emon and Rumee Ahmed (Oxford: Oxford University Press, 2018), 232.
32 Güler, *Sabit Din*, 109.
33 Güler, *Kuş Bakışı*, 229. Also, Eliaçık, *Kur'an'a Giriş*, 90.
34 Yaşar Nuri, *İslam Nasıl*, 294.
35 Öztürk, *Siyaset İtikad*, 272. Rationalists argue that Muslims today can resort to *ma'ruf* by adopting good practices from various societies. Öztürk, *Kur'an ve Tefsir*, 187.
36 Yaşar Nuri, *Ses Birgün*, 135; Eliaçık, *Demokratik*, 13; Kırbaşoğlu, *Ahirzaman*, 19.
37 Azimli, *Cahiliyye'yi Farklı*, 15.
38 Güler, *Kur'an'ın Ahlak*, 80; Eliaçık, *İslam'ın Üç*, 19.
39 Öztürk, *Kur'an, Vahiy Nüzul*, 147; Eliaçık, *Demokratik*, 58–9.
40 R. İhsan Eliaçık, *Bu Belde: Türkiye Yazıları* (Istanbul: İnşa, 2015), 183; Güler, *Politik Teoloji*, 194.
41 Öztürk, *Tefsir Tarihi*, 27.
42 Güler, *İsimsiz*, 94.
43 Güler, *Kuş Bakışı*, 234.
44 Kırbaşoğlu, *Ahirzaman*, 71–2.
45 Yaşar Nuri, *400 Soruda*, 70.
46 Yaşar Nuri, *Ses Birgün*, 194 ; Güler, *Sabit Din*, 103 ; Eliaçık, *Çağdaş Dünyada*, 272.
47 Güler, *Kur'an'ın Mahiyeti*, 50; Yaşar Nuri, *İnsanlığı Kemiren*, 104–16.

48　Güler, *Realpolitik*, 88.
49　Güler, *Sabit Din*, 157.
50　Güler, *Sünniliğin Eleştirisine*, 51.
51　Atay, *Ben*, 242.
52　Yaşar Nuri, *Türkiye'ye Mektuplar*, 70.
53　Rahman, *Major Themes*, 33.
54　Mohammad Hashim Kamali, *Crime and Punishment in Islamic Law: A Fresh Interpretation* (Oxford: Oxford University Press, 2019), 105–7.
55　Brunei Sharia Penal Code Order 2013, http://www.agc.gov.bn/AGC%20Images/LAWS/Gazette_PDF/2013/EN/S069.pdf (November 5, 2019).
56　Robin Simcox, "Ansar al-Sharia and Governance in Southern Yemen," *Current Trends in Islamist Ideology* 14, no. 1 (2012): 63.
57　Hayrettin Karaman, Mustafa Çağrıcı, İ. Kafi Dönmez and Sadrettin Gümüş, *Kur'an Yolu Türkçe Meal ve Tefsiri Vol. II* (Ankara: Diyanet İşleri Başkanlığı, 2012), 268–9.
58　İlhan Akbulut, "İslam Hukukunda Suçlar ve Cezalar," *Ankara Universitesi Hukuk Fakültesi Dergisi* 52, no. 1 (2003): 167–81.
59　al-Shafi'i, *al-Shafi'i's Risala*, 138.
60　Kırbaşoğlu, *İslam'ın Kurucu*, 67; Yaşar Nuri, *Çıplak Uyarı*, 48. Chopping hands was adapted from *jahilliya* Arabic culture. Mustafa Ölmez, "Şer'i Naslarda Lügavii Yorumlamadan Kaynaklanabilecek Hataların Engellenmesinde Hadislerin Rolü— Serika Ayeti Örneği," *Marife Dini Araştırmalar Dergisi* 18, no. 1 (2018): 274.
61　Kırbaşoğlu, *İslam'ın Kurucu*, 67; Yaşar Nuri, *İslam Nasıl*, 131.
62　This is *zajr*, i.e., deterrence, the underlying principle of all fields of Islamic criminal law. Rudolph Peters, *Crime and Punishment in Islamic Law Theory and Practice from the Sixteenth to the Twenty-first Century* (Cambridge: Cambridge University Press, 2005), 30; Eliaçık, *İhyadan İnşaya*, 345.
63　Güler, *Aklın İçindeki*, 109.
64　Fazlur Rahman, "The Concept of Hadd in Islamic Law," *Islamic Studies* 4, no. 3 (1965): 239.
65　"Kur'an'da Kölelik de Kadın Dövme de El Kesme de Vardır," https://www.youtube.com/watch?v=O3JQ-jbNRkE&t=200s (December 25, 2016).
66　Öztürk, *Siyaset İtikad*, 272. Also, Azimli, *Halifelik Tarihine*, 26. Abu Yusuf's methodology has a strong emphasis on customs in interpreting the shari'a. Gideon Libson, "On the Development of Custom as a Source of Law in Islamic Law: Al-ruju'u ila al-'urfi aḥadu al-qawa'idi al-khamsi allati yatabanna 'alayha al-fiqhu," *Islamic Law and Society* 4, no. 2 (1997): 144; Z. Ishaq Ansari, "The Early Development of Islamic Fiqh in Kufah with Special Reference to the Works of Abu Yusuf and Shaybani," *Islamic Studies* 57, no. ½ (2018): 103–58.
67　Güler, "Fazlurrahman'ın Tarihselciliği," http://www.islamianaliz.com/m/3608/fazlurrahmanin-tarihselciligi (February 22, 2020).
68　Kırbaşoğlu, *Üçüncü Yol*, 148.
69　Kırbaşoğlu, *İslam Düşüncesinde Sünnet*, 32. According to Forte, the motivation for the penalty of amputation among "modern Islamic states" is different from that of the jurists of classical times. David. F. Forte, "Islamic Law and the Crime of Theft: An Introduction," *Cleveland State Law Review* 34, no. 1 (1985): 48.
70　Eliaçık, *Devrimci*, 26–7.
71　Yaşar Nuri, *Merak Edilen*, 112.
72　Laury Silvers, "'In the Book We Have Left Out Nothing': The Ethical Problem of the Existence of Verse 4:34 in the Quran," *Comparative Islamic Studies* 2, no. 2 (2006): 173.

73 Atay, *Ben*, 247.
74 Güler, "Fazlurrahman'ın Tarihselciliği."
75 Hüseyin Atay, "Dinde Reformun Yöntemi ve Bir Örnek: Hırsızlık," *AÜİFD* 43, no. 2 (2002): 15–16.
76 Eliaçık, *Çağdaş Dünyada*, 210.
77 "Laws Criminalizing Apostasy in Selected Jurisdiction" (Washington: The Law Library, Global Research Center, 2014).
78 Mohamed Azam Mohamed Adil, "Law of Apostasy and Freedom of Religion in Malaysia," *Asian Journal of Comparative Law* 2, no. 1 (2007): 1–36; Nazila Ghanea, "Apostasy and Freedom to Change Religion or Belief," *Current Issues in Law and Religion* 4, no. 1 (2017): 139–58.
79 https://www.pewforum.org/2013/04/30/the-worlds-muslims-religion-politics-society-overview/ (March 25, 2020).
80 Rudolph Peters and Gert J. J. De Vries, "Apostasy in Islam," *Die Welt des Islams* 17, no. ¼ (1976/7): 1–2.
81 Christine Schirrmacher, *Let There Be No Compulsion in Religion (Sura 2:256): Apostasy from Islam as Judged by Contemporary Islamic Theologians* (Bonn: Verlag für Kultur und Wissenschaft Culture and Science, 2016), 127–283 and 401–556.
82 "Mürtedin ve Namaz Kılmayanın Öldürülmesi" https://www.youtube.com/watch?v=T0WT47SgFMs (April 19, 2019).
83 https://sorularlaislamiyet.com/dinimizde-murted-olana-neden-hayat-hakki-taninmaz (November 9, 2019).
84 Said Nursi, *Mesnevi-i Nuriye* (Istanbul: Yeni Asya, 2018), 134.
85 Hayrettin Karaman, Mustafa Çağrıcı, İ. Kafi Dönmez and Sadrettin Gümüş, *Kur'an Yolu Türkçe Meal ve Tefsiri Vol. I* (Ankara: Diyanet İşleri Başkanlığı, 2012), 341–3.
86 https://kurul.diyanet.gov.tr/Cevap-Ara/868/dinden-cikmayi-gerektiren-sozleri--elfaz-i-kufru--soylemenin-nikaha-etkisi-nedir- (December 13, 2019).
87 Hayreddin Karaman, Ali Bardakoğlu and İ. Kafi Dönmez, *İlmihal II* (Ankara: Diyanet, 1998), 223.
88 Yaşar Nuri, *Dinde Reform II*, 253.
89 Kırbaşoğlu, *İslami İlimlerde Metot*, 371.
90 "Mürtedin Öldürülmesi İle İlgili," https://www.youtube.com/watch?v=VR_TCjcwwAE (February 14, 2015).
91 Güler, *Dine Yeni*, 156–7.
92 Kırbaşoğlu, *İslam'ın Kurucu*, 195.
93 Güler, *Dine Yeni*, 157; Eliaçık, *Çağdaş Dünyada*, 88.
94 This is the confusion of political apostasy and religious apostasy according to Al-Alwani. Taha Jabir Al-Alwani, *Apostasy in Islam: A Historical and Scriptural Analysis* (London: International Institute of Islamic Thought, 2011), 98.
95 M. J. Akbar, *The Shade of Swords: Jihad and the Conflict Between Islam and Christianity* (London: Routledge, 2002), 190.
96 Sayyid Qutb, *Milestones* (Birmingham: Maktabah, 2006), 65–81.
97 https://www.diyanethaber.com.tr/hutbeler/son-dakika-28-subat-2020-cuma-hutbesinde-degisiklik-h9316.html (March 26, 2020).
98 Majid Khadduri, *War and Peace in the Law of Islam* (Baltimore: John Hopkins University Press, 1955), 55–73; Asma Afsaruddin, *Striving in the Path of God* (Oxford: Oxford University Press, 2013), 10.
99 Adnan A. Musallam, *From Secularism to Jihad: Sayyid Qutb and the Foundation of Radical Islamism* (London: Praeger, 2005), 182.

100 Güler, *Vicdan*, 208.
101 W. Montgomery Watt, "Islamic Conceptions of the Holy War," in *The Holy War*, edited by Thomas P. Murphy (Columbus: Ohio State University Press, 1976), 145.
102 Güler, *İsimsiz*, 87.
103 Öztürk, *Kur'an ve Tarihsellik*, 114.
104 Ibid., 54. Also, see Kırbaşoğlu, *İslam'ın Kurucu*, 182.
105 al-Waqidi, *The Life of Muhammad [Kitab al-Maghazi]*. Translated by Rizwi Faizer (London: Routledge, 2011), 5.
106 Güler, *Derin Ahlak*, 49; Ibn Ishaq, *Sirat*, 22.
107 Güler, *Kuş Bakışı*, 129. Stetkevych's studies on pre-Islamic Arab poetry provide crystal clear examples of war, blood, and sacrifice among Arabs and how they were coded in that culture. Suzanne Pinckney Stetkevych, *Immortals Speak: Pre-Islamic Poetry and the Poetics of Ritual* (Ithaca: Cornell University Press, 1993), 55–86.
108 Leone Caetani, "The Art of War of the Arabs, and the Supposed Religious Fervor of the Arab Conquests," in *The Expansion of the Early Islamic State*, edited by Fred M. Donner (London: Routledge, 2016), 1. Also, see John Kelsay, *Arguing the Just War in Islam* (Cambridge, MA: Harvard University Press, 2007), 15.
109 Sadık Kirazlı, "Conflict and Conflict Resolution in the pre-Islamic Arab Society," *Islamic Studies* 50, no. 1 (2011): 26.
110 G. E. Von Grunebaum, "The Nature of Arab Unity Before Islam," *Arabica* 10, no. 1 (1963): 5–23.
111 Güler, *Kuş Bakışı*, 131.
112 Güler, *Evrensel Ümmetçiliğe*, 13. Ibn Ishaq wrote that the Prophet was given the permission of fight after Arabs persecuted them to the point that "they had to choose whether to give up the religion, be maltreated at home." Ibn Ishaq, *Sirat*, 212.
113 al-Shafi'i, *al-Shafi'i's Risala*, 84.
114 İsrafil Balcı, *İlk İslam Fetihleri: Savaş-Barış İlişkisi* (Istanbul: Pınar, 2011), 26–9.
115 Güler, *Sünniliğin Eleştirisine*, 53.
116 Güler, *Evrensel Ümmetçiliğe*, 17.
117 Güler, *Direniş Teolojisi*, 10; İsrafil Balcı, *Hz. Peygamber'in Savaşlarında İlahi Yardım* (Ankara: Ankara Okulu, 2014), 23–6.
118 Güler, *Aklın İçindeki*, 18.
119 Kırbaşoğlu, *Ahirzaman*, 125.
120 Balcı, *İlk İslam Fetihleri*, 34.
121 Yaşar Nuri, *Kur'an'ın Yarattığı*, 188.
122 Eliaçık, *Demokratik*, 199.
123 Balcı, *İlk İslam Fetihleri*, 25.
124 Eliaçık, *Çağdaş Dünyada*, 166.
125 Güler, *Realpolitik*, 43. Kennedy classifies early Muslims' wars in the period 632–83 as "the conquests." Hugh Kennedy, *The Armies of the Caliphs: Military and Society in the Early Islamic State* (London: Routledge, 2005), 1–17.
126 Kırbaşoğlu, *Müslüman Kalarak*, 166; Öztürk, *Kur'an ve Tarihsellik*, 197–218.
127 Güler, *Dine Yeni*, 221.
128 "Kur'an'da Kölelik de Kadın Dövme de El Kesme de Vardır," https://www.youtube.com/watch?v=O3JQ-jbNRkE&t=200s (December 25, 2016).
129 "Kölelik ve Cariyelik," https://www.youtube.com/watch?v=Vp_ifPRipnw (November 9, 2018).
130 Ehud R. Toledano, "Abolition and Anti-slavery in the Ottoman Empire: A Case to Answer?" In *A Global History of Anti-slavery Politics in the Nineteenth Century*,

edited by William Mulligan and Maurice Bric (New York: Palgrave Macmillan, 2013), 118. Cooper wrote that "slavery was so embedded in Muslim society through religious law, custom and culture, that it was self-explanatory. Slavery was in some way 'Islamic' simply by virtue of existing in a culture that defined itself as being Islamic." Quoted in E. Ann McDougall, "What Is Islamic About Slavery in Muslim Societies? Cooper, Concubinage and Contemporary Legacies of Islamic Slavery in North, West and East Africa," in *Slavery in the Islamic World: Its Characteristics and Commonality*, edited by Mary Ann Fay (London: Palgrave Macmillan, 2019), 7.

131   Öztürk, *Cahiliyeden İslamiyet'e Kadın*, 26. While summarizing the Islamic slavery in Africa, Willis notes that they were seen as lacking a major attachment of lineage and genealogy, which were esteemed values by Arabs. John Ralph Willis, "Introduction: The Ideology of Enslavement in Islam," in *Slaves and Slavery in Muslim Africa Vol. 2 The Servile Estate*, edited by John Ralph Willis (London and New York: Routledge, 1985), 3–4. While studying what he calls Ottoman colonialism, Deringil writes that it subscribed to the belief that "the savages and heretics" in Africa were in need of "the true faith." Selim Deringil, "They Live in a State of Nomadism and Savagery: The Late Ottoman Empire and the Post-Colonial Debate," *Comparative Studies in Society and History* 45, no. 2 (2003): 312–3 and 341. There is an alternate view that refrains from describing any form of slavery as "benign," which, however, again argues that there might me differences between Islamic and Western slavery in terms of how slaves are treated "in various ways including the regulation of slavery by the law, the community consensus on how slaves should be treated, and the particular way that household slavery endowed the enslaved." Mary Ann Fay, "Introduction: What Is Islamic About Slavery in the Islamic World?" In *Slavery in the Islamic World: Its Characteristics and Commonality*, edited by Mary Ann Fay (London: Palgrave Macmillan, 2019), 2.

132   Özsoy, *Kur'an ve Tarihsellik Yazıları*, 73–4.
133   William Gervase Clarence-Smith, *Islam and the Abolition of Slavery* (Oxford: Oxford University Press, 2006), 1.
134   Karaman is coauthor of both *İlmihal* and *Tefsir*.
135   Hayrettin Karaman, "İslam'da Köle ve Talan var mı?," *Yeni Şafak*, 5 April 2009.
136   The benign discourse of slavery reaches a climax in Islamists. Mawdudi says that it was Islam that first abolished slavery. S. Abul A'la Maududi, *Human Rights in Islam* (Leicester: Islamic Foundation, 1976), 172.
137   Cf. Chouki El Hamel, *Black Morocco: A History of Slavery, Race, and Islam* (Cambridge: Cambridge University Press, 2013), 17.
138   Kırbaşoğlu, *İslami İlimlerde Metot*, 140.
139   Yaşar Nuri, *İnsanlığı Kemiren*, 169.
140   Karaman et al., *İlmihal II*, 16.
141   Öztürk, *Kur'an'ı Kendi*, 196–9 ; Eliaçık, *Sosyal İslam*, 298.
142   Rahman, *Islam and Modernity*, 7.
143   Rahman, *Major Themes*, 32.
144   Özsoy, *Sünnetullah*, 19.
145   "Kölelik ve Cariyelik," https://www.youtube.com/watch?v=Vp_ifPRipnw (November 9, 2018)
146   Kırbaşoğlu, *İslam'ın Kurucu*, 192–3.
147   Güler, *Dine Yeni*, 221.
148   Eliaçık, *Sosyal İslam*, 298; Eliaçık, *Mülk Yazıları*, 130–47.
149   Kırbaşoğlu, *Müslüman Kalarak*, 166.

150 Öztürk, *Kur'an ve Tarihsellik*, 267.
151 Güler, *Realpolitik*, 193.
152 Öztürk, *Kur'an'ı Kendi*, 120–2.
153 Öztürk, *Kur'an ve Tarihsellik*, 196.
154 Judith E. Tucker, *Women, Family, and Gender in Islamic Law* (Cambridge: Cambridge University Press, 2008), 2.
155 İlhami Güler, "Kur'an'da Kadın Erkek Eşitsizliğinin Temelleri," *İslami Araştırmalar* 10, no. 4 (1997): 298–300. It is worth translating the title of this article: "The Foundations of the Inequality Between Man and Woman in Quran."
156 Öztürk, *Kur'an'ı Kendi*, 194.
157 Güler, *Realpolitik*, 11; Atay, *Kur'an'a Göre IV*, 180.
158 Güler, "Kur'an'da Kadın Erkek," 297.
159 Özsoy, *Kur'an ve Tarihsellik Yazıları*, 14.
160 Balcı, *Peygamberlik Öncesi*, 72; Atay, *Kur'an'da İman*, 60.
161 Özsoy, *Kur'an ve Tarihsellik Yazıları*, 14. Öztürk is inspired heavily by Darwaza, who is known for his hermeneutical approach to Quran. Ismail K. Poonawala, "Muhammad 'Izzat Darwaza's Principles Modern Exegesis: A Contribution towards Quranic hermeneutics," in *Approaches to the Quran*, edited by G. R. Hawting and Abdul-Kader A. Shareef (London and New York: Routledge, 1993), 225–46. Darwaza wrote a biography of Muhammad in which he narrated his life within a continuity of the Arab society. İzzet Derveze, *Kur'an'a Göre Hz. Muhammed'in Hayatı Vol. I* (Istanbul: Düşün, 2011), 11.
162 Öztürk, *Söyleşiler*, 91.
163 Atay, *Kur'an'a Göre I*, 103.
164 "Kur'an Sana Hitap Etmiyor," https://www.youtube.com/watch?v=q_rVDCI2bSQ (July 14, 2015). For apologetics, the verse is metaphorical expression of parallels between womanhood and earth, which is "inconceivable for orientalists, and people who are unaware of Arabic language." Saleha Fatima and Musferah Mehfooz, Similarities Between Woman and Earth: A Study of Quranic Metaphorical Comprehensiveness in the Light of Al-Baqara 223," *Jihad al-Islam* 9, no. 2 (2016): 5.
165 Yaşar Nuri, *İnsanlığı Kemiren*, 169.
166 Kırbaşoğlu, *İslami İlimlerde Metot*, 76.
167 Cf. Fatima Mernissi, *Women and Islam: A Historical and Theological Enquiry* (Oxford: Basil Blackwell, 1991), 4–5.
168 Öztürk, *Kur'an'ı Kendi*, 109–11.
169 Öztürk, *Kur'an ve Tarihsellik*, 276–7.
170 Öztürk, *Kur'an'ı Kendi*, 123–202.
171 Ibid., 128.
172 Yaşar Nuri Öztürk, *Asrı Saadetin Büyük Kadınları* (Istanbul: Yeni Boyut, 2013), 6.
173 Atay, *Kur'an'a Göre I*, 103; Yaşar Nuri, *Türkiye'ye Mektuplar*, 109.
174 Öztürk, *Kur'an'ı Kendi*, 191.
175 Narendra Subramanian, "Legal Change and Gender Equality: Changes in Muslim Family Law in India," *Law & Social Inquiry* 33, no. 3 (2008): 632.
176 Atay, *İslam'ı Yeniden*, 105.
177 "İslami Alemi Boşanma Konusunda," https://www.youtube.com/watch?v=qq_LZtyAIjE (December 3, 2013).
178 Atay, *Kur'an'a Göre I*, 20–6.
179 Eliaçık, *Sosyal İslam*, 150.
180 Yaşar Nuri, *Kur'an'daki İslam*, 434.

181 In Chapter 2, I wrote that the universalists argue that scientific developments may require new interpretations in the Islamic law. A relevant case is related to divorce. Verse 2:228 requires that "divorced women must wait for three monthly periods before remarrying." Given the developments in medical technology, Yaşar Nuri proposes that the period can be shortened, according to a scientific report. Yaşar Nuri, *Dinde Reform II*, 75. (Kırbaşoğlu shares this view. See Kırbaşoğlu, *Müslüman Kalarak*, 227.) Another example is the prohibition meant to stop women's circumambulation Ka'ba while menstruating. THCRA ruled that women cannot circumambulate Ka'ba when they are on menstruation. https://kurul.diyanet.gov.tr/Cevap-Ara/111/adetli-kadin-ziyaret--veda-ve-umre-tavaflarini-yapabilir-mi- (October 30, 2019). Atay, given the changes in the medical field, rules that the prohibition is now irrelevant. Atay, *Kur'an'a Göre IV*, 180.
182 Lawal Muhammad Bani and Hamza A. Pate, "Dissolution of Marriage (Divorce) Under Islamic Law," *Journal of Law, Policy and Globalization* 42, no. 1 (2015): 139–42.
183 Güler, "Kur'an'da Kadın Erkek," 296–303. "Kadının Boşanma Hakkı," https://www.youtube.com/watch?v=0zQgKo4Kzx4&t=39s (October 21, 2018).
184 Jamal J. Nasir, *The Islamic Law of Personal Status* (London: Graham and Trotman, 1990), 112; Somepalli Alekhya, "Comparative Analysis of Islamic Divorce Laws: Socio-legal Analysis," *Journal of Family and Adoption Law* 2, no. 2 (2019): 20.
185 See: https://www.ius.uzh.ch/dam/jcr:00000000-74d3-1f02-ffff-ffff87068da3/Law_22_2006_2558.pdf (October 29, 2019).
186 Rakesh Kumar Singh, *Textbook on Muslim Law* (New Delhi: Universal, 2011), 128.
187 Karaman et al., *İlmihal II*, 17.
188 İsmail Köksal, "İslam Hukukunda Zıhar," *Dini Araştırmalar* 3, no. 7 (2000): 258.
189 Özsoy, *Sünnetullah*, 18.
190 Ibid. Also, see Muhammad ibn Hasan ibn Ali Ja'far al-Tusi, *A Concise Description of Islamic Law and Legal Opinions [al-Nihayah fi Mujarrad al-Fiqh wa al-Fatawa]*. Translated by A. Ezzati (London: ICAS Press, 2008), 371.
191 Öztürk, *Cahiliyeden İslamiyet'e Kadın*, 52.
192 Ibid., 51.
193 Cf. Gerald R. Hawting, "An Ascetic Vow and an Unseemly Oath? Ila and Zihar in Muslim Law," *Bulletin of the School of Oriental and African Studies* 57, no. 1 (1994): 114.
194 Özsoy, *Sünnetullah*, 18.
195 "Kadının Boşanma Hakkı," https://www.youtube.com/watch?v=0zQgKo4Kzx4&t=39s (October 21, 2018).
196 Güler, "Kur'an'da Kadın Erkek," 318.
197 https://kurul.diyanet.gov.tr/Cevap-Ara/905/kadinin-mirastaki-durumu-nedir- (February 6, 2020).
198 Karaman et al., *İlmihal II*, 248.
199 See Hülya Özay, "İslam Miras Hukukunun Özellikleri," *İslam Medeniyeti Araştırmaları Dergisi* 3, no. 2 (2018): 209.
200 Ahmet Efe, "İslam Miras Hukukunda Kadın-Erkek Hisselerinin Farklı Oluşu Üzerine Bir Değerlendirme," *İslam Hukuku Araştırmaları Dergisi* 18, no. 1 (2011): 157–68.
201 M. Hayri Kırbaşoğlu, "Kadın Konusunda Kur'an'a Yöneltilen Başlıca Eleştiriler," *İslami Araştırmalar* 10, no. 4 (1997): 265–6.
202 Güler, "Kur'an'da Kadın Erkek," 301 ; "Kadın ve Miras," https://www.youtube.com/watch?v=YLiNFRZmd_8 (April 20, 2016).

203 "Sola mal olan bütün değerler Kuran'da vardır," *Sabah*, February 7, 2010. "Mirsat Kadına," https://www.youtube.com/watch?v=SM5HIeLA-b0 (November 6, 2013)
204 Öztürk, *Cahiliyeden İslamiyet'e Kadın*, 69.
205 Kırbaşoğlu, *Müslüman Kalarak*, 289; Güler, *Dine Yeni*, 72. Güler quotes Hüseyin Kazım Kadri (d. 1934), an Ottoman reformist, who in 1917 analyzed the status of Universal Declaration of Human Rights from an Islamic perspective. To Kadri, many principles of the declaration were contained by Islam. Kadri also explained the unequal distribution of inheritance between the two sexes based on the economic realities of the early Muslim societies. Hüseyin Kazım Kadri, *İnsan Hakları Beyannamesi'nin İslam Hukukuna Göre İzahı [Prepared by Osman Ergin]* (Istanbul: Sinan, 1949), 41–2.
206 Yaşar Nuri, *İslam Nasıl*, 250.
207 "O ayetler artık geçersiz," *Gazete Vatan*, April 21, 2012.
208 Hüseyin Atay, *Kur'an: Türkçe Çeviri* (Ankara: Atay, 2013), 77.
209 https://kuran.diyanet.gov.tr/tefsir/Nisâ-suresi/504/11-12-ayet-tefsiri (February 23, 2020).
210 Özsoy, *Sünnetullah*, 21–2. Öztürk, *Cahiliyeden İslamiyet'e Kadın*, 74–5.
211 Mustafa Öztürk, "Modern Döneme Özgü Bir Kur'an Tasavvuru: Kur'ancılık ve Kur'an İslami Söyleminin Tahlil ve Tenkidi," *Marife* 10, no. 3 (2010): 9–43.
212 Wael B. Hallaq, *Shari'a: Theory, Practice, Transformations* (Cambridge: Cambridge University Press, 2012), 350; Nadira Mustapha, "Law: Women as Witness," in *Encyclopedia of Women and Islamic Cultures Family, Law and Politics Vol. II*, edited by Suad Joseph (Leiden and Boston: Brill, 2005), 476.
213 The Iranian penal law (Article 199) informs that "the standard [of proof] for testimony in all offenses shall be two male witnesses." https://www.refworld.org/docid/518a19404.html (February 8, 2020). Marziyeh Bakhshizadeh, *Changing Gender Norms in Islam: Between Reason and Revelation* (Berlin: Budrich, 2018), 97.
214 https://kurul.diyanet.gov.tr/Cevap-Ara/803/nikahta-sahitligin-hukmu-nedir- (November 7, 2019).
215 Öztürk, *Cahiliyeden İslamiyet'e Kadın*, 110–1.
216 Atay, *Kur'an'a Göre I*, 29–30; Yaşar Nuri, *İslam Nasıl*, 250.
217 Atay, *Kur'an'a Göre I*, 29–30.
218 "Kadının Şahitliği," https://www.youtube.com/watch?v=Nr2L3QEbGuU (March 15, 2019).
219 Eliaçık, *İhyadan İnşaya*, 32.
220 Eliaçık, *Çağdaş Dünyada*, 190; Yaşar Nuri, *İslam Nasıl*, 250; Güler, "Kur'an'da Kadın Erkek," 301. Cf. Amina Wadud, *Quran and Woman: Reading the Sacred Text from a Woman's Perspective* (Oxford: Oxford University Press, 1999), 85–6.
221 "İki Kadın Bir Erkek," https://www.youtube.com/watch?v=Vq7bthU83RA (February 1, 2019).
222 Kırbaşoğlu, *İslam'ın Kurucu*, 149; Yaşar Nuri, *Türkiye'ye Mektuplar*, 109. Kırbaşoğlu also finds that regulations against women's traveling alone are no longer relevant. Kırbaşoğlu, *Müslüman Kalarak*, 46.
223 Yusuf al-Qaradawi, *The Lawful and the Prohibited in Islam* (Kuwait: International Islamic Federation of Student Organization, 1984), 205.
224 S. Douki, F. Nacef, A. Belhadj, A. Bouasker, and R. Ghachem, "Violence against women in Arab and Islamic Countries," *Archives of Women's Mental Health* 6, no. 1 (2003): 167; Muhammad M. Haj-Yahia, "Beliefs of Jordanian Women About Wife-Beating," *Psychology of Women Quarterly* 26, no. 1 (2002): 283.

225 Kecia Ali, *Sexual Ethics and Islam: Feminist Reflections on Quran, Hadith, and Jurisprudence* (Oxford: Oneworld, 2006), 125.
226 Atay, *Cehaletin*, 325.
227 Eliaçık, *Demokratik*, 285.
228 Yaşar Nuri, *Kur'an'daki İslam*, 387.
229 Atay, *Kur'an'a Göre II*, 34.
230 Özsoy, *Kur'an ve Tarihsellik Yazıları*, 135–8.
231 Öztürk, *Tefsirin Halleri*, 18.
232 Öztürk, *Söyleşiler*, 201.
233 "Kadın dövmek," https://www.youtube.com/watch?v=Poy55PIGa_8 (January 11, 2016).
234 Öztürk, *Cahiliyeden İslamiyet'e Kadın*, 165.
235 Öztürk, *Söyleşiler*, 211.
236 Özsoy, *Kur'an ve Tarihsellik Yazıları*, 139–42.
237 Öztürk, *Cahiliyeden İslamiyet'e Kadın*, 167.
238 "Peygamberin Yaptığı," https://www.youtube.com/watch?v=XgwTQPrsAVs (June 14, 2016).
239 Güler, *Kuş Bakışı*, 246.
240 Elizabeth Özdalga, *The Veiling Issue, Official Secularism, and Popular Islam in Modern Turkey* (London: Routledge, 2015).
241 Jen'nan Ghazal Read, "Introduction: The Politics of Veiling in Comparative Perspective," *Sociology of Religion* 68, no. 3 (2007): 231–6.
242 Anastasia Vakulenko, *Islamic Veiling in Legal Discourse* (London: Routledge, 2012), 2.
243 Karaman et al, *İlmihal II*, 71.
244 H. Yunus Apaydın, "Tesettür," in *İslam Ansiklopedisi Vol. 40*, edited by commission (Ankara: TDV, 2011), 543–5.
245 Güler, *Direniş Teolojisi*, 122. *İlmihal* also does not find such forms of veiling as Islamic. Karaman et al., *İlmihal II*, 72.
246 Yaşar Nuri, *Çıplak Uyarı*, 179.
247 Eliaçık, *Çağdaş Dünyada*, 196.
248 Yaşar Nuri, *İnsanlığı Kemiren*, 213.
249 Hüseyin Atay, *Kur'an'a Göre Araştırmalar VI* (Ankara: Atay, 2017), 60–1; Yaşar Nuri, *Cevap Veriyorum*, 74.
250 Yaşar Nuri, *Kur'an'ın Temel Buyrukları*, 188–91.
251 "Mustafa Öztürk'ün Başörtüsü Yorumu." https://www.youtube.com/watch?v=a7d3hzHaGFs (November 30, 2018). "Kur'anda Başörtüsü," https://www.youtube.com/watch?v=fudaYxI0wh4 (January 19, 2015).
252 Öztürk, *Cahiliyeden İslamiyet'e Kadın*, 101.
253 Öztürk, *Kur'an'ı Kendi*, 107–20.
254 Öztürk, *Cahiliyeden İslamiyet'e Kadın*, 104–5.
255 Ibid., 102–4.
256 Universalists also employ the historicist argument which explains the regulation on veiling in reference to the social status of women. Yaşar Nuri, *İslam Nasıl*, 235.
257 Öztürk, *Cahiliyeden İslamiyet'e Kadın*, 104–5.
258 Güler, *Direniş Teolojisi*, 123.
259 Güler, *Aklın İçindeki*, 58.
260 Jamal J. Nasir, *The Status of Women under Islamic Law and Modern Islamic Legislation* (London: Brill, 2009), 25–8; Lynn Welchman, *Women and Muslim Family*

Laws in Arab States: A Comparative Overview of Textual Development and Advocacy (Amsterdam: Amsterdam University Press, 2007).
261 Karaman et al., *İlmihal II*, 216.
262 Katharine Charsley and Anika Liversage, "Transforming Polygamy: Migration, Transnationalism and Multiple Marriages among Muslim Minorities," *Global Networks* 13, no. 1 (2013): 63.
263 Semra Ulaş, "İslam'da Çok Kadınla Evlilik," *İslami Araştırmalar* 6, no. 1 (1991): 61.
264 "Kur'an Sana Hitap Etmiyor," https://www.youtube.com/watch?v=q_rVDCI2bSQ (July 14, 2015).
265 Eliaçık, *Kur'an'a Giriş*, 69. Rahman, too, explains the rationale of polygamy as the orphan problems of the early Muslim society. Rahman, *Major Themes*, 32.
266 Öztürk, *Kur'an ve Tarihsellik*, 294–9.
267 Yaşar Nuri, *Din ve Fıtrat*, 296. Also see Öztürk, *Kur'an ve Tarihsellik*, 117.
268 "Çok Eşlilik Ayeti," https://www.youtube.com/watch?v=yb_Aooy6efY&t=376s (April 15, 2016).
269 "Çok Eşlilik Konusunda," https://www.youtube.com/watch?v=0D4835b7J-o (April 20, 2016).
270 Öztürk, *Kur'an ve Tarihsellik*, 294–9.
271 This is a popular argument shared by contemporary reformists. Nisrine Abiad, *Sharia, Muslim States and International Human Rights Treaty Obligations: A Comparative Study* (London: The British Institute of International and Comparative Law, 2008), 19; Zainab Chaudry, "The Myth of Misogyny: A Reanalysis of Women's Inheritance in Islamic Law," *Albany Law Review* 61, no. 2 (1998): 512–3.
272 Eliaçık, *Kur'an'a Giriş*, 68–71. Cf. Jehad G. Issa, "Introduction to Islamic Legislation," *Woodrow Wilson Journal of Law* 2, no. 1 (1979): 36.
273 Öztürk, *Cahiliyeden İslamiyet'e Kadın*, 42.
274 Eliaçık, *İhyadan İnşaya*, 90.
275 Yohanan Friedmann, *Tolerance and Coercion in Islam: Interfaith Relations in the Muslim World* (Cambridge: Cambridge University Press, 2003), 161.
276 "Prohibition of Interfaith Marriage," A Report by Staff of the Global Legal Research Directorate, (Washington: The Law Library of Congress, 2015).
277 https://kurul.diyanet.gov.tr/Cevap-Ara/800/musluman-kadin-gayrimuslim-bir-erkekle-evlenebilir-mi-(November 7, 2019).
278 Nihat Doğan, "İslam Hukuku Açısından Müslüman Bayanın Ehl-i Kitap Erkekle Evliliği," *İslam Hukuku Araştırmaları Dergisi* 2, no. 1 (2003): 155.
279 Atay, *Kur'an'a Göre III*, 62.
280 See Azizah al-Hibri and Raja' M. El Habti, "Islam," in *Sex, Marriage, and Family in World Religions*, edited by Don S. Browning, M. Christian Green and John Witte Jr. (New York: Columbia University Press, 2006), 224.
281 Güler, *Sabit Din*, 81.
282 Güler, "Kur'an'da Kadın Erkek," 303.
283 Yaşar Nuri, *Kur'an'ın Temel Buyrukları*, 273.
284 Yaşar Nuri, *Kur'an'daki İslam*, 312. "Müşriklerle Evlenmek," https://www.youtube.com/watch?v=-QEuEMJZLnQ (February 17, 2017).
285 Alex B. Leeman, "Interfaith Marriage in Islam: AN Examination of the Legal Theory Behind the Traditional and Reformist Positions," *Indiana Law Journal* 84, no. 2 (2009): 758.
286 Eliaçık, *Bana Dinden*, 165.

287 Öztürk, *Cahiliyeden İslamiyet'e Kadın*, 144.
288 Ibid., 145.
289 Joseph Chinyong Liow, *Piety and Politics: Islamism in Contemporary Malaysia* (Oxford: Oxford University Press, 2009), 192.
290 Fred M. Donner, *Narratives of Islamic Origins: The Beginning of Islamic Historical Writing* (Princeton: Darwin Press, 1998), 101.
291 Nimrod Hurvitz, *The Formation of Hanbalism Piety in Power* (London: Routledge, 2002), 9.
292 Karaman et al., *İlmihal I*, 218.
293 Cf. Louis Bouyer, *Liturgical Piety* (Notre Dame: University of Notre Dame Press, 1954), 1.
294 Megan H. Reid, *Law and Piety in Medieval Islam* (Cambridge: Cambridge University Press, 2013), 7–8; Marshall G. S. Hodgson, *The Venture of Islam Vol. II. Concise and History in a World of Civilization* (London: The University of Chicago Press, 1977), 249 and 360; Daniella Talmon-Heller, *Islamic Piety in Medieval Syria: Mosques, Cemeteries and Sermons under the Zangids and Ayubis* (Leiden: Brill, 2007), 221; Sarah A. Tobin, *Everyday Piety: Islam and Economy in Jordan* (New York: Cornell University Press, 2016), 5–6.
295 Kırbaşoğlu, *İslami İlimlerde Metot*, 65; Eliaçık, *Yaşayan Kur'an*, 156.
296 Güler, *Kuş Bakışı*, 14.
297 Atay, *İslam'ı Yeniden*, 114.
298 Güler, *Sünniliğin Eleştirisine*, 53.
299 Eliaçık, *Bana Dinden*, 13; Yaşar Nuri, *Konferanslarım*, 57.
300 Atay, *İslam'ı Yeniden*, 141.
301 Güler, *Özgürlükçü Teoloji*, 16.
302 On this debate, see Webb Keane, "Ethics as Piety," *Numen* 61, no. 2/3 (2014): 233.
303 M. Hayri Kırbaşoğlu, *Eskimez Yeni: Hz. Peygamber'in Sünneti* (Ankara: Otto, 2017), 48.
304 Atay, *Kur'an'a Göre IV*, 141.
305 Eliaçık, *Yaşayan Kur'an*, 156; Özsoy, *Sünnetullah*, 88.
306 Yaşar Nuri, *Kur'an Penceresinden*, 27.
307 Eliaçık, *Demokratik*, 41.
308 M. Hayri Kırbaşoğlu, *Destursuz Çağa Girenler* (Ankara: Otto, 2014), 22.
309 Güler, *Kur'an'ın Ahlak*, 137.
310 Yaşar Nuri, *Konferanslarım*, 20; Güler, *Kuş Bakışı*, 74.
311 Atay, *Kur'an'a Göre II*, 81.
312 Güler, *Aklın İçindeki*, 83.
313 Atay, *Kur'an'a Göre Araştırmalar V*, 51.
314 Atay, *İslam'da İşçi*, 86.
315 Eliaçık, *Demokratik*, 41.
316 Eliaçık, *Bana Dinden*, 31; Yaşar Nuri, *Ses Birgün*, 16; Güler, *Kuş Bakışı*, 76; Atay, *Kur'an'a Göre II*, 69.
317 Eliaçık, *Sosyal Islam*.
318 Karaman et al., *İlmihal I*, 221.
319 M. Kamil Yaşaroğlu, "Namaz," in *İslam Ansiklopedisi Vol. XXXII*, edited by commission (Ankara: TDV, 2006), 350–7.
320 Eliaçık, *Bana Dinden*, 17–25; Kırbaşoğlu, *Destursuz*, 71.
321 Özsoy, *Sünnetullah*, 88; Güler, *Derin Ahlak*, 16; Eliaçık, *Çağdaş Dünyada*, 318.
322 Yaşar Nuri, *Tanrı, Akıl*, 316.

323 Eliaçık, *Bana Dinden*, 17–25; Kırbaşoğlu, *Destursuz*, 71.
324 Eliaçık, *Mülk Yazıları*, 10.
325 Güler, *Özgürlükçü Teoloji*, 75.
326 Güler, *Aklın İçindeki*, 17.
327 Cf. Saba Mahmoud, *Politics of Piety: The Islamic Revival and the Feminist Subject* (Princeton: Princeton University Press, 2005), 4 and 122.
328 Eliaçık, *Bana Dinden*, 28.
329 Eliaçık, *Devrimci*, 35; Güler, *Sabit Din*, 68; Yaşar Nuri, *Kur'an Verilerine*, 134.
330 Atay, *İslam'da İşçi*, 56.
331 Eliaçık, *Mülk Yazıları*, 10.
332 Güler, *Özgürlükçü Teoloji*, 41.
333 Yaşar Nuri, *Kur'an'ı Kerim'de Lanetlenen*, 138.
334 Güler, *Vicdan*, 155 and 232.
335 Güler, *Kuş Bakışı*, 88 and 114.
336 Eliaçık, *Çağdaş Dünyada*, 80. For Atay, ritualistic piety weakens Muslims' interest into arts. Atay, *Cehaletin*, 238.
337 Güler, *Kur'an'ın Ahlak*, 137.
338 Yaşar Nuri, *Kur'an Penceresinden*, 37.
339 Eliaçık, *Bana Dinden*, 89.
340 Eliaçık, *Sosyal İslam*, 219.
341 Yaşar Nuri, *Kur'an'ın Yarattığı*, 131.
342 Güler, *Özgürlükçü Teoloji*, 8; Kırbaşoğlu, *Destursuz*, 21.
343 İlhami Güler, *İman Ahlak İlişkisi* (Ankara: Ankara Okulu, 2003), 134.
344 Güler, *İtikaddan İmana*, 12. Eliaçık, too, compares ritualistic piety to shamanism. Eliaçık, *Bana Dinden*, 10.
345 Kırbaşoğlu, *Destursuz*, 23.
346 Yaşar Nuri, *Kur'an'ı Kerim'de Lanetlenen*, 245.
347 Güler, *Aklın İçindeki*, 121.
348 Eliaçık, *Bana Dinden*, 12.
349 Güler, *İsimsiz*, 73.
350 Eliaçık, *Bana Dinden*, 10.
351 Eliaçık, *Kur'an'a Giriş*, 90.
352 Kırbaşoğlu, *Destursuz*, 22.
353 Güler, *Dine Yeni*, 60.
354 Jennifer Hitchcock, "The 5 Pillars of Islam," *Verbum* 2, no. 2 (2005): 43–5.
355 Eliaçık, *Bu Belde*, 170; Öztürk, *Merak Edilen*, 48.
356 Kırbaşoğlu, *İslami İlimlerde Metot*, 62. "Islamin Şartı," https://www.youtube.com/watch?v=e_nJCUsTKSY (December 17, 2017).
357 Eliaçık, *Bu Belde*, 170.
358 Güler, *Politik Teoloji*, 193.
359 Yaşar Nuri, *Konferanslarım*, 52.
360 Kırbaşoğlu, *İslami İlimlerde Metot*, 64.
361 Kırbaşoğlu, *Destursuz*, 78.
362 Kırbaşoğlu, *Ahirzaman*, 11 and 34.
363 Kırbaşoğlu, *Üçüncü Yol*, 60; M. Hayri Kırbaşoğlu, "Son Muhalifin İzinde: Yeryüzünün Son Göksel Muhalifi: Hz. Muhammed (sav)," *Milel ve Nihal* 15, no. 2 (2018): 47. On the Mu'tazila's five doctrines, see Martin et al., *Defenders of Reason*, 53; Gabriel Said Reynolds, *A Muslim Theologian in the Sectarian Milieu 'Abd al-Jabbar and the Critique of Christian Origins* (Leiden: Brill, 2004), 64.

364 Güler, *Özgürlükçü Teoloji*, 8; Güler, *İtikaddan İmana*, 149.
365 "Aktif İbadetten," https://www.youtube.com/watch?v=HFCMAqYHXzI (March 16, 2018).
366 Yaşar Nuri, *Dinde Reform II*, 120.
367 Ahmad Hasan, "The *Sunnah*—Its Early Concept and Development," *Islamic Studies* 7, no. 1 (1968): 47.
368 Fazlur Rahman, "Concepts, Sunnah, Ijtihad, and Ijma' in the Early Period," *Islamic Studies* 1, no. 1 (1962): 5; M. Hayri Kırbaşoğlu, "İslami İlimlerde Şafi'nin Rolü Üzerine," in *Sünni Paradigmanın Oluşumunda Şafi'i'nin Rolü*, edited by M. Hayri Kırbaşoğlu, (Istanbul: Otto, 2016), 254.
369 Yusuf al-Qaradawi, *Approaching the Sunna: Comprehension and Controversy* (London: The International Institute of Islamic Thought, 2006), 1–6; Kırbaşoğlu, *İslam Düşüncesinde Sünnet*, 367.
370 al-Shafi'i, *Risala*, 112.
371 Kırbaşoğlu, *İslam Düşüncesinde Sünnet*, 37.
372 al-Shafi'i, *al-Shafi'i's Risala*, 118–9. See Abrahamov, *Islamic Theology*, 1–3.
373 Kelsay, "Divine Command Ethics," 107.
374 Fazlur Rahman, *Islamic Methodology in History* (Islamabad: Islamic Research Institute, 1995), 23.
375 M. Hayri Kırbaşoğlu, "Klasik Sünnet Tanımlarının Eleştirisi ve Yeni Bir Sünnet Tanımı Denemesi," *Journal of Islamic Research* 5, no. 1 (1991): 23-4.
376 Kırbaşoğlu, *İslam Düşüncesinde Sünnet*, 43.
377 Yaşar Nuri, *Dinde Reform I*, 265.
378 Yaşar Nuri, *Kur'an'ı Anlamaya*, 49; Kırbaşoğlu, *Müslüman Kalarak*, 47.
379 Yaşar Nuri, *Tanrı, Akıl*, 200–201; Kırbaşoğlu, *Müslüman Kalarak*, 271.
380 Yaşar Nuri, *Din Maskeli*, 100–1.
381 Güler, *Aklın İçindeki*, 121.
382 "İslami Kıyafet," https://www.youtube.com/watch?v=J3LPOQO7To0 (February 20, 2017).
383 Kırbaşoğlu, *Müslüman Kalarak*, 264; Güler, *Kur'an'ın Mahiyeti*, 56 and 17; Yaşar Nuri, *Konferanslarım*, 148.
384 Azimli, *Cahiliyye'yi Farklı*, 140.
385 Güler, *Aklın İçindeki*, 60.
386 Kırbaşoğlu, *Müslüman Kalarak*, 74; Atay, *İslam'ı Yeniden*, 162.
387 Taha Jabir Al-Alwani and 'Imad al Din Khalil, *The Quran and the Sunnah: The Time-Space Factor* (London: The Institute of Islamic Thought, 1995), 39.
388 Kırbaşoğlu, *İslam Düşüncesinde Sünnet*, 105. "Mustafa Öztürk'ün Hadislere ve Sünnete Bakışı" https://www.youtube.com/watch?v=AdtGkKkbk5k (February 27, 2016).
389 Kırbaşoğlu, *İslam Düşüncesinde Sünnet*, 267; Güler, *Kur'an'ın Mahiyeti*, 131; Yaşar Nuri, *İnsanlığı Kemiren*, 36.
390 Yaşar Nuri, *Kur'an Verilerine*, 133.
391 Kırbaşoğlu, *İslam Düşüncesinde Sünnet*, 92; Yaşar Nuri, *Din Maskeli*, 100–1.
392 Yaşar Nuri, *Çıplak Uyarı*, 89.
393 Cf. Adis Duderija, "Understanding the Nature and Scope of the Concept of Sunnah," *Arab Law Quarterly* 21 no. 3 (2007): 279–80.
394 Kırbaşoğlu, *İslam Düşüncesinde Sünnet*, 20.
395 Kırbaşoğlu, *Müslüman Kalarak*, 260–1; Yaşar Nuri Öztürk, *Yeniden Yapılanmak: Kur'an'a Dönüş* (Istanbul: Yeni Boyut, 1996), 57.

396 Güler, *Özgürlükçü Teoloji*, 23.
397 See William F. McCants, *Founding Gods, Inventing Nations* (Princeton: Princeton University Press, 2011), 123.
398 Ghada Karmi, "Al-Tıbb al-Nabawi: The Prophet's Medicine," in *Technology Tradition and Survival: Aspects of Material Culture in the Middle East and Central Asia*, edited by Richard Tapper and Keith McLachlan (London: Frank Cass, 2003), 32.
399 Irmeli Perho, *The Prophet's Medicine: A Creation of Muslim Traditionalist Scholars* (Helsinki: Finish Oriental Society, 1985), 34; al-Jawziyya, *The Prophetic Medicine [Al-Tıbb al-Nabawi]*. Translated by Abd al-Qadir bin Abd al-Aziz (Al-Mansoura: Dar al-Ghadd, 2003), 6.
400 Kırbaşoğlu, *Müslüman Kalarak*, 267. For Rahman "the prophetic medicine" is "a vulgarization of the scientific medical tradition." Fazlur Rahman, "Islam and Medicine: A General Overview," *Perspectives in Biology and Medicine* 27, no. 4 (1984): 588.
401 Azimli, *Cahiliyye'yi Farklı*, 142.
402 Öztürk, *Siyaset İtikad*, 62.
403 Kırbaşoğlu, *Müslüman Kalarak*, 268.
404 M. Mustafa Al-A'zami, *Studies in Hadith Methodology and Literature* (Kuala Lumpur: Islamic Trust Books, 2002), 16.
405 https://dinhizmetleri.diyanet.gov.tr/Documents/Kur%E2%80%99an%20ve%20S%C3%BCnnet%20Bir%20B%C3%BCt%C3.BCnd%C3%BCr.pdf (November 12, 2019).
406 See Ann K. S. Lambton, *State and Government in Medieval Islam* (London: Routledge, 1991).
407 Öztürk, *Siyaset İtikad*, 7 and 11.
408 Jack Miles and Sohail H. Hashmi, *Islamic Political Ethics* (Princeton: Princeton University Press, 2009), 7.
409 Jan Michiel Otto, "Introduction: Investigating the Role of Sharia in National Law," in *Sharia Incorporated: A Comparative Overview of the Legal Systems of Twelve Muslim Countries in Past and Present*, edited by Jan Michiel Otto, 17–50 (Leiden: Leiden University Press, 2010), 27.
410 Khatab, *The Power of Sovereignty*, 119–72; Imam Ruhullah Khomeini. "The Necessity for Islamic Government," in *Islam and Revolution: Writings and Declarations of Imam Khomeini*, edited by Hamid Algar (Berkeley: Mizan Press, 1981), 40–54.
411 PEW Research Center, "The World's Muslims," http://www.pewforum.org/2013/04/30/the-worlds-muslims-religion-politics-societyoverview/ (August 8, 2018).
412 Eliaçık, *Demokratik*, 16; Yaşar Nuri, *İnsanlığı Kemiren*, 118; Güler, *Kur'an'ın Mahiyeti*, 108.
413 Güler, *Realpolitik*, 95.
414 Eliaçık, *Demokratik*, 129.
415 Yaşar Nuri, *400 Soruda*, 227.
416 Güler, *Realpolitik*, 190.
417 Muhammad Assad, *The Principles of State and Government in Islam* (Kuala Lumpur: Islamic Trust Book, 2007), 4 and 30–68.
418 Yaşar Nuri, *Yeniden Yapılanmak*, 29.
419 Güler, *Direniş Teolojisi*, 74.
420 Eliaçık, *Bu Belde*, 84.
421 Andreas Anter, *Max Weber's Theory of the Modern State: Origins, Structure and Significance* (New York: Palgrave, 2014), 13.

422 Hans Kelsen, *General Theory of Law and State* (London: Transactions, 2006), 189.
423 When read literally, for al-Mawardi, the political leadership is Islamic only insofar as it meets the criterion of overt fidelity to the prescribed rituals and practices of Sunni Islam. Abu'l-Hasan al-Mawardi, *al-Ahkam as-Sultaniyyah [The Laws of Islamic Governance]*. Translated by A. Yate (London: Ta-Ha, 1996), 10.
424 Kırbaşoğlu, *Ahirzaman*, 61.
425 Atay, *Ben*, 301.
426 Azimli, *Ömer*, 38.
427 Kırbaşoğlu, *Ahirzaman*, 62.
428 Eliaçık, *Çağdaş Dünyada*, 163–4.
429 W. Montgomery Watt, *Muhammad: Prophet and Statesman* (Oxford: Oxford University Press, 1961), 212–5.
430 Muhammad Hamidullah, *The Prophet's Establishing A State and His Succession* (Hyderabad: Habib, 1986), 1–14 and 40–2.
431 Mohammed Abed al-Jabri, *Democracy, Human Rights and Law in Islamic Thought* (London: I. B. Tauris, 2009), 34.
432 Shahab Ahmad, *Before Orthodoxy: The Satanic Verses in Early Islam* (Cambridge, MA: Harvard University Press, 2017), 3; Ahmed El Shamsy, "The Social Construction of Orthodoxy," in *The Cambridge Companion to Classical Islamic Theology*, edited by Tim Winter (Cambridge: Cambridge University Press, 2008), 97.
433 Yaşar Nuri, *Emevi*, 217.
434 Güler, *Politik Teoloji*, 75–6.
435 Eliaçık, *İslam'da Sosyal*, 63.
436 Yaşar Nuri, *Türkiye'ye Mektuplar*, 81.
437 Asma Afsaruddin, "Obedience to Political Authority: An Evolutionary Concept," in *Islamic Democratic Discourse: Theory, Debates, and Philosophical Perspectives*, edited by M. A. Muqtedar Khan (New York: Lexington Books, 2006), 37–62; Karaman et al., *İlmihal II*, 295; E. I. J. Rosenthal, *Political Thought in Medieval Islam: An Introductory Outline* (Cambridge: Cambridge University Press, 1962), 42; Khaled Abou El Fadl, *Religion and Violence in Islamic Law* (Cambridge: Cambridge University Press, 2001), 164.
438 Yaşar Nuri, *Kur'an'ın Temel Buyrukları*, 163.
439 Kırbaşoğlu, *Alternatif Hadis*, 400–2.
440 Yaşar Nuri, *Kur'an Verilerine*, 41.
441 Güler, *Özgürlükçü Teoloji*, 41 and 74.
442 Eliaçık, *Sosyal İslam*, 26–32.
443 Eliaçık, *Kur'an'a Giriş*, 103.
444 Kırbaşoğlu, "Son Muhalifin," 35–6.
445 Eliaçık, *Sosyal İslam*, 174; Güler, *İman Ahlak*, 131.
446 Öztürk Yaşar Nuri, *Saltanat Dinciliğinin Öncüsü Firavun: Çağdaş Firavunları Tanıma Kılavuzu* (Istanbul: Yeni Boyut, 2015), 62–6. Yaşar Nuri borrows from Eric Fromm, particularly in criticizing passive masses who endorse authoritarian regimes. Similarly, while Islamizing the right to revolt against the unjust ruler, he quotes from Proudhon. Yaşar Nuri, *Saltanat Dinciliğinin*, 107.
447 Kırbaşoğlu, "Son Muhalifin İzinde," 39.
448 Yaşar Nuri, *Kur'an Penceresinden*, 369.
449 Eliaçık, *Sosyal İslam*, 52.
450 Güler, *Direniş Teolojisi*, 57.
451 Yaşar Nuri, *Kur'an'ın Yarattığı*, 51.
452 Kırbaşoğlu, "Son Muhalifin," 36.

453 Güler, *Sabit Din*, 40.
454 Kırbaşoğlu, "Son Muhalifin," 36.
455 Rahman, *Major Themes*, 25; Rahman, *Islam and Modernity*, 5.
456 Yaşar Nuri, *Emevi*, 235; Eliaçık, *Çağdaş Dünyada*, 34.
457 Rahman, *Major Themes*, 25.
458 Yaşar Nuri, *İmamı Azam*, 153 and 277. Yaşar Nuri was influenced by Muhammad Abu Zahra, the author of popular and influential biography of Abu Hanifa. Abu Zahra argued that the standard approach to Abu Hanifa among Muslims ignores his political ideas and legacy. Abu Zahra's book was translated in Turkish in 1959. Abu Zahra, *Ebu Hanife* (Ankara: Diyanet, 2018).
459 Yaşar Nuri, *Arapçılığa Karşı*, 480.
460 Atay, *Kur'an'a Göre IV*, 98.
461 Öztürk, *Siyaset İtikad*, 55; Yaşar Nuri, *İnsanlığı Kemiren*, 172.
462 Kırbaşoğlu, "Son Muhalifin," 47.
463 Eliaçık, *Mülk Yazıları 2*, 48.
464 Yaşar Nuri, *Saltanat Dinciliğinin,* 13. Öztürk dedicated *Saltanat Dinciliğinin* to M. Muhammad Taha (d. 1985), a Sudanese reformist who was brutally killed for his reformist opinions.
465 Yaşar Nuri, *Saltanat Dinciliğinin*, 14.
466 Güler, *İtikaddan İmana*, 64.
467 Güler, *Kur'an'ın Ahlak*, 59.
468 Eliaçık, *Mülk Yazıları 2*, 8.
469 Yaşar Nuri, *Saltanat Dinciliğinden*, 16–29.
470 Kırbaşoğlu, *Destursuz*, 68–9.
471 Kırbaşoğlu, *Destursuz*, 21; Güler, *Politik Teoloji*, 40; Eliaçık, *Mülk Yazıları 2*, 8.

Chapter 3

1 Tobias Andersson, *Early Sunni Historiography: A Study of the Tarikh of Khalifa b. Khayyat* (Leiden: Brill, 2018), 2.
2 H. A. R. Gibb, "An Interpretation of Islamic History I," *The Muslim World* 45, no. 1 (1955): 5.
3 Aziz Al-Azmeh, *The Times of History: Universal Topics in Islamic Historiography* (Budapest: Central European University Press, 2007), 67.
4 Andreas Görke, "The Relationship between Maghazi and Hadith in Early Islamic Scholarship," *Bulletin of SOAS* 74, no. 2 (2011): 172.
5 Mehmet Azimli, *Hz. Ali Neslinin İsyanları: X. Yüzyıla kadar Şii Karakterli Hareketler* (Konya: Çizgi, 2017), 9.
6 Öztürk, *Siyaset İtikad*, 14–15.
7 Güler, *Politik Teoloji*, 176–7.
8 Chase F. Robinson, "The Study of Islamic Historiography: A Progress Report," *Journal of the Royal Asiatic Society of Great Britain & Ireland* 7, no. 2 (1997): 201. Also, see Khalidi, *Arab Historical Thought*, 22.
9 A. C. S. Peacock, *Medieval Islamic Historiography and Political Legitimacy* (London and New York: Routledge, 2007), 8.
10 Said Amir Arjomand, "'Abd Allah Ibn al-Muqaffa' and the 'Abbasid Revolution,'" *Iranian Studies* 27, no. ¼ (1994): 21; M. A. Shaban, *The 'Abbasid Revolution* (Cambridge: Cambridge University Press, 1970), 159–62.

11 Saleh Said Agha, *The Revolution Which Toppled the Umayyads: Neither 'Arab nor Abbasids* (Leiden: Brill, 2003), xv–xxxiii.
12 Elton L. Daniel, *The Political and Social History of Khurasan under Abbasid Rule* (Chicago: Bibliotheca Islamica, 1979), 26; Bernard Lewis, "On the Revolutions in Early Islam," *Studia Islamica* 32, no. 1 (1970): 227.
13 Muhammad Qasim Zaman, *Religion and Politics Under the Early 'Abbasids the Emergence of the Proto-Sunni Elite* (Leiden: Brill, 1997), 71.
14 Eric J. Hanne, "Abbasid Politics and the Classical Theory of the Caliphate," in *Writers and Rulers: Perspectives on Their Relationship from Abbasid to Safavid Times*, edited by Beatrice Gruendler and Louise Marlow (Wiesbaden: Reichert Verlag, 2004), 50.
15 Chase F. Robinson, *Islamic Historiography* (Cambridge: Cambridge University Press, 2003), 26.
16 Mehmet Azimli, *Dört Halifeyi Farklı Okumak-3: Hz. Osman* (Ankara: Ankara Okulu, 2018), 12.
17 Boaz Shoshan, *Poetics of Islamic Historiography: Deconstructing Tabari's History* (London and Boston: Brill, 2004), 3.
18 Chase F. Robinson, "The Violence of the Abbasid Revolution," in *Living Islamic History*, edited by Yasir Suleiman, 226–51 (Edinburgh: Edinburgh University Press, 2010), 231.
19 Abdelkader I. Tayob, "Ṭabari on the Companions of the Prophet: Moral and Political Contours in Islamic Historical Writing," *Journal of the American Oriental Society* 119, no. 2 (1999): 206.
20 Rizwi Faizer and Andrew Rippin, "Introduction," in *The Life of Muhammad: Al-Waqidi's Kitab al-Maghazi*, edited by Rizwi Faizer (London: Routledge, 2011), xii.
21 Claude Cahen, "History and Historians," in *Religion, Learning, and Science in the 'Abbasid Period*, edited by M. J. L. Young, J. D. Latham and R. B. Serjeant (Cambridge: Cambridge University Press, 1990), 196.
22 İsrafil Balcı, "Rivayetin Metne Dönüştürülmesinde Ravi Tasavvurunua Seyf b. Ömer'den Örnekler," *İslami İlimler Dergisi* 3, no. 2 (2008): 105.
23 Güler, *Politik Teoloji*, 163.
24 Yaşar Nuri, *Dinde Reform Değil II*, 98.
25 For definitions, see Giovanni C. Cattini, "Historical Revisionism," *Transfer: Journal of Contemporary Culture* 6, no. 1 (2011): 30.
26 For definitions, see Aviezer Tucker, "Historiographic Revision and Revisionism: The Evidential Difference," in *Past in the Making*, edited by Michal Kopecek (Budapest: Central European University Press, 1989), 1–2.
27 I paraphrase Seed, here. John Seed, "Secular and Religious: Historical Perspectives," *Social History* 39, no. 1 (2014): 3.
28 Mehmet Azimli, "Mekke Fethi'nden Tebuk Savaşı'na Bazı Mülahazalar," *Journal of Islamic Research* 21, no. 3 (2010): 198; Öztürk, *Siyaset İtikad*, 66.
29 Mehmet Azimli, *Dört Halifeyi Farklı Okumak-3: Hz. Osman* (Ankara: Ankara Okulu, 2018), 13; Güler, *Kuş Bakışı*, 137.
30 Magid Fakhry, *A History of Islamic Philosophy* (New York: Columbia University Press, 2004), 38; Lenn E. Goodman, "Ghazali's Argument from Creation (I)," *International Journal of Middle East Studies* 2, no. 1 (1971): 69.
31 al-Ash'ari, *Kitab al-Lum'a*, 33–4.
32 Richard M. Frank, *Creation and the Cosmic System: Al Ghazali and Avicenna* (Heidelberg: Carl Winter, 1992), 22.
33 al-Ash'ari, *Kitab al Lum'a*, 35.

34. al-Ghazali, *Tahafut*, 58.
35. al-Ash'ari, *Al-Ibanah*, 53.
36. Güler, *Sabit Din*, 82.
37. Kırbaşoğlu, *Alternatif Hadis*, 389.
38. Özsoy, *Sünnetullah*, 67.
39. Güler, *Kuş Bakışı*, 137 ; Öztürk, *Siyaset İtikad*, 69–70.
40. Azimli, *Tarih Okumaları*, 14–16. Laroui wrote on Arab history that "history ... does not constitute a level of reality possessing an autonomous consistency, where actions fall into place and by their very configuration cause other actions to appear." Abdallah Laroui, *The Crisis of the Arab Intellectual Traditionalism or Historicism?* (Berkeley: University of California Press, 1976), 23.
41. Güler, *Vicdan*, 117.
42. Eliaçık, *Daru's-Selam*, 15–16.
43. Öztürk, *Meal Kültürümüz*, 20.
44. Güler, *Sabit Din*, 90.
45. Eliaçık, *Çağdaş Dünyada*, 159.
46. Yaşar Nuri, *Yeniden Yapılanmak*, 51.
47. On salvation history, see John Wansbrough, *The Sectarian Milieu: Content and Composition of Islamic Salvation History* (Oxford: Oxford University Press, 1978), 31.
48. Güler, *Politik Teoloji*, 176–7.
49. Kırbaşoğlu, *Alternatif Hadis*, 388; Eliaçık, *Daru's-Selam*, 158; Azimli, *Tarih Okumaları*, 12. Cf. Tarif Khalidi, "The Idea of Progress in Classical Islam," *Journal of Near Eastern Studies* 40, no. 4 (1981): 277–89.
50. Özsoy, *Sünnetullah*, 125.
51. Güler, *İman Ahlak*, 7.
52. Öztürk, *Kur'an ve Tarihsellik*, 101.
53. Mehmet Azimli, *Siyer Okumaları* (Ankara: Ankara Okulu, 2017), 28. Also see Eliaçık, *İhyadan İnşaya*, 74; Güler, *Derin Ahlak*, 25.
54. I paraphrase this from: Navid Kermani, "From Revelation to Interpretation: Nasr Hamid Abu Zayd and the Literary Study of the Quran," in *Modern Muslim Intellectuals and The Quran*, edited by Suha Taji-Farouki (Oxford: Oxford University Press, 2004), 177.
55. Ibn Rushd, *Tahafut al-Tahafut*, 88–91 and 325. We see the impact of Ibn Rushd on the rationalists. Güler writes that a God that is not bound by morality is a tyrant. Güler, *Allah'ın Ahlakiliği*, 13.
56. Glasner, *Averroes's Physics*, 172.
57. Maria De Cillis, *Free Will and Predestination in Islamic Thought: Theoretical Compromises in Islamic Thought Theoretical Compromises in the Works of Avicenna, al-Ghazali and Ibn-'Arabi* (London and New York: Routledge, 2014), 11; Muhammad b. al-Shahrastani, *Muslim Sects and Divisions: The Section on Muslim Sects in Kitab al-Milal wa'l-Nihal*. Translated and Edited by A. Kazi and J. G. Flynn (London and New York: Routledge, 2014), 42.
58. al-Maturidi, *Kitab al-Tawhid*, 455–63 and 100–1.
59. Öztürk, *Siyaset İtikad*, 70.
60. Yaşar Nuri, *Merak*, 41.
61. Güler, *Politik Teoloji*, 170.
62. Özsoy, *Sünnetullah*, 115. Also see Eliaçık, *Kur'an'a Giriş*, 147; Balcı, *Peygamber ve Mucize*, 23.

63 Balcı, *Hz. Peygamber'in Savaşlarında*, 93 and 52; Eliaçık, *Kur'an'a Giriş*, 14; Atay, *Cehaletin*, 292.
64 Eliaçık, *Çağdaş Dünyada*, 290.
65 M. Mustafa Al-A'zami, *The History of the Quranic Text: From Revelation to Compilation* (Leicester: UK Islamic Academy, 2003), 69; Aliza Shnizer, "Sacrality and Collection," in *The Blackwell Companion to the Quran*, edited by Andrew Rippin (Oxford: Blackwell, 2006), 165-7.
66 Karaman et al., *İlmihal I*, 106.
67 https://www.diyanet.gov.tr/tr-TR/Kurumsal/Detay/13240/basin-aciklamasi (April 11, 2020).
68 Öztürk and Ünsal, *Kur'an Tarihi*, 7–8 and 46–62. Though this book is an edition, only the third chapter is written by Ünsal. I quote only the chapters written by Öztürk.
69 Güler, *Kuş Bakışı*, 113.
70 Azimli, *Siyer Okumaları*, 135–46.
71 Mehmet Azimli, "Hz. Peygamber'in Hastalığından Kuran'ın Cemine Kadar Meydana Gelen Bazı Olaylar Üzerine Mülahazalar," *Şarkiyat İlmi Araştırmalar Dergisi* 1, no. 1 (2009): 78.
72 Öztürk, *Kur'an, Vahiy Nüzul*, 7–12; Ibid., 79. Yaşar Nuri, *Kur'an'daki İslam*, 27–8.
73 Eliaçık, *Kur'an'a Giriş*, 35–8.
74 Azimli, *Osman*, 131–2.
75 Azimli, *Ebu Bekir*, 138–9. "Ancak sonuçta Hz. Peygamber'e indirilen ayetlerin hepsinin bize ulaşmadığı ortaya çıkmaktadır."
76 Öztürk and Ünsal, *Kur'an Tarihi*, 19–20.
77 Mehmet Azimli, *Siyeri Farklı Okumak* (Ankara: Ankara Okulu, 2018), 26.
78 Azimli, "Peygamber'in Hastalığından," 79.
79 Ali Ahmad al Imam, *Variant Readings of the Quran: A Critical Study of Their Historical and Linguistic Origins* (Herndon, VA: International Institute of Islamic Thought, 1998), 23.
80 Öztürk and Ünsal, *Kur'an Tarihi*, 47–56.
81 See F. E. Peters, *The Voice, The Word, the Books: The Sacred Scripture of the Jews, Christians, and Muslims* (Princeton: Princeton University Press, 2007), 147.
82 Öztürk and Ünsal, *Kur'an Tarihi*, 28.
83 Graham, *Divine Word*, 15 and 3; William A. Graham, "The Earliest Meaning of Quran," *Die Welt des Islams* 23/24, no. 1 (1984): 362. "Clearly, the Arabs who first heard Muhammad reciting the Quran did not immediately recognize or accept it as divine revelation." Tarık R. Kassam, "Signifying Revelation in Islam," in *Theorizing Scriptures: New Critical Orientations to a Cultural Phenomenon*, edited by Vincent L. Wimbush (New Brunswick, NJ: Rutgers University Press, 2008), 32.
84 Azimli, *Osman*, 130; Yaşar Nuri, *Fatiha*, 8.
85 Behnam Sadeghi and Uwe Bergmann, "The Codex of a Companion of the Prophet and the Quran of the Prophet," *Arabica* 57, no. 4 (2010): 343–436; Theodor Nöldeke, F. Schwally, G. Bergstrasser and O. Pretzl, *The History of Quran* (Leiden: Brill, 2013), 238; Yvonne Yazbeck Haddad, "An Exegesis of Sura Ninety-Eight," *Journal of the American Oriental Society* 97, no. 4 (1977): 522.
86 Yaşar Nuri, *Fatiha*, 8. Also, see Jeffrey, *Materials for the History*, 21.
87 Öztürk and Ünsal, *Kur'an Tarihi*, 58.
88 Ibid., 71.

89 Etan Kohlberg and Mohammad Ali Amir-Moezzi, *Revelation and Falsification: The Kitab al-qira'at of Ahmad b. Muhammad al-Sayyari* (Leiden: Brill, 2009), 2; Ruqayya Y. Khan, "Did a Women Edit the Quran? Hafsa and her Famed Codex," *Journal of the American Academy of Religion* 82, no. 1 (2014): 205.
90 Öztürk and Ünsal, *Kur'an Tarihi*, 73–81. Cf. M. J. Kister, "The Struggle against Musaylima and the Conquest of Yamama," *Jerusalem Studies in Arabic and Islam* 27, no. 1 (2002): 1–56. Al-Tabari gives the number of companions who were killed in the Battle of Yamama as 360. However, his *History* is not clear, as it also gives different statistical accounts. al-Tabari, *The History of Al-Taberi Vol. XI*. Translated by K. Yahya Blankinship (New York: The State University of New York, 1985), 128.
91 We read similar reservations about the Yamama account in Watt and Bell. See W. Montgomery Watt and R. Bell, *Introduction to Quran* (Edinburgh: Edinburgh University Press, 1977), 40–2.
92 Azimli, *Osman*, 131.
93 Azimli, *Ebu Bekir*, 124.
94 For example, in analyzing the *Codex Parisino-petropolitanus* (dated to the Umayyad period, i.e., late seventh century), Déroche concludes that "many problems, for instance that of the *hamza*, had not been resolved yet." François Déroche, *Qurans of the Umayyads: A First Overview* (Leiden: Brill, 2014), 25–7.
95 Abu 'Abdullah al-Qurtubi, *Tafsir Al-Qurtubi Classical Commentary of the Holy Quran*. Translated by Aisha Bewley (London: Dar Al Taqwa, 2003), 74.
96 al-Bukhari, *Sahih al-Bukhari Vol. VI* (Riyadh: Darussalaam, 1997), 426.
97 Öztürk and Ünsal, *Kur'an Tarihi*, 165.
98 Standardization of Quran and political dynamics have always been linked. See Matthias Radscheit, "The Quran—Codification and Canonization," in *Self-Referentiality in the Quran*, edited by Stefan Wild (Wiesbaden: H. Verlag, 2007), 98. The final text was "promulgated by official state action." John Burton, "Collection of the Quran," in *Encyclopedia of the Quran Volume One A-D.*, edited by Jane Dammen McAuliffe (Leiden: Brill, 2001), 352.
99 Nicolai Sinai, "When Did the Consonantal Skeleton of the Quran Reach Closure? Part II," *Bulletin of the School of Oriental and African Studies* 77, no. 3 (2014): 512.
100 Öztürk, *Siyaset İtikad*, 33.
101 Yaşar Nuri, *Arapçılığa Karşı*, 99.
102 Öztürk and Ünsal, *Kur'an Tarihi*, 138–47. On the codex of Ali ibn Abi Talib, see Seyfeddin Kara, *In Search of Ali Ibn Abi Talib's Codex: History and Traditions of the Earliest Copy of the Quran* (Berlin: Gerlach, 2018), 59–74; J. Eliash, "The Shiite Quran: A Reconsideration of Goldziher's Interpretation," *Arabica* 16, no. 1 (1969): 15–24.
103 Azimli, *Osman*, 129–32.
104 Öztürk and Ünsal, *Kur'an Tarihi*, 155–9. al-Suyuti, too, wrote that the number of copies sent by Uthman to the cities is unknown. However, he suggests five. al-Suyuti, *Al-Itqan*, 143.
105 For a detailed analysis of political tensions before the assassination of Uthman, see Gerald R. Hawting, "The Significance of the Slogan la hukma illa lillah and the References to the Hudud in the Traditions about the Fitna and the Murder of Uthman," *Bulletin of the School of Oriental and African Studies* 41, no. 3 (1978): 453–63.
106 Azimli, *Ebu Bekir*, 125–6. We read the stance of Ali from a Shi'a Ayatollah as follows: "No record of historical value shows that Ali . . . took part in this official collection."

Ayatollah Haji Mirza Mahdi Pooya, *Essence of the Holy Quran: The Eternal Light* (Freehold, NJ: Imam Shae-bu-Zaman Association, 1990), 23.
107 Al-A'zami, *The History of the Quranic Text*, 78.
108 Öztürk and Ünsal, *Kur'an Tarihi*, 79.
109 Ibid., 100–11. Öztürk writes that similar reports were also proposed later, against Ubay ibn Ka'b. Ibid., 92–5.
110 Azimli, *Osman*, 108.
111 Öztürk and Ünsal, *Kur'an Tarihi*, 97–100.
112 Nöldeke, *The History of Quran*, 236; Michael Lecker, "Zayd B. Thabit, A Jew with Two Sidelocks: Judaism and Literacy in Pre-Islamic Medina (Yathrib)," *Journal of Near Eastern Studies* 56, no. 4 (1997): 259–73.
113 Ahmet Yaman, "Abdullah bin Mesud'un Hanefi Mezhebinin Oluşumunda Rolü," *Marife* 4, no. 2 (2004): 8.
114 Azimli, *Osman*, 131. When Uthman ordered that the copies of his *codex* be sent to each of the main centers of the empire, his order was executed everywhere, save in Kufa, where the Abdullah ibn Mas'ud and his partisans refused to obey it. Claude Gilliot, "Creation of a Fixed Text," in *The Cambridge Companion to the Quran*. Cambridge, edited by Jane Dammen McAuliffe (Cambridge: Cambridge University Press, 2006), 45. The codex of Abdullah ibn Mas'ud was already the main copy well before in Kufa. See M. Kemal Atik, "Abdullah bin Mesud ve Mushafının Tarihteki Yeri," *KSÜ İlahiyat Fakültesi Dergisi* 5, no. 1 (2005): 21.
115 Yaşar Nuri, *Fatiha*, 8.
116 Déroche, *Qurans of the Umayyads*, 137.
117 Öztürk and Ünsal, *Kur'an Tarihi*, 92–5.
118 Ibid., 135–6.
119 Azimli, "Hz. Peygamber'in Hastalığından," 75–8.
120 Öztürk, *Cevap Veriyorum* 3, 33.
121 al-Bukhari, *Sahih Vol. VI*, 425; al-Suyuti, *Al-Itqan*, 142.
122 Öztürk and Ünsal, *Kur'an Tarihi*, 35 and 85–6.
123 Azimli, *Ebu Bekir*, 123–8. Öztürk and Ünsal, *Kur'an Tarihi*, 137.
124 Azimli, *Ebu Bekir*, 131. al-Bukhari, *Sahih Vol. VI*, 393.
125 Azimli, "Peygamber'in Hastalığından," 78.
126 Öztürk and Ünsal, *Kur'an Tarihi*, 113. al-Bukhari, *Sahih Vol. VI*, 426.
127 Öztürk and Ünsal, *Kur'an Tarihi*, 93–4, 113 and 21. Also, Gilliot, "Creation of a Fixed Text," 47.
128 Öztürk, *Kur'an Dili*, 65.
129 Azimli, *Osman*, 134.
130 Öztürk and Ünsal, *Kur'an Tarihi*, 154.
131 Ibid., 114–5.
132 Öztürk, *Kur'an Dili*, 87.
133 Said Nursi, *The Flashes Collection* (Istanbul: Sozler, 2009), 207.
134 Massimo Campanini, *The Quran: Basics* (London: Routledge, 2007), 16.
135 Öztürk, *Kur'an Dili*, 64. Also see Amidu Sanni, "New Perspectives on the Phenomenology of Error (Lahn) in Scriptural Quran," in *Oriental Studies*, edited by Zeki Dilek (Ankara: AKDTYK, 2007), 336.
136 Öztürk and Ünsal, *Kur'an Tarihi*, 154. Also see Z. I. Oseni, "An Examination of Al-Hajjaj B. Yusuf Al-Thaqafi's Major Policies," *Islamic Studies* 27, no. 4 (1988): 318.
137 Öztürk and Ünsal, *Kur'an Tarihi*, 116–7.
138 Öztürk, *Tefsir Tarihi*, 48.

139 al-Bukhari, *Sahih Vol. VI*, 428.
140 Öztürk, *Tefsir Tarihi*, 35.
141 Öztürk and Ünsal, *Kur'an Tarihi*, 117; John Gilchrist, *Jam' Al-Quran: The Codification of the Quran Text* (Mondeor: MERCSA, 1989), 53; al-Suyuti, *Al-Itqan*, 142.
142 Öztürk, *Kur'an, Vahiy Nüzul*, 214.
143 Travis Zadeh, "Touching and Ingesting: Early Debates over the Material Quran," *Journal of the American Oriental Society* 129, no. 3 (2009): 461.
144 Öztürk, *Tefsir Tarihi*, 34–7.
145 Balcı, *Peygamberlik Öncesi*, 176.
146 Kırbaşoğlu, *Alternatif Hadis*, 361. Balcı describes this as an "inflation of miracles." Balcı, *Peygamber ve Mucize*, 137.
147 Balcı, *Peygamber'in Savaşlarında*, 96 and 212. Azimli, *Siyer Okumaları*, 32.
148 Kırbaşoğlu, *İslam'ın Kurucu*, 282; Yaşar Nuri, *Kur'an'daki İslam*, 454; Güler, *Sünniliğin Eleştirisine*, 65. Azimli, *Osman*, 9; Atay, *Kur'an'a Göre III*, 131.
149 On this approach see F. E. Peters, "The Quest of the Historical Muhammad," in *The Quest for the Historical Muhammad*, edited by Ibn Warraq (New York: Prometheus, 2000), 444–75.
150 Azimli, *Siyeri Farklı*, 13–14; Güler, *Realpolitik*, 43.
151 Eliaçık, *Hangi Muhammed*, 39.
152 Yaşar Nuri, *İslam Dünyasında Akıl*, 81.
153 Güler, *Özgürlükçü Teoloji*, 38; Balcı, *Peygamber ve Mucize*, 77; Yaşar Nuri, *Kur'an'ın Yarattığı*, 66.
154 Gerhard Böwering, "The Light Verse: Quranic Text and Sufi Interpretation," *Oriens* 36, no. 1 (2010): 127; Mustafa Akman, "Hakikat-i Muhammedi Düşüncesi ve Bu Düşüncenin Referanslarını Aktaran İki Kaynak ve Müellifleri," *Yalova Sosyal Bilimler Dergisi* 1, no. 2 (2011): 108.
155 Eliaçık, *Hangi Muhammed*, 12–21; Yaşar Nuri, *İslam Dünyasında Akıl*, 235.
156 Güler, *Dine Yeni*, 42.
157 Güler, *Sabit Din*, 79.
158 Azimli, *Siyeri Farklı*, 24–6.
159 Harold Motzki, "Introduction," in *The Biography of Muhammad*, edited by Harold Motzki (Leiden: Brill, 2000), xiv.
160 Azimli, *Siyeri Farklı*, 24–6.
161 Güler, *Politik Teoloji*, 176–7.
162 Azimli, *Siyeri Farklı*, 24–6. Also see Balcı, *Peygamber ve Mucize*, 137. On angels informing Muhammad about plots against him, see Ibn Ishaq, *Sirat*, 222.
163 Marc Bloch, *Feudal Society 1: The Growth and Ties of Dependence* (London: Routledge, 2004), 73.
164 Ernst Breisach, *Historiography: Ancient, Medieval and Modern* (Chicago: The University of Chicago Press, 1994), 128.
165 Peter Ainsworth, "Legendary History: *Historia* and *Fabula*," in *Historiography in the Middle Ages*, edited by Deborah Mauskopf Deliyannis (Leiden: Brill, 2003), 412.
166 Öztürk, *Meal Kültürümüz*, 20.
167 al-Tabari, *The History of al-Tabari Vol. VI*. Translated by W. M. Watt and M. V. McDonald (New York: The State University of New York, 1988), 140–2; Ibn Ishaq, *Sirat*, 221.
168 Ibn Ishaq, *Sirat*, 82.
169 al-Waqidi, *Kitab al-Maghazi*, 17.

170 On the argument that some factual historical data on Muhammad were produced after his death, see Isaiah Goldfeld, "The Illiterate Prophet (Nabi Ummi)," *Der Islam* 57, no. 1 (1980): 58–67.
171 Eliaçık, *Yaşayan Kur'an*, 11.
172 Sebastian Günther, "Muhammad, the Illiterate Prophet: An Islamic Creed in the Quran and Quran Exegesis," *Journal of Quranic Studies* 4, no. 1 (2002): 1–5.
173 Öztürk, *Kur'an, Vahiy Nüzul*, 40.
174 Eliaçık, *Hangi Muhammed*, 59.
175 Azimli, *Siyeri Farklı*, 111. The age difference between Muhammad and Khadija is taken as a referencing of various credentials, such as "not consumed by lust" or being "comfortable with a powerful woman." Kecia Ali, *The Lives of Muhammad* (Harvard: Harvard University Press, 2014), 119.
176 Balcı, *Peygamberlik Öncesi*, 153.
177 Ibid., 19; Eliaçık, *Kur'an'a Giriş*, 29; Azimli, *Siyeri Farklı*, 125.
178 Balcı, *Peygamberlik Öncesi*, 9.
179 Yaşar Nuri, *Din Maskeli*, 285.
180 Eliaçık, *Sosyal İslam*, 141.
181 Güler, *Politik Teoloji*, 124–5. "Nietzsche describes monumental history as aiming to guide and motivate present conduct by considering past agents and events." Scott Jenkins, "Nietzsche's Use of Monumental History," *Journal of Nietzsche Studies* 45, no. 2 (2014): 170.
182 Balcı, *Peygamber ve Mucize*, 53–4.
183 Güler, *Dine Yeni*, 41–3.
184 Balcı, *Peygamber ve Mucize*, 58.
185 al-Tabari wrote: "She called her father to her house, plied him with wine until he was drunk." al-Tabari, *The History Vol. VI*, 49.
186 Azimli, *Siyeri Farklı*, 108–10.
187 Ibn Ishaq wrote that Khadija was informed about a monk who identified Muhammad as the expected prophet. Ibn Ishaq, *Sirat*, 82. Also, see al-Tabari, *The History Vol. VI*, 48.
188 Azimli, *Siyeri Farklı*, 21.
189 "Cahilliye döneminde ortalama bir insan." Balcı, *Peygamberlik Öncesi*, 290.
190 Atay, *Kur'an'a Göre IV*, 85.
191 Azimli, *Siyeri Farklı*, 355.
192 Ibid., 472.
193 Balcı, *Peygamberlik Öncesi*, 96–8.
194 Öztürk, *Tefsirin Halleri*, 21. Lings's once popular biography of Muhammad was also famous for its romanticized account of this case. Muhammad Lings, *Muhammad: His Life Based on the Earliest Sources* (London: Islamic Text Society, 1983), 213. Such accounts are rejected in the Sunni narrative. See İbrahim Sarıçam, *Hz. Muhammed ve Evrensel Mesajı* (Ankara: Diyanet, 2014), 290.
195 Güler, *Politik Teoloji*, 125.
196 Azimli, *Siyeri Farklı*, 125. Ibn Ishaq wrote that confinement in a cave was the custom of Quraysh. Ibn Ishaq, *Sirat*, 105.
197 Balcı, *Peygamberlik Öncesi*, 75.
198 Öztürk and Ünsal, *Kur'an Tarihi*, 19.
199 Ibid., 66.
200 Abu-Zayd, "The Others in the Quran," 286.

201 Azimli, "Bedir Savaşı," 12. According to Ibn Ishaq, Muhammad saw the trade caravan before the Badr War as a prey given by God. Ibn Ishaq, Sirat, 289.
202 Leila Azzam and Aisha Gouverneur, *The Life of the Prophet Muhammed* (London: The Islamic Text Society, 1985), 22.
203 The account of Ibn Kathir supports Balcı's *force major* thesis, as we read that when Muhammad was sent to Halima, "it was a year of famine," and Halima's household was extremely poor. Ibn Kathir, *Al-Sira al-Nabawiyya [The Life of the Prophet Muhammad] Vol. I*. Translated by T. Le Gassick (Reading: Garnet, 2006), 161.
204 Balcı, *Peygamberlik Öncesi*, 185.
205 Azimli, *Siyeri Farklı*, 80.
206 Sarıçam, *Hz. Muhammed*, 81.
207 Azimli, *Cahiliyye'yi Farklı*, 73.
208 Azimli, *Siyeri Farklı*, 90.
209 Ibid., 52. Balcı, *Peygamberlik Öncesi*, 103.
210 Balcı, *Peygamberlik Öncesi*, 104 and 74.
211 Azimli, *Cahiliyye'yi Farklı*, 65; Ibn Ishaq, *Sirat*, 38.
212 Azimli, *Cahiliyye'yi Farklı*, 43; Ibn Ishaq, *Sirat*, 53.
213 Azimli, *Siyeri Farklı*, 119–21.
214 Ibid., 121–3. Also, see M. J. Kister, "The Sons of Khadija," *Jerusalem Studies in Arabic and Islam* 16, no. 1 (1993): 78.
215 Balcı, *Peygamberlik Öncesi*, 64; Hisham Ibn al-Kalbi, *The Book of Idols Being a Translation from the Arabic of the Kitab al-Asnam*. Translated by N. Amin Faris (Princeton, NJ: Princeton University Press, 2015), 17–18.
216 On the miracles before and during the birth of Muhammad, see Ibn Ishaq, *Sirat*, 90–104. On the miracles regarding the signs of approaching prophethood, see al-Tabari, *The History Vol. VI*, 63–4; Ibn Kathir, *Al-Sira al-Nabawiyya Vol. I*, 145–59.
217 David Thomas, "Miracles in Islam," in *The Cambridge Companion to Miracles*, edited by Graham H. Tewelftree (Cambridge: Cambridge University Press, 2011), 203.
218 Karaman et al., *İllmihal I*, 115.
219 Güler, *Kuş Bakışı*, 234; Özsoy, *Sünnetullah*, 54; Balcı, *Peygamber ve Mucize*, 22. Cf. Rahman, *Major Themes*, 53.
220 Azimli, *Siyeri Farklı*, 15; Güler, *Sabit Din*, 74.
221 Yaşar Nuri, *400 Soruda*, 34.
222 Balcı, "Erken Dönem," 118–21.
223 Atay, *Ben*, 129; Balcı, *Peygamber ve Mucize*, 14.
224 Öztürk, *Siyaset İtikad*, 63. Also Balcı, *Peygamber ve Gayb*, 54; Yaşar Nuri, *Din Maskeli*, 97; Kırbaşoğlu, *Alternatif Hadis*, 362.
225 Azimli, *Siyeri Farklı*, 35. The Bahira miracle is a major one in the list of miracles. See Ibn Ishaq, *Sirat*, 79–81.
226 Kırbaşoğlu, *Ahirzaman*, 98. Also see Balcı, *Peygamber ve Gayb*, 153.
227 Balcı, *Peygamber ve Gayb*, 36.
228 Yaşar Nuri, *Kur'an'ın Yarattığı*, 69; Atay, *Kur'an'da İman*, 104; Balcı, *Peygamber ve Gayb*, 14.
229 Balcı, *Peygamber ve Gayb*, 63–5.
230 Güler, *Sünniliğin Eleştirisine*, 97; Balcı, *Peygamber ve Gayb*, 121.
231 Balcı, *Peygamber ve Gayb*, 67.
232 Ibid., 106–7.
233 Azimli, "İsra Miraç," 44–55.
234 Balcı, *Peygamber ve Mucize*, 35–6.

235 Balcı, *Peygamber ve Gayb*, 146.
236 Yaşar Nuri, *İslam Nasıl*, 327.
237 Balcı, *Tartışmalı Siyer*, 33–5.
238 Güler, *Vicdan*, 37. Also see Eliaçık, *Çağdaş Dünyada*, 291.
239 Atay, *Kur'an'a Göre V*, 78.
240 Taylor, *A Secular Age*, 25.
241 Seyyed Hossein Nasr, *An Introduction to Islamic Cosmological Doctrines* (London: Thames and Hudson, 1964), 1–10.
242 For Balcı, the incorporation of fabricated stories on Muhammad's sexual power is also a result of the Medieval mentality. Balcı, *Peygamber ve Mucize*, 84.
243 Yaşar Nuri, *Kur'an Penceresinden*, 20.
244 Yusuf Acara, "Saadet Asrı Model Toplum Tecrübesinin Engellilere İlişkin Kodları," *Dinbilimleri* 13, no. 1 (2013): 312.
245 Öztürk, *Söyleşiler*, 75.
246 Balcı, *Tartışmalı Siyer*, 250.
247 Güler, *Sabit Din*, 83.
248 William A. Graham, "Traditionalism in Islam: An Essay in Interpretation," *The Journal of Interdisciplinary History* 23, no. 3 (1993): 503.
249 Karaman et al., *İlmihal I*, 153.
250 Yaşar Nuri, *Kur'an Penceresinden*, 255.
251 Fu'ad Jabali, *The Companions of the Prophet: A Study of Geographical Distribution and Political Alignments*. (Leiden: Brill, 2003), 42.
252 Kırbaşoğlu, *İslam Düşüncesinde Hadis*, 59–69. This definition traces back to al-Bukhari. Ignaz Goldziher, *Muslim Studies II* (Albany: State University of New York Press, 1971), 222.
253 Azimli, *Osman*, 13; Balcı, *Tartışmalı Siyer*, 262; Kırbaşoğlu, *İslam Düşüncesinde Hadis*, 59–69.
254 Yaşar Nuri, *Lanetlenen Soy*, 305; Balcı, *Tartışmalı Siyer*, 262.
255 Güler, *Politik Teoloji*, 125. Also see Yaşar Nuri, *İnsanlığı Kemiren*, 467.
256 Eliaçık, *Demokratik*, 48.
257 Atay, *Kur'an'a Göre V*, 11.
258 Yaşar Nuri, *İmamı Azam*, 99.
259 Atay, *Kur'an'a Göre V*, 213.
260 Azimli, "Mekke Fethi'nden," 197.
261 Öztürk, *Siyaset İtikad*, 34.
262 Azimli, *Farklı Okumalar: Hasan ve Muaviye*, 87.
263 Azimli, "Bedir Savaşı," 15.
264 Yaşar Nuri, *İslam Dünyasında Akıl*, 83.
265 Kırbaşoğlu, *İslam Düşüncesinde Hadis*, 83.
266 Azimli, *Ömer*, 151; Eliaçık, *Bana Dinden*, 145.
267 Azimli, *Ebu Bekir*, 111.
268 Güler, *Aklın İçindeki*, 14.
269 Kırbaşoğlu, *İslam Düşüncesinde Hadis*, 71–4; Azimli, "Bedir Savaşı," 10.
270 Azimli, *Siyeri Farklı*, 331.
271 Karaman et al., *İlmihal II*, 281; Muhamad Yusuf Faruqi, "Legal Authority of the Sunnah: Practice of Rightly-Guided Caliphs and Views of the Early Fuqaha," *Islamic Studies* 31, no. 4 (1992): 397; Christopher Melchert, "The Rightly Guided Caliphs: The Range of Views Preserved in Hadith," in *Sunni and Shi'i Practice and Thought*, edited by Saud al-Sarhan (London: I. B. Tauris, 2019), 63.

272 Balcı, *Tartışmalı Siyer*, 250; Azimli, *Ali*, 47–8.
273 Atay, *Ben*, 284.
274 Azimli, *Ali*, 64.
275 Atay, *Ben*, 286.
276 Azimli, *Ali*, 27.
277 Tayeb El-Hibri, *Parable and Politics in Early Islamic History: The Rashidun Caliphs* (New York: Columbia University Press, 2010), 77.
278 Atay, *Ben*, 207.
279 Yaşar Nuri, *Lanetlenen Soy*, 31. Also, Atay, *Ben*, 288.
280 Öztürk, *Siyaset İtikad*, 33.
281 Mehmet Azimli, *Dört Halifeyi Doğru Okumak-2: Hz. Ömer* (Ankara: Ankara Okulu, 2017), 139.
282 Yaşar Nuri, *Merak Edilen*, 184.
283 R. İhsan Eliaçık, *Adalet Devleti: Ortak İyinin İktidarı* (Istanbul: İnşa, 2017), 207.
284 Yaşar Nuri, *Arapçılığa Karşı*, 83. Cf. A. S. Tritton, *Caliphs and Their Non-Muslim Subjects: A Critical Study of the Covenant of Umar* (London: Routledge, 2008), 5–17.
285 Azimli, *Ömer*, 145.
286 Balcı, *İlk İslam Fetihleri*, 133–41.
287 Güler, *Evrensel Ümmetçiliğe*, 75.
288 Abd al-Aziz Duri, *Early Islamic Institutions: Administration and Taxation from the Caliphate to the Umayyads and 'Abbasids* (London: I. B. Tauris, 2011), 90.
289 Yaşar Nuri, *Maun Suresi*, 189; Azimli, *Osman*, 48.
290 Azimli, *Ömer*, 87–9.
291 Atay, *Ben*, 201. According to several studies, Khalid was sacked because he and his soldiers were no longer compatible with the new tribal formation of the Islamic army during Umar. Khalil Athamina, "The Appointment and Dismissal of Khalid b. Walid: A Study of the Political Strategy of the Early Muslim Caliphs in Syria," *Arabica* 41, no. 2 (1994): 265.
292 Atay, *Ben*, 272–81.
293 Najm al-Din Yousefi, "Islam without Fuqaha: Ibn al-Muqaffa and His Perso-Islamic Solution to the Caliphate's Crisis of Legitimacy (70–142 AH/ 690–760 CE)," *Iranian Studies* 50, no. 1 (2015): 2 and 18; C. E. Bosworth, "The Persian Impact on Arabic Literature," in *Arabic Literature to the End of the Umayyad Period*, edited by A. F. L. Beeston, T. M. Johnstone, R. B. Serjeant and G. R. Smith (Cambridge: Cambridge University Press, 1983), 488.
294 Azimli, *Ebu Bekir*, 92.
295 Güler, *Aklın İçindeki*, 14.
296 Jakob Skovgaard-Petersen, "Heirs of Abu Bakr: On the Ideology and Conception of History in al-Qaeda and Islamic State," *Connections* 16, no. 1 (2017): 32.
297 Atay, *Ben*, 205.
298 Güler, *Evrensel Ümmetçiliğe*, 39. Also see Donna E. Arzt, "The Role of Compulsion in Islamic Conversion: Jihad, Dhimma and Ridda," *Buffalo Human Rights Law Review* 8, no. 1 (2002): 31.
299 Azimli, *Ebu Bekir*, 90.
300 Öztürk and Ünsal, *Kur'an Tarihi*, 95; Yaşar Nuri, *Maun Suresi*, 206.
301 Yaşar Nuri, *İmamı Azam*, 283; Azimli, *Halifelik Tarihine*, 38.
302 Azimli, *Hz. Ali Neslinin*, 13; Yaşar Nuri, *Emevi*, 50–5.
303 Azimli, *Osman*, 51.
304 Yaşar Nuri, *Lanetlenen Soy*, 44; Eliaçık, *Mülk Yazıları*, 333; Azimli, *Osman*, 118.

305 Yaşar Nuri, *Emevi*, 60–8; Eliaçık, *Mülk Yazıları 2*, 148.
306 Eliaçık, *Mülk Yazıları 2*, 149; Azimli, *Osman*, 72.
307 Yaşar Nuri, *Maun Suresi*, 207.
308 Azimli, *Osman*, 70–1; Yaşar Nuri, *Maun Suresi*, 200.
309 Azimli, *Osman*, 72; Eliaçık, *Mülk Yazıları*, 333.
310 Azimli, *Osman*, 107.
311 Eliaçık, *Mülk Yazıları*, 334; Yaşar Nuri, *Arapçılığa Karşı*, 99.
312 Eliaçık, *Mülk Yazıları 2*, 150.
313 Azimli, *Halifelik Tarihine*, 101.
314 Azimli, *Ali*, 70–3. Also see Kırbaşoğlu, *İslam Düşüncesinde Hadis*, 83. Aisha, however, later became critical of Uthman's assassination when her rival Ali became the next caliph. al-Tabari, *The History of Al-Taberi Vol. XVI*. Translated by A. Brockett (New York: The State University of New York, 1997), 52. Also, see Martin Hinds, "The Murder of the Caliph Uthman," *International Journal of Middle East Studies* 3, no. 4 (1972): 464.
315 Azimli, *Osman*, 169. Also see al-Tabari, *The History of al-Tabari Vol. XV*. Translated by R. S. Humphreys (New York: The State University of New York, 1992), 218–9.
316 Azimli, *Osman*, 176–87. Al-Tabari, *The History Vol. XV*, 250.
317 Yaşar Nuri, *Dinde Reform Değil II*, 121.
318 Al-Azmeh, *The Times of History*, 7.
319 Güler, *Sünniliğin Eleştirisine*, 25.
320 Balcı, *İlk İslam Fetihleri*, 293. Yaşar Nuri asserts that the Khattab, the clan of Caliph Umar, was famous for its Arabism. Yaşar Nuri, *Lanetlenen Soy*, 31.
321 Azimli, *Ömer*, 89; al-Tabari, *The History of Al-Taberi Vol. XII*. Translated by Y. Friedman (New York: The State University of New York, 1992), 42–5.
322 Balcı, *İlk İslam Fetihleri*, 321–6.
323 Ibid., 109.
324 Yaşar Nuri, *Lanetlenen Soy*, 89.
325 Güler, *Vicdan*, 347.
326 Yaşar Nuri, *Din Maskeli*, 150.
327 Balcı, *İlk İslam Fetihleri*, 27.
328 Güler, *Kuş Bakışı*, 47.
329 Güler, *Aklın İçindeki*, 15.
330 Azimli, "Mekke Fethi'nden," 198.
331 Balcı, *İlk İslam Fetihleri*, 324.
332 Azimli, *Osman*, 59.
333 Eliaçık, *Mülk Yazıları*, 29.
334 Azimli, *Osman*, 49.
335 Azimli, *Ömer*, 63–4.
336 Bernard Lewis, "The Concept of Islamic Republic," *Die Welt des Islams* 4, no. 1 (1955): 4.
337 Ahmet Şeyhun, *Islamic Thinkers in the Late Ottoman Empire and the Early Turkish Republic* (Leiden: Brill, 2014), 39.
338 As a typical example, see Metin Kural, *Dört Halife: Hz. Ebubekir, Hz. Ömer, Hz. Osman, Hz. Ali* (Istanbul: Kar, 2006).
339 Atay, *Cehaletin*, 181.
340 The critique by the rationalists of the early caliphate is very much like al-Jabri's analysis of the early caliphate. al-Jabri, *Democracy*, 38–41.

341 Azimli reminds that opposing people like Sa'd ibn Ubade—the looser candidate of Ansar, who never submitted to Abu Bakar and Umar—lived in isolation and were later sent into exile. Azimli, *Ebu Bekir*, 66.
342 Azimli, *Halifelik Tarihine*, 36.
343 Güler, *Sünniliğin Eleştirisine*, 24.
344 Yaşar Nuri, *Merak Edilen*, 180; Mehmet Azimli, "Hulefa-i Raşidin Dönemi Halife Seçimleri," *Dinbilimleri Akademik Araştırma Dergisi* 7, no. 2 (2007): 39.
345 Wayel Azmeh, Misconceptions About the Caliphate in Islam," *Digest of Middle East Studies* 25, no. 2 (2016): 186.
346 Öztürk, *Siyaset İtikad*, 31.
347 Eliaçık, *İhyadan İnşaya*, 113; Azimli, *Halifelik Tarihine*, 70.
348 Azimli, *Halifelik Tarihine*, 67.
349 Atay, *Cehaletin*, 180.
350 Atay, *Ben*, 206; al-Tabari, *The History of Al-Taberi Vol. XIV*. Translated by G. R. Smith (New York: The State University of New York, 1994), 144–5.
351 Azimli, *Ömer*, 189. Uthman later appointed the members of the electoral council to important posts. Recep Doğan, "Discussion over Theological and Political Foundations of Caliphate in Islam," *Journal of Islamic Studies and Culture* 6, no. 2 (2018): 2. For Lewis, the election Uthman was a victory of the old Meccan oligarchy. Bernard Lewis, *The The Arabs in History* (Oxford: Oxford University Press, 1993), 59.
352 Atay, *Ben*, 188–90. For the election of a tribal leader in pre-Islamic Arab society, see W. Montgomery Watt, *The Early Caliphate* (Edinburgh: Edinburgh University, 1968), 35.
353 Azimli, *Halifelik Tarihine*, 76–7.
354 al-Jabri, *The Formation of Arab Reason*, 124.
355 Azimli, *Cahiliyye'yi Farklı*, 9–10.
356 Öztürk, *Cahiliyeden İslamiyet'e Kadın*, 13.
357 Yaşar Nuri, *Yeniden Yapılanmak*, 51.
358 Balcı, *Peygamberlik Öncesi*, 806.
359 Güler, *Dine Yeni*, 68.
360 Güler, *Vicdan*, 115; Eliaçık, *Kur'an'a Giriş*, 58; Balcı, *Peygamberlik Öncesi*, 65.
361 Öztürk, *Cahiliyeden İslamiyet'e Kadın*, 14–15.
362 Azimli, *Cahiliyye'yi Farklı*, 75; Güler, *Dine Yeni*, 17. Allah was recognized as god before Islam, albeit not as the only god, but at least a supreme god. Joseph Henninger, "Pre-Islamic Bedouin Religion," in *The Arabs and Arabia on the Eve of Islam*, edited by F. E. Peters (London: Routledge, 1999), 118; W. Montgomery Watt, "Belief in a High God in Pre-Islamic Arabia," in *The Arabs and Arabia on the Eve of Islam*, edited by F. E. Peters (London: Routledge, 1999), 310.
363 Balcı, *Peygamberlik Öncesi*, 80–1. The verse 12:106: "most of them will only believe in God while also joining others with Him."
364 Eliaçık, *Demokratik*, 47.
365 Azimli, *Cahiliyye'yi Farklı*, 10.
366 Eliaçık, *Yaşayan Kur'an*, 63. In Ibn Ishaq, we read that rituals such as visiting Ka'ba with one's shaved head, and sacrificing animals during their stay, were known well before Islam. Ibn Ishaq, *Sirat*, 36–9.
367 Azimli, *Cahiliyye'yi Farklı*, 91.
368 Balcı, "İslam'ın İlk," 91. "Their prayers before the House [Ka'ba] are nothing but whistling and clapping."
369 Öztürk, *Cahiliyeden İslamiyet'e Kadın*, 19.

370 Balcı, *Peygamberlik Öncesi*, 25–31; Azimli, *Siyeri Farklı*, 45; Also see Ibn Ishaq, *Sirat*, 55; Michael Lecker, Pre-Islamic Arabia," in *New Cambridge History of Islam Vol. I: The Formation of the Islamic World Sixth to Eleventh Centuries*, edited by Chase F. Robinson (Cambridge: Cambridge University Press, 2010), 161.
371 Balcı, *Peygamberlik Öncesi*, 67.
372 Ibn Ishaq, *Sirat*, 9.
373 Gerald R. Hawting, The Religion of Abraham and Islam," in *Abraham, the Nations, and the Hagarites: Jewish, Christian, and Islamic Perspectives on Kinship with Abraham*, edited by Martin Goodman, George H. van Kooten and Jacques T. A. G. M. van Ruiten (Leiden: Brill, 2010), 488; Shari L. Lewin, *The Making of a Forefather: Abraham in Islamic and Jewish Exegetical Narratives* (Leiden: Brill, 2006), 245.
374 Karaman et al., *İlmihal I*, 514.
375 Yaşar Nuri, *Kur'an Penceresinden*, 20; Azimli, *Osman*, 77.
376 Atay, *Ben*, 230.
377 Frank Rosenthal, *A History of Muslim Historiography* (Leiden: Leiden University Press, 1968), 131.
378 Atay, *Kur'an'a Göre II*, 12; Güler, *Politik Teoloji*, 165; Eliaçık, *Daru's-Selam*, 155.
379 Konrad Hirschler, *Medieval Arabic Historiography: Authors as Actors* (London: Routledge, 2006), 2.
380 Ziauddin Sardar, *The Future of Muslim Civilization* (London: Croom Helm, 1979), 167–88.
381 Özsoy, *Sünnetullah*, 118. Cf. Khalidi, *Arab Historical Thought*, 8.

Chapter 4

1 Timur Kuran, "The Absence of the Corporation in Islamic Law: Origins and Persistence," *American Journal of Comparative Law* 53, no. 4 (2005): 785–834; Timur Kuran, *The Long Divergence: How Islamic Law Held Back the Middle East* (Princeton: Princeton University Press, 2011), 7.
2 Wilfred Cantwell Smith, *Islam in Modern History* (Princeton: Princeton University Press, 1957), 41.
3 Kırbaşoğlu, *Destursuz*, 51; Atay, *Ben*, 29; Güler, *Dine Yeni*, 110.
4 George Makdisi, "The Sunni Revival," in *Islamic Civilization, 950-1150*, edited by D. H. Richards (Oxford: Bruno Cassirer, 1973), 155–68; Gibb, "An Interpretation of Islamic History," in *Studies of the Civilization of Islam*, edited by S. Shaw and W. Polk (Princeton: Princeton University Press, 1982), 3–33; Ahmet T. Kuru, *Islam, Authoritarianism, Underdevelopment: A Global and Historical Comparison* (Cambridge: Cambridge University Press, 2019), 118–63.
5 Ann K. S. Lambton, *Landlord and Peasant in Persia: A Study of Land Tenure and Land Revenue Administration* (London and New York: I. B. Tauris, 1969), 61; D. G. Tor, "The Islamisation of Iranian Kingly Ideals in the Persianate Fürstenspiegel," *Iran* 49, no. 1 (2011): 116.
6 Mustafa Öztürk, *Kur'an ve Aşırı Yorum: Tefsirde Batinilik ve Batini Te'vil Geleneği* (Ankara: Ankara Okulu, 2016), 266; Frederick Starr, *Lost Enlightenment: Central Asia's Golden Age from the Arab Conquest to Tamerlane* (Princeton, NJ: Princeton University Press, 2013), 405; A. L. Tibawi, "Origin and Character of al-madrasah," *Bulletin of the School of Oriental and African Studies* 25, no. 1/3 (1962): 225–38.

7   Massima Campanini, "In Defense of Sunnism: Al Ghazali and the Seljuqs," in *The Seljuqs: Politics, Society and Culture*, edited by Christian Lange and Songül Mecit (Edinburgh: Edinburg University Press, 2011), 228–39; Daphna Ephrat, "The Seljuqs and the Public Sphere in the Period of Sunni Revivalism: The View from Baghdad," in *The Seljuqs: Politics, Society and Culture*, edited by Christian Lange and Songül Mecit (Edinburgh: Edinburgh University Press, 2011), 139–45.
8   Öztürk, *Kur'an ve Aşırı Yorum*, 277.
9   On the other hand, the Sunni revival thesis accepts that the origins of Sunni paradigm trace back to well before the eleventh century. Hamid Dabashi, *Authority in Islam: From the Rise of Muhammad to the Establishment of the Umayyads* (London: Transactions, 1989), 71–5.
10 Atay, *Cehaletin*, 146; Eliaçık, *Demokratik*, 57–8.
11 Azimli, *Halifelik Tarihine*, 18–55; Öztürk, *Dinde Reform Değil II*, 195; Eliaçık, *Kur'an'a Giriş*, 75.
12 Atay, *Kur'an'a Göre II*, 78.
13 Güler, *Evrensel Ümmetçiliğe*, 73; Öztürk, *Kur'an, Tefsir*, 157.
14 Güler, *Politik Teoloji*, 116.
15 Güler, *Özgürlükçü Teoloji*, 7.
16 Atay, *Cehaletin*, 243.
17 Atay, *Kur'an'a Göre V*, 19; Yaşar Nuri, *Saltanat Dinciliğinin*, 144.
18 Güler, *Sabit Din*, 90.
19 Yaşar Nuri, *Saltanat Dinciliğinin*, 135.
20 Atay, *Kur'an'a Göre V*, 42.
21 Yaşar Nuri, *Din Maskeli*, 162.
22 On this thesis, see Eric Ormsby, *Ghazali* (London: Oneworld, 2000), 66; Watt W. Montgomery, *Muslim Intellectual: A Study of Al-Ghazali* (Edinburgh: Edinburgh University Press, 1963), 59; Fakhry, *A History of Islamic Philosophy*, 323.
23 Güler, *Politik Teoloji*, 201; Atay, *Cehaletin*, 142; Yaşar Nuri, *Emevi*, 297; Atay, *Kur'an'a Göre IV*, 54. Though critical of al-Ghazali on various accounts, however, Kırbaşoğlu also appreciates him for borrowing philosophical methods from the Greek philosophy. Kırbaşoğlu, *Üçüncü Yol*, 75.
24 Güler, *İtikaddan İmana*, 135; Yaşar Nuri, *Emevi*, 292. On this, see Margaret Smith, *Al-Ghazali: The Mystic* (Lahore: HIP, 1983), 225.
25 Öztürk, *Kur'an, Vahiy Nüzul*, 95. The esoteric methods proposed by al-Ghazali also assert that Quran has the knowledge of everything. Özsoy, *Sünnetullah*, 63.
26 al-Ghazali, *Al Munkidh*, 25.
27 Al-Attas, *Islam and Secularism*, 146.
28 Atay, *Cehaletin*, 129.
29 Öztürk, *Tefsir Tarihi*, 59. Öztürk "Kur'an Vahyinin," 30–2. Öztürk notes that one factor that motivated al-Ghazali to incorporate Sufism into mainstream Islam is his strategy to weaken the connection of Sufism with Shi'a esoterism. Öztürk, *Tefsirin Halleri*, 88.
30 Güler, *Sünniliğin Eleştirisine*, 36. For the rationalists, the incorporation of Sufism into the mainstream Islam gave way to other negative consequences, such as promoting asceticism so far as to make Muslims indifferent to worldly affairs. Güler in this vein criticizes al-Ghazali's books like *The Alchemy of Happiness*. Öztürk asserts that al-Ghazali's legacy is therefore a key factor also in the popularity of ritualistic piety. Güler, *Allah'ın Ahlakiliği*, 16; Eliaçık, *Bana Dinden*, 375; Öztürk, *Siyaset İtikad*, 234.

31 Yaşar Nuri, *Din Maskeli*, 168. See Leonard Binder, "Al-Ghazali's Theory of Islamic Government," *The Muslim World* 45, no. 3 (1995): 232. al-Ghazali lists kings as the second group of superior people, after the prophets. For al-Ghazali, the sultan is the shadow of God on earth. Abu Hamid al-Ghazali, *Nasihat al-Muluk [Ghazali's Book of Council for Kings]*. Translated by F. R. C. Bagley (London: Oxford University Press, 1964), 45.
32 Eliaçık, *İslam'ın Üç*, 106. Eliaçık here refers to the tradition that likens religion and state to twins. See E. I. J. Rosenthal, *Political Thought in Medieval Islam: An Introductory Outline* (Cambridge: Cambridge University Press, 1962), 39. Lambton, *State and Government in Medieval Islam*, 108.
33 Eliaçık, *İhyadan İnşaya*, 118. See Paul Weithman, "Augustine's Political Philosophy," in *The Cambridge Companion to Augustine*, edited by Eleonore Stump and Norman Kretzmann (Cambridge: Cambridge University Press, 2001), 234–52.
34 Eliaçık, *İhyadan İnşaya*, 310.
35 Yaşar Nuri, *İslam Dünyasında Akıl*, 120; Eliaçık, *Bu Belde*, 128; Güler, *Politik Teoloji*, 279.
36 Yaşar Nuri, *İslam Dünyasında Akıl*, 124.
37 Öztürk, *Kur'an ve Aşırı Yorum*, 39. Ebrahim Moosa has written that al-Ghazali used sometimes theology in the service of Seljuqi politics. Ebrahim Moosa, *Ghazali and the Poetics of Imagination* (Chapel Hill: The University of North Caroline Press, 2005), 163. The rationalists' observations in the case of al-Ghazali also remind of what Safi wrote of the new Sunni orthodoxy in the post-Abbasid period: It is a new paradigm where "the semantics of state and religion now overlap." See Omid Safi, *The Politics of Knowledge in Premodern Islam: Negotiating Ideology and Religious Inquiry* (Chapel Hill: The University of North Caroline Press, 2006), 5.
38 Yaşar Nuri, *Kur'an'ın Yarattığı*, 137.
39 Güler, *Politik Teoloji*, 96.
40 Güler, *Kuş Bakışı*, 134.
41 Atay, *Osmanlılarda Yüksek*, 77–9.
42 Öztürk, *Kur'an ve Tarihsellik*, 283; Güler, *İtikaddan İmana*, 9; Yaşar Nuri, *Konferanslarım*, 90; Kırbaşoğlu, *Alternatif Hadis*, 155; Balcı, *Peygamber ve Mucize*, 134.
43 Öztürk, *Cumhuriyet Türkiyesi'nde*, 312.
44 Güler, *Özgürlükçü Teoloji*, 15. See W. Montgomery Watt, *Islamic Philosophy and Theology* (Edinburgh: Edinburgh University Press, 1985), 79–80; George Makdisi, "Ash'ari and the Ash'arites in Islamic Religious History," *Studia Islamica* 17, no. 1 (1962): 38.
45 Güler, *Dine Yeni*, 117–9; Atay, *Osmanlılarda Yüksek*, 151.
46 Güler, *Özgürlükçü Teoloji*, 91.
47 Atay, *Ben*, 150; Eliaçık, *İhyadan İnşaya*, 310. Güler writes that al-Ghazali synthesized dogmatism of Ash'arism and al-Shafi'i's method. Güler, *Sabit Din*, 86. Rahman uses "Ash'ari anti-rationalism" as a frame. Fazlur Rahman, *Revival and Reform in Islam: A Study of Islamic Fundamentalism* (Oxford: Oneworld, 2000), 61.
48 Eliaçık, *İhyadan İnşaya*, 31.
49 Güler, *Sabit Din*, 131.
50 Özsoy, *Kur'an ve Tarihsellik Yazıları*, 105; Güler, *İsimsiz*, 73; Öztürk, *Kur'an ve Tarihsellik*, 85–8.
51 Atay, *İslam'da İşçi*, 48.
52 Güler, *Vicdan*, 171.
53 Atay, *İslam'ı Yeniden*, 31; Öztürk, *Siyaset İtikad*, 66.

54 Kırbaşoğlu, "İslami İlimlerde Şafi'nin Rolü," 225; Öztürk, *Tefsir Tarihi*, 14–25; Güler, *Sünniliğin Eleştirisine*, 17; M. Hayri Kırbaşoğlu, "Er-Risale'nin Şekil ve Muhteva Açısından Eleştirisi," in *Sünni Paradigmanın Oluşumunda Şafi'i'nin Rolü*, edited by M. Hayri Kırbaşoğlu (Istanbul: Otto, 2016), 317; Özsoy, *Kur'an ve Tarihsellik Yazıları*, 29. Also see Kelsay, "Divine Command Ethics," 115; Scott C. Lucas, *The Legacy of the Generation of Ibn Sa'd, Ibn Ma'in, and Ibn Hanbal* (Leiden: Brill, 2004), 151–3.
55 Taha Jabir Kırbaşoğlu, *Ehl-i Sünnet'in Kurucu*, 14. See al-Awani, *Source Methodology in Islamic Jurisprudence: Usul al-Fiqh al-Islami* (London: The International Institute of Islamic Thought, 2003), 43–52.
56 Özsoy, *Kur'an ve Tarihsellik Yazıları*, 105; Güler, *Evrensel Ümmetçiliğe*, 73.
57 Güler, *Politics Teoloji*, 192.
58 Güler, *Özgürlükçü Teoloji*, 88.
59 Kırbaşoğlu, *İslami İlimlerde*, 229.
60 Yaşar Nuri, *Din Maskeli*, 12.
61 Gerald R. Hawting, *The First Dynasty of Islam: The Umayyad Caliphate AD 661–759* (London: Routledge, 2000), 14.
62 Yaşar Nuri, *Kur'an Verilerine*, 34–5.
63 Yaşar Nuri, *Arapçılığa Karşı*, 102.
64 Güler, *Sünniliğin Eleştirisine*, 23.
65 Eliaçık, *İslam'ın Üç*, 78; Azimli, *Halifelik Tarihine*, 136; Güler, *Politik Teoloji*, 141.
66 Eliaçık, *Daru's-Selam*, 97.
67 Azimli, *Halifelik Tarihine*, 37.
68 Yaşar Nuri, *İnsanlığı Kemiren*, 429.
69 Öztürk, *Siyaset İtikad*, 21; Yaşar Nuri, *Din Maskeli*, 218; Güler, *Realpolitik*, 78.
70 Güler, *Politik Teoloji*, 26.
71 Yaşar Nuri, *Saltanat Dinciliğinin*, 136.
72 H. A. R. Gibb, "The Evolution of Government in Early Islam," *Studia Islamica* 4, no. 1 (1955): 6.
73 Öztürk, *Dinde Reform Değil II*, 122; Azimli, *Halifelik Tarihine*, 125; Güler, *Politik Teoloji*, 133.
74 Güler, *Dine Yeni*, 80.
75 Güler, *İsimsiz*, 95; Eliaçık, *Demokratik*, 49.
76 On the Umayyads' resorting to sheer power. See Andrew Marsham, *Rituals of Islamic Monarchy: Accession and Succession in First Muslim Empire* (Edinburgh: Edinburgh University Press, 2009), 82.
77 Güler, *Özgürlükçü Teoloji*, 75. Also, see Khalid Yahya Blankinship, *The End of the Jihad State: The Reign of Hisham 'Abd al-Malik and the Collapse of the Umayyads* (New York: State University of New York Press, 1994), 24.
78 Yaşar Nuri, *Türkiye'ye Mektuplar*, 102.
79 Eliaçık, *Çağdaş Dünyada*, 43; Yaşar Nuri, *Kur'an Penceresinden*, 19.
80 Eliaçık, *Sosyal İslam*, 223; Yaşar Nuri, *Maun Suresi*, 34.
81 Öztürk, *Siyaset İtikad*, 19; Eliaçık, *Sosyal İslam*, 294; Azimli, *Osman*, 80. Cf. Rahman, *Revival and Reform in Islam*, 40–4.
82 Atay, *Kur'an'da İman Esasları*, 12; Güler, *Derin Ahlak*, 43.
83 Yaşar Nuri, *Dinde Reform Değil I*, 420; Atay, *Kur'an'a Göre I*, 19; Güler, *Dine Yeni*, 120.
84 Güler, *Derin Ahlak*, 43.
85 Eliaçık, *Bana Dinden*, 172; Yaşar Nuri, *400 Soruda*, 55.

86 Güler, *Allah'ın Ahlakiliği*, 84; Md. Modiur Rahman, Responsibility for Action in an Early Historical Document of Islam: Al-Hasan bin Ali's Risala," *Islamic Quarterly* 34, no. 4 (1990): 235–48. Also, see Michael Schwarz, "The Letter of al-Hasan al-Basri," *Oriens* 20, no. 1 (1967): 15–30.
87 Yaşar Nuri, *400 Soruda*, 59.
88 Ziauddin Ahmed, "A Survey of the Development of Theology in Islam," *Islamic Studies* 11, no. 2 (1972): 97.
89 Öztürk, *Siyaset İtikad*, 19; Balcı, *Peygamber ve Gayb*, 141; Eliaçık, *Bana Dinden*, 147; Atay, *Ben*, 127; Güler, *Allah'ın Ahlakiliği*, 84; Steven C. Judd, "The Early Qadariyya," in *The Oxford Handbook of Islamic Theology*, edited by Sabine Schmidtke (Oxford: Oxford University Press, 2016), 49; Steven C. Judd, "Ghaylan al-Dimashqi: The Isolation of a Heretic in Islamic Historiography," *International Journal of Middle East Studies* 31, no. 2 (1999): 161–84.
90 Güler, *Allah'ın Ahlakiliği*, 84; Eliaçık, *Bana Dinden*, 147; Balcı, *Peygamber ve Gayb*, 139–40.
91 Steven C. Judd, "Competitive Hagiography in Biographies of al-Awza'i and Sufyan al-Thawri," *Journal of the American Oriental Society* 122, no. 1 (2002): 26.
92 Güler, *İtikaddan İmana*, 35. The executed scholars agreed on "justice" as one of God's divine attributes, which became an essential creed of the Mu'tazilite's system. Abu-Zayd, "The Dilemma of the Literary Approach," 36.
93 Öztürk, *Siyaset İtikad*, 22; Yaşar Nuri, *Lanetlenen Soy*, 53; Atay, *Kur'an'da İman Esasları*, 13; Balcı, *Peygamber ve Gayb*, 139; Azimli, *Cahiliyye'yi Farklı*, 84.
94 Güler, *Politik Teoloji*, 80. Also see Suleiman Ali Mourad, "Theology: Free Will and Predestination," in *The Islamic World*, edited by Andrew Rippin (London: Routledge, 2008), 180.
95 Yaşar Nuri, *Kur'an Penceresinden*, 83; Güler, *Allah'ın Ahlakiliği*, 83.
96 Balcı, *Peygamber ve Gayb*, 138.
97 Güler, *Allah'ın Ahlakiliği*, 83; Balcı, *Peygamber ve Gayb*, 138.
98 Balcı, *Peygamber ve Gayb*, 56; Azimli, *Siyeri Farklı*, 62; Güler, *Kur'an'ın Ahlak*, 171.
99 Yaşar Nuri, *400 Soruda*, 54.
100 Yaşar Nuri, *Türkiye'ye Mektuplar*, 116.
101 Güler, *İsimsiz*, 51.
102 Güler, *Allah'ın Ahlakiliği*, 161.
103 Balcı, *Peygamber ve Gayb*, 139.
104 Kırbaşoğlu, *Alternatif Hadis*, 494–5. Also, see Güler, *Dine Yeni*, 115.
105 Eliaçık, *Kur'an'a Giriş*, 82.
106 Atay, *Ben*, 138.
107 Güler, *İsimsiz*, 33; Azimli, "Bedir Savaşı," 16.
108 Güler, *Vicdan*, 18.
109 Ibid., 243–4; Eliaçık, *Demokratik*, 57–8.
110 Elizabeth Sirriyeh, *Sufis and Anti-Sufis: The Defense, Re-thinking and Rejection of Sufism in the Modern World* (London: Routledge, 2013), 1–3; Michael Laffan, Understanding Al-Imam's Critique of Tariqa Sufism," in *Varieties of Religious Authority Changes and Challenges in 20th Century Indonesian Islam*, edited by Azyumardi Azra, Kees Van Dijk and Nico J. G. Kaptein (Pasir Panjang: ISEAS, 2010), 18.
111 Öztürk, *Kur'an, Vahiy Nüzul*, 96 and 131; Atay, *İslam'ı Yeniden*, 80; Yaşar Nuri, *İslam Dünyasında Akıl*, 97; Balcı, *Peygamber ve Gayb*, 8; Güler, *Vicdan*, 246–55.

112 Rahman also entertains the idea that Sufism was good in the origin; however, it later corrupted. Rahman, *Revival and Reform in Islam*, 82.
113 Güler, *Aklın İçindeki*, 354. Rahman, too, defined Sufism as "religion within religion." Rahman, *Islamic Methodology*, 106.
114 Öztürk, *Siyaset İtikad*, 83; Kırbaşoğlu, *Ahirzaman*, 273; Yaşar Nuri, *Kur'an'ın Yarattığı*, 81. But, Öztürk underlines that several Sunni scholars' interest in Sufism like al-Kalabadhi (d. 995) helped keeping Sufism within a controlled zone. Öztürk, *Kur'an ve Aşırı Yorum*, 265. Accordingly, the Sufi interpretations of jihad verses are always softer for they redefine jihad as one's struggle with his/her own ego rather than the conventional war. Öztürk, *Kur'an ve Tarihsellik*, 131.
115 Yaşar Nuri Öztürk, *Tasavvufun Ruhu ve Tarikatlar* (Istanbul: Yeni Boyut, 1990), 15.
116 Yaşar Nuri, *Yeniden Yapılanmak*, 120.
117 Kırbaşoğlu, *Üçüncü Yol*, 180; Yaşar Nuri, *Çıplak Uyarı*, 65.
118 Kırbaşoğlu, *Ahirzaman*, 272; Yaşar Nuri, *Tasavvufun Ruhu*, 255; Öztürk, *Siyaset İtikad*, 249.
119 Kırbaşoğlu, *Üçüncü Yol*, 177–8.
120 Güler, *Vicdan*, 208.
121 Öztürk, *Siyaset İtikad*, 252; Güler, *Vicdan*, 150; Atay, *Ben*, 132.
122 Güler, *Kur'an'ın Mahiyeti*, 86.
123 Eliaçık, *İslam'ın Üç*, 68.
124 Yaşar Nuri, *Kur'an Penceresinden*, 56; Güler, *Realpolitik*, 19; Atay, *Kur'an'a Göre V*, 118.
125 Eliaçık, *Kur'an'a Giriş*, 207; Öztürk, *Cumhuriyet Türkiyesi'nde*, 203.
126 Yaşar Nuri, *Ses Birgün*, 76.
127 Atay, *Cehaletin*, 67–9.
128 Eliaçık, *Bana Dinden*, 9.
129 Balcı, *Peygamber ve Gayb*, 8. For Atay, this is a case to observe the ongoing impact of al-Ghazali upon contemporary Islamic movements. Atay, *Kur'an'a Göre IV*, 86.
130 Yaşar Nuri, *Yeniden Yapılanmak*, 62; Öztürk, *Siyaset İtikad*, 57.
131 Eliaçık, *Kur'an'a Giriş*, 115; Öztürk, *Siyaset İtikad*, 55; Yaşar Nuri, *İnsanlığı Kemiren*, 30.
132 Öztürk, *Siyaset İtikad*, 49.
133 Güler, *Özgürlükçü Teoloji*, 45.
134 Yaşar Nuri, *Çıplak Uyarı*, 39; Kırbaşoğlu, *Üçüncü Yol*, 176.
135 Güler, *Derin Ahlak*, 14.
136 Öztürk, *Siyaset İtikad*, 249. Also see Eliaçık, *Sosyal İslam*, 65.
137 Güler, *Realpolitik*, 23.
138 Atay, *Kur'an'a Göre II*, 13.
139 The rise of Islamic groups in Turkey, too, occurred in the context of the worldwide shift to neoliberalism. Valentine M. Moghadam, *Globalization and Social Movements Islamism, Feminism, and The Global Justice Movement* (New York: Rowman and Littlefield, 2009), 44.
140 Kırbaşoğlu, *Ahirzaman*, 275.
141 Güler, *Realpolitik*, 17; Eliaçık, *Sosyal İslam*, 285.
142 Güler, *Dine Yeni*, 148.
143 Yaşar Nuri, *İslam Dünyasında Akıl*, 239.
144 Güler, *Kur'an'ın Ahlak*, 136.
145 Rahman, *Revival and Reform in Islam*, 60.

Conclusion

1 Kırbaşoğlu, *İslam Düşüncesinde Sünnet*, 31.
2 Mustafa Akyol, "A New Secularism Is Appearing in Islam," *New York Times*, December 23, 2019.
3 İştar Gözaydın, *Diyanet: Türkiye Cumhuriyeti'nde Dinin Tanzimi* (Istanbul: İletişim, 2009), 1–24.
4 "Tarihselcilik," https://www.youtube.com/watch?v=2owSqHzTMRg (March 10, 2018).
5 Şerif Mardin, *Türk Modernleşmesi Makaleler IV* (Istanbul: İletişim, 1991), 356–61.
6 Güler, *Vicdan*, 117.

BIBLIOGRAPHY

Abdul-Rauf, Hussein. *Quran Translation: Discourse, Texture and Exegesis*. London: Routledge, 2001.

Abiad, Nisrine. *Sharia, Muslim States and International Human Rights Treaty Obligations: A Comparative Study*. London: The British Institute of International and Comparative Law, 2008.

Abrahamov, Binyamin. *Islamic Theology: Traditionalism and Rationalism*. Edinburgh: Edinburgh University Press, 1998.

Abu Rida, Muhammad A. "Norms and Values". In *The Different Aspects of Islamic Culture: The Individual and Society in Islam*, edited by A. Bouhdiba and M. M. al-Dawalibi, 19–60. Paris: UNESCO, 1998.

Abu Zahra, Muhammad. *Ebu Hanife*. Ankara: Diyanet, 2018.

Abu-Zayd, Nasr. "The Dilemma of the Literary Approach to the Quran." *Alif: Journal of Comparative Poetics* 23, no. 1 (2003): 8–47.

Abu-Zayd, Nasr. *Rethinking the Quran: Towards a Humanistic Hermeneutics*. Utrecht: Humanistic University Press, 2004.

Abu-Zayd, Nasr. "The Others in the Quran: A Hermeneutical Approach." *Philosophy and Social Criticism* 36, no. ¾ (2010): 281–94.

Acara, Yusuf. "Saadet Asrı Model Toplum Tecrübesinin Engellilere İlişkin Kodları." *Dinbilimleri* 13, no. 1 (2013): 131–71.

Adil, Mohamed Azam Mohamed. "Law of Apostasy and Freedom of Religion in Malaysia." *Asian Journal of Comparative Law* 2, no. 1 (2007): 1–36.

Afsaruddin, Asma. "Obedience to Political Authority: An Evolutionary Concept." In *Islamic Democratic Discourse: Theory, Debates, and Philosophical Perspectives*, edited by M. A. Muqtedar Khan, 37–62. New York: Lexington Books, 2006.

Afsaruddin, Asma. *Striving in the Path of God*. Oxford: Oxford University Press, 2013.

Agha, Saleh Said. *The Revolution Which Toppled the Umayyads: Neither 'Arab nor Abbasids*. Leiden: Brill, 2003.

Ahmad, Furqan. "Understanding the Islamic Law of Divorce." *Journal of the Indian Law Institute* 45, no. ¾ (2003): 484–508.

Ahmad, Shahab. *Before Orthodoxy: The Satanic Verses in Early Islam*. Cambridge, MA: Harvard University Press, 2017.

Ahmat, Aziz. *Islamic Modernism in India and Pakistan, 1857–1964*. Bombay: Oxford University Press, 1967.

Ahmed, Rumee. "Which Comes First, the *Maqasid* or the *Shariʿa*?" In *The Objectives of Islamic Law: The Promises and Challenges of the Maqasid al-Shariʿa*, edited by Idris Nassery, Rumee Ahmed, and Muna Tatari, 239–62. London: Lexington, 2018.

Ahmed, Ziauddin. "A Survey of the Development of Theology in Islam." *Islamic Studies* 11, no. 2 (1972): 93–111.

Ainsworth, Peter. "Legendary History: *Historia* and *Fabula*." In *Historiography in the Middle Ages*, edited by Deborah Mauskopf Deliyannis, 387–416. Leiden: Brill, 2003.

Akbar, M. J. *The Shade of Swords: Jihad and the Conflict Between Islam and Christianity*. London: Routledge, 2002.

Akbulut, İlhan. "İslam Hukukunda Suçlar ve Cezalar." *Ankara Universitesi Hukuk Fakültesi Dergisi* 52, no. 1 (2003): 167–81.

Akman, Mustafa. "Hakikat-i Muhammedi Düşüncesi ve Bu Düşüncenin Referanslarını Aktaran İki Kaynak ve Müellifleri." *Yalova Sosyal Bilimler Dergisi* 1, no. 2 (2011): 107–31.

Al-A'zami, M. Mustafa. *Studies in Hadith Methodology and Literature*. Kuala Lumpur: Islamic Trust Books, 2002.

Al-A'zami, M. Mustafa. *The History of the Quranic Text: From Revelation to Compilation*. Leicester: UK Islamic Academy, 2003.

Al-Alwani, Taha Jabir. *Source Methodology in Islamic Jurisprudence: Usul al-Fiqh al-Islami*. London: The International Institute of Islamic Thought, 2003.

Al-Alwani, Taha Jabir. *Apostasy in Islam: A Historical and Scriptural Analysis*. London: International Institute of Islamic Thought, 2011.

Al-Alwani, Taha Jabir and 'Imad al Din Khalil. *The Quran and the Sunnah: The Time-Space Factor*. London: The Institute of Islamic Thought, 1995.

al-Ash'ari. *Al-Ibanah. 'An Usul Ad-Diyanah [The Elucidation of Islam's Foundation]*. Translated by Walter C. Klein. New Haven: American Oriental Society, 1940.

al-Ash'ari. *Kitab al-Luma' [The Luminous Book]*. Translated by Richard J. McCarthy. Beirut: Imprimerie Catholique, 1953.

Al-Attas, Syed Muhammad Naquib. *Islam and Secularism*. Kuala Lumpur: ISTAC, 1993.

Al-Azmeh, Aziz. *The Times of History: Universal Topics in Islamic Historiography*. Budapest: Central European University Press, 2007.

Al-Azmeh, Wayel. "Misconceptions About the Caliphate in Islam." *Digest of Middle East Studies* 25, no. 2 (2016): 186–209.

Al-Baghdadi, 'Abd Qahir ibn-Tahir. *Moslim Schism and Sects [Al-Fark Bain al-Firak]*. Translated by K. Chambers Seelye. New York: New York University Press, 1920.

al-Bukhari. *Sahih al-Bukhari Vol. V*. Riyadh: Darussalaam, 1997.

al-Bukhari. *Sahih al-Bukhari Vol. VI*. Riyadh: Darussalaam, 1997.

Al-Faruqi, Ismail R. *Al-Tawhid: Its Implications for Thought and Life*. London: The International Institute of Islamic Thought, 2000.

Al-Faruqi, Ismail R. *Selected Essays*. London: The International Institute of Islamic Thought, 2018.

al-Ghazali, Abu Hamid. *Deliverance from Error [Al Munkidh min Ad Dallal]*. Translated by W. M. Watt. Lahore: Sh. M. Ashraf, 1963.

al-Ghazali, Abu Hamid. *Nasihat al-Muluk [Ghazali's Book of Council for Kings]*. Translated by F. R. C. Bagley. London: Oxford University Press, 1964.

al-Ghazali, Abu Hamid. *Tahafut al-Falasifa [The Incoherence of the Philosophers]*. Translated by Michael E. Marmura. Provo: Brigham Young University Press, 2000.

al-Ghazali, Abu Hamid. *The Jewels of the Quran: Al-Ghazali's Theory [Kitab Jawahir al-Quran]*. Translated by Muhammad Abul Quasem. Kuala Lumpur: University of Malaya Press, 1977.

al-Ghazali, Abu Hamid. *The Just Balance [Al-Qistas Al-Mustaqim]*. Translated by D. P. Brewster. Lahore: Sh. M. Ashraf, 1978.

al-Ghazali, Abu Hamid. *The Incoherence of the Philosophers [Tahafut al-falasifa]*. Translated by Michael E. Marmura. Utah: Brigham Young University Press, 2000.

al-Hibri, Azizah and Raja' M. El Habti. "Islam." In *Sex, Marriage, and Family in World Religions*, edited by Don S. Browning, M. Christian Green and John Witte Jr., 150–225. New York: Columbia University Press, 2006.

al Imam, Ahmad. 'Ali. *Variant Readings of the Quran: A Critical Study of Their Historical and Linguistic Origins*. Herndon, VA: International Institute of Islamic Thought, 1998.

al-Jabri, Mohammed Abed. *Democracy, Human Rights and Law in Islamic Thought*. London: I. B. Tauris, 2009.

al-Jabri, Mohammed Abed. *The Formation of Arab Reason: Text, Tradition and the Construction of Modernity in the Arab World*. London: I. B. Tauris, 2011.

al-Jawziyya. *The Prophetic Medicine [Al-Tibb al-Nabawi]*. Translated by Abd al-Qadir bin Abd al-Aziz. Al-Mansoura: Dar al-Ghadd, 2003.

al-Kalbi, Hisham Ibn. *The Book of Idols Being a Translation from the Arabic of the Kitab al-Asnam*. Translated by N. Amin Faris. Princeton, NJ: Princeton University Press, 2015.

al-Maturidi. *Kitabü't-Tevhid Açıklamalı Tercüme [Kitab al-Tawhid]*. Translated by Bekir Topaloğlu. Ankara: ISAM, 2018.

al-Mawardi, Abu'l-Hasan. *al-Ahkam as-Sultaniyyah [The Laws of Islamic Governance]*. Translated by A. Yate. London: Ta-Ha, 1996.

al-Qaradawi, Yusuf. *The Lawful and the Prohibited in Islam*. Kuwait: International Islamic Federation of Student Organization, 1984.

al-Qaradawi, Yusuf. *Approaching the Sunna: Comprehension and Controversy*. London: The International Institute of Islamic Thought, 2006.

al-Qurtubi, Abu 'Abdullah. *Tafsir Al-Qurtubi Classical Commentary of the Holy Quran*. Translated by Aisha Bewley. London: Dar Al Taqwa, 2003.

Al-Raysuni, Ahmad. *Imam al-Shatibi's Theory of the Higher Objectives and Intents of the Islamic Law*. London: The International Institute of Islamic Thought, 2005.

al-Shafi'i. *al-Shafi'i's Risala Treatise on the Foundations of Islamic Jurisprudence*. Translated by Majid Khadduri. London: The Islamic Text Society, 1997.

al-Shahrastani, Muhammad b. 'Abd al-Karim. *Muslim Sects and Divisions: The Section on Muslim Sects in Kitab al-Milal wa'l-Nihal*. Translated and Edited by A. Kazi and J. G. Flynn. London and New York: Routledge, 2014.

al-Shatibi, Ibrahim Ibn Musa Abu Ishaq. *Al-Muwafaqat fi Usul al-Shari'a Vol. II [The Reconciliation of the Fundamentals of the Islamic Law]*. Translated by Imran Ahsan Khan Nyazee. Reading: Garnett, 2014.

al-Sulami, Mishal Fahm. *The West and Islam: Western Liberal Democracy versus the System of Shura*. London: Routledge, 2003.

al-Suyuti, Imam Jalal-al-Din 'Abd al-Rahman. *The Perfect Guide to the Sciences of the Quran Volume I [Al-Itqan fi 'Ulum al-Quran]*. Translated by Hamid Algar, Michael Schub and Ayman Abdel Haleem. Reading: Garnet, 2011.

al-Tabari. *The History of Al-Taberi Vol. XI*. Translated by K. Yahya Blankinship. New York: The State University of New York, 1985.

al-Tabari. *The History of Al-Taberi Vol. XXVII*. Translated by J. A. Williams. New York: The State University of New York, 1985.

al-Tabari. *The History of al-Tabari Vol. VI*. Translated by W. M. Watt and M. V. McDonald. New York: The State University of New York, 1988.

al-Tabari. *The History of Al-Tabari Vol. XV*. Translated by R. S. Humphreys. New York: The State University of New York, 1992.

al-Tabari. *The History of Al-Taberi Vol. XII*. Translated by Y. Friedman. New York: The State University of New York, 1992.

al-Tabari. *The History of Al-Taberi Vol. XIV*. Translated by G. R. Smith. New York: The State University of New York, 1994.

al-Tabari. *The History of Al-Taberi Vol. XVI*. Translated by A. Brockett. New York: The State University of New York, 1997.

al-Tusi, Muhammad ibn Hasan ibn Ali Ja'far. *A Concise Description of Islamic Law and Legal Opinions [al-Nihayah fi Mujarrad al-Fiqh wa al-Fatawa]*. Translated by A. Ezzati. London: ICAS Press, 2008.

Al-Wahidi. *Al-Wahidi's Asbab al-Nuzul*. Translated by Mokrane Guezzou. Louisville, KY: Fons Vitae, 2008.

Al-Waqidi. *The Life of Muhammad [Kitab al-Maghazi]*. Translated by Rizwi Faizer. London: Routledge, 2011.

Alekhya, Somepalli. "Comparative Analysis of Islamic Divorce Laws: Socio-legal Analysis." *Journal of Family and Adoption Law* 2, no. 2 (2019): 18–26.

Ali, Kecia. *Sexual Ethics and Islam: Feminist Reflections on Quran, Hadith, and Jurisprudence*. Oxford: Oneworld, 2006.

Ali, Kecia. *The Lives of Muhammad*. Harvard: Harvard University Press, 2014.

Amin, Kamaruddin. "The Reliability of the Traditional Science of Hadith: A Critical Consideration." *Al-Jami'ah Journal of Islamic Studies* 43, no. 2 (2005): 255–81.

An-Na'im, Abdullahi Ahmed. "Islamic Law, International Relations, And Human Rights: Challenge and Response." *Cornell International Law Journal* 20, no. 2 (1987): 317–36.

An-Na'im, Abdullahi Ahmed. *Toward an Islamic Reformation Civil Liberties Human Rights, and International Law*. New York: Syracuse University Press, 1990.

An-Nai'im, Abdullahi Ahmed. "What Do We Mean by Universal?" *Index on Censorship* 4/5, no. 1 (1994): 120–8.

Andersson, Tobias. *Early Sunni Historiography: A Study of the Tarikh of Khalifa b. Khayyat*. Leiden: Brill, 2018.

Ansari, Z. Ishaq. "The Early Development of Islamic Fiqh in Kufah with Special Reference to the Works of Abu Yusuf and Shaybani." *Islamic Studies* 57, no. ½ (2018): 103–58.

Anter, Andreas. *Max Weber's Theory of the Modern State: Origins, Structure and Significance*. New York: Palgrave, 2014.

Apaydın, H. Yunus. "Tesettür." In *İslam Ansiklopedisi Vol. 40*, edited by commission, 543–5. Ankara: TDV, 2011.

Arberry, A. J. *Revelation and Reason in Islam*. London: Routledge, 2008.

Arjomand, Said Amir. "'Abd Allah Ibn al-Muqaffa' and the 'Abbasid Revolution.'" *Iranian Studies* 27, no. ¼ (1994): 9–36.

Arkoun, Muhammad. *The Unthought in Contemporary Islamic Thought*. London: Saqi, 2002.

Arzt, Donna E. "The Role of Compulsion in Islamic Conversion: Jihad, Dhimma and Ridda." *Buffalo Human Rights Law Review* 8, no. 1 (2002): 15–44.

Aşlamacı, İbrahim, and Recep Kaymakcan. "A Model for Islamic Education from Turkey: The Imam-Hatip Schools." *British Journal of Religious Education* 39, no. 3 (2017): 279–92.

Assad, Muhammad. *The Principles of State and Government in Islam*. Kuala Lumpur: Islamic Trust Book, 2007.

Atay, Falih Rıfkı. *Baş Veren İnkılapçı*. Istanbul: Cumhuriyet, 1997.

Atay, Hüseyin. *İslam'da Bilgi Teorisi*. Istanbul: Furkan, 1982.

Atay, Hüseyin. "Dinde Reform." *AÜİFD* 43, no. 1 (2001): 1–26.

Atay, Hüseyin. "Dinde Reformun Yöntemi ve Bir Örnek: Hırsızlık." *AÜİFD* 43, no. 2 (2002): 1–18.

Atay, Hüseyin. *Kur'an'a Göre Araştırmalar I*. Ankara: Atay, 2012.
Atay, Hüseyin. *Kur'an'a Göre Araştırmalar II*. Ankara: Atay, 2012.
Atay, Hüseyin. *Kur'an'a Göre Araştırmalar III*. Ankara: Atay, 2012.
Atay, Hüseyin. *Kur'an'a Göre Araştırmalar IV*. Ankara: Atay, 2012.
Atay, Hüseyin. *Kur'an'a Göre Araştırmalar V*. Ankara: Atay, 2012.
Atay, Hüseyin. *Kur'an: Türkçe Çeviri*. Ankara: Atay, 2013.
Atay, Hüseyin. *İslam'da İşçi-İşveren İlişkileri*. Ankara: Atay, 2015.
Atay, Hüseyin. *İslam'ı Yeniden Anlama*. Ankara: Atay, 2017.
Atay, Hüseyin. *Kur'an'a Göre Araştırmalar VI*. Ankara: Atay, 2017.
Atay, Hüseyin. *Cehaletin Tahsili*. Ankara: Atay, 2018.
Atay, Hüseyin. *Kur'an'da İman Esasları ve Kader*. Ankara: Atay, 2018.
Atay, Hüseyin. *Osmanlılarda Yüksek Din Eğitimi: Medrese Programları İcazetnameler Islahat Hareketleri*. Istanbul: Atay, 2018.
Atay, Hüseyin. *Ben: Akıl ve Kuran Işığında 1400 Yıllık Süreçte İslam'ın Serüveni*. Istanbul: Destek, 2019.
Athamina, Khalil. "The Appointment and Dismissal of Khalid b. Walid: A Study of the Political Strategy of the Early Muslim Caliphs in Syria." *Arabica* 41, no. 2 (1994): 253–72.
Atik, M. Kemal. "Abdullah bin Mesud ve Mushafının Tarihteki Yeri." *KSÜ İlahiyat Fakültesi Dergisi* 5, no. 1 (2005): 1–64.
Auda, Jasser. *Maqasid al-Sharia of Islamic Law: A Systems Approach*. London: The International Institute of Islamic Thought, 2008.
Ayoub, Mahmoud M. *The Quran and Its Interpreters Vol. I*. Albany: State University of New York Press, 1984.
Ayoub, Mahmoud. "Uzayr in the Quran and Muslim Tradition." In *Studies in Islamic and Judaic Traditions*, edited by W. M. Brinner and S. D. Ricks, 3–18. Atlanta, GA: Scholars Press, 1986.
Azimli, Mehmet. "Hulefa-i Raşidin Dönemi Halife Seçimleri." *Dinbilimleri Akademik Araştırma Dergisi* 7, no. 2 (2007): 35–59.
Azimli, Mehmet. "Hz. Peygamber'in Hastalığından Kuran'ın Cemine Kadar Meydana Gelen Bazı Olaylar Üzerine Mülahazalar." *Şarkiyat İlmi Araştırmalar Dergisi* 1, no. 1 (2009): 67–80.
Azimli, Mehmet. "İsra Miraç Olayları Üzerine Bazı Mülahazalar." *Bilimname* 1, no. 1 (2009): 43–58.
Azimli, Mehmet. "Bedir Savaşı Çerçevesinde Bazı Mülahazalar." *Bilimname* 8, no. 1 (2010): 7–20.
Azimli, Mehmet. "Mekke Fethi'nden Tebuk Savaşı'na Bazı Mülahazalar." *Journal of Islamic Research* 21, no. 3 (2010): 194–201.
Azimli, Mehmet. *Farklı Okumak: Hasan ve Muaviye*. Ankara: Ankara Okulu, 2016.
Azimli, Mehmet. *Halifelik Tarihine Giriş: Başlangıcından IX. Asra Kadar*. Istanbul: Cizgi, 2016.
Azimli, Mehmet. *Cahiliyye'yi Farklı Okumak*. Ankara: Ankara Okulu, 2017.
Azimli, Mehmet. *Dört Halifeyi Doğru Okumak-2: Hz. Ömer*. Ankara: Ankara Okulu, 2017.
Azimli, Mehmet. *Dört Halifeyi Farklı Okumak-4: Hz. Ali*. Ankara: Ankara Okulu, 2017.
Azimli, Mehmet. *Hz. Ali Neslinin İsyanları: X. Yüzyıla kadar Şii Karakterli Hareketler*. Konya: Çizgi, 2017.
Azimli, Mehmet. *Siyer Okumaları*. Ankara: Ankara Okulu, 2017.
Azimli, Mehmet. *Dört Halifeyi Farklı Okumak-1: Hz. Ebu Bekir*. Ankara: Ankara Okulu, 2018.

Azimli, Mehmet. *Dört Halifeyi Farklı Okumak-3: Hz. Osman*. Ankara: Ankara Okulu, 2018.
Azimli, Mehmet. *Siyeri Farklı Okumak*. Ankara: Ankara Okulu, 2018.
Azimli, Mehmet. *Tarih Okumaları*. Ankara: Ankara Okulu, 2018.
Azzam, Leila and Aisha Gouverneur. *The Life of the Prophet Muhammed*. London: The Islamic Text Society, 1985.
Bakhshizadeh, Marziyeh. *Changing Gender Norms in Islam: Between Reason and Revelation*. Berlin: Budrich, 2018.
Balcı, İsrafil. "Erken Dönem Arap Kültüründe Peygamberlik Tasavvuru." *Ekev Akademi Dergisi* 10, no. 29 (2006): 111–34.
Balcı, İsrafil. "Rivayetin Metne Dönüştürülmesinde Ravi Tasavvurunua Seyf b. Ömer'den Örnekler." *İslami İlimler Dergisi* 3, no. 2 (2008): 105–25.
Balcı, İsrafil. "Bedir Savaşı Ile İlgili Mucizevi Rivayetlerin Kur'an, Hadis ve Tarih Verilerine Göre Kritiği." *İstem* 7, no. 13 (2009): 85–124.
Balcı, İsrafil. *İlk İslam Fetihleri: Savaş-Barış İlişkisi*. Istanbul: Pınar, 2011.
Balcı, İsrafil. "İslâm'ın İlk Kıblesinin el-Mescidü'l-Aksâ Olduğu İddialarının Kritiği ve Kıble Değişikliğinin Tarihsel Arka Planı." *İslam Araştırmaları Dergisi* 28, no. 2 (2012): 85–116.
Balcı, İsrafil. *Hz. Peygamber ve Mucize*. Ankara: Ankara Okulu, 2013.
Balcı, İsrafil. *Peygamberlik Öncesi Hz. Muhammed*. Ankara: Ankara Okulu, 2014.
Balcı, İsrafil. *Hz. Peygamber ve Gayb*. Ankara: Ankara Okulu, 2016.
Balcı, İsrafil. *Hz. Peygamber ve Namaz*. Ankara: Ankara Okulu, 2018.
Balcı, İsrafil. *Tartışmalı Siyer Meseleleri*. Istanbul: Düşün, 2018.
Balcı, İsrafil. *Hz. Peygamber'in Savaşlarında İlahi Yardım*. Ankara: Ankara Okulu, 2014.
Bani, Lawal Muhammad and Hamza A. Pate. "Dissolution of Marriage (Divorce) Under Islamic Law." *Journal of Law, Policy and Globalization* 42, no. 1 (2015): 138–43.
Bano, Masooda. *The Revival of Islamic Rationalism: Logic, Metaphysics and Mysticism in Modern Muslim Societies*. Cambridge: Cambridge University Press, 2020.
Berg, Herbert. "Competing Paradigms in Islamic Origins: Quran 15:89-91 and the Value of Isnads." In *Method and Theory in the Study of Islamic Origins*, edited by Herbert Berg, 259–92. Leiden: Brill, 2003.
Binder, Leonard. "Al-Ghazali's Theory of Islamic Government." *The Muslim World* 45, no. 3 (1995): 229–41.
Blankinship, Khalid Yahya. *The End of the Jihad State: The Reign of Hisham 'Abd al-Malik and the Collapse of the Umayyads*. New York: State University of New York Press, 1994.
Bloch, Marc. *Feudal Society 1: The Growth and Ties of Dependence*. London: Routledge, 2004.
Bostom, Andrew G. *Sharia versus Freedom: The Legacy of Islamic Totalitarianism*. London: Prometheus, 2012.
Bosworth, C. E. "The Persian Impact on Arabic Literature." In *Arabic Literature to the End of the Umayyad Period*, edited by A. F. L. Beeston, T. M. Johnstone, R. B. Serjeant and G. R. Smith, 483–94. Cambridge: Cambridge University Press, 1983.
Bouyer, Louis. *Liturgical Piety*. Notre Dame: University of Notre Dame Press, 1954.
Bowen, John R. *Why the French Don't Like the Headscarf*. Princeton: Princeton University Press, 2010.
Böwering, Gerhard. "The Light Verse: Quranic Text and Sufi Interpretation." *Oriens* 36, no. 1 (2010): 113–44.
Breisach, Ernst. *Historiography: Ancient, Medieval and Modern*. Chicago: The University of Chicago Press, 1994.

Brown, Jonathan A. C. *Hadith: Muhammad's Legacy in the Medieval and Muslim World.* Oxford: Oneworld, 2009.

Brown, Jonathan A. C. "Is the Devil in the Details? Tension Between Minimalism and Comprehensiveness in the Shariah." *Journal of Religious Ethics* 39, no. 3 (2011): 458–72.

Burton, John. "Collection of the Quran." In *Encyclopedia of the Quran Volume One A-D.*, edited by Jane Dammen McAuliffe, 351–61. Leiden: Brill, 2001.

Burton, John. *An Introduction to Hadith.* Edinburgh: Edinburgh University Press, 2001.

Caetani, Leone. "The Art of War of the Arabs, and the Supposed Religious Fervor of the Arab Conquests." In *The Expansion of the Early Islamic State*, edited by Fred M. Donner, 1–14. London: Routledge, 2016.

Cahen, Claude. "History and Historians." In *Religion, Learning, and Science in the 'Abbasid Period*, edited by M. J. L. Young, J. D. Latham and R. B. Serjeant, 188–232. Cambridge: Cambridge University Press, 1990,

Campanini, Massimo. *The Quran: Basics.* London: Routledge, 2007.

Campanini, Massimo. "Quranic Hermeneutics and Political Hegemony: Reformation of Islamic Thought." *The Muslim World* 99, no. 1 (2009): 124–33.

Campanini, Massima. "In Defense of Sunnism: Al Ghazali and the Seljuqs." In *The Seljuqs: Politics, Society and Culture*, edited by Christian Lange and Songül Mecit, 228–39. Edinburgh: Edinburg University Press, 2011.

Campanini, Massimo. "The Mu'tazila in Islamic History and Thought." *Religion Compass* 6, no. 1 (2012): 41–50.

Candan, Abdulcelil. *Kur'an-ı Kerim'de Anlaşılması Güç Ayetler.* Istanbul: Seyda, 2016.

Çapçıoğlu, İhsan. "Türkiye'deki İlahiyat Fakültelerinde Din Sosyolojisi Alanında Tamamlanmış Lisansüstü Tezler Üzerine Bir Araştırma." *AÜİFD* 45, no. 1 (2004): 203–24.

Catovic, Sami. "Finding a Principled Approach to *Matn* Analysis." In *Contemporary Approaches to the Quran and Sunnah*, edited by Mahmoud Ayoub, 155–71. London: The International Institute of Islamic Thought, 2012.

Cattini, Giovanni C. "Historical Revisionism." *Transfer: Journal of Contemporary Culture* 6, no. 1 (2011): 28–38.

Cengiz, Yunus. "Türkiye'de Mu'tezile Hakkında Yapılan Çalışmaların Değerlendirilmesi." *İslami İlimler Dergisi* 12, no. 12 (2017): 103–44.

Charsley, Katharine and Anika Liversage. "Transforming Polygamy: Migration, Transnationalism and Multiple Marriages among Muslim Minorities." *Global Networks* 13, no. 1 (2013): 60–78.

Chaudry, Zainab. "The Myth of Misogyny: A Reanalysis of Women's Inheritance in Islamic Law." *Albany Law Review* 61, no. 2 (1998): 511–56.

Ciddi, Sinan. *Kemalism in Turkish Politics: The Republican People's Party, Secularism and Nationalism.* New York: Routledge, 2009.

Cillis, Maria De. *Free Will and Predestination in Islamic Thought: Theoretical Compromises in Islamic Thought Theoretical Compromises in the Works of Avicenna, al-Ghazali and Ibn-'Arabi.* London and New York: Routledge, 2014.

Clarence-Smith, William Gervase. *Islam and the Abolition of Slavery.* Oxford: Oxford University Press, 2006.

Clark, Stephen R. L. *Plotinus Myth, Metaphor, and Philosophical Practice.* Chicago: The Chicago University Press, 2016.

Cleve, Felix M. *The Philosophy of Anaxagoras.* New York: King's Crown Press, 1949.

Crone, Patricia. *Roman, Provincial, and Islamic Law: The Origins of the Islamic Patronate.* Cambridge: Cambridge University Press, 1987.

Culson, Noel J. *A History of Islamic Law*. Edinburgh: Edinburgh University Press, 2005.
Dabashi, Hamid. *Authority in Islam: From the Rise of Muhammad to the Establishment of the Umayyads*. London: Transactions, 1989.
Daniel, Elton L. *The Political and Social History of Khurasan under Abbasid Rule, 747–820*. Chicago: Bibliotheca Islamica, 1979.
Delaney, Carol. *The Seed and The Soil: Gender and Cosmology in Turkish Village Society*. Berkeley: University of California Press, 1991.
Deringil, Selim. "They Live in a State of Nomadism and Savagery: The Late Ottoman Empire and the Post-Colonial Debate." *Comparative Studies in Society and History* 45, no. 2 (2003): 311–42.
Déroche, François. *Qurans of the Umayyads: A First Overview*. Leiden: Brill, 2014.
Derveze, İzzet. *Kur'an'a Göre Hz. Muhammed'in Hayatı Vol. I*. Istanbul: Düşün, 2011.
Dickinson, Eeric. *The Development of Early Sunnite Hadith Criticism: The Taqdima of Ibn Abi Hatim al-Razi (240/854-327/938)*. Leiden: I. B. Tauris, 2001.
Dickinson, Eeric. "Ibn al-Salah al-Shahrazuri and the Isnad." *Journal of the American Oriental Society* 122, no. 3 (2002): 481–505.
Doğan, Nihat. "İslam Hukuku Açısından Müslüman Bayanın Ehl-i Kitap Erkekle Evliliği." *İslam Hukuku Araştırmaları Dergisi* 2, no. 1 (2003): 131–56.
Doğan, Recep. "Discussion over Theological and Political Foundations of Caliphate in Islam." *Journal of Islamic Studies and Culture* 6, no. 2 (2018): 1–8.
Donner, Fred M. *Narratives of Islamic Origins: The Beginning of Islamic Historical Writing*. Princeton: Darwin Press, 1998.
Donner, Fred M. *Muhammed and the Believers at the Origins of Islam*. Cambridge, Massachusetts: The Belknap Press of Harvard University Press, 2010.
Douki, S., F. Nacef, A. Belhadj, A. Bouasker, and R. Ghachem. "Violence against women in Arab and Islamic Countries." *Archives of Women's Mental Health* 6, no. 1 (2003): 165–71.
Drozdek, Adam. "Anaxagoras' Cosmic Mind." *Estudios clásicos* 47, no. 127 (1971): 23–36.
Dubetsky, A. "Class and Community in Urban Turkey." In *Commoners, Climbers and Notables A Sampler of Studies on Social Ranking in the Middle East*, edited by C. A. O. Van Nieuwenhuijze, 360–71. Leiden: E. J. Brill, 1971.
Duderija, Adis. "Understanding the Nature and Scope of the Concept of Sunnah." *Arab Law Quarterly* 21 no. 3 (2007): 269–80.
Duri, Abd al-Aziz. *Early Islamic Institutions: Administration and Taxation from the Caliphate to the Umayyads and 'Abbasids*. London: I. B. Tauris, 2011.
Dusuki, Asyraf Wajdi, and Nurdianawati Irwani Abdullah. "Maqasid al-Shari'ah, Maslahah, and Corporate Social Responsibility." *American Journal of Islamic Social Sciences* 24, no. 1 (2007): 25–45.
Efe, Ahmet. "İslam Miras Hukukunda Kadın-Erkek Hisselerinin Farklı Oluşu Üzerine Bir Değerlendirme." *İslam Hukuku Araştırmaları Dergisi* 18, no. 1 (2011): 157–68.
El Fadl, Khaled Abou. *Religion and Violence in Islamic Law*. Cambridge: Cambridge University Press, 2001.
El Fadl, Khaled Abou. *Speaking in God's Name: Islamic Law, Authority, and Women*. Oxford: One World, 2001.
El Hamel, Chouki. *Black Morocco: A History of Slavery, Race, and Islam*. Cambridge: Cambridge University Press, 2013.
El Shamsy, Ahmed. "The Social Construction of Orthodoxy." In *The Cambridge Companion to Classical Islamic Theology*, edited by Tim Winter, 97–118. Cambridge: Cambridge University Press, 2008.

El-Awa, Mohamed. "The Place of Custom (Urf) in Islamic Legal Theory." *Islamic Quarterly* 17, no. 3 (1973): 177–82.
El-Cheikh, Nadia Maria. "Muhammad and Heraclius: A Study in Legitimacy." *Studia Islamica* 89, no. 1 (1999): 5–21.
El-Hibri, Tayeb. *Parable and Politics in Early Islamic History: The Rashidun Caliphs*. New York: Columbia University Press, 2010.
Eliaçık, R. İhsan. *İslam'ın Üç Çağı: İnşa Çağında Yeni-İslamcılık Söylemleri*. Istanbul: Çıra, 2004.
Eliaçık, R. İhsan. *Mülk Yazıları 2*. Istanbul: İnşa, 2010.
Eliaçık, R. İhsan. *Sosyal İslam: Dinin Direği Paylaşımdır*. Istanbul: Destek, 2011.
Eliaçık, R. İhsan. *Yaşayan Kur'an: İlk Mesajlar*. Istanbul: İnşa, 2012.
Eliaçık, R. İhsan. *Devrimci İslam*. Istanbul: Doğu, 2013.
Eliaçık, R. İhsan. *İslam'da Sosyal Değişim ve Devrimler*. Istanbul: Doğu, 2013.
Eliaçık, R. İhsan. *Demokratik Özgürlükçü İslam*. Istanbul: Tekin, 2014.
Eliaçık, R. İhsan. *Bu Belde: Türkiye Yazıları*. Istanbul: İnşa, 2015.
Eliaçık, R. İhsan. *Daru's-Selam: Evrensel Adalet ve Barış Yurdu*. Istanbul: İnşa, 2015.
Eliaçık, R. İhsan. *İhyadan İnşaya İslam Düşüncesi*. Istanbul: İnşa, 2015.
Eliaçık, R. İhsan. *Mülk Yazıları: Göklerde ve Yerde Mülkiyet Allah'a Aittir*. Istanbul: İnşa, 2016.
Eliaçık, R. İhsan. *Adalet Devleti: Ortak İyinin İktidarı*. Istanbul: İnşa, 2017.
Eliaçık, R. İhsan. *Bana Dinden Bahset*. Istanbul: İnşa, 2017.
Eliaçık, R. İhsan. *Çağdaş Dünyada İslam*. Istanbul: İnşa, 2017.
Eliaçık, R. İhsan. *Hangi Muhammed: Sihirbaz, Kahin, Ruhban Değil Arkadaş Peygamber*. Istanbul: İnşa, 2017.
Eliaçık, R. İhsan. *Kur'an'a Giriş: Gerçeğe, Hayata ve Topluma Dönüş*. Istanbul: İnşa, 2017.
Eliash, J. "The Shiite Quran: A Reconsideration of Goldziher's Interpretation." *Arabica* 16, no. 1 (1969): 15–24.
Emerson, Ralph Waldo. *English Traits*. Boston and New York: H. Mifflin Company, 1903.
Ephrat, Daphna. "The Seljuqs and the Public Sphere in the Period of Sunni Revivalism: The View from Baghdad." In *The Seljuqs: Politics, Society and Culture*, edited by Christian Lange and Songül Mecit, 139–56. Edinburgh: Edinburgh University Press, 2011.
Ernst, Carl W. *How to Read the Quran*. Edinburgh: Edinburgh University Press, 2011.
Espada, Joao Carlos. "The Tradition of Liberty and Why It Does Matter." In *The Liberal Tradition in Focus Problems and New Perspectives*, edited by Joao Carlos Espada, Marc F. Plattner and Adam Wolfson, 10–15. New York: Lexington Books, 2000.
Euben, Roxanne L. *Enemy in the Mirror: Islamic Fundamentalism and the Limits of Modern Rationalism*. Princeton: Princeton University Press, 1999.
Faizer, Rizwi, and Andrew Rippin. "Introduction." In *The Life of Muhammad: Al-Waqidi's Kitab al-Maghazi*, edited by Rizwi Faizer, xi–xvii. London: Routledge, 2011.
Fakhry, Magid. *A History of Islamic Philosophy*. New York: Columbia University Press, 2004.
Faruqi, Muhamad Yusuf. "Legal Authority of the Sunnah: Practice of Rightly-Guided Caliphs and Views of the Early Fuqaha." *Islamic Studies* 31, no. 4 (1992): 393–409.
Fatima, Saleha and Musferah Mehfooz. "Similarities Between Woman and Earth: A Study of Quranic Metaphorical Comprehensiveness in the Light of Al-Baqara 223." *Jihad al-Islam* 9, no. 2 (2016): 5–17.
Fatoohi, Louay. *Abrogation in the Quran and Islamic Law: A Critical Study of the Concept of "Naskh" and Its Impact*. London and New York: Routledge, 2013.

Fay, Mary Ann. "Introduction: What Is Islamic About Slavery in the Islamic World?" In *Slavery in the Islamic World: Its Characteristics and Commonality*, edited by Mary Ann Fay, 1–6. London: Palgrave Macmillan, 2019.

Findley, Carter Vaughn. *Ottoman Civil Officialdom: A Social History*. Princeton: Princeton University Press, 1989.

Forte, David. F. "Islamic Law and the Crime of Theft: An Introduction." *Cleveland State Law Review* 34, no. 1 (1985): 47–67.

Frank, Richard M. *Creation and the Cosmic System: Al Ghazali and Avicenna*. Heidelberg: Carl Winter, 1992.

Friedmann, Yohanan. *Tolerance and Coercion in Islam: Interfaith Relations in the Muslim World*. Cambridge: Cambridge University Press, 2003.

Geiss, Bernard W. *The Spirit of Islamic Law*. Athens: The University of Georgia Press, 1998.

Georgeon, François. "La formation des élites à la fin de l'Empire ottoman : le cas de Galatasaray." *Revue des mondes musulmans et de la Méditerranée* 72, no. 1 (1994): 15–25.

Gesink, Indira Falk. *Islamic Reform and Conservatism: Al-Azhar and the Evolution of Modern Sunni Islam*. London: I. B. Tauris, 2010.

Ghanea, Nazila. "Apostasy and Freedom to Change Religion or Belief." *Current Issues in Law and Religion* 4, no. 1 (2017): 139–58.

Ghobadzadeh, Naser. *Religious Secularity: A Theological Challenge to the Islamic State*. Oxford: Oxford University Press, 2005.

Gibb, H. A. R. "An Interpretation of Islamic History I." *The Muslim World* 45, no. 1 (1955): 4–15.

Gibb, H. A. R. "The Evolution of Government in Early Islam." *Studia Islamica* 4, no. 1 (1955): 5–17.

Gibb, H. A. R. "An Interpretation of Islamic History." In *Studies of the Civilization of Islam*, edited by S. Shaw and W. Polk, 3–33. Princeton: Princeton University Press, 1982.

Gilchrist, John. *Jamʿ Al-Quran: The Codification of the Quran Text*. Mondeor: MERCSA, 1989.

Gilliot, Claude. "Creation of a Fixed Text." In *The Cambridge Companion to the Quran*. Cambridge, edited by Jane Dammen McAuliffe, 41–58. Cambridge: Cambridge University Press, 2006.

Glasner, Ruth. *Averroes' Physics: A Turning Point in Medieval Natural Philosophy*. Oxford: Oxford University Press, 2009.

Goldfeld, Isaiah. "The Illiterate Prophet (Nabi Ummi)." *Der Islam* 57, no. 1 (1980): 58–67.

Goldziher, Ignaz. *Muslim Studies II*. Albany: State University of New York Press, 1971.

Goldziher, Ignaz. *The Zahiris Their Doctrine and Their History: A Contribution to the History of Islamic Thought*. Leiden: E. J. Brill, 1971.

Goldziher, Ignaz. *On the History of Grammar Among Arabs: An Essay in Literary History*. Philadelphia: John Benjamins, 1994.

Göle, Nilüfer. "Secularism and Islamism in Turkey: The Making of Elites and Counter-Elites." *The Middle East Journal* 51, no. 1 (1997): 46–8.

Goodman, Lenn E. "Ghazali's Argument from Creation (I)." *International Journal of Middle East Studies* 2, no. 1 (1971): 67–85.

Görke, Andreas. "The Relationship between Maghazi and Hadith in Early Islamic Scholarship." *Bulletin of SOAS* 74, no. 2 (2011): 171–85.

Gözaydın, İştar. *Diyanet: Türkiye Cumhuriyeti'nde Dinin Tanzimi*. Istanbul: İletişim, 2009.

Graham, William A. *Divine Word and Prophetic Word in Early Islam*. Paris: Mouton, 1977.

Graham, William A. "The Earliest Meaning of Quran." *Die Welt des Islams* 23/24, no. 1 (1984): 361–77.
Graham, William A. "Traditionalism in Islam: An Essay in Interpretation." *The Journal of Interdisciplinary History* 23, no. 3 (1993): 495–522.
Griffel, Frank. "Introduction." In *Islamic Law in the Contemporary Context: Shari'a*, edited by Abbas Amanat and Frank Griffel, 1–19. Stanford: Stanford University Press, 2002.
Güler, İlhami. "Kur'an'da Kadın Erkek Eşitsizliğinin Temelleri." *İslami Araştırmalar* 10, no. 4 (1997): 296–303.
Güler, İlhami. *İman Ahlak İlişkisi*. Ankara: Ankara Okulu, 2003.
Güler, İlhami. "Kur'an Metnini Yormadan (Tefsir) Olayların Yorumuna (Tevil)." *Kelam Araştırmaları* 7, no. 2 (2009): 11–18.
Güler, İlhami. *Özgürlükçü Teoloji Yazıları*. Ankara: Ankara Okulu, 2011.
Güler, İlhami. *Direniş Teolojisi*. Ankara: Ankara Okulu, 2015.
Güler, İlhami. *Kur'an'ın Ahlak Metafiziği*. Ankara: Ankara Okulu, 2015.
Güler, İlhami. *Derin Ahlak: Teolojik Siyasi Ahlak Analizleri*. Ankara: Ankara Okulu, 2016.
Güler, İlhami. *Dine Yeni Yaklaşımlar*. Ankara: Ankara Okulu, 2016.
Güler, İlhami. *Evrensel Ümmetçiliğe Doğru: Türkiye İslamcılığının Eleştirisi*. Ankara: Ankara Okulu, 2016.
Güler, İlhami. *Kuş Bakışı*. Ankara: Ankara Okulu, 2016.
Güler, İlhami. *Realpolitik ve Muhafazakarlık*. Ankara: Ankara Okulu, 2016.
Güler, İlhami. *Allah'ın Ahlakiliği Sorunu: Ehl-i Sünnet'in Allah Tasavvuruna Ahlaki Açıdan Eleştirel Bir Yaklaşım*. Ankara: Ankara Okulu, 2017.
Güler, İlhami. *İsimsiz İlhamlar*. Ankara: Ankara Okulu, 2017.
Güler, İlhami. *İtikaddan İmana*. Ankara: Ankara Okulu, 2017.
Güler, İlhami. *Sabit Din Dinamik Şeriat*. Ankara: Ankara Okulu, 2017.
Güler, İlhami. *Sünniliğin Eleştirisine Giriş*. Ankara: Ankara Okulu, 2017.
Güler, İlhami. *Aklın İçindeki İlhamlar*. Ankara: Ankara Okulu, 2018.
Güler, İlhami. *Kur'an'ın Mahiyeti ve Yorumu*. Ankara: Ankara Okulu, 2018.
Güler, İlhami. *Politik Teoloji Yazıları*. Ankara: Ankara Okulu, 2018.
Güler, İlhami. *Vicdan Böyle Buyurdu*. Ankara: Ankara Okulu, 2018.
Gündüz, Şinasi. "From Apology to Phenomenology: The Contemporary State of the Studies of History of Religions in Turkey." In *Change and Essence: Dialectic Relations Between Change and Continuity in the Turkish Intellectual Tradition*, edited by Şinasi Gündüz and Cafer S. Yaran, 25–44. Washington: The Council for Research in Values and Philosophy, 2005.
Günther, Sebastian. "Muhammad, the Illiterate Prophet: An Islamic Creed in the Quran and Quran Exegesis." *Journal of Quranic Studies* 4, no. 1 (2002): 1–26.
Haddad, Yvonne Yazbeck. "An Exegesis of Sura Ninety-Eight." *Journal of the American Oriental Society* 97, no. 4 (1977): 519–30.
Haider, Tazeem. "Universality in the Message of Quran." *Journal of South Asian Studies* 4, no. 2 (2016): 61–5.
Haj-Yahia, Muhammad M. "Beliefs of Jordanian Women About Wife-Beating." *Psychology of Women Quarterly* 26, no. 1 (2002): 282–91.
Haleem, M. A. S. Abdel. *The Quran*. Oxford: Oxford University Press, 2005.
Hallaq, Wael B. *A History of Islamic Legal Theories*. Cambridge: Cambridge University Press, 1997.
Hallaq, Wael B. *The Origins and Evolution of Islamic Law*. Cambridge: Cambridge University Press, 2005.

Hallaq, Wael B. *Shari'a: Theory, Practice, Transformations*. Cambridge: Cambridge University Press, 2012.

Hamdani, Sumaiya A. *Between Revolution and State: The Path to Fatimid Statehood*. London: I. B. Tauris, 2006.

Hamidullah, Muhammad. *The Prophet's Establishing A State and His Succession*. Hyderabad: Habib, 1986.

Hamilton, Paul. *Historicism*. London: Routledge, 1996.

Hanne, Eric J. "Abbasid Politics and the Classical Theory of the Caliphate." In *Writers and Rulers: Perspectives on Their Relationship from Abbasid to Safavid Times*, edited by Beatrice Gruendler and Louise Marlow, 49–71. Wiesbaden: Reichert Verlag, 2004.

Hasan, Ahmad. "The *Sunnah*—Its Early Concept and Development." *Islamic Studies* 7, no. 1 (1968): 47–69.

Hatiboğlu, Mehmed S. "İslam'da İlk Siyasi Kavmiyetçilik Hilafetin Kureyşiliği." *AÜİFD* 23, no. 1 (1979): 121–223.

Hatiboğlu, Mehmed S. *İslami Tenkid Zihniyeti ve Hadis Tenkidinin Doğuşu*. Ankara: Otto, 2016.

Hawting, Gerald R. "The Significance of the Slogan la hukma illa lillah and the References to the Hudud in the Traditions about the Fitna and the Murder of Uthman." *Bulletin of the School of Oriental and African Studies* 41, no. 3 (1978): 453–63.

Hawting, Gerald R. "An Ascetic Vow and an Unseemly Oath? Ila and Zihar in Muslim Law." *Bulletin of the School of Oriental and African Studies* 57, no. 1 (1994): 113–25.

Hawting, Gerald R. *The First Dynasty of Islam: The Umayyad Caliphate AD 661–759*. London: Routledge, 2000.

Hawting, Gerald R. "The Religion of Abraham and Islam." In *Abraham, the Nations, and the Hagarites: Jewish, Christian, and Islamic Perspectives on Kinship with Abraham*, edited by Martin Goodman, George H. van Kooten and Jacques T. A. G. M. van Ruiten, 477–501. Leiden: Brill, 2010.

Henninger, Joseph. "Pre-Islamic Bedouin Religion." In *The Arabs and Arabia on the Eve of Islam*, edited by F. E. Peters, 109–28. London: Routledge, 1999.

Himmelfarb, Gertrude. *The Roads to Modernity: The British, French and American Enlightenments*. New York: Vintage Books, 2004.

Hinds, Martin. "The Murder of the Caliph Uthman." *International Journal of Middle East Studies* 3, no. 4 (1972): 450–69.

Hirschler, Konrad. *Medieval Arabic Historiography: Authors as Actors*. London: Routledge, 2006.

Hitchcock, Jennifer. "The 5 Pillars of Islam." *Verbum* 2, no. 2 (2005): 43–50.

Hodgson, Marshall G. S. *The Venture of Islam Vol. I. Concise and History in a World of Civilization*. London: The University of Chicago Press, 1977.

Hodgson, Marshall G. S. *The Venture of Islam Vol. II. Concise and History in a World of Civilization*. London: The University of Chicago Press, 1977.

Holtzman, Livnat. "Human Choice, Divine Guidance and the Fitra Tradition." In *Ibn Taymiyya and His Times*, edited by Yossef Rapaport and Shahab Ahmet, 163–88. Karachi: Oxford University Press, 2010.

Hourani, George F. *Reason and Tradition in Islamic Ethics*. Cambridge: Cambridge University Press, 1985.

Hurvitz, Nimrod. *The Formation of Hanbalism Piety in Power*. London: Routledge, 2002.

Ibn Ashur, Muhammad bin Tahir. *Treatise on Maqasid al-Shari'a*. London: The International Institute of Islamic Thought, 2006.

Ibn Ishaq. *Sirat Rasul Allah [The Life of Muhammad: A Translation of Ibn Ishaq's Sirat Rasul Allah]*. Translated by. A. Guillaume. Oxford: Oxford University Press, 1955.
Ibn Kathir. *Al-Sira al-Nabawiyya [The Life of the Prophet Muhammad] Vol. I*. Translated by T. Le Gassick. Reading: Garnet, 2006.
Ibn Rushd. *The Incoherence of the Incoherence [Tahafut al-Tahafut]*. Translated by Simon Van Den Bergh. Cambridge: EJW Gibb Memorial Trust, 1987.
Issa, Jehad G. "Introduction to Islamic Legislation." *Woodrow Wilson Journal of Law* 2, no. 1 (1979): 34–76.
İzmirli, İsmail Hakkı. *'Ilm-i Kelam: Birinci Kitab*. Istanbul: Şehzadebaşı Evkaf-ı İslamiyye Matbaası, 1925.
Izutsu, Toshihiko. *God and Man in the Quran: Semantics of the Quranic Weltanschauung*. Tokyo: Keio University Press, 1964.
Izutsu, Toshiko. *Creation and the Timeless Order of Things: Essays in Islamic Mystical Philosophy*. Ashland: White Cloud Press, 1994.
Jabali, Fu'ad. *The Companions of the Prophet: A Study of Geographical Distribution and Political Alignments*. Leiden: Brill, 2003.
Jakson, Roy. *Mawlana Mawdudi and Political Islam Authority and Islamic State*. London and New York: Routledge, 2011.
Janin, Hunt, and Andre Kahlmeyer. *Islamic Law: The Sharia from Muhammad's Time to the Present*. London: McFarland and Company, 2007.
Jeffrey, Arthur. *Materials for the History of the Text of Quran: The Old Codices*. Leiden: Brill, 1937.
Jeffrey, Arthur. *Islam, Muhammad and His Religion*. New York: The Bobbs-Merrill, 1958.
Jenkins, Scott. "Nietzsche's Use of Monumental History." *Journal of Nietzsche Studies* 45, no. 2 (2014): 169–81.
Judd, Steven C. "Ghaylan al-Dimashqi: The Isolation of a Heretic in Islamic Historiography." *International Journal of Middle East Studies* 31, no. 2 (1999): 161–84.
Judd, Steven C. "Competitive Hagiography in Biographies of al-Awza'i and Sufyan al-Thawri." *Journal of the American Oriental Society* 122, no. 1 (2002): 25–37.
Judd, Steven C. "The Early Qadariyya." In *The Oxford Handbook of Islamic Theology*, edited by Sabine Schmidtke, 44–54. Oxford: Oxford University Press, 2016.
Juynboll, G. H. A. *Muslim Tradition: Studies in Chronology, Provenance and Authorship of Early Hadith*. Cambridge: Cambridge University Press, 1983.
Kadri, Hüseyin Kazım. *İnsan Hakları Beyannamesi'nin İslam Hukukuna Göre İzahı [Prepared by Osman Ergin]*. Istanbul: Sinan, 1949.
Kallek, Cengiz. "Kaffal, Muhammed bin Ali." In *İslam Ansiklopedisi Vol. 24*, edited by commission, 146–8. Ankara: TDV, 2001.
Kamali, Muhammad Hashim. "Maqasid al-Shari'ah: The Objectives of Islamic Law." *Islamic Studies* 38, no. 2 (1999): 193–208.
Kamali, Mohammad Hashim. *Crime and Punishment in Islamic Law: A Fresh Interpretation*. Oxford: Oxford University Press, 2019.
Kara, İsmail. "Diyanet İşleri Başkanlığı." In *İslamcılık*, edited by Yasin Aktay, Tanıl Bora and Murat Gültekingil, 45–66. Istanbul: İletişim: 2005.
Kara, Seyfeddin. *In Search of Ali Ibn Abi Talib's Codex: History and Traditions of the Earliest Copy of the Quran*. Berlin: Gerlach, 2018.
Karaman, Hayreddin, Ali Bardakoğlu and İ. Kafi Dönmez. *İlmihal I*. Ankara: Diyanet, 1998.
Karaman, Hayreddin, Ali Bardakoğlu and İ. Kafi Dönmez. *İlmihal II*. Ankara: Diyanet, 1998.

Karaman, Hayrettin, Mustafa Çağrıcı, İ. Kafi Dönmez and Sadrettin Gümüş. *Kur'an Yolu Türkçe Meal ve Tefsiri Vol. I.* Ankara: Diyanet İşleri Başkanlığı, 2012.

Karaman, Hayrettin, Mustafa Çağrıcı, İ. Kafi Dönmez and Sadrettin Gümüş. *Kur'an Yolu Türkçe Meal ve Tefsiri Vol. II.* Ankara: Diyanet İşleri Başkanlığı, 2012.

Karmi, Ghada. "Al-Tıbb al-Nabawi: The Prophet's Medicine." In *Technology Tradition and Survival: Aspects of Material Culture in the Middle East and Central Asia*, edited by Richard Tapper and Keith McLachlan, 32–9. London: Frank Cass, 2003.

Karpat, Kemal. "Some Historical and Methodological Considerations Concerning Social Stratification in the Middle East." In *Commoners, Climbers and Notables A Sampler of Studies on Social Ranking in the Middle East*, edited by C. A. O. Van Nieuwenhuijze, 83–101. Leiden: E. J. Brill, 1977.

Karpat, Kemal. *Studies on Ottoman Social and Political History: Selected Articles and Essays.* Leiden: Brill, 2002.

Kassam, Tarık R. "Signifying Revelation in Islam." In *Theorizing Scriptures: New Critical Orientations to a Cultural Phenomenon*, edited by Vincent L. Wimbush, 29–40. New Brunswick, NJ: Rutgers University Press, 2008.

Kaya, Ibrahim. *Social Theory and Later Modernities: The Turkish Experience.* Liverpool: Liverpool University Press, 2004.

Kayıkça, Sabrina, "'Cumhuriyet'in Kuruluşundan Günümüze Kadar Köye ve Köylüye Yönelik Olarak İzlenen Politikalar." *Türk İdare Dergisi* 448, no. 1 (2005): 1–22.

Keane, Webb. "Ethics as Piety." *Numen* 61, no. 2/3 (2014): 221–36.

Keddie, Nikki R. *Response to Imperialism: Political and Religious Writings of Sayyid Jamal ad-Din "al-Afghani."* Berkeley, Los Angeles: University of California Press, 1983.

Kelsay, John. "Divine Command Ethics in Early Islam: Al-Shafi'i and the Problem of Guidance." *The Journal of Religious Ethics* 22, no. 1 (1994): 101–26.

Kelsay, John. *Arguing the Just War in Islam.* Cambridge, MA: Harvard University Press, 2007.

Kelsen, Hans. *General Theory of Law and State.* London: Transactions, 2006.

Kennedy, Hugh. *The Prophet and the Age of Caliphates: The Islamic Near East from the Sixth to the Eleventh Century.* London: Longman, 2004.

Kennedy, Hugh. *The Armies of the Caliphs: Military and Society in the Early Islamic State.* London: Routledge, 2005.

Kenney, T. Jeffrey. *Muslim Rebels: Kharijites and the Politics of Extremism in Egypt.* Oxford: Oxford University Press, 2006.

Kermani, Navid. "From Revelation to Interpretation: Nasr Hamid Abu Zayd and the Literary Study of the Quran." In *Modern Muslim Intellectuals and The Quran*, edited by Suha Taji-Farouki, 169–92. Oxford: Oxford University Press, 2004.

Khadduri, Majid. *War and Peace in the Law of Islam.* Baltimore: John Hopkins University Press, 1955.

Khalidi, Tarif. *Arab Historical Thought in the Classical Period.* Cambridge: Cambridge University Press, 1994.

Khalidi, Tarif. "The Idea of Progress in Classical Islam." *Journal of Near Eastern Studies* 40, no. 4 (1981): 277–89.

Khan, Israr Ahmad. *Authentication of Hadith: Redefining the Criteria.* London: The International Institute of Islamic Thought, 2010.

Khan, Ruqayya Y. "Did a Women Edit the Quran? Hafsa and her Famed Codex." *Journal of the American Academy of Religion* 82, no. 1 (2014): 175–216.

Khatab, Sayed. *The Power of Sovereignty: The Political and Ideological Philosophy of Sayyid Qutb.* London: Routledge, 2006.

Khomeini, Imam Ruhullah. "The Necessity for Islamic Government." In *Islam and Revolution: Writings and Declarations of Imam Khomeini*, edited by Hamid Algar, 40–54. Berkeley: Mizan Press, 1981.

Kingberg, Leah. "Muhkamat and Mutashabihat (Koran 3/7): Implications of a Koranic Pair of Terms in Medieval Exegesis." *Arabica* 35, no. 2 (1988): 143–72.

Kirazlı, Sadık. "Conflict and Conflict Resolution in the pre-Islamic Arab Society." *Islamic Studies* 50, no. 1 (2011): 25–53.

Kister, M. J. "The Sons of Khadija." *Jerusalem Studies in Arabic and Islam* 16, no. 1 (1993): 69–75.

Kister, M. J. "The Struggle against Musaylima and the Conquest of Yamama." *Jerusalem Studies in Arabic and Islam* 27, no. 1 (2002): 1–56.

Kırbaşoğlu, M. Hayri. "Klasik Sünnet Tanımlarının Eleştirisi ve Yeni Bir Sünnet Tanımı Denemesi." *Journal of Islamic Research* 5, no. 1 (1991): 21–37.

Kırbaşoğlu, M. Hayri. "Kadın Konusunda Kur'an'a Yöneltilen Başlıca Eleştiriler." *İslami Araştırmalar* 10, no. 4 (1997): 259–70.

Kırbaşoğlu, M. Hayri. *Ehl-i Sünnet'in Kurucu Ataları*. Istanbul: Otto, 2011.

Kırbaşoğlu, M. Hayri. *Destursuz Çağa Girenler*. Ankara: Otto, 2014.

Kırbaşoğlu, M. Hayri. *Üçüncü Yol Mukaddimesi*. Ankara: Otto, 2014.

Kırbaşoğlu, M. Hayri. *Alternatif Hadis Metodolojisi*. Istanbul: Otto, 2015.

Kırbaşoğlu, M. Hayri. *İslam'ın Kurucu Metni: Kur'an Araştırmaları*. İstanbul: Otto, 2015.

Kırbaşoğlu, M. Hayri. *İslami İlimlerde Metot Sorunu*. Istanbul: Otto, 2015.

Kırbaşoğlu, M. Hayri. "Er-Risale'nin Şekil ve Muhteva Açısından Eleştirisi." In *Sünni Paradigmanın Oluşumunda Şafi'i'nin Rolü*, edited by M. Hayri Kırbaşoğlu, 263–322. Istanbul: Otto, 2016.

Kırbaşoğlu, M. Hayri. "İmam Şafi'i'nin Er-Risalesi'nin Hadis İlmindeki Etkileri." In *Sünni Paradigmanın Oluşumunda Şafi'i'nin Rolü*, edited by M. Hayri Kırbaşoğlu, 323–58. Istanbul: Otto, 2016.

Kırbaşoğlu, M. Hayri. "İslami İlimlerde Şafi'nin Rolü Üzerine." In *Sünni Paradigmanın Oluşumunda Şafi'i'nin Rolü*, edited by M. Hayri Kırbaşoğlu, 237–62. Istanbul: Otto, 2016.

Kırbaşoğlu, M. Hayri. "Şaf'i'in Er-Risale'deki Hadisçiliği." In *Sünni Paradigmanın Oluşumunda Şafi'i'nin Rolü*, edited by M. Hayri Kırbaşoğlu, 359–72. Istanbul: Otto, 2016.

Kırbaşoğlu, M. Hayri. *Ahirzaman İlmihali*. Ankara: Otto, 2017.

Kırbaşoğlu, M. Hayri. *Eskimez Yeni: Hz. Peygamber'in Sünneti*. Ankara: Otto, 2017.

Kırbaşoğlu, M. Hayri. "Son Muhalifin İzinde: Yeryüzünün Son Göksel Muhalifi: Hz. Muhammed (sav)." *Milel ve Nihal* 15, no. 2 (2018): 34–49.

Kırbaşoğlu, M. Hayri. *İslam Düşüncesinde Hadis Metodolojisi*. Ankara: Ankara Okulu, 2018.

Kırbaşoğlu, M. Hayri. *İslam Düşüncesinde Sünnet: Eleştirel Bir Yaklaşım*. Ankara: Ankara Okulu, 2018.

Kırbaşoğlu, M. Hayri. *Müslüman Kalarak Yenilenmek*. Istanbul: Otto, 2019.

Kohlberg, Etan and Mohammad Ali Amir-Moezzi. *Revelation and Falsification: The Kitab al-qira'at of Ahmad b. Muhammad al-Sayyari*. Leiden: Brill, 2009.

Köksal, İsmail. "İslam Hukukunda Zıhar." *Dini Araştırmalar* 3, no. 7 (2000): 257–69.

Koştaş, Münir. "Ankara Üniversitesi İlahiyat Fakültesi." *AÜİFD* 31, no. 1 (1989): 1–27.

Kramer, Gudrun. "Islamists Notions of Democracy." *Middle East Report* 183, no. 1 (1992): 2–8.

Kural, Metin. *Dört Halife: Hz. Ebubekir, Hz. Ömer, Hz. Osman, Hz. Ali*. Istanbul: Kar, 2006.

Kuran, Timur. "The Absence of the Corporation in Islamic Law: Origins and Persistence." *American Journal of Comparative Law* 53, no. 4 (2005): 785–834.

Kuran, Timur. *The Long Divergence: How Islamic Law Held Back the Middle East*. Princeton: Princeton University Press, 2011.

Kuru, Ahmet T. *Islam, Authoritarianism, Underdevelopment: A Global and Historical Comparison*. Cambridge: Cambridge University Press, 2019.

Laffan, Michael. "Understanding Al-Imam's Critique of Tariqa Sufism." In *Varieties of Religious Authority Changes and Challenges in 20th Century Indonesian Islam*, edited by Azyumardi Azra, Kees Van Dijk and Nico J. G. Kaptein, 17–53. Pasir Panjang: ISEAS, 2010.

Lambton, Ann K. S. *Landlord and Peasant in Persia: A Study of Land Tenure and Land Revenue Administration*. London and New York: I. B. Tauris, 1969.

Lambton, Ann K. S. *State and Government in Medieval Islam*. London: Routledge, 1991.

Lapidus, Ira M. *History of Islamic Societies*. Cambridge: Cambridge University Press, 2014.

Larkin, Margaret. "The Inimitability of the Quran: Two Perspectives." *Religion and Literature* 20, no. 1 (1998): 31–47.

Laroui, Abdallah. *The Crisis of the Arab Intellectual Traditionalism or Historicism?* Berkeley: University of California Press, 1976.

Lecker, Michael. "Zayd B. Thabit, A Jew with Two Sidelocks: Judaism and Literacy in Pre-Islamic Medina (Yathrib)." *Journal of Near Eastern Studies* 56, no. 4 (1997): 259–73.

Lecker, Michael. "Pre-Islamic Arabia." In *New Cambridge History of Islam Vol. I: The Formation of the Islamic World Sixth to Eleventh Centuries*, edited by Chase F. Robinson, 153–70. Cambridge: Cambridge University Press, 2010.

Leeman, Alex B. "Interfaith Marriage in Islam: An Examination of the Legal Theory Behind the Traditional and Reformist Positions." *Indiana Law Journal* 84, no. 2 (2009): 743–73.

Lennon, Thomas M. "The Rationalist Conception of Substance." In *A Companion to Rationalism*, edited by Alan Nelson, 12–30. Oxford: Blackwell, 2005.

Lewin, Shari L. *The Making of a Forefather: Abraham in Islamic and Jewish Exegetical Narratives*. Leiden: Brill, 2006.

Lewis, Bernard. "The Concept of Islamic Republic." *Die Welt des Islams* 4, no. 1 (1955): 1–9.

Lewis, Bernard. "On the Revolutions in Early Islam." *Studia Islamica* 32, no. 1 (1970): 215–31.

Lewis, Bernard. *The Arabs in History*. Oxford: Oxford University Press, 1993.

Libson, Gideon. "On the Development of Custom as a Source of Law in Islamic Law: Al-rujuʿu ila al-ʿurfi aḥadu al-qawaʿidi al-khamsi allati yatabannaʿalayha al-fiqhu." *Islamic Law and Society* 4, no. 2 (1997): 131–55.

Lings, Muhammad. *Muhammad: His Life Based on the Earliest Sources*. London: Islamic Text Society, 1983.

Liow, Joseph Chinyong. *Piety and Politics: Islamism in Contemporary Malaysia*. Oxford: Oxford University Press, 2009.

Lucas, Scott C. *The Legacy of the Generation of Ibn Saʿd, Ibn Maʿin, and Ibn Hanbal*. Leiden: Brill, 2004.

Madelung, Wilfred. "The Shiite and Kharijite Contribution to Pre-Ashʿarite Kalam." In *Islamic Philosophical Theology*, edited by Parviz Morewedge, 120–41. Albany, NY: The State University of New York, 1979.

Madelung, Wilfred. *Religious Trends in Early Islamic Iran*. Albany, NY: Bibliotheca Persica, 1988.

Madelung, Wilfred. "Al-Ghazali's Changing Attitude to Philosophy." In *Islam and Rationality: The Impact of al-Ghazali Papers Collected on His 900th Anniversary*, edited by Georges Tamer, 23–44. London: Brill, 2015.

Mahdi, Muhsin. "Rationalist Tradition in Islam." In *Intellectual Traditions in Islam*, edited by Farhad Daftary, 43–65. London: I. B. Tauris, 2001.

Mahmoud, Saba. *Politics of Piety: The Islamic Revival and the Feminist Subject*. Princeton: Princeton University Press, 2005.

Makdisi, George. "Ash'ari and the Ash'arites in Islamic Religious History." *Studia Islamica* 17, no. 1 (1962): 37–80.

Makdisi, George. "The Sunni Revival." In *Islamic Civilization, 950–1150*, edited by D. H. Richards, 155–68. Oxford: Bruno Cassirer, 1973.

Makdisi, George. "The Significance of the Sunni Schools of Law in Islamic Religious History." *IJMES* 10, no. 1 (1979): 1–8.

Makdisi, George. *The Rise of the Colleges: Institutions of Learning in Islam and the West*. Edinburgh: Edinburgh University Press, 1981.

Makdisi, George. "The Juridical Theology of Shafi'i: Origins and Significance of Usul al-Fiqh." *Studia Islamica* 59, no. 1 (1984): 5–47.

Mardin, Şerif. "Center-Periphery Relations: A Key to Turkish Politics?" *Daedalus* 102, no. 1 (1973): 169–90.

Mardin, Şerif. *Türk Modernleşmesi Makaleler IV*. Istanbul: İletişim, 1991.

Marsham, Andrew. *Rituals of Islamic Monarchy: Accession and Succession in First Muslim Empire*. Edinburgh: Edinburgh University Press, 2009.

Marsham, Andrew. "Public Execution in the Umayyad Period: Early Islamic Punitive Practice and Its Late Antique Context." *Journal of Arabic and Islamic Studies* 11, no. 1 (2011): 101–36.

Martin, Richard C., Mark R. Woodward and Dwi S. Atmaja. *Defenders of Reason in Islam: Mu'tazilism from Medieval School to Modern Symbol*. London: Oneworld, 1997.

Martin, Vanessa. *Creating an Islamic State: Khomeini and the Making of New Iran*. London and New York: I.B. Tauris, 2003.

Maududi, S. Abul A'la. *Human Rights in Islam*. Leicester: Islamic Foundation, 1976.

McCants, William F. *Founding Gods, Inventing Nations*. Princeton: Princeton University Press, 2011.

McDougall, E. Ann. "What Is Islamic About Slavery in Muslim Societies? Cooper, Concubinage and Contemporary Legacies of Islamic Slavery in North, West and East Africa." In *Slavery in the Islamic World: Its Characteristics and Commonality*, edited by Mary Ann Fay, 7–36. London: Palgrave Macmillan, 2019.

Melchert, Christopher. "The Rightly Guided Caliphs: The Range of Views Preserved in Hadith." In *Sunni and Shi'i Practice and Thought*, edited by Saud al-Sarhan, 63–80. London: I. B. Tauris, 2019.

Melchert, Christopher. *The Formation of Sunni Schools of Law, 9th–10th Centuries. C.E.* Leiden: Brill, 1997.

Melchert, Christopher. "Ahmad Ibn Hanbal and the Quran." *Journal of Quranic Studies* 6, no. 2 (2004): 22–34.

Melchert, Christopher. "Traditionists-Jurisprudents and the Framing of Islamic Law." *Islamic Law and Society* 8, no. 3 (2017): 383–406.

Mernissi, Fatima. *Women and Islam: A Historical and Theological Enquiry*. Oxford: Basil Blackwell, 1991.

Miles, Jack and Sohail H. Hashmi. *Islamic Political Ethics*. Princeton: Princeton University Press, 2009.

Moghadam, Valentine M. *Globalization and Social Movements Islamism, Feminism, and The Global Justice Movement.* New York: Rowman and Littlefield, 2009.
Moosa, Ebrahim. *Ghazali and the Poetics of Imagination.* Chapel Hill: The University of North Caroline Press, 2005.
Motzki, Harold. "Introduction." In *The Biography of Muhammad*, edited by Harold Motzki, xi–xvi. Leiden: Brill, 2000.
Mourad, Suleiman Ali. "Theology: Free Will and Predestination." In *The Islamic World*, edited by Andrew Rippin, 179–90. London: Routledge, 2008.
Mukti, Mohd Fakhrudin Abdul. "Al-Ghazali and His Refutation of Philosophy." *Journal Usuluddin* 21, no. 1 (2005): 1–22.
Musa, Aisha Y. *Hadith as Scripture: Discussions on the Authority of Prophetic Traditions in Islam.* New York: Palgrave Macmillan, 2008.
Musallam, Adnan A. *From Secularism to Jihad: Sayyid Qutb and the Foundation of Radical Islamism.* London: Praeger, 2005.
Mustapha, Nadira. "Law: Women as Witness." In *Encyclopedia of Women and Islamic Cultures Family, Law and Politics Vol. II*, edited by Suad Joseph, 475–7. Leiden and Boston: Brill, 2005.
Mutluer, Mustafa. "Gelişimi, yapısı ve sorunlarıyla Türkiye'de enerji sektörü." *Ege Coğrafya Dergisi* 5, no. 1 (1990): 184–214.
Narin, İsmail, and Abdulnasir Süt. "Prof. Dr. M. Hayri Kırbaşoğlu ile Problemlerimiz ve Çıkış Yolu Üzerine Söyleşi." *Bingöl Üniversitesi İlahiyat Fakültesi Dergisi* 3, no. (2014): 221–38.
Nasir, Jamal J. *The Islamic Law of Personal Status.* London: Graham and Trotman, 1990.
Nasir, Jamal J. *The Status of Women under Islamic Law and Modern Islamic Legislation.* London: Brill, 2009.
Nasr, Seyyed Hossein. *An Introduction to Islamic Cosmological Doctrines.* London: Thames and Hudson, 1964.
Nawas, John A. "The Miḥna of 218 A. H./833 A. D. Revisited: An Empirical Study." *Journal of the American Oriental Society* 116, no. 4 (1996): 698–708.
Nazıroğlu, Bayramali. "İlahiyat Fakültelerinde Din Eğitimi ve Sorunları." In *Türkiye'de Din Eğitimi ve Sorunları*, edited by Mustafa Köylü, 169–208. Istanbul: Dem, 2018.
Nelson, Alan. "The Rationalist Impulse." In *A Companion to Rationalism*, edited by Alan Nelson, 3–11. Oxford: Blackwell, 2005.
Neuwirth, Angelika. "Quran and History—A Disputed Relationship. Some Reflections on Quranic History and History in the Quran." *Journal of Quranic Studies* 5, no. 1 (2010): 1–18.
Nöldeke, Theodor, F. Schwally, G. Bergstrasser and O. Pretzl. *The History of Quran.* Leiden: Brill, 2013.
Nursi, Said. *The Words.* Istanbul: Sözler, 2008.
Nursi, Said. *The Flashes Collection.* Istanbul: Sozler, 2009.
Nursi, Said. *Mesnevi-i Nuriye.* Istanbul: Yeni Asya, 2018.
Ölmez, Mustafa. "Şer'i Naslarda Lügavii Yorumlamadan Kaynaklanabilecek Hataların Engellenmesinde Hadislerin Rolü—Serika Ayeti Örneği." *Marife Dini Araştırmalar Dergisi* 18, no. 1 (2018): 259–78.
Omer, Spahic. "Theological Conflicts in Early Islamic Era: The Execution of Ghaylan ibn Muslim al-Dimashqi al-Qadari." *Intellectual Discourse* 9, no. 2 (2002): 205–17.
Öncü, Ayşe. "Becoming Secular Muslims: Yaşar Nuri Öztürk as a Super-Subject on Turkish Television." In *Religion, Media and the Public Sphere*, edited by Birgit Meyers and Annelis Moors, 227–50. Bloomington: Indiana University Press, 2006.

Ormsby, Eric. *Ghazali*. London: Oneworld, 2000.
Oseni, Z. I. "An Examination of Al-Hajjaj B. Yusuf Al-Thaqafi's Major Policies." *Islamic Studies* 27, no. 4 (1988): 317–27.
Othman, Muhammad Zain bin Haji, and Muhammad Bakhit al-Muti'i. "Urf as a Source of Islamic Law." *Islamic Studies* 20, no. 4 (1981): 343–55.
Otto, Jan Michiel. "Introduction: Investigating the Role of Sharia in National Law." In *Sharia Incorporated: A Comparative Overview of the Legal Systems of Twelve Muslim Countries in Past and Present*, edited by Jan Michiel Otto, 17–50. Leiden: Leiden University Press, 2010,
Özay, Hülya. "İslam Miras Hukukunun Özellikleri." *İslam Medeniyeti Araştırmaları Dergisi* 3, no. 2 (2018): 203–24.
Özbudun, Ergun. "State Elites and Democratic Political Culture in Turkey." In *Political Culture and Democracy in Developing Countries*, edited by Larry Diamond, 189–210. Boulder: Lynne Rienner, 1993.
Özdalga, Elizabeth. *The Veiling Issue, Official Secularism, and Popular Islam in Modern Turkey*. London: Routledge, 2015.
Özsoy, Ömer. *Kur'an ve Tarihsellik Yazıları*. Ankara: Kitabiyat, 2004.
Özsoy, Ömer. *Sünnetullah: Bir Kur'an İfadesinin Kavramsallaşması*. Ankara: Fecr, 2017.
Öztürk, Mustafa. *Kur'an Dili ve Retoriği*. Ankara: Ankara Okulu, 2015.
Öztürk, Mustafa. "Modern Döneme Özgü Bir Kur'an Tasavvuru: Kur'ancılık ve Kur'an İslami Söyleminin Tahlil ve Tenkidi." *Marife* 10, no. 3 (2010): 9–43.
Öztürk, Mustafa. *Kur'an'ı Kendi Tarihinde Okumak: Tefsirde Anakronizme Ret Yazılar*. Ankara: Ankara Okulu, 2013.
Öztürk, Mustafa. *Tefsir Tarihi Araştırmaları*. Ankara: Ankara Okulu, 2014.
Öztürk, Mustafa. *Cumhuriyet Türkiyesi'nde Meal ve Tefsir'in Serencamı*. Ankara: Ankara Okulu, 2015.
Öztürk, Mustafa. *Kur'an'ın Mu'tezili Yorumu: Ebu Müslim el-İsfehani Örneği*. Ankara: Ankara Okulu, 2015.
Öztürk, Mustafa. *Osmanlı Tefsir Mirası*. Ankara: Ankara Okulu, 2015.
Öztürk, Mustafa. *Söyleşiler Polemikler*. Ankara: Ankara Okulu, 2015.
Öztürk, Mustafa. *Kur'an ve Aşırı Yorum: Tefsirde Batinilik ve Batini Te'vil Geleneği*. Ankara: Ankara Okulu, 2016.
Öztürk, Mustafa. *Meal Kültürümüz*. Ankara: Ankara Okulu, 2016.
Öztürk, Mustafa. *Tefsirin Halleri*. Ankara: Ankara Okulu, 2016.
Öztürk, Mustafa. "Kur'an Vahyinin Anlaşılması ve Yorumlanması." In *Tefsir Geleneğinde Anlam-Yorum Nüzul-Siret İlişkisi*, edited by Mustafa Öztürk, 13–42. Ankara: Ankara Okulu, 2017.
Öztürk, Mustafa. *Cahiliyeden İslamiyet'e Kadın*. Ankara: Ankara Okulu, 2017.
Öztürk, Mustafa. *Kur'an ve Tefsir Kültürümüz*. Ankara: Ankara Okulu, 2017.
Öztürk, Mustafa. *Kur'an, Tefsir ve Usul Üzerine Problemler, Tespitler, Teklifler*. Ankara: Ankara Okulu, 2017.
Öztürk, Mustafa. *Kur'an ve Tarihsellik Üzerine Çerçeve Yazılar, Örnek Konular*. Ankara: Ankara Okulu, 2018.
Öztürk, Mustafa. *Kur'an, Vahiy Nüzul*. Ankara: Ankara Okulu, 2018.
Öztürk, Mustafa. *Siyaset İtikad, Din*. Ankara: Ankara Okulu, 2018.
Öztürk, Mustafa. *Kur'an'a Çağdaş Yaklaşımlar*. Ankara: Ankara Okulu, 2019.
Öztürk, Mustafa, and Hadiye Ünsal. *Kur'an Tarihi*. Ankara: Ankara Okulu, 2018.
Öztürk, Yaşar Nuri. *İslam Nasıl Yozlaştırıldı*. Istanbul: Yeni Boyut, 1988.
Öztürk, Yaşar Nuri. *Din ve Fıtrat*. Istanbul: Yeni Boyut, 1990.

Öztürk, Yaşar Nuri. *Tasavvufun Ruhu ve Tarikatlar*. Istanbul: Yeni Boyut, 1990.
Öztürk, Yaşar Nuri. *Kur'an'ı Anlamaya Doğru*. Istanbul: Yeni Boyut, 1995.
Öztürk, Yaşar Nuri. *Konferanslarım: Bir İmanın Destanlaşması*. Istanbul: Yeni Boyut, 1996.
Öztürk, Yaşar Nuri. *Yeniden Yapılanmak: Kur'an'a Dönüş*. Istanbul: Yeni Boyut, 1996.
Öztürk, Yaşar Nuri. *Fatiha Suresi Tefsiri*. Istanbul: Yeni Boyut, 1997.
Öztürk, Yaşar Nuri. *Çıplak Uyarı*. Istanbul: Yeni Boyut, 1998.
Öztürk, Yaşar Nuri. *Ses Birgün Yankılanır*. Istanbul: Yeni Boyut, 1998.
Öztürk, Yaşar Nuri. *Cevap Veriyorum: Gerçek Din Arayanlarla Baş Başa*. Istanbul: Yeni Boyut, 2001.
Öztürk, Yaşar Nuri. *Cevap Veriyorum 3: Gerçek Din Arayanlarla Baş Başa*. Istanbul: Yeni Boyut, 2003.
Öztürk, Yaşar Nuri. *Türkiye'ye Mektuplar*. Istanbul: Yeni Boyut, 2004.
Öztürk, Yaşar Nuri. *Arapçılığa Karşı Akılcılığın Öncüsü İmam Azam Ebu Hanife: Esas Fikirleri Gölgelenen Önder*. Ankara: Yeni Boyut, 2009.
Öztürk, Yaşar Nuri. *Asrı Saadetin Büyük Kadınları*. Istanbul: Yeni Boyut, 2013.
Öztürk, Yaşar Nuri. *Din Maskeli Allah Düşmanlığı: Şirk ve Şirke Tepkinin Felsefeleşmesi: Deizm*. Istanbul: Yeni Boyut, 2013.
Öztürk, Yaşar Nuri. *Kur'an'ın Yarattığı Mucize Devrimler*. Istanbul: Yeni Boyut, 2014.
Öztürk, Yaşar Nuri. *İnsanlığı Kemiren İhanet: Dincilik*. Istanbul: Yeni Boyut, 2015.
Öztürk, Yaşar Nuri. *Kur'an Penceresinden Özgürlük ve İsyan: Teofilozofik Bir Tahlil*. Istanbul: Yeni Boyut, 2015.
Öztürk, Yaşar Nuri. *Kur'an Verilerine Göre Kötülük Toplumu*. Istanbul: Yeni Boyut, 2015.
Öztürk, Yaşar Nuri. *Saltanat Dinciliğinin Öncüsü Firavun: Çağdaş Firavunları Tanıma Kılavuzu*. Istanbul: Yeni Boyut, 2015.
Öztürk, Yaşar Nuri. *Tanrı, Akıl ve Ahlaktan Başka Kutsal Tanımayan İnanç Deizm Teofilozofik Bir Tahlil*. Istanbul: Yeni Boyut, 2015.
Öztürk, Yaşar Nuri. *400 Soruda İslam*. Istanbul: Yeni Boyut, 2016.
Öztürk, Yaşar Nuri. *Emevi Dinciliğine Karşı Mücadelenin Öncüsü: Ebu Zer*. Istanbul: Yeni Boyut, 2016.
Öztürk, Yaşar Nuri. *İslam Dünyasında Akıl ve Kur'an Nasıl Dışlandı?* Istanbul: Yeni Boyut, 2016.
Öztürk, Yaşar Nuri. *İmamı Azam Savunması Şehit Bir Önder İçin Apolocya*. Istanbul: Yeni Boyut, 2017.
Öztürk, Yaşar Nuri. *Kur'an-i Kerim'de Lanetlenen Soy*. Istanbul: Yeni Boyut, 2017.
Öztürk, Yaşar Nuri. *Kur'an'ın Temel Buyrukları Emirler ve Yasaklar*. Istanbul: Yeni Boyut, 2017.
Öztürk, Yaşar Nuri. *Maun Suresi Böyle Buyurdu: Din Maskeli Zulme Tanrı'nın Vuruşu*. Istanbul: Yeni Boyut, 2017.
Öztürk, Yaşar Nuri. *Dinde Reform Değil İslam'da Tecdit: Peygamber'in Yüklediği Görev Volume II*. Istanbul: Yeni Boyut, 2018.
Öztürk, Yaşar Nuri. *Dinde Reform Değil İslam'da Tecdit: Peygamber'in Yüklediği Görev Volume I*. Istanbul: Yeni Boyut, 2018.
Öztürk, Yaşar Nuri. *Kur'an'daki İslam*. Istanbul: Yeni Boyut, 2018.
Öztürk, Yaşar Nuri. *Merak Edilen Yönleriyle İslam*. Istanbul: Kaynak, 2018.
Pak, Soon-Yong. "Articulating the Boundary Between Secularism and Islamism: The Imam-Hatip Schools of Turkey." *Anthropology and Education Quarterly* 35, no. 3 (2004): 324–44.
Peacock, A. C. S. *Medieval Islamic Historiography and Political Legitimacy*. London and New York: Routledge, 2007.

Perho, Irmeli. *The Prophet's Medicine: A Creation of Muslim Traditionalist Scholars*. Helsinki: Finish Oriental Society, 1985.

Peters, F. E. "The Quest of the Historical Muhammad." In *The Quest for the Historical Muhammad*, edited by Ibn Warraq, 444–75. New York: Prometheus, 2000.

Peters, F. E. *The Voice, The Word, the Books: The Sacred Scripture of the Jews, Christians, and Muslims*. Princeton: Princeton University Press, 2007.

Peters, J. R. T. M. *God's Created Speech: A Study in the Speculative Theology of the Mu'tazili Qadi al-Qudat Abu l-Hasan 'Abd al-Jabbar bn Ahmad al-Hamadani*. Leiden: Brill, 1976.

Peters, Rudolph. *Crime and Punishment in Islamic Law Theory and Practice from the Sixteenth to the Twenty-first Century*. Cambridge: Cambridge University Press, 2005.

Peters, Rudolph, and Gert J. J. De Vries. "Apostasy in Islam." *Die Welt des Islams* 17, no. ¼ (1976/7): 1–24.

Poonawala, Ismail K. "Muhammad 'Izzat Darwaza's principles modern exegesis: a contribution towards Quranic hermeneutics." In *Approaches to the Quran*, edited by G. R. Hawting and Abdul-Kader A. Shareef, 225–46. London and New York: Routledge, 1993.

Pooya, Ayatollah Haji Mirza Mahdi. *Essence of the Holy Quran: The Eternal Light*. Freehold, NJ: Imam Shae-bu-Zaman Association, 1990.

Power, E. S. J. *Umayya Ibn Abi-s Salt*. Beyrouth: Imprimerie Catholique, 1906.

Qasmi, Ali Usman. "Towards a New Prophetology: Maulwi 'Abdullah Cakralawi's Ahl al-Quran Movement." *The Muslim World* 99, no. 1 (2009): 155–80.

Qutb, Sayyid. *Milestones*. Birmingham: Maktabah, 2006.

Radscheit, Matthias. "The Quran—Codification and Canonization." In *Self-Referentiality in the Quran*, edited by Stefan Wild, 93–102. Wiesbaden: H. Verlag, 2007.

Rahami, Mohsen. "Development of Criminal Punishment in the Iranian Post-Revolutionary Penal Code." *European Journal of Crime, Criminal Law and Criminal Justice* 13, no. 4, (2005): 585–602.

Rahman, Fazlur. "Concepts, Sunnah, Ijtihad, and Ijma' in the Early Period." *Islamic Studies* 1, no. 1 (1962): 5–21.

Rahman, Fazlur. "The Concept of Hadd in Islamic Law." *Islamic Studies* 4, no. 3 (1965): 237–51.

Rahman, Fazlur. *Islam*. Ankara: Selcuk, 1981.

Rahman, Fazlur. *Islam and Modernity Transformation of an Intellectual Tradition*. Chicago: The University of Chicago Press, 1982.

Rahman, Fazlur. "Islam and Medicine: A General Overview." *Perspectives in Biology and Medicine* 27, no. 4 (1984): 585–97.

Rahman, Fazlur. "Translating the Quran." *Religion & Literature* 20, no. 1 (1988): 23–30.

Rahman, Fazlur. *Islamic Methodology in History*. Islamabad: Islamic Research Institute, 1995.

Rahman, Fazlur. *Revival and Reform in Islam: A Study of Islamic Fundamentalism*. Oxford: Oneworld, 2000.

Rahman, Fazlur. *Major Themes of Quran*. Chicago: The University of Chicago Press, 2009.

Rahman, Md. Modiur. "Responsibility for Action in an Early Historical Document of Islam: Al-Hasan bin Ali's Risala." *Islamic Quarterly* 34, no. 4 (1990): 235–48.

Read, Jen'nan Ghazal. "Introduction: The Politics of Veiling in Comparative Perspective." *Sociology of Religion* 68, no. 3 (2007): 231–6.

Reed, Howard A. "Turkey's New Imam-Hatip Schools." *Die Welt des Islams* 4, no. 2/3 (1955): 150–63.

Reid, Megan H. *Law and Piety in Medieval Islam*. Cambridge: Cambridge University Press, 2013.

Reynolds, Gabriel Said. *A Muslim Theologian in the Sectarian Milieu 'Abd al-Jabbar and the Critique of Christian Origins*. Leiden: Brill, 2004.
Ricoeur, Paul. *The Interpretation Theory: Discourse and the Surplus of Meaning*. Texas: The Texas Christian University Press, 1976.
Robinson, Chase F. "The Study of Islamic Historiography: A Progress Report." *Journal of the Royal Asiatic Society of Great Britain & Ireland* 7, no. 2 (1997): 199-227.
Robinson, Chase F. *Islamic Historiography*. Cambridge: Cambridge University Press, 2003.
Robinson, Chase F. "The Violence of the Abbasid Revolution." In *Living Islamic History*, edited by Yasir Suleiman, 226-51. Edinburgh: Edinburgh University Press, 2010.
Rosenthal, E. I. J. *Political Thought in Medieval Islam: An Introductory Outline*. Cambridge: Cambridge University Press, 1962.
Rosenthal, Frank. *A History of Muslim Historiography*. Leiden: Leiden University Press, 1968.
Sadeghi, Behnam and Uwe Bergmann. "The Codex of a Companion of the Prophet and the Quran of the Prophet." *Arabica* 57, no. 4 (2010): 343-436.
Saeh, Bassam. *The Miraculous Language of the Quran: Evidence of Divine Origin*. London: International Institute of Islamic Thought, 2015.
Safi, Omid. *The Politics of Knowledge in Premodern Islam: Negotiating Ideology and Religious Inquiry*. Chapel Hill: The University of North Caroline Press, 2006.
Sanni, Amidu. "New Perspectives on the Phenomenology of Error (Lahn) in Scriptural Quran." In *Oriental Studies*, edited by Zeki Dilek, 333-44. Ankara: AKDTYK, 2007.
Sardar, Ziauddin. *The Future of Muslim Civilization*. London: Croom Helm, 1979.
Sarıçam, İbrahim. *Hz. Muhammed ve Evrensel Mesajı*. Ankara: Diyanet, 2014.
Scheibe, Erhard. *Between Rationalism and Empiricism: Selected Papers in the Philosophy of Physics*. New York: Springer, 2001.
Schirrmacher, Christine. *Let There Be No Compulsion in Religion (Sura 2:256): Apostasy from Islam as Judged by Contemporary Islamic Theologians*. Bonn: Verlag für Kultur und Wissenschaft Culture and Science, 2016.
Schleiermacher, Friedrich. *On Religion: Speeches to Its Cultured Despisers*. Cambridge: Cambridge University Press, 1996.
Schluchter, Wolfgang. *The Rise of Western Rationalism: Max Weber's Developmental History*. Berkeley: University of California Press, 1991.
Schmidtke, Sabine. "Theological Rationalism in the Medieval World of Islam." *Al-'Usur al Wusta* 20, no. 1 (2008): 17-22.
Schwarz, Michael. "The Letter of al-Hasan al-Basri." *Oriens* 20, no. 1 (1967): 15-30.
Searle, John R. *Speech Acts: An Essay in the Philosophy of Language*. Cambridge: Cambridge University Press, 1969.
Searle, John R. *Expression and Meaning: Studies in the Theory of Speech Acts*. Cambridge: Cambridge University Press, 1979.
Seed, John. "Secular and Religious: Historical Perspectives." *Social History* 39, no. 1 (2014): 3-13.
Şeyhun, Ahmet. *Islamic Thinkers in the Late Ottoman Empire and the Early Turkish Republic*. Leiden: Brill, 2014.
Sezgin, İpek Gencel. "Islamist Party Identity in Right-Wing Milieus: The Case of the National Outlook Movement in Kayseri (1960-1980)." In *Contemporary Turkey at a Glance Interdisciplinary Perspectives on Local and Translocal Dynamics*, edited by Kristina Kamp, Ayhan Kaya, E. Fuat Keyman and Özge Onursal Beşgül, 93-110. Wiesbaden: Springer, 2014.
Shaban, M. A. *The 'Abbasid Revolution*. Cambridge: Cambridge University Press, 1970.

Shabana, Ayman. "Custom in the Islamic Legal Tradition." In *The Oxford Handbook of Islamic Law*, edited by Anver R. Emon and Rumee Ahmed, 231–48. Oxford: Oxford University Press, 2018.
Shah, Mustafa. "Introduction." In *The Hadith Critical Concepts in Islamic Studies*, edited by Mustafa Shah, 1–56. London: Routledge, 2009.
Sharif, Adel Omer. "Generalities on Criminal Procedure under Islamic Shariʿa." In *Criminal Justice in Islam Judicial Procedure in the Shariʿa*, edited by Muhammad Abdel Halim, Adel Omar Sharif and Kate Daniels, 3–16. London: I.B. Tauris, 2003.
Shavit, Uriya. "Is Shura a Muslim Form of Democracy? Roots and Systemization of a Polemic." *Middle Eastern Studies* 46, no. 3 (2010): 349–74.
Shaw, Stanford J., and Ezel Kural Shaw. *History of the Ottoman Empire and Modern Turkey Volume II Reform, Revolution, and Republic: The Rise of Modern Turkey, 1808–1975*. Cambridge: Cambridge University Press, 1977.
Shnizer, Aliza. "Sacrality and Collection." In *The Blackwell Companion to the Quran*, edited by Andrew Rippin, 159–71. Oxford: Blackwell, 2006.
Shoshan, Boaz. *Poetics of Islamic Historiography: Deconstructing Tabari's History*. London and Boston: Brill, 2004.
Shuʿayb, Fiazuddin. "Al-Ghazzali's Final Word on Kalam." *Islam & Science* 9, no. 2 (2011): 151–72.
Silvers, Laury. "'In the Book We Have Left Out Nothing': The Ethical Problem of the Existence of Verse 4:34 in the Quran." *Comparative Islamic Studies* 2, no. 2 (2006) 171–80.
Simcox, Robin. "Ansar al-Sharia and Governance in Southern Yemen." *Current Trends in Islamist Ideology* 14, no. 1 (2012): 58–72.
Sinai, Nicolai. "When Did the Consonantal Skeleton of the Quran Reach Closure? Part II." *Bulletin of the School of Oriental and African Studies* 77, no. 3 (2014): 509–21.
Singh, Rakesh Kumar. *Textbook on Muslim Law*. New Delhi: Universal, 2011.
Sirriyeh, Elizabeth. *Sufis and Anti-Sufis: The Defense, Re-thinking and Rejection of Sufism in the Modern World*. London: Routledge, 2013.
Skovgaard-Petersen, Jakob. "Heirs of Abu Bakr: On the Ideology and Conception of History in al-Qaeda and Islamic State." *Connections* 16, no. 1 (2017): 25–36.
Smith, Barry. "John Searle: From Speech Acts to Social Reality." In *John Searle*, edited by Barry Smith, 1–33. Cambridge: Cambridge University Press, 2003.
Smith, Margaret. *Al-Ghazali: The Mystic*. Lahore: HIP, 1983.
Smith, Wilfred Cantwell. *Islam in Modern History*. Princeton: Princeton University Press, 1957.
Smith, Wilfred Cantwell. "Can Believers Share the Quran and the Bible as the Word of God?" In *On Sharing Religious Experience: Possibilities for Interfaith Mutuality*, edited by J. D. Gort, H. M. Vroom, R. Fernhout, and A. Wessels, 55–63. Amsterdam: Rodopi, 1992.
Sorokin, Pitirim. *Social Mobility Vol. 3*. London: Routledge, 1998.
Spectorsky, Susan. "Hadith in the Responses of Ishaq b. Rahwayh." *Islamic Law and Society* 8, no. 3 (2002): 407–31.
Starr, Frederick. *Lost Enlightenment: Central Asia's Golden Age from the Arab Conquest to Tamerlane*. Princeton, NJ: Princeton University Press, 2013.
Stetkevych, Suzanne Pinckney. *Immortals Speak: Pre-Islamic Poetry and the Poetics of Ritual*. Ithaca: Cornell University Press, 1993.
Subramanian, Narendra. "Legal Change and Gender Equality: Changes in Muslim Family Law in India." *Law & Social Inquiry* 33, no. 3 (2008): 631–72.

Takim, Liyakat A. "From Bid'a to Sunna: The Wilaya of 'Ali in the Shi'i Adhan." *Journal of the American Oriental Society* 120, no. 2 (2000): 166–77.

Talmon-Heller, Daniella. *Islamic Piety in Medieval Syria: Mosques, Cemeteries and Sermons under the Zangids and Ayubis*, 1146–260. Leiden: Brill, 2007.

Tamer, Georges. "Preface." In *Islam and Rationality: The Impact of al-Ghazali Papers Collected on His 900th Anniversary*, edited by Georges Tamer, ix–xix. London: Brill, 2015.

Taylor, Charles. *A Secular Age*. New York: Belknap, 2007.

Taylor, Richard C. "Ibn Rushd/Averroes and "Islamic" Rationalism." *Medieval Encounters* 15, no. 1 (2009): 225–35.

Tayob, Abdelkader I. "Ṭabari on the Companions of the Prophet: Moral and Political Contours in Islamic Historical Writing." *Journal of the American Oriental Society* 119, no. 2 (1999): 203–10.

Thomas, David. "Miracles in Islam." In *The Cambridge Companion to Miracles*, edited by Graham H. Tewelftree, 199–215. Cambridge: Cambridge University Press, 2011.

Tibawi, A. L. "Origin and Character of al-madrasah." *Bulletin of the School of Oriental and African Studies* 25, no. 1/3 (1962): 225–38.

Timani, Hussam S. *Modern Intellectual Readings of the Kharijites*. New York: Peter Lang, 2008.

Tobin, Sarah A. *Everyday Piety: Islam and Economy in Jordan*. New York: Cornell University Press, 2016.

Toledano, Ehud R. "Abolition and Anti-slavery in the Ottoman Empire: A Case to Answer?" In *A Global History of Anti-slavery Politics in the Nineteenth Century*, edited by William Mulligan and Maurice Bric, 117–36. New York: Palgrave Macmillan, 2013.

Tor, D. G. "The Islamisation of Iranian Kingly Ideals in the Persianate Fürstenspiegel." *Iran* 49, no. 1 (2011): 115–22.

Tritton, A. S. *Caliphs and Their Non-Muslim Subjects: A Critical Study of the Covenant of Umar*. London: Routledge, 2008.

Tucker, Aviezer. "Historiographic Revision and Revisionism: The Evidential Difference." In *Past in the Making*, edited by Michal Kopecek, 1–15. Budapest: Central European University Press, 1989.

Tucker, Judith E. *Women, Family, and Gender in Islamic Law*. Cambridge: Cambridge University Press, 2008.

Ulaş, Semra. "İslam'da Çok Kadınla Evlilik." *İslami Araştırmalar* 6, no. 1 (1991): 52–63.

Ushama, Thameem. "Issues in the Understanding of Muhkam and Muteshabih Passages of the Quran." *Al-Shajarah: Journal of the International Institute of Islamic Thought and Civilization* 16, no. 1 (2011): 85–112.

Vakulenko, Anastasia. *Islamic Veiling in Legal Discourse*. London: Routledge, 2012.

Vasalau, Sophia. *Moral Agents and Their Deserts: The Character of Mu'tazilite Ethics*. Princeton: Princeton University Press, 2008.

Vial, Theodore. "Friedrich Schleiermacher." In *Nineteenth-Century Philosophy of Religion*, edited by Graham Oppy and N. N. Trakakis, 31–47. London: Routledge, 2013.

Von Grunebaum, G. E. "The Nature of Arab Unity Before Islam." *Arabica* 10, no. 1 (1963): 5–23.

Wadud, Amina. *Quran and Woman: Reading the Sacred Text from a Woman's Perspective*. Oxford: Oxford University Press, 1999.

Wansbrough, John. *The Sectarian Milieu: Content and Composition of Islamic Salvation History*. Oxford: Oxford University Press, 1978.

Watt, W. Montgomery. *Muhammad: Prophet and Statesman*. Oxford: Oxford University Press, 1961.

Watt, W. Montgomery. *Muslim Intellectual: A Study of Al-Ghazali*. Edinburg: Edinburgh University Press, 1963.
Watt, W. Montgomery. *The Early Caliphate*. Edinburgh: Edinburgh University, 1968.
Watt, W. Montgomery. "Islamic Conceptions of the Holy War." In *The Holy War*, edited by Thomas P. Murphy, 141–56. Columbus: Ohio State University Press, 1976.
Watt, W. Montgomery. *Islamic Philosophy and Theology*. Edinburgh: Edinburgh University Press, 1985.
Watt, W. Montgomery. "Belief in a High God in Pre-Islamic Arabia." In *The Arabs and Arabia on the Eve of Islam*, edited by F. E. Peters, 307–12. London: Routledge, 1999.
Watt, W. Montgomery and R. Bell. *Introduction to Quran*. Edinburgh: Edinburgh University Press, 1977.
Weiss, Bernard G. *The Search for God's Law: Islamic Jurisprudence in the Writings of Sayf al-Din al-Amidi*. Salt Lake City: University of Utah Press, 2010.
Weithman, Paul. "Augustine's Political Philosophy." In *The Cambridge Companion to Augustine*, edited by Eleonore Stump and Norman Kretzmann, 234–52. Cambridge: Cambridge University Press, 2001.
Welchman, Lynn. *Women and Muslim Family Laws in Arab States: A Comparative Overview of Textual Development and Advocacy*. Amsterdam: Amsterdam University Press, 2007.
White, Jenny B. "The End of Islamism? Turkey's Muslimhood Model." In *Remaking Muslim Politics Pluralism, Contestation, Democratization*, edited by Robert W. Hefner, 87–111. Princeton: Princeton University Press, 2005.
Wild, Stefan. "Islamic Enlightenment and the Paradox of Averroes." *Die Welt des Islam* 36, no. 3 (1996): 379–90.
Willis, John Ralph. "Introduction: The Ideology of Enslavement in Islam." In *Slaves and Slavery in Muslim Africa Vol. 2 The Servile Estate*, edited by John Ralph Willis, 1–15. London and New York: Routledge, 1985.
Witt, R. E. "The Plotinian Logos and the Stoic Basis." *The Classical Quarterly* 25, no. 2 (1931): 103–11.
Wymann-Landgraf, Umar F. Abd-Allah. *Malik and Medina: Islamic Legal Reasoning in the Formative Period*. Leiden: Brill, 2003.
Yaman, Ahmet. "Abdullah bin Mesud'un Hanefi Mezhebinin Oluşumunda Rolü." *Marife* 4, no. 2 (2004): 7–26.
Yaran, Rahmi. "Karafi'den Şatibi'ye Makasıd/Maslahat Söylemi." *Marmara Üniversitesi İlahiyat Fakültesi Dergisi* 45, no. 1 (2013): 5–30.
Yardım, Ali. "Dihye bin Halife." In *İslam Ansiklopedisi Vol. IX*, edited by commission, 294–4. Ankara: TDV, 1999.
Yaşaroğlu, M. Kamil. "Namaz." In *İslam Ansiklopedisi Vol. XXXII*, edited by commission, 350–7. Ankara: TDV, 2006.
Yavuz, Hakan. "Political Islam and the Welfare (Refah) Party in Turkey." *Comparative Politics* 30, no. 1 (1997): 63–82.
Yousefi, Najm al-Din. "Islam without Fuqaha: Ibn al-Muqaffa and His Perso-Islamic Solution to the Caliphate's Crisis of Legitimacy (70–142 AH/ 690–760 CE)." *Iranian Studies* 50, no. 1 (2015): 9–44.
Zadeh, Travis. "Touching and Ingesting: Early Debates over the Material Quran." *Journal of the American Oriental Society* 129, no. 3 (2009): 443–66.
Zaman, Muhammad Qasim. *Religion and Politics Under the Early 'Abbasids the Emergence of the Proto-Sunni Elite*. Leiden: Brill, 1997.

INDEX

Abbasids, the   26, 103–4, 136
Abdullah ibn Mas'ud   111–14, 116, 126
Abu Davud   55, 114, 123
Abu Hanifa   7, 9, 31, 50, 52, 55, 57, 100, 143, 147
Abu Hurayra   56–7, 127
Abu Yusuf   66
Ahl hadith   6–7, 51, 57
ahl ra'y   6–7, 9, 57
Ahl-i Quran Movement   43
Ahmad ibn Hanbal   7, 54, 114, 123
al-Ash'ari   13, 97, 103, 106–7, 112
  on causality   34, 105
  as traditionalist   7, 9
al-Baghdadi, Abd al-Qahir   33
al-Bukhari   54, 56–7, 112, 114–15, 123
al-Dimashqi, Gaylan   142–3
al-Ghazali
  on causality   34
  the critique of   54, 56, 138
  on *maqasid*   50
  on piety   94
  and politics   138
  on Quran's content   31
  and Sufism   144
  as traditionalist   7–9, 136, 137
  on women   75
al-Isfahani, Abu Muslim   9, 31
al-Jabbar, Qadi abd   10, 49, 150
al-Jabri, Muhammad   8, 61, 98–9, 131
al-Juhani, Ma'bad   142
al-Maturidi   7–9, 107, 147, 150
  on causality   108
al-Mawardi   98
al-Qurtubi   33, 54, 75, 85, 112, 114
al-Razi   75
  on Quran   31, 33
  on revelation   34
al-Shafi'i   56–7, 65, 103, 131, 139
  the critique of   52, 70, 75, 107, 139–40
  on hadith (*and* sunnah)   52–3, 94–6
  on jihad   70
  his legacy   31
  on piety   94
  on Quran   31, 43
  as traditionalist   7–9, 50, 53
  on women   75
al-Shatibi   7, 32, 50–1
al-Suyuti   33, 54–5, 117
  on Quran   31, 112
Anaxagoras   49
apostasy   67–9
Arab
  culture   28–9, 50, 55, 63, 66, 70, 74, 83, 86, 95–6, 121
  mythology   32, 58, 64
Aristotle   31, 36, 45, 49
Ash'ari school   7, 29, 139
authoritarianism   5–6, 23, 92, 100, 102
Ayas, M. Rami   20

Baltacıoğlu, İ. Hakkı   20
Başgil, Ali Fuat   19
Bilmen, Ömer Nasuhi   94

caliphate   111–12, 127–8, 130–1
causality   11, 34
  in Ash'arism   11
  in history   105–8, 118, 129
  in Ibn Rushd   11
Chakralawi, M. Abdullah   43
chopping   63, 65–7
Christians/Christianity   29, 33, 44, 67, 89
companions   7, 9, 111, 124
  the definition of   54

destiny   19, 123, 132, 141–3
Dilthey, William   7, 41
divorce   76
Diyanet   18, 65, 68–9

empiricism   10–12, 26, 42, 46
Erdoğan, Recep Tayyip   5, 18, 72, 101

fatalism   107, 139
freedom   43, 48, 72, 74, 88, 91, 93, 101, 139, 145
free will   11, 34

the Gülen movement   2, 5, 141

hadith   51
   the critique of   53–8
   the interpretation of   53
   methodology   56–7
   the nature of   53
   and science   58
   the status of   52
Hamidullah, Muhammad   98
hanif   27, 121
Hatiboğlu, M. Said   19
hermeneutics   41–2, 44
hijab   83
historicism/historicists   11–12, 26–8, 34, 40–1
history
   under Abbasids   104
   revisionism   105
   Sunni   103, 105

Ibn Kullab   26
Ibn Rushd   7, 11, 107
İlahiyat   18–20
Imam-Hatip Schools   17–18
individualism   3, 145–7
inner knowledge   8, 46, 137
Iran   61, 80
ISIS   65
Islamic movements   145–6
Islamic state   97
Islamism   61, 97
isnad   56–7
istihsan   50, 52

jahilliya   32, 132
Jesus   17, 64
Jews
   in Quran   27–8, 33
jihad   69–70, 130
jizyah   28
justice   6, 38, 43, 47, 51, 55, 89, 91, 97
the Justice and Development Party   2, 5, 141

Kemalism   5, 14–15, 18–19, 83, 151–3
Khalafallah, Muhammad Ahmad   32
Khomeini, Ayatollah   61, 97

lahn   115

madrasa   20, 136–7
   the Saljuqi   136–8, 140
maqasid   50–1
ma'ruf   48, 50, 63
Mawdudi, Abu A'la   61, 67
Mihna   26
miracles
   the rejection of   57, 122
mobilization   15
modernization/modernity   14, 60, 149, 153
moral principles/morality   62, 88, 93, 99, 101
Mu'tazila   50, 52, 54, 94, 140
   on causality   107
   on Quran   26–7, 43
   as rationalist   9

nash   39, 40
natural law   11, 31, 35, 63, 106–8, 122, 154
Nursi, Said   14, 68, 115

occasionalism   11, 105–6, 139

patriarchalism   74–5
peace, *see* jihad
philosophy   19–21, 131, 137
piety   88–91, 93
   moral   91–2
   ritualistic   89–92
political opposition   97–100
political pacifism   145
polygamy   63, 86

qissas   32
Qur'an
   authentic meaning of   41
   compilation of   39, 109
   its content   30–1, 33, 45
   as created   26
   as historical   27–8, 44
   its history   108–9

its interpretation   40–1, 47–9
  as local   29, 30
  moral objectives of   42
  its nature   26–7, 43, 46
  and science   32–3, 45
  as speech act   35–8
Qutb, Sayyid   61
  on jihad   69

Rahman, Fazlur   1, 9
  on interpreting Quran   42, 66, 73
  on revelation   34
  on Turkey   20–1
rationalism   7, 11, 43, 153
  classical Islamic   7, 10
  contemporary Islamic rationalism
    2–8, 11–14
  Western/classical   7, 9–10, 12
reasoning   8, 10, 12, 26, 42–3, 47, 49
reform   1, 3, 6, 19, 102
revelation   10, 36
  the nature of   34–5, 46, 110
revisionism
  on Abu Bakr   127
  on Ali   126
  on companions   124
  on early Islamic history   124
  in the history of Qur'an   108–11
  on Muhammad   116, 118
  on Umar   126
  on Uthman   128

Salah/Namaz   90
Sassanid   127, 129, 136, 138
Schleiermacher, Friedrich   48
science   4, 13, 31–3, 45–6, 54–5, 96, 124,
    139, 150–1, 154
Searle, John   7
secularism   5–6, 14, 18–19, 83, 105, 107,
    118, 151–3
shari'a   61–3
  interpretation of   64–5
  as local   64
  the nature of   62–3
slavery   28, 71–3
  in Sunnism   72
Smith, W. Cantwell   27

speech act theory   41
state
  Islamic   98–9
  theory of   99
Sufism   144
  the critique of   145
Sunnah   96
  comprehensive   94
  and science   96
Sunni
  clergy   18
  the crisis   151
  fundamentalism   6
  orthodoxy   18
  revival   5, 145
Sunnism
  the critique of   3, 4, 6
supernatural   105

Tanci, Muhammad   20
tradition, *see* hadith
traditionalism   7, 9, 43
traditionists   7, 54

Ubay ibn Ka'b   111
Umar   9, 50, 55, 71–2
Umayyads, the   140
  on hadith   56
universalism/universalists   12, 43
Uthman   39
  the assassination of   128
  commission   109–14

veiling, *see* hijab
violence   70, 82, 91, 104, 152

women
  beating   82
  inheritance   79
  marrying non-Muslim men   87
  in shari'a   74, 79, 80
  testimony   80–1

Yemame War   111

Zayd ibn Thabit   113
zihar   75–8

www.ingramcontent.com/pod-product-compliance
Lightning Source LLC
Chambersburg PA
CBHW062142300426
44115CB00012BA/2005